Women *in the* Middle

2nd Edition

Their Parent Care Years

Elaine M. Brody, MSW, DSc(Hon), for many years, Mrs. Brody was Director of the Department of Human Resources and Associate Director of Research at the Philadelphia Geriatric Center. She also was Clinical Professor of Psychiatry in the Department of Psychiatry at the Medical College of Pennsylvania and Adjunct Associate Professor of Social Work in Psychiatry in the School of Medicine at the University of Pennsylvania. Mrs. Brody is a past President of The Gerontological Society of America (1980). She received an honorary doctorate, D.Sc., from The Medical College of Pennsylvania in 1987, and has been elected a Distinguished Scholar of the National Academies of Social Work Practice. Among the many awards she received are the 1985 Brookdale Award of The Gerontological Society of America, the 1983 Donald P. Kent Award of The Gerontological Society of America, and the 1982 Distinguished Alumni Award of the University of Pittsburgh School of Social Work. Mrs. Brody was selected as a Woman of the Year by *Ms. Magazine*, January 1986. She has served on the editorial boards of many professional journals and on Peer Review Committees at the National Institute of Mental Health, the Administration on Aging, and a number of foundations. She was a member of the Congressional Advisory Panel on Alzheimer's Disease and of the Brookings Institution Advisory Panel on Long Term Care. Her publications include six books, many book chapters, and over 200 journal articles. She has directed 18 federally financed research studies on subjects such as Individualized Treatment of Mentally Impaired Aged; Mental and Physical Health Practices of Older People; The Dependent Elderly and Women's Changing Roles; Women, Work, and Care of the Aged; Parent Care, Sibling Relationships and Mental Health; and Marital Status, Parent Care and Mental Health. She directed a large demonstration of a multi-service respite program for family caregivers of older people with Alzheimer's disease. Mrs. Brody has lectured at scores of universities; consulted with many foundations, hospitals, governmental and voluntary agencies; and testified many times before Committees of the United States House of Representatives and the United States Senate.

Women *in the* Middle
2nd Edition
Their Parent Care Years

Elaine M. Brody, MSW, DSc (Hon.)

Springer Publishing Company, Inc.
11 West 42nd Street
New York, NY 10036

Acquisitions Editor: Sheri W. Sussman
Production Editor: Jeanne Libby
Cover design by Mimi Flow

06 07 08 09 / 5 4 3 2 1

New ISBN 0-8261-6382-3 © 2006 by Springer Publishing Company, Inc.

Library of Congress Cataloging-in-Publication Data

Brody, Elaine M.
Women in the middle : their parent-care years / Elaine M. Brody, with contributions by Avalie R. Saperstein.—2nd ed.
p. cm.— (Springer series on life styles & issues in aging)
Includes bibliographical references and index.
ISBN 0-8261-6381-5
1. Aging parents—Home care-United States. 2. Adult children of aging parents—United States. 3. Women—United States—Family relationships. 4. Caregivers—United States—Family relationships. 5. Parent and adult child—United States. I. Saperstein, Avalie R. II. Title. III. Series: Springer series on life styles and issues in aging.
HV1461 .B77 2004
362.6'085'4—dc44 2003065668

Printed in Canada at Transcontinental Printing.

This book is dedicated to my late beloved husband
Stanley J. (Steve) Brody

Contents

Foreword

Regardless of living arrangement, family contact remains intense for virtually all older people. Family issues are at the foundation of clinical practice in gerontology. It is common for clinicians to report that they spend more time with the family than with the older patient in the assessment and long-term management of late life disorders. It is, unfortunately, also common for clinicians to report that there is no good way to be paid for the time they need to spend with the family.

The death of the family, one of the most common misconceptions in our culture, was stated as a simple fact in the 1965 report of the Committee on Aging of the Group for Advancement of Psychiatry (GAP, 1965) and was amplified in the important 1968 Research Report of the American Psychiatric Association (Simon & Epstein, 1968). Families were seen as geographically and emotionally distant, distracted by issues of employment and mobility, disintegrated, reduced in size, and generally indifferent to the concerns of the older generation.

At roughly the same time, a different conclusion was building from the social and behavioral science literature. The work of Margaret Blenkner (1965), Elaine Brody (1966), Ethel Shanas and Gordon Streib (1965) and others were beginning to establish a framework for what later came to be called caregiving. A large study of service use (Comptroller General, 1977) documented the important contributions of family members to the ongoing care and support of disabled older persons in the community.

The landmark publication of *The 36-Hour Day* in 1981 (Mace & Rabins, 1981), now in its third edition, dramatically altered our understanding of family issues. The family was now more properly seen as the fundamental structure providing care to its older members. The title of Elaine Brody's 1984 Kent Award Lecture, "Parent Care as Normative Family Stress" (Brody, 1985) summarized the new conceptualization of the centrality of the family.

This evolving role of the family was not without challenges, however, and the stresses and burdens associated with this care were identified as being substantial (Light, Niederehe, & Lebowitz, 1994). The correlations of the stresses of caregiving with depression and anxiety in caregivers were consistently shown to be high and clinically significant (Schulz, Bookwala, O'Brien, & Fleissner, 1995). In an important line of research, Kiecolt-Glaser and colleagues (1996) demonstrated that caregiver stress was significantly associated with immune system suppression and that this stress was an independent risk factor for mortality (Schulz & Beach, 1999). Interestingly, caregiver-based interventions were shown to have significant effects on patient outcomes (Mittelman, Ferris, & Shulman, 1993).

Nor was care exclusively unidirectional from the younger to the older members of the family. Extensions of life expectancy for the chronically ill and disabled created caregiving situations that lasted for decades into old age for the parents of these individuals (Cohler, Pickett, & Cook, 1991; Seltzer, Greenberg, & Krauss, 1995). Social and parental dislocations produced by substance abuse, incarceration, or HIV/AIDS have also increased caregiving responsibilities of grandparents toward their grandchildren (Minkler & Roe, 1993).

It is now taken as a fact that older people are not typically abandoned, alone or solo actors in a complex world. We now acknowledge that families, and not isolated individuals, are the norm in our society.

Elaine Brody has led us on this important journey. More than 20 years ago, she alerted us to the fact that families were not corporations with common missions and a division of labor tailored to the achievement of that mission. She pointed out that women—the spouses of those with disabling conditions and especially their daughters—were the ones upon whom our care systems relied.

Much research has been launched from these fundamental observations. A skim of the program of the annual scientific meeting of the Gerontological Society of America will confirm the activity and excitement that still exists in the area that most refer to as caregiving. Indeed, the whole topic has moved beyond research and has entered our language and our overall awareness. Through the work of Rosalynn Carter and the Carter Center in Atlanta, caregiving has been placed at the center of our national discussions of long-term care.

But in this process of moving the issue of caregiving to center stage, we have lost Elaine Brody's fundamental message regarding the critical role of women as carers and as beneficiaries of the care. Her revisiting the issue serves as a reminder that care must be provided to someone by someone and those "someones" are, more often than not, adult daughters of disabled older women. And more than ever before, daughters with careers in the paid labor force, daughters with outstanding loans from their own education, and with families of their own and all the issues related to that. These women are truly "in the middle" and Elaine Brody's perspective on the issues in the lives of these women is timely and highly welcome at this time.

WHY AT THIS TIME IN PARTICULAR?

In October 2002, the Public Policy Institute of AARP issued an important report on long-term care (Redfoot & Pandya, 2002). The report makes the startling observation that if rates of long-term care service use had followed the pattern observed in the mid 1970s there would be half a million more people in nursing homes than we actually have. Where have these 500,000 people gone? For one thing, there have been sharp declines in the rates of disability, thanks largely to improved strategies of chronic disease management and greater access to community services. Due to overall growth in the population, however, the number of people with significant disabilities has stayed high. Care is provided to people, not to rates, and so the need for care remains at a high level.

Much has been written about this caregiving situation, and the emphasis has been on things like the stresses associated with the burdens of care. There is no question that being a caregiver is hard—the case studies in this book certainly reflect that. But what is often lost in the surveys is the upside of caregiving—the joys, the sense of fulfillment, the accomplishment, and the humor. Elaine Brody captures this, and much more in her case studies and narratives she presents.

Women in the Middle, Second Edition reminds us all of the continued importance of the lesson that the Brody's—Elaine and her late husband Professor Stanley "Steve" J. Brody—taught us all. That is, that policy and planning is easy when all it entails is moving boxes and arrows around a grid. What is fundamentally most important, however, is that individuals never quite fit into these boxes. Caring, not "providing assistance," but really caring for an older person, is not easy at all.

The book acknowledges that caring is both tough and fulfilling. Through her work, and through her life, Elaine Brody has celebrated the heroic contributions of the women in this role. She has enriched our field and our lives, and for this we are all profoundly in her debt.

Barry D. Lebowitz, Ph.D.
National Institute of Mental Health

REFERENCES

Blenkner, M. (1965). Social work and family relationships in later life with some thoughts on filial maturity, in social structure and the family: *Generational relations.* Edited by Shanas, E., Streib, G. Englewood Cliffs: Prentice-Hall.

Brody, E. M. (1966). The aging family. *The Gerontologist, 6,* 201–206.
Brody, E. M. (1985). Parent care as normative family stress. The Donald P. Kent Memorial Lecture. *The Gerontologist, 25,* 19–29.
Cohler, B. J., Pickett, S. A., & Cook, J. A. (1991). The psychiatric patient grows older. In *The Elderly with Chronic Mental Illness*. Edited by Light, E., Lebowitz, B. D. New York: Springer Publishing, pp. 82–110.
Comptroller General of the United States. (1977). *Report to Congress on home health—The need for a national policy to better provide for the elderly*. US General Accounting Office, HRD-78-19, Washington, DC.
Group for the Advancement of Psychiatry (GAP) (1965). Psychiatry and the aged: an introductory approach. New York, NY.
Kiecolt-Glaser, J., Glaser, R., Gravenstein, S., Malarkey, W., & Sheridan, J. (1996). Chronic stress alters the immune response to influenza virus vaccine in older adults. *Proc Nat Acad Sci USA 93,* 3043–3047.
Light, E., Niederehe, G., & Lebowitz, B. D. (Eds.) (1994). *Stress effects on family caregivers of Alzheimer's patients*. New York: Springer Publishing Company.
Mace, N. L., & Rabins, P. V. (1981). *The 36-hour day*. Baltimore: Johns Hopkins University Press.
Minkler, M., & Roe, K. M. (1993). *Grandmothers as caregivers: Raising children of the crack cocaine epidemic*. Newbury Park, CA: Sage Publications.
Mittelman, M. S., Ferris, S. H., Shulman, E., et al. (1996). A family intervention to delay nursing home placement of patients with Alzheimer's disease: A randomized, controlled trial. *JAMA, 276,* 1725–1731.
Redfoot, D. L., & Pandya, S. M. (2002). Before the boom. *Trends in long-term supportive services for older Americans with disabilities*. Washington, DC: AARP Public Policy Institute Report 2002-2015.
Schulz, R., & Beach, S. R. (1999). Caregiving as a risk factor for mortality: The caregiver health effects study. *JAMA, 282,* 2215–2219.
Schulz, R., O'Brien, A. T., Bookwala, J., & Fleissner, K. (1995). Psychiatric and physical morbidity effects of dementia caregiving: Prevalence, correlates, and causes. *The Gerontologist, 35,* 771–791.
Seltzer, M. M., Greenberg, J. S., & Krauss, M. W. (1995). A comparison of coping strategies of aging mothers of adults with mental illness or mental retardation. *Psychology and Aging, 10,* 64–75.
Shanas, E., & Streib, G. F. (Eds.) (1965). *Social structure and the family: Intergenerational relations*. Englewood Cliffs, NJ: Prentice-Hall.
Simon, A., & Epstein, L. J. (1968). Aging in modern society. *Psychiatric Research Report 23*. Washington DC, American Psychiatric Association.

Acknowledgments

The first edition of this book acknowledged my indebtedness to my husband, Professor Stanley J. "Steve" Brody, for having been my colleague and mentor during all of our 55 years together. Steve prompted me to start on a professional path long before the "new" values encouraged women to work. Though he died in 1997, the influence of his thinking is still powerful in whatever work I do.

I owe appreciation that is difficult to express to the unparalleled Philadelphia Geriatric Center (PGC) (recently renamed the Madlyn and Leonard Abramson Center for Jewish Life) and to the extraordinary people who shaped its development. Its history is described in a recent publication, *The Philadelphia Geriatric Center: How Did It Happen?* (Brody, E. M., 2001).

The funding that made possible the research studies described in this book came primarily from the National Institute of Mental Health, but also from the Administration on Aging, the Frederick and Amelia Schimper Foundation of New York, the John A. Hartford Foundation of New York, and the Pew Charitable Trusts (The Medical Trust) of Philadelphia. Barry Lebowitz of the National Institute of Mental Health is unique in the mentorship and encouragement he provides scientists in the field of research in aging. I have been a grateful beneficiary of his wisdom.

Caran Hardy's superb secretarial skills, critical eye, and warm friendship made my task in writing this book immeasurably easier than it might have been.

Most of all, my loving thanks go to my children, children-in-law, and grandchildren. They have validated on a personal level the loyalty, caring, and emotional support that all gerontologists know are the most valuable gifts that can be given to an elderly parent and grandparent (me!). So thank you, my daughter and son, Laurel Ann Karpman and Peter Robert Brody, your husband and wife, Robert K. and Debra B., and my granddaughters, Hannah and Jodi Karpman, Jocelyn and Rachel Brody, and Deb Heimel.

They all encouraged (no, urged) me to do this second edition. Indeed, they were the crucial variable in my decision to do so.

Finally, since I moved to La Jolla when I retired 16 years ago, I no longer "collaborate" in the usual sense with the people listed in the acknowledgments in the first edition. But they are always present in my memory and affections. Some of their names slipped into the list below because I could not bear to leave them out. Colleagues all over the country were more than generous in responding to requests for information needed to fill in the 15 intervening years between the two books. I am deeply appreciative.

Here they are:

Steven Albert, Shelley Benedict, Peninah Berdugo, Bob Binstock, Larry Corder, Robert Frieldland, Alan Glicksman, Chris Hoffman, Ira Katz, Mort Kleban, M. Powell Lawton, Barry Lebowitz, George Maddox, Miriam Moss, Greg O'Neill, Sheryl Panka-Bryman, Miriam Rose, Avalie Saperstein, Carol Schutz, Al Sirrocco, Abigail Spector, Robyn Stone, Richard Suzman, Arthur Waldman, and the staff of the Counseling for Caregivers program at the Madlyn and Leonard Abramson Center for Jewish Life.

THANK YOU!
Elaine M. Brody

Introduction

"Women in the middle" were so-named because daughters, who are the main caregivers to elderly disabled parents, are most often in their middle years, are caught in the middle of multiple competing demands on their time and energy (husbands, children, parents, and work), and are often in the middle emotionally between elderly parents on the one hand and husbands and children on the other. The negative consequences of their situation are among the most consistently documented findings in a multiplicity of research studies throughout the past few decades—consequences to their own mental and physical health, family well-being, vocational activities, and other aspects of their lives.

The impetus for revisiting those women (the first edition was published in 1990) derives from the fact that *change*—that inevitable and inexorable process—has occurred in their personal and social environments. And while change was occurring, there was also *continuity* of some aspects of their lives as well as increasing *diversity* among them (Brody, E. M., 1995a). It is now almost a full generation later since the original book was published. The generation called "Baby Boomers" has arrived at the parent care ages and stages, while their mothers—the providers of parent care who were the original women in the middle—have entered old age and even advanced old age. And, due to dramatic demographic changes, these now-elderly mothers and fathers are part of the largest population of people 65 or over in history. Elderly people are projected to constitute 70 million people by 2030, or 20% of the population (up from 13% in the year 2000). Among this group is the largest proportion of *very* old people that ever existed—those who most need the care given primarily by women in the middle.

The group of elderly who are 85 or over is growing more rapidly than any other age group in our population. The U.S. Bureau of the Census reports that the number of such people increased by 275% between 1960 and 1994. Moreover, the Bureau projects that by 2050, thanks to the arrival of surviving Baby Boomers at the stage of advanced old age, there will be 19 million of those "oldest old" people! *Change*, then, has been radical in terms of demographic developments.

Continuity has been evidenced by the fact that most of the help the old require is still given by adult children—mainly by daughters—who are the women in the middle. (Daughters outnumber sons three to one as the main caregivers to disabled elderly parents, a ratio that is four to one when the parents are extremely disabled.)

Not least among the changes that have occurred is the increasing ethnic *diversity* of our population and therefore among the caregivers and care recipients.

Simply counting the number of people needing or providing care at any given time does not tell the whole story, of course. *The subject of parent-care concerns virtually all of us, including those who have had or may in the future have children and hope to grow old ourselves.*

Other changes, too, have occurred that serve to increase the pressures on caregiving daughters and daughters-in-law—changes such as the rapid entry of women into the workforce and changes in family patterns such as high rates of divorce and lower birth rates. The later years at which women have been having children serve to place many of them in situations of "double dependency"—caring for their own children and their parents at the same time. And some women continue to have what in the first edition of this book were called "caregiving careers," helping several old people simultaneously or sequentially.

While Baby Boomers are in the forefront among contemporary parent-caregivers, the task is by no means exclusive to them. Almost 20% of the women who are primary caregivers and who are the women immersed in that situation are under 45, and more than 15% are over 65.

Baby Boomers have still another reason to be deeply interested in parent care: they have fewer children than did past generations (except for their own parents) and therefore will have fewer family resources upon whom to depend when they become old. That is, the ratio between the dependent elderly and potential caregivers has changed radically and is continuing to change, portending ever greater demands on the caring generation(s).

Thus, during the intervening years since the first edition of *Women in the Middle* was published, change, continuity, and diversity have proceeded. Women's responsibilities and the pressures they experience have increased and intensified. Taken together, all information serves to show that women right now are even more in the middle and there are more such women than ever before. There has been a huge sea-change in women's lives.

This edition will include much new information, for change has also has occurred in a wide variety of social, economic, and environmental conditions as well as in demography. Highly visible now, for example, are a wide variety of new housing arrangements for older people, new family forms, geographic mobility, and many other developments. Gerontological research has not been idle. Numerous studies have been reported that serve to enrich and fill out the picture. The new relevant findings that have emerged are included in this book. There are also changes that should have taken place via appropriate social policy, but did not happen.

Recent research—including cross-national studies—affirms earlier findings about continuity in the loyalty of families to their elderly members. Not a shred of evidence exists to imply that families have ceased to care for their elderly or that the strains of doing so have been alleviated. Caring for and about the family's elderly is a human universal. Along with *change* and *diversity*, there has been *continuity* in the inner or subjective experiences of the daughters and daughters-in-law who are the majority of those who provide care for the dependent elderly.

This book will focus squarely on the women themselves—daughters and daughters-in-law—and tell the caregiving story from *their* perspective. Many books about parent care have been written. Overwhelmingly, they are self-help books that instruct family caregivers about ways of caring for the disabled elderly—methods and techniques of providing help, dealing with problems presented, and understanding the older person's aging processes, health problems, personality difficulties, and so on. Such books are desirable and necessary. However, they are very different from *Women in the Middle* which describes and discusses the caregiving women's subjective feelings, experiences, and problems, and the effects on their mental and physical well being, life styles, family relationships, and vocational activities. The women in the middle will tell their stories in their own words so that we hear from them in the own voices.

My interest in such women began in the late 1950s when my work at the Philadelphia Geriatric Center (PGC) involved interviewing older people who were applying for admission to the Center's home for the aged. Those who had daughters were almost invariably accompanied by an adult daughter; those who did not were accompanied by a son, and usually by his wife as well. Virtually all of the adult children were painfully disturbed by the need to place the parent. Most had been caring for the elderly person for long periods of time and with enormous difficulty. Some had taken the parent into their own homes with all the disruption entailed. In many instances, the application to the institution was precipitated by something that happened in the caregiver's family, such as her own or her husband's illness (or death) or problems with one of her own children.

Despite the efforts these women had amply demonstrated and despite reality factors that made it impossible for them to go on doing the day-to-day, hands-on parent care tasks, they felt guilty, conflicted, and even ashamed. Deeply ingrained values—personal and social—emphasize that taking care of a parent is a daughter's responsibility. Now they felt that somehow they had failed to fulfill that responsibility and had failed the parent. After all, the widespread myth tells us that "nowadays, families don't take care of their elderly parents as they did in the good old days," and women see themselves as the ones whose job it is to provide the care. (The myth still exists, by the way, despite the accumulation of evidence to the contrary.)

I was, of course, seeing the women when they had reached the point of no return, after enduring many hard years of parent care that often had exacted a toll on their emotional and physical well-being. What had those years been like? What were the forces that compelled them to wait so long before considering nursing home placement? How could they be helped?

Those questions caused a shift in my activities. They set in motion the research studies that focused on the problems and dilemmas of women who had not yet reached the nursing home's doors. In addition to conducting thousands of personal interviews, 14 of my research projects (11 funded by the National Institute of Mental Health and 3 by the Administration on Aging) surveyed about 1,500 women, 300 of their husbands, and 100 of their siblings. Another valued source of information derived from tape-recorded, in-depth interviews with 62 women conducted with the help of a grant from the Amelia Schimper Foundation of New York. The Pew Charitable Trust of Philadelphia and the John A. Hartford Foundation of New York shared funding of still another project. Together, the various sources of information permitted in-depth exploration of the feelings and situations of groups of women in diverse circumstances.

Among the circumstances my research explored were the women's diversity in marital status (some are married, some have never married, some are divorced or separated, and some are widowed); diversity in work status (some are in the labor force and some are not); diversity in that the parents of some women require nursing home care and other women continue to provide care in their own or their parents' homes; and diversity in the ages and stages of life of the parent-caring women. My clinical experience and research studies together prompted me to write the original *Women in the Middle* book.

Fortunately, Avalie Saperstein joined the PGC staff in 1975 when the PGC turned its face outward to older people living in the community.

Eventually, she became Senior Vice President of that organization and played a major role in developing and administering a variety of programs for such older people and their families. Her innovative Counseling for Caregivers program that has been replicated nationally was designed to mitigate the negative consequences caregivers experience. It was an outgrowth of a large demonstration/research project of respite care Dr. M. Powell Lawton and I conducted in which she participated. For this book, Ms. Saperstein wrote chapter 15 on Ethnic/Racial Diversity and chapter 17 on Services and Residential Services. (Additional aspects of her resume appear on the first page of chapter 15).

Before outlining the chapters to follow, the author reiterates the request made in the original book. The reader is asked to keep the feelings and experiences of the older people themselves in mind. Though their problems are not dealt with directly from their perspectives, they are the other side of the caregiving equation. The disabled aged undergo painful losses of independence and function, they often lose their homes and possessions, and, most important of all, they lose people they love. What are their inner experiences when they need to depend on others, when they are aware of the disruptions their dependency occasions in the lives of their families, when they become "guests" (welcome or unwelcome) in the homes of their children or residents of nursing homes?

Finally, a disclaimer. The fact that this book is about daughters who unquestionably bear the overwhelming burden of caregiving does not constitute criticism of sons. Change may indeed be desirable in the allocation of responsibilities between the sexes—what Weithorn (1975) called a "revised contract." But that contract cannot be only between women and men, but must include government in the form of social policy and services as well. There is reason to affirm sons' affection, loyalty, devotion, and responsibility, and there is reason to affirm the caregiving efforts of elderly husbands and wives who care for and about each other and the efforts of other relatives and friends as well. It is well to remember that the well-being of all generations and both genders is linked inextricably in common cause. All of us as individuals, as families, and collectively as a society must be involved in negotiating that revised contract. Surely, knowledge of what caregiving women experience should inform efforts to help them.

Part I. Background

The four chapters in the Background section of the book describe the powerful trends, pressures, and values that combine to create the personal and social crises of the women of the middle.

Chapter 1. Women in the Middle: How It Happened documents the relevant dramatic demographic and socio-economic trends that account for millions of women occupying their difficult "middle" position.

Chapter 2. Scope of Parent Care describes the needs of the elderly recipients of care for help in their daily lives. How many of the older people need help? What kinds of assistance do they need? And, in a question central to this book: Who provides that help?

Chapter 3. Effects of Caregiving contains information derived from research about (1) the effects of parent care on the emotional and physical health of the woman and on their family and vocational lives; and (2) the external or objective factors that predict or mitigate the strains they experience.

Chapter 4. Values About Women's Roles elaborates on one of the potent forces influencing the women's behavior: the values they hold. Those values are reinforced by religious, social, cultural and even professional and political convictions about what constitutes appropriate filial behavior for women. Tension between values the women hold that may compete constitute part of the emotional soil from which these filial caregivers' problems spring.

Part II. Subjective Experiences

The chapters in this section turn to the heart of the book's message.

Chapter 5. Introduction. This chapter looks closely at the women who appeared as statistics in Part One. We listen to the voices of women in many different circumstances as they tell us of their long caregiving careers and their subjective experiences—that is, the "internals" of caregiving and the effects on their lives and family relationships. In describing those subjective aspects of caregiving, I relied on my own experiences conducting thousands of clinical interviews and also on long, verbatim tape-recorded accounts of their caregiving journeys by the women themselves. Not one of the caregivers' words has been altered, though their identities have been carefully disguised.

Chapter 6. On Becoming the Primary Caregiver: The Caregiving Daughters and Their Siblings. How does it happen that one individual in a sibling set becomes the principal caregiver to a disabled parent? There are, of course, a variety of explanations, and the caregivers describe their perceptions of the situations. Chapter 3 describes the effects of caregiving on the primary caregiver, but her siblings do not go unaffected or unscathed. In this chapter, we hear from them about the effects they experience during the parent care years, when they live close by and also when they live at a distance.

Chapter 7. Six Major Subjective Themes and a Variation. After introducing the subject of the major subjective themes experienced by the women in the middle, each of the fundamental and pervasive themes is described in detail, illustrated by the women's own interpretations and comments. The first theme begins with the overarching, profound, and social conviction that "It's a Woman's Role" to care for the disabled elderly. After the next five themes are described, the "variation" ends the chapter. The variation is a tentative beginning explanation of some subjective differences that exist when daughters provide care to mothers and when they provide care to fathers.

Part III. Diversity Among Caregivers

Women in the middle come from all walks of life, and there are a multitude of ways in which they are diverse. This central section of the book deals in detail with major sources of diversity and the ways in which the parent-care years affect and are affected by that particular form of diversity. Included are 25 illustrative case narratives that had been tape recorded.

Chapter 8. Diversity in Ages and Stages. Since the need to provide parent care may arise for a daughter when she is 30 or 50 or 70, this chapter speaks to the reciprocal effects of her age and stage of life with the parent care years.

Chapter 9. Diversity in Marital Status:Introduction and a Research Survey. Women in the middle may be married, or widowed, or divorced or separated, or may never have married. There are some similarities in the subjective experiences of these groups of women, but there are also distinct differences that derive from their marital status. This chapter contains an introduction and a report on the findings of my longitudinal survey of about 500 caregiving daughters who occupied different marital statuses. The survey was at its midpoint when the first edition of this book appeared and is therefore new to this edition.

Chapter 10. Married Daughters and Their Husbands and Children is about women who are married during their parent care years. Because the members of their immediate families are intimately and profoundly affected and often contribute to the caregivers' feelings of being in the middle, their husbands and children appear as well. It is virtually impossible to describe the subjective experiences of these women without the husbands (the sons-in-law, whom I call the "unsung heroes") and children being included in the picture. Those family members also play active caregiving roles at times and might legitimately take their places among those who are called "secondary" caregivers.

Chapter 11. Daughters Without Partners is about those who are widowed, divorced/separated, or have never married. Some have family networks and some are relatively alone in caregiving, either because they were "only" children or their sibling(s) have died. And there are daughters who are completely alone because they are only children, have no husbands, and are childless. There is also a small section on not-married daughters who have a "significant other."

Chapter 12. Caregiving Daughters-in-law. Though many aspects of the care given to older people are similar for daughters and daughters-in-law, there are also striking differences in their subjective experiences that will become apparent. Because it is their husbands—the sons of the disabled parent—who are often named as the "primary" caregivers even though their wives do most of the actual caregiving, the daughters-in-law are characterized as "proxy primaries."

Chapter 13. Commentary on the Marital Status Case Studies ends the marital status part of the book.

Chapter 14. Diversity in Work Status. This chapter deals with still another source of diversity among caregiving daughters: their work status. Employment has become a major role for a large majority of women. The chapter compares the effects of parent care on women who are employed, those who left their jobs because of parent-care responsibilities, and those who do not work outside their homes. It also compares the parent care activities of those groups of women. The interplay between responsibilities to jobs and to parents is examined. Since the business world has become increasingly aware of the predicament of the many employees who are involved in parent care, its relevant activities are described.

Chapter 15. Ethnic and Racial Diversity. This chapter, written by Avalie R. Saperstein, recognizes that racial and ethnic diversity is increasing very rapidly in the United States. Various ethnic and racial groups enact the caregiving role in some ways somewhat differently from each other, but they also are similar in their commitment to caring for their elderly. This book cannot, of course, deal comprehensively with the vast and changing scene, but the major information available on the subject is reviewed.

Part IV. Nursing Homes, Community Services, and Living Arrangements for Older People

Chapter 16. Nursing Home Placement: A Painful Decision. The initial focus of this chapter is on that most painful decision of all—the decision some children must make to place the parent in a nursing home. The conditions that lead to such placement are described as are the effects on their family caregivers during and after that placement. The chapter contains information new to this edition, as my research study on the subject was still underway when the first edition of this book was being written.

Chapter 17. Community Services and Residential Settings. This chapter, by Avalie R. Saperstein, describes some of the helpful community services and newer forms of living arrangements that have been developed for older people—for example, assisted living (AL), continuing care retirement communities (CCRS), and naturally occurring retirement communities (NORCs).

Part V

Chapter 18. Unfinished Business on the Parent-Care Agenda summarizes the major issues that were discussed in the book and identifies some of the unfinished business with regard to women in the middle and parent care. Various trends that affect parent care have been occurring and will be identified. Since there is a scarcity of information about the effects of some of those important trends on parent care and on women in the middle, some research needs to explore those effects are suggested. There will be comments on the directions being taken by public policy (or that policy is failing to take) that bear on our subject. The book ends with an agenda for all of us.

Part I

Background

Chapter 1

Women in the Middle: How It Happened

It took me five years to get my master's degree to prepare for working when I reached the "empty nest" stage of life. But last year, my mother left the stove on and started a fire. She has been getting more and more forgetful and confused and can't be alone at all. I'm depressed, and I don't sleep well. How can I go to work when she needs constant supervision?

* * *

Mom moved in with us because she had a bad stroke. Our whole lives are disrupted. She criticizes my 15-year-old son for the way he dresses and makes my 17-year-old daughter and her friends turn off the music. The kids and my husband complain, and I'm caught in the middle. I have to be the peacemaker and keep them all happy.

* * *

My two brothers and I are attorneys. When our mother, who lives in Florida, fractured a hip, everyone assumed that I would fly down and stay for a while. My brothers are good sons, but my suggestion that we take turns met with surprise. They said they had "to earn a living." And do you know something? I can't figure out why, but I do it. I don't know how long I can keep up this juggling act.

* * *

I'm divorced and work as a secretary to earn a living. My 90-year-old mother has rheumatoid arthritis and has to be lifted. I had to place her in a nursing home, but I felt terribly guilty. Now I'm in terrible conflict. My son and his wife are pressing me to move near them, 3,000 miles

> away. I'm 64, and that's all I have to look forward to. But I can't move my mother now, and I can't leave her here alone. My visits are all she has.

* * *

> I retired after teaching for 30 years, and my husband is tapering off his medical practice. We thought we'd travel a bit at this stage of our lives. Money doesn't seem to solve the problem of my 89-year-old mother-in-law. She has three shifts of nurses, but we can't even get away for a vacation. If a nurse doesn't turn up, I have to fill in and spend hours trying to get another. On top of that, our daughter is getting a divorce and she and her two-year-old have come back to live with us.

In a situation unprecedented in history, such women in this country and in other nations are confronted with the need to help their disabled elderly parents, parents-in-law, and other elderly relatives. In addition to their traditional family roles as wives, homemakers, mothers, and grandmothers, many women nowadays assume the role of caregiver to the vastly increased number of older people who need help. And still another role has been added for those women who have entered or reentered the labor force.

Whether or not they work outside of their homes, the dilemma of these women lies in trying to fulfill all of those roles—to respond to the competing demands and to sort out their priorities. Some of them suffer intensely and are bewildered by the situations in which they find themselves. The pressures they experience come not only from multiple claims on their time and energy, but from the emotional aspects of their situations. There is a negative impact on the health and financial status of some of these women, but the most severe and pervasive effects that have been documented are emotional strains such as anxiety, depression, frustration, conflict, anger, feelings of guilt about not being able to "do it all," and stress from trying to do so. (These effects are discussed in detail in Chapter 3.)

Such women have been characterized as "women in the middle" (Brody, E. M., 1981) because:

- They are most often in their middle years, though they range in age from their 20s to their 70s;
- They are, in the main, a middle generation in three- or four-generation families;
- They are caught in the middle of the requirements of their various roles;
- Many are in the middle between conflicting values: the powerful, deeply rooted traditional value that care of older people—indeed,

care of all people in the family who need help—is *their* responsibility, and the newer value that it is all right—even desirable—for women to work or to pursue other interests outside the home; and
- Some are in the middle emotionally when the elderly people they are helping become rivals for their attention with their husbands and children.

The phrase "women in the middle" is, of course, a metaphor for all family members who find themselves in that position—the husbands and wives of the disabled elderly, their sons and daughters, children-in-law, grandchildren, and, at times, even other relatives. And, because problems affecting one family member inevitably affect the others, the entire family is often in the middle. Research evidence shows clearly, however, that the vast majority of caregivers to the old—about three-quarters—are women—primarily wives and daughters, but also daughters-in-law and other female relatives (Stone, Cafferata, & Sangl, 1987; Stone, 2000).

The predicament of those who care for the elderly is a salient personal issue. It is also an issue of major importance for older people themselves, for the entire family, and for society as a whole. The capacity of close family members, called the "informal" support system, to provide the required assistance determines what services and supports they need that should be provided or financed by what is called the "formal" support system of government and social agencies.

Such non-family services and supports are also called the "long-term support system." The government's role in long term care is often hotly debated. Certainly, some modest advances have been made during the years since the first edition of this book was published in 1990. But at times, such progress has been threatened by proposals for (and sometimes actual) cutbacks, and the government did not enact legislation for long-term care insurance as had been expected in the 1990s.

Women in the middle are extremely diverse not only in age but also in their stages of life, ranging from those with young children to those who are old themselves. They vary in their economic situations, social, racial, and ethnic backgrounds, and in marital and family status. They have different personalities, adaptive capacities, and combinations of personal circumstances. The quality of their relationships with their parents varies widely. The nature and amount of assistance they provide varies in accordance with the older people's functional capacities and cognitive status. Some of the women have lived "traditional" lives as homemakers and volunteer workers. Nowadays, most are in the labor force. Some women worked when they were young and gave up their jobs for marriage and motherhood, whereas others have worked all of their adult lives. Some move in and out of the work force as their own and their families' needs dictate. Still others are part of the huge number who in the last half century have entered or reentered the labor force or wish to do so. Many women work because they and their families need the money for day-to-day expenses or to send children to college, for example. Others work because of commitment to careers, and still others because their jobs give them various kinds of satisfaction. Most work because of combinations of such reasons.

The problems of parent-caring women were virtually ignored for many years. Publicity about women who work usually focused on young women—their achievement of advanced educational levels, their entry into occupations formerly considered the domain of men, the "glass ceiling," and their rise up the corporate ladder. Both the professional literature and the media reflected concern primarily with the effects of women's working on their marital relationships, on the emotional development of their young children, and on the young women themselves. Social policy too often tended to take the position that caring for the aged should be solely a family responsibility. In that context, since "family" is a euphemism for women, women are expected to be the caregivers, and services to help them to do the caregiving are grossly underdeveloped. The Women's Movement devoted much effort to matters such as eliminating sex discrimination in educational institutions and in the workplace, the abortion issue, and the provision of services such as daycare for children. It has not given equal priority to the problems of the elder-caring middle generations of women.

Some progress has been made, however. The helping professions—medicine, psychiatry, social work, and psychology—have been moving rapidly in recent years to develop information about the elderly and the processes of aging. A growing number of professionals are focusing their interests and efforts on the aged. This is a highly desirable trend, of course. But the family caregivers are too often viewed as people to be instructed in how to implement professional recommendations for the older people and trained in their care. The caregivers' strains are often regarded as deriving only from their personal, intrapsychic, or interpersonal problems.

Gerontological research has developed rapidly, and there has been an acceleration of studies and publications about parent care. Such research received major impetus in the last quarter of the 20th century from funding from newly established government agencies such as the Center on Aging at NIMH, the Administration on Aging, and the National Institute on Aging.

The pressures experienced by women in the middle are exacerbated by misconceptions concerning the behavior of the modern family with respect to caring for its dependent older members. A persistent myth adds to these women's problems—specifically the widespread misconception that, nowadays, adult children do not take care of their elderly parents the way they used to in the "good old days." Despite several decades during which a massive and consistent body of evidence to the contrary was developed (e.g., see Shanas, 1979a), that myth still stubbornly refuses to be dispelled in popular belief. It is ironic that many contemporary parent-caring women themselves believe the myth, even though nowadays they do much more parent care than their counterparts in the past (Brody, E. M., 1985b). A close relative of the myth is the thoroughly disproved notion that financing public services leads to a reduction in family care and unleashes unmanageable and costly demand for non-family services. (See Penning, 2002 for a recent review.)

Whatever their individual situations, what parent-caring women have in common is that they are feeling the stunning impact of massive demographic and socioeconomic trends that have converged to place them in the middle. Those trends have made "nowadays" very different from the so-called good old days. Two of the trends are demographic—the vast increase in the aging population and the falling birth rate. In particular, the increase of very old people has increased the need for the provision of help in their daily lives. A third trend is socioeconomic—the large-scale entry of women into the workplace. Still other influential trends are the changing patterns of marriage and childbearing. Those trends will be described in order to explain how the situations of women in the middle came about and how the women are being affected.

DEMOGRAPHIC TRENDS

In the current climate in which care of old people has become a major focus of interest for researchers and professionals as well as an important social issue, it is well to remember that prior to the 1960s there was virtually no interest at all in that subject. A major factor stimulating interest in the families of older people was, of course, the emergence and growing visibility of a large aging population.

The rise in the number and proportion of older people in our population was one of the most dramatic and influential developments of the 20th century. The number of people 65 years of age and over has grown rapidly and steadily in proportion to the number who are under the age of 65. At the turn of the century, there were 3.1 million older people, representing 4% of the population. In a five-fold increase, by 1960 there were 16.6 million older people (9.2% of the population), and by 1985 there were 28.6 million. By 1997, there were more than 34 million older people—one in eight of all persons in the United States (U.S. AOA, 1998).

That demographic revolution was brought about by public health measures, improved welfare programs, better nutrition, antibiotics, and discoveries of ways to prevent the great epidemic diseases such as cholera, smallpox, diphtheria, and poliomyelitis. As a result, more people have been able to survive longer, because such illnesses used to prevent them from ever reaching old age. It gives one perspective to realize that in ancient Greece, life expectancy at birth was only 21 years; it took 2,000 years to increase life expectancy to 49 years by 1900. Now, a century later, a new baby can expect to live to 76 years of age! The trend will continue. Life expectancy is expected to reach 83 years by the year 2050, and the number of elderly is projected to increase to 70 million by the year 2030, or 20% of the total population (AOA, 1998).

Another aspect of the demographic revolution affected the issue of filial care even more directly. The number and proportion of *very* old people—those aged 75 and over, and particularly those 85 and over—has increased more rapidly than the older population in general. This came about because of hi-tech medicine, coupled with Medicare (1965), which made such medical care available to older people. Together, hi-tech medicine and Medicare account for the fact that the number and proportion of people at those advanced ages will continue to grow the most rapidly.

To quote the Bureau of the Census:

> The "oldest old"—those 85 and over—are the most rapidly growing elderly age group. Between 1960 and 1994, their members rose 274%. In contrast, the elderly population in general rose 100%, and the entire U.S. population grew only 45%. The oldest old numbered 3 million in 1994, making them 10% of the elderly and just over 1% of the total population. Thanks to the arrival of the baby boom generation, it is expected the oldest old will number 19 million in 2050. That would make them 24% of elderly Americans and 5% of all Americans. (U.S. Bureau of the Census, SB 95-8, May 1995)

The report also notes that by 1994, due to men having higher death rates than women, elderly women outnumbered elderly men by a ratio of three to two (20 million to 14 million), a difference that grew with advancing age to a ratio of five to two at age 85 and over.

The net result of those statistics is that in the year 2000, older men were much more likely to be married than older women—74% of men and 43% of women. There were more than four times as many widows (8.5 million) as widowers (2 million) (U.S. Bureau of the Census, June 2001). Thus (and also because men tend to marry women younger than they are), wives are more likely than husbands to care for disabled spouses. For those who do not have a spouse available for caregiving, divorced older persons represented only 8% of all older people in 2000, but their numbers (2.6 million) had increased significantly since 1900, when about 1.5 million older people were divorced or separated (ibid).

The result of these radical changes will be a continuing increase in the need for filial care, since it is the very old who are the ones most vulnerable to the chronic illnesses that lead to disability and dependence on others. In addition, since rates of widowhood soar as people move toward advanced old age, fewer of the very old have a surviving spouse on whom to depend. When a spouse is present, he or she is also likely to be in advanced old age, to have health problems and be less able to provide care, and, therefore, to be more dependent on adult children for help in doing so.

Thus, demographic trends that have been called the "greying of America" have had and will continue to have a direct impact on the demand for parent care.

While that powerful trend was occurring, another major and influential demographic trend was also taking place. As the aging population increased, fertility rates declined. The falling birth rate made even more pronounced the alteration in the ratio between the old and younger generations. Birth rates fell steadily between the year 1800 and the late 1930s, when a new low was reached (Uhlenberg, 1974); the average number of children born to a mother surviving to at least the age of 40 declined from eight children to fewer than three. This decline accounts in part for the proportionate growth of older people in the population. By 1981, the percentage of women who had borne four or more children had dropped to 25.5% (Heuser, 1976). By 1979, lifetime birth expectations for married women in the main childbearing years of ages 18 to 34 was 2.2 births (U.S. Department of Commerce, 1982).

An exception to the decreasing fertility rates occurred during the Baby Boom years. The National Center for Health Statistics reported that " . . . birth and fertility rates—which increased dramatically in the 1940s and 1950s (the Baby Boom years), declined rapidly in the 1960s and early 1970s—have been declining in the 1990s. The lifetime number of children per women dropped to 2.07—below the level needed to maintain the population. The 1997 birthrate is the lowest ever recorded . . . " (National Center for Health Statistics, July 1998). However, for the first time in eight years, the numbers of births in the U.S. rose in 1998 by 2% from 1997, with birthrates rising to their highest point in decades among women in their 30s. The result is that older people nowadays have many fewer adult children to share the responsibilities of parent care than was true early in the last century. That is, the pool of children on whom they can rely is much smaller now than used to be the case. Fewer children means fewer daughters. And since many women are daughters-in-law as well as daughters, the chances of being called upon for parent or parent-in-law care, or both, increase greatly.

Those trends—the increase in the elderly population and low fertility rates—have radically altered the structure of the family and the conformation of the family tree. The four-generation family has become commonplace rather than a rare phenomenon, a change that affects all generations. In the mid-1960s, a major scientific conference was called to consider the implications of the fact that the three-generation family had become so common (Shanas & Streib, 1965). At the very time that the social scientists were deliberating, however, Shanas and her colleagues were conducting a major cross-national study that would show that 40% of older people with children had great-grandchildren (Shanas et al., 1968)! By the latter part of the 20th century, the four-generation family had become even more commonplace, with more than half of all people 65 and older having great-grandchildren.

If one looks at the new family tree upward from the perspective of the younger generations, it is obvious that at every age beginning with birth, people nowadays have more parents, grandparents, and great-grandparents than used to be the case. Many more children now can expect to have both of their parents survive until they reach maturity, and many have grandparents who survive to become great-grandparents. The pattern of having more parents and grandparents alive continues through young adulthood and into middle age. Now, three out of five of all women 50 years old have at least one living parent and one living child (Soldo, 1996).

The U.S. Bureau of the Census (1986), in making projections for the 21st century, pointed out that more people will find themselves caring for very old persons after they themselves have reached retirement age. By 2050, every third person 60 to 74 years old could have a surviving parent.

From the standpoint of filial care, then, very old people are more likely to have adult children who also are old or are approaching old age, a phenomenon that will be even more widespread in the future. At the same time, the growing proportion of births to women in their 30s means that more women in the future will be providing parent care while they still have young children at home.

The American Association of Retired Persons (AARP) survey (2002) of the "Sandwich Generation," which that organization defined as 45 to 55-year-old Baby Boomers, found that 70% of the Boomers have at least one living parent, and nearly 4 out of every 10 still have children living at home with them. In view of the fact that in 1999 more than two-thirds of caregiving daughters of the elderly were between the years of 45 and 64 and more than 15% were over the age of 65 (Center on an Aging Society, 1999), it is obvious that there are also many families for whom the "sandwich" has an additional layer.

The situation is much more complex, however, than even those data indicate. Some people in the parent-care years have both parents alive, and, since many of those aging children are married, a roughly comparable proportion of their spouses could also have a surviving parent. A middle-aged couple may find themselves looking after two sets of elderly parents. And, when there are two generations in the aging phase of life, adult grandchildren may find themselves helping both their parents and grandparents. Some such situations arise even now, but it is not known how frequently they occur.

One must be careful in looking at the future, however. Biomedical breakthroughs could occur, for example, that would reduce dependency among the aged by preventing or ameliorating age-related and disability-causing chronic ailments such as Alzheimer's disease and arthritis. If that should happen, the needs of very old people for help in their daily lives would decrease. At the same time, it is impossible to foresee population changes and the new groups of disabled people that conceivably could occur because new diseases [such as acquired immune deficiency syndromes (AIDS)] arise and spread. In addition, economic as well as social conditions may change, making extrapolation of needs and resources a high-risk enterprise.

A PERSPECTIVE ON CHANGING NEEDS

In the context of the massive demographic and socio-economic changes, the vastly increased needs for help by older people began to become apparent about half a century ago. Not everyone remembers what the socio-economic scene was like for older people in the 1950s and 1960s.

The phrase "old people" was almost synonymous with "poor people." Though the Social Security Act had been passed in 1935, there had not been time for it to alleviate that poverty to any significant extent. During the Great Depression (even as late as 1938), half of all older people were totally dependent economically on their children and another quarter were dependent on public or private welfare (Brody, S. J., 1987). In the 1950s, for the first time more older people were receiving Social Security benefits than were receiving public assistance (though this does not speak to adequacy of income) and not everyone was covered. The proportion who were totally dependent on their adult children (the family in the middle) had dropped from half in 1938 to 1.5% by 1979. In the 1950s and 1960s, many older people were still applying to homes for aged, which were mandated to be for the "well" aged, simply because they could not afford to live in the community. The income floor was low and incomplete, and there was no social insurance against the costs of catastrophic illness or disability in old age.

Medicare and Medicaid would not come into being until 1965. Most states still had legislation holding adult children responsible for the financial support of their parents in the form of the harsh Legally Responsible Relatives (LRR) provisions of public assistance programs. These persisted until they were eliminated first by Medicaid (1965) and later by Supplemental Security Income (SSI) (1972), which was the successor program to Old Age Assistance.

It was not only providing money to support the elderly that was a strain on adult children. In those days, the landscape was barren in terms of services and facilities for the elderly. There were no assisted living facilities (ALs), no life care communities (CCRCs), no diagnostic centers for elderly, no in-home services, and certainly no special facilities for Alzheimer's patients in or out of homes for the aged or nursing homes. There were no research units focusing on aging and virtually no attention to aging in professional schools. The phrases "long-term care" and "continuum of care" did not exist.

The family—the women in the middle—was on its own to care for the rapidly increasing number of disabled elderly. During those years, Alzheimer's disease was emerging to a position of prominence among the ailments affecting the very old. The sufferers were described as "senile," a term which yielded sequentially to labels such as organic brain syndrome, senile dementia, chronic organic brain syndrome, mental impairment, and, ultimately, Alzheimer's disease.

The overall, rather chaotic picture was exacerbated by widespread initiatives in public policy to discharge the elderly from state mental hospitals.

Earlier they had been admitted in old age because they were "mentally disturbed" or had been admitted with functional mental disorders when younger and had grown old in the hospitals. Even in 1965, 70% of people 65 and over, for whom admission to Pennsylvania state hospitals was being sought, had a diagnosis of "senility." The Mental Health and Retardation Acts of 1963 and 1965 aimed to shift the major locus of care for the mentally ill from hospitals to the community. The popular slogan "back to the community" sounded benevolent, but there was no community to go back to in terms of facilities or services.

One major effect of all those demographic and socio-economic developments was to put enormous pressure on voluntary sectarian homes for the aged to admit the impaired aged. Another result was a spurt in the growth of proprietary nursing homes and in bootleg nursing homes, often euphemistically called "boarding homes." Since community services were virtually non-existent, the burden of care for the dependent older people remained on their families. The latter responded heroically, but often suffered severely as a result.

Against that background, the 1960s witnessed the growth of long waiting lists for facilities such as homes for the aged, and community agencies experienced increasing pressure for services such as homemakers, which traditionally had been geared towards helping young families. What was happening was that the increased numbers of older people, particularly very old people, were experiencing the chronic illnesses that are associated with age—Alzheimer's disease and related disorders, cardiovascular diseases, and arthritis, for example. The demand for health care was shifting radically from acute care to chronic care.

The phrase "long-term care" emerged to describe the system of government and private agencies and facilities that are needed to provide the variety of continuous, sustained services required by people with chronic disabilities. Attempts to define long-term care were not made until the late 1970s (Brody, E. M., 1977; U.S. National Committee on Vital and Health Statistics, 1978). Such care was defined as one or more services provided on a sustained basis to enable individuals whose functional capacities are chronically impaired to be maintained at their maximum levels of health and well-being. Efforts began to develop the components of the continuum of long-term care—in-home services, semi-independent living facilities, different types and levels of institutional care, and linkages of one to the other so that care plans could change as the older people's capacities changed. During the last decades of the 20th century, many more services and living facilities were invented. Though some programs proliferated (see chapter 17), they by no means are adequate either in number or accessibility as yet and are uneven regionally.

Though community and government agencies were slow to respond to the new needs, those needs now receive more attention than used to be the case. But the family did respond by inventing long-term care well before the phrase was articulated by professionals. In making the shift from episodic, short-term acute care to long-term care, the family proved to be more flexible, willing, and effective than professionals and policy-makers. While the family was struggling to meet the vastly increased needs of the old, however, its capacities to do so were being exceeded.

If we are to understand the predicament of parent-caring women, it is important to recognize that elder care has become a "normative" experience—an experience with which most people will be confronted at some time during their lives. Taken together, the increased number and proportion of very old people in the population, the rise in chronic ailments and the disabilities that result, and the falling birth rate mean that *contemporary adult children provide more care and more difficult care to more parents and parents-in-law over much longer periods of time than ever has been the case before* (Brody, E. M., 1985b). And, as the next chapter will show, "adult children" translates mainly to daughters and daughters-in-law.

WOMEN'S CHANGING LIFE-STYLES

While the demography and the kinds of help needed by older people were changing, so too were the lifestyles of the women who are the main caregivers to the old. The life patterns of women were becoming increasingly heterogeneous, and a "decrystallization" of rigid life patterns was occurring (Lopata & Norr, 1980). To a greater extent than ever before in history, women then began to follow divergent paths in the pursuit of personal lifestyles.

One of the most visible changes in women's lifestyles has been the vastly increased number of women who are employed or who do volunteer work. Among the factors that have contributed to that trend are the smaller number of children to keep women at home, economic pressures, the high divorce rate that sends many women to work, delayed ages at which marriages and motherhood occur, and, of course, the women's movement and changes in attitudes about gender-appropriate roles. Not only do contemporary women have fewer children to keep them at home than did women in previous generations, but they have more time for out-of-home activities such as employment and volunteer work because so many labor-saving devices for the home have been invented—washing machines, dish-washers, prepared foods, packaged goods, and throwaway paper products such as napkins and diapers, for example. Increased educational levels have stimulated career interests. Not least among reasons by any means, changes in the economy—the rising cost of living—compel many women to seek paid work.

Reinforced by the culture, work satisfaction and economic need form a powerful combination that motivates women to do paid work. Moreover, people have higher expectations for their children to have longer periods of education that require more money, and many couples enjoy and want to continue the higher standard of living that becomes accessible to the double-income family.

The proportion of women of all ages who work outside the home has soared. In 1930, for example, 24% of all women of working age worked outside the home. By 1950, one-third did so, and by 1998, 60% of women were working (compared to 75% of men) (U.S. Department of Labor, February 16, 2000). It is projected that by the year 2008, about 62% of women will be in the labor force (U.S. Department of Labor, Winter 1999). At present, approximately 74% of working women work full time. Increasing educational levels are evidenced by the fact that between 1900 and 2000, the percentages of women lawyers and doctors had risen from 1% to 29% and from 6% to 26% respectively.

A large proportion of the increase in women's labor force participation was attributable to the entry of middle-aged women into the workforce, and those are the women most likely to be in the parent-care years. In 1998, 76% of women aged 45 to 54 were working!

CHANGING PATTERNS OF MARRIAGE AND CHILDBEARING

The changes described thus far—demographic changes, changes in the nature of older people's health conditions, and the large-scale entry of middle-generation women into the labor force—are the broad trends that have combined to produce the women-in-the-middle phenomenon. (The problems of parent-caring women who work and the effects they experience are discussed in detail in chapter 11.)

But those trends do not tell the whole story. Women's lifestyles have been taking increasingly diverse paths in ways other than their labor force participation. Patterns of marriage, divorce, remarriage, and childbearing have been changing rapidly. Data reported in 1961 indicated that almost three-fourths of people (other than spouses) to whom older people turned for help in a health crisis were middle-generation married women (Shanas, 1961). By the time of the U.S. Long-Term Care Survey of 1982, 44% of daughter caregivers were not married. These not-married women either had never married (13.4%), were widowed (14.2%), or were divorced or separated (16.2%) (Stone, Cafferata, & Sangl, 1987). Married primary caregiving daughters in the 1999 National Long-Term Care Survey were 58.6% of the total, with 19% being divorced or separated, 11.1% widowed, and 10.3% never married (Center on an Aging Society, 1999).

A selection process appears to go on in many families so that an elderly parent tends to rely on the child with fewest competing responsibilities (Ikels, 1983; Shanas et al., 1968; Stoller, 1983). The high rates of widowhood among middle-aged women (the primary caregivers to the old), the soaring rates of divorce, and the rise in the proportion of women who do not marry probably account for the increase that occurred in the proportion of women who are not married during their years of parent care.

Though the divorce rate in the United States has been rising almost continuously since the early 1900s, the rise gradually accelerated, with divorce rate almost tripling in the years between 1962 and 1981 (U.S. National Center for Health Statistics, 1985). By 1980, approximately one marriage in four had ended in divorce for women born between 1908 and 1912. However, one-third of the first marriages of women born between 1923 and 1927 had ended in divorce by that year, and 42% of the marriages of females born between 1948 and 1950 were projected to do so. Many of those women are now in the parent-care years (Schoen, 1985). In the year 1996, there were almost half as many divorces as there were marriages (U.S. Bureau of the Census, 2001).

Although statistics on divorce have frequently been cited as evidence of the seeming unpopularity of marriage and family life, data on remarriage tend to refute this assertion. Remarriages have always been common in the United States, but until the 1900s, almost all remarriages were after the death of a spouse. Since then, remarriage after divorce has increased and became the predominant form of remarriage.

Remarriage after divorce implies a complexity of family life unknown to other types of families. Unique and compounded problems of kinship, family authority and responsibility, and legal relationships represent added opportunities for disagreement, strain, and divisions among family members. The fragility of these "blended" families may be due to the fact that the institution of the family offers no standardized norms or solutions for problems faced by the remarried—that the institution of "family" developed primarily in response to the needs of first families. Consequently, the institutionalized patterns of family behavior are not in place for families of remarriage. There is no information about the patterns of parent care that occur in such situations. Nor is there information about those patterns when the parents now in need of help had remarried. To which parent or set of elderly parents do the filial loyalties go?

It is likely that widowed daughters will constitute an increasing proportion of caregiving daughters. The disabled elderly come primarily from the ranks of the rising number and proportion of *very* old people whose children are older and therefore more likely to be widowed. Rates of widowhood soar beginning in middle age. And, of course, more women are remaining unmarried, with the marriage rate for all unmarried women aged 15 and over declining (U.S. National Center for Health Statistics, 1986).

If those trends continue, in the future there will be even more daughter caregivers without husbands during their parent care years. Expectations about parent care that are placed upon not-married daughters may be greater than for their married peers. In addition, not-married women experience strains specific to their marital status that are unrelated to parent care, but that may complicate the picture when they are helping a parent. Those strains are described in Chapter 11 and are apparent in the case studies in that chapter.

MYTH AND THE EVIDENCE

Despite all those trends that have increased the needs for parent care and increased women's responsibilities, and no matter how much evidence is assembled about the women's filial reliability, the myth of the "good old days" persists. It is so stubborn that Ethel Shanas called it a "hydra-headed monster" (Shanas, 1979a). (The hydra monster of Greek mythology had nine heads and could not be killed because it grew two new heads in place of each one that was cut off.)

It is very likely that the myth has multiple determinants. Undoubtedly, it was reinforced by the sociological theory of the "isolated nuclear family." That widely accepted theory held that the nuclear family (parents and growing children) was the main and most effective family form in modern industrialized society, having replaced the extended family of the United States of an earlier time (Parsons & Bales, 1955). As a result, the aged were believed to be isolated from and even rejected by their families.

Research on these questions began slowly with studies that examined the relationship of older people in general with their families. The findings of those studies challenged a variety of assumptions related to the myth of family alienation from the aged. It was generally thought, for example, that the elderly rarely saw their families, that intergenerational bonds had become weaker, and even that families "dumped" disabled old people into institutions. In the early 1960s, broad surveys of non-institutionalized older people across the nation began to assemble the facts. Those surveys were mainly conducted by Ethel Shanas and her colleagues here and abroad (Reid, 1966; Rosow, 1965; Shanas, 1960, 1979b; Shanas & Streib, 1965; Shanas et al., 1968; Strieb, 1958). Their findings are still valid today:

- Virtually all older people do have some family members, with only a tiny proportion having absolutely no kin.
- Ties between the generations are strong and viable. Adult children do not abdicate their responsibilities, and continuing contacts are the rule rather than the exception.
- Just over two-thirds of elderly care recipients live within an hour's distance of at least one adult child (Spillman & Pezzin, 2000). They and their children prefer to live near but not with each other, a preference that had been described as a wish for "intimacy at a distance" (Rosenmayhr & Kockeis, 1963). Most of the elderly not only live close to a child, but see those children (and grandchildren) frequently.
- Intergenerational exchanges of services are the rule rather than the exception. Those exchanges are reciprocal, with the aged giving as well as receiving the garden-variety of help that family members give each other on a day-to-day basis.
- When families are unable to care for their disabled elderly, a constellation of personal, social, and economic factors are at work. In the main, institutionalization of older people is the last resort of families after all possible alternatives have been explored. (See chapter 16.)

There are no indications at all that the situation is any different today. In 1997, of the 34 million older people living in the community (that is, not in an institution), two-thirds lived in a family setting (80% of older men and 57% of older women). Almost 10 million (about 31%) lived alone (80% of whom were women) (U.S. Administration on Aging, 1998). Older people have frequent contacts with relatives. Despite increased geographic mobility, those with children frequently see and talk with them on the phone. In 1984 and again in 1994, slightly over two-thirds of potential caregivers (i.e., adult children in addition to spouses) lived within an hour of the care recipient: 97% of primary caregivers and 93% of secondaries (Spillman & Pezzin, 2000, p. 8).

Parenthetically, it is interesting that very recently a study in England revisited three urban areas there in order to detect trends that might have occurred since they were studied a half century ago (Phillipson, Bernard, Phillips, & Ogg, 2001). Despite the passage of time and major population changes which included significant immigration of minority ethnic groups, the conclusion drawn was that " . . . kinship ties have held up well to the developments effecting urban societies over the past fifty years . . . " and that the central core of supports (spouses and daughters especially) is crucial to distributing help in a variety of ways (Phillipson et al., 2001, p. 251).

When, in 1963, The Gerontological Society of America and Duke University sponsored the symposium mentioned above in order to examine the facts about the family relationships of older people (Shanas & Streib, 1965), the conveners felt that the three-generation family required consideration because it had become so common. They agreed that many programs for older people were based on social myths that had persisted because the assumptions on which they were founded had not been scrutinized by scholars.

That symposium was a significant watershed in the study of intergenerational relations. There was such consensus among the social scientists, that one of them called the conference a "bench mark of the final respects paid to the isolated nuclear family before its interment" (Rosow, 1965, p. 341). A consistent theme was the responsible behavior of adult children in helping their parents.

The scholars who participated in the conference were so certain that discovery of the facts would put an end to the notion of the isolated nuclear family that one of them stated flatly, "The isolated nuclear family is a myth. This has already been conclusively demonstrated. It does not merit any further attention from the field, and I, for one, refuse to waste any more time even discussing it" (Sussman in Shanas & Streib, 1965, p. 341). Unfortunately, however, the notion of the isolated nuclear family is still firmly entrenched.

A reason for the persistence of the myth at that time may have related to nursing homes. The number of elderly people placed in nursing homes was increasing rapidly during the 1960s and 1970s because of the increase of the very old who were disabled. Such facilities became highly visible on the American scene. Though this did not represent family abandonment (see chapter 16), it was often interpreted in that way. Moreover, institutions were (and often still are) viewed negatively in reaction to abuses both in institutions of an earlier day (such as poorhouses and mental hospitals) and in those of today about which periodic scandals continue to erupt. It is interesting to note, however, that during the decade between 1984 and 1994, the percentage of the 65+ population in nursing homes has remained constant at about 5% of the elderly population (Spillman & Pezzin, 2000).

A powerful force in perpetuating the myth that families do not do enough for their elderly is political motivation. It permits legislators to avoid funding needed services and programs using the rationale that it is up to families to do the caregiving.

More subtle psychological forces may also be at work in keeping the myth alive. The many role losses and interpersonal losses of aged people may be experienced psychologically as abandonment. The elderly may be expressing an unconscious fear of additional losses or a wish for more attention and care than their children are able to provide. The myth is also consonant with the strength of the values of "home" and "family." Phrases such as, "There's no place like home" and "Home is where the heart is," reflect those deeply entrenched values and feelings. In psychological terms, then, the myth may be translated as the fear of losing one's own home, lifestyle, and independence.

The myth may also be an expression of the guilt of a youth-oriented society in need of a scapegoat for the general social neglect of its old. Certainly, it represents a lag in social expectations that have not changed to keep pace with the changing socioeconomic and demographic developments described above. The "etiquette of filial behavior"—that is, the outmoded conventions and stereotyped attitudes of an earlier phase of history—has persisted rather than responded to current realities (Brody, E. M., 1970). Value-laden words like "abandonment" and "dumping" are used to describe a situation in which older people do not always receive the services they need or wish for from adult children because the latter are unable—not unwilling—to provide them.

In addition, there is the tendency to romanticize and idealize the past. A good example of that tendency is the notion that in the past, three-generational living was preferred, whereas, nowadays, older people long wistfully to be taken into their children's home but are rejected. This is epitomized in the bitter saying, "One mother had room for all her children, but none of them has room for her." Yet information showed that "the three-generation family to which contemporary commentators often point with nostalgia, in some cases may have been forced on poor families for lack of any palatable substitute" (Rosenheim, 1965). Kent (1965) characterized as the illusion of the "Golden Past" the fact that "the three-generation family pictured as a farm idyll is common, yet all evidence indicates that at no time in any society was a three-generation family ever the common mode, and even less evidence that it was idyllic." In the same vein, when Laslett (1976) studied historical documents such as legal records, household census data, and parish registries, he referred to the "world-we-have-lost syndrome." He pointed to the rarity of three-generation families and households in the past, the instances of severe family conflict, and the impoverished neglect suffered by some old people.

Where multigeneration households did exist in the past, it was likely that young couples, on marrying, lived in the homes of their parents. Such arrangements were considerably more feasible in the rural communities of the old days than in the more crowded quarters of our urbanized, industrialized society. They also reflected the economic inability of young marrieds to live on their own. The modern pattern is for a young couple to set up a separate home.

Bengtson and Treas (1980) pointed out the influence of social, economic, and demographic consideration in shaping intergenerational relations in the past. Not only were multigeneration households uncommon, but when they did exist, they were of short duration. Economics played a major role, since older people often could not afford to live separately. Moreover, an older person with income was an asset to poor families, and grandparents (particularly grandmothers) could provide much assistance with childcare and housekeeping. Prosperous old people could exercise much control over the lives of adult children. Parental power was formidable when day-to-day subsistence and even the chance to marry depended on parents' willingness to provide dowries to daughters and to turn over the family farm or business to sons. Many historical accounts show that considerable, even bitter, conflicts occurred at times between elderly parents and their adult children.

It bears repetition that, by their own account, the elderly prefer to live *near* but not *with* their children. Financial problems limit choices about living arrangements, however. With the improved levels of income older people have nowadays, more of them are able to live the way they prefer—separately from their children. Though they would prefer to live close geographically to their children, increasing mobility has been making that proximity less feasible for some.

It is interesting that, as the generations were freed in the main from financial obligations to each other, emotional bonds rose in relative importance and apparently are stronger, rather than weaker, than they were in the past. In a study of three generations of women, for example, it was found that middle-generation women were giving more emotional support to their elderly mothers than the latter had given to *their* mothers when at the same ages (Brody, E. M., Johnsen, Fulcomer, & Lang, 1983). Those elderly mothers, however, had given more financial help to *their* mothers than they were receiving from their daughters. At the same time, the younger women had more competing responsibilities than did their mothers at comparable ages and had helped their own adult children longer both financially and emotionally. More of the middle-aged women studied were in the labor force or were more involved in volunteer work than their mothers had been at comparable ages.

To summarize: the major trends that brought about the phenomenon of women in the middle have been the development of a large population of chronically disabled older people, the falling birth rate, and the changing lifestyles of women (including labor-force participation and changing patterns of marriage and divorce). Despite the trends, however, there is strong consensus among scholars that family ties are as strong as ever, and family members make strenuous efforts to meet their responsibilities in caring for their elderly.

The next chapter looks at the scope of the need for parent care at present—how many older people need help, the kinds of assistance they need, and the role of adult daughters and daughters-in-law in providing it—that is, the role of women in the middle who nowadays have more elderly parents and more competing responsibilities than ever before in history.

Chapter 2

The Scope of Parent Care

Information relevant to the scope of parent care includes:

1. The number and proportion of older people who need help to function in their daily lives and the various kinds of help they need;
2. The distribution of helping services between the family or informal system of care and the formal system of government, voluntary agencies, and paid workers; and
3. The identity and characteristics of the particular members of the family who provide care, with special reference to the roles of adult daughters and daughters-in-law.

OLDER PEOPLE'S NEEDS FOR CARE

The previous chapter noted that the needs of the increasing population of old and very old people have changed because chronic ailments have replaced acute diseases as their major health problems. By definition, chronic diseases cannot be cured and can last for many years. In contrast to acute ailments, they may result in disabilities that require ongoing dependency on others. As acute diseases such as pneumonia, tuberculosis, poliomyelitis, childbed fever, and smallpox were brought under control by advances in public health and by the development of antibiotics and vaccines, a dramatic drop occurred in the proportions of deaths due to such illnesses. Between 1900 and 1980, the percentage of deaths due to infectious diseases dropped from 40% to 6%! It is well to remember, however, that trends often take unexpected directions. Between 1980 and 1992, deaths from infectious diseases increased to more than 9% of all deaths (a 58% increase) (U.S. National Center for Infectious Diseases,

2001). The Center report commented that infectious disease rates are volatile.

When so many people were enabled to surmount the barriers that previously had caused deaths at earlier ages, there was a rise in the incidence and prevalence of chronic, age-related ailments such as Alzheimer's disease and related disorders, rheumatoid arthritis, diabetes, osteoporosis, and cardiovascular and cerebrovascular disease. The postponement of death by medical interventions has been called the "Failures of Success" (Gruenberg, 1977). That is, disabled people's lives have been prolonged into more years of dependency that in turn mean more years during which there must be someone on whom to depend. The result has been a radical change in the nature of the health services needed by elderly people from acute (i.e., temporary) care to chronic (i.e., sustained) care. Nowadays, 34% of people between the ages of 65 and 74 and 45% of those 75 and over are limited in activities by chronic conditions (Trupin & Rice, June 1995). That is not to say, however, that their limitations necessarily mean that help from others is needed or that acute care is never needed.

The rise of chronic disease and resultant disabilities gave impetus to the development of ways of assessing people's capacities to function in their daily lives. Such assessment has been defined as any systematic attempt to measure objectively the level at which an individual is functioning in a variety of areas (Lawton, 1971). The phrase "functional assessment," so widely used today, has its roots in the field of rehabilitation. The orientation to *function* rather than to *diagnosis* recognizes that diagnosis (although of vital importance to medical treatment) does not indicate the nature of the day-to-day, ongoing services required. People with the same diagnosis—arthritis, for example—may require vastly different kinds of help. One person with some arthritis in a shoulder or hand may be completely independent, whereas another may be so disabled as to be in a wheelchair and require help with toileting, getting in and out of bed, and other personal activities.

Functional assessment serves many purposes. Originally, it was seen as the basis for setting treatment goals when aiming to improve an individual's level of functioning. It can also indicate the amount and nature of the help an individual needs from others and makes it possible to estimate the numbers of people who have various levels of disability. When assessment data on many individuals are aggregated, the information can be used to plan services and programs and to indicate what health and social policy should do to meet the needs (Lawton & Brody, E. M., 1969).

First came ways of measuring people's capacities for what are called "activities of daily living" (ADL)—that is, basic functions such as bathing, dressing, eating, toileting, transferring, and ambulating (getting around inside) (Katz, Ford, Moskowitz, Jackson, & Jaffee, 1963). Then came assessment of the higher order capabilities that are called "instrumental activities of daily living" (IADL): the ability to use a telephone, shopping, food preparation, housekeeping, laundry, transportation, taking medications, and handling finances (Lawton & Brody, E. M., 1969). If the ADL and IADL capacities of older people are assessed and the people who help with the various tasks are identified, it becomes possible to estimate not only the numbers of the elderly who are in need of help, but also to determine the sources of the assistance they receive. It must be kept in mind, however, that while older people with ADL deficits clearly are more disabled than those who have only IADL deficits, there are variations within each of these categories. Needing help to shop and cook, for example, is considerably less demanding of a caregiver than needing assistance in all IADLs.

Information concerning older people's functional status is of central importance to the subject of this book, since most of the required care is provided by the adult daughters who are the women in the middle. There are a variety of categories of services needed by disabled older people that will be discussed in turn. Because functional status is used almost universally to determine the level and type of need, that category of assistance will be discussed first.

FUNCTIONAL ASSISTANCE NEEDED BY OLDER PEOPLE

Assessment instruments have been used in many studies to estimate the dependencies in the elderly population. (The assessment instruments themselves, however, do not address the matter of who helps older people. This will be discussed later.) When looking at the proportions of old people who need various levels of help, it should be kept in mind that the data are cross-sectional. That is, the data tell us how many individuals need various kinds of help at any given time—the time at which the particular survey was done. But people's capacities change over time. An older person who needs help only with transportation and shopping today may need help with those tasks plus housekeeping and cooking tomorrow. Still further in the future, she may need all of those forms of help plus assistance with bathing and dressing. Still later, help with feeding and toileting may be needed as well.

Not all people develop increasing disabilities gradually, of course. Some may make a rapid transition from total independence to considerable dependency if they experience a sudden catastrophic illness such as a massive stroke. That is not to say that the direction of change is invariably downward, though it often is. Functioning levels may be improved as people recover from acute episodes of disease or with good care and rehabilitative measures (Brody, S. J., 1990). Careful evaluation is always important, therefore, so that the older person can be enabled to reach his or her maximum level of functioning. When an older person is helped to move from an inability to walk to being able to walk with a walker, or from being unable to get in and out of bed to being able to do so independently, it makes a tremendous difference to the caregiver as well as to the disabled individual.

Estimates of the number and proportion of older people who need help, the kinds of help they need, and the sources of that help derive from a variety of surveys and reports. Various surveys often use different criteria for definitions and descriptions of both the populations in need of help and those who provide the help. For example, the age criterion for needing help in one survey may be age 50 or over, age 65 or over in another, and 70 or over in still another. Even the definition of "help" may vary. Help may be defined as chronic and ongoing or it may include temporary or sporadic assistance. Caregivers are generally called "primary" (the individual who provides most of the care) and "secondary" (those who provide additional help to assist the primary), and are sorted at times into "active" and "potential." "Active" caregivers are those who are usually defined as actually providing care, and "potentials" are spouses or children who exist and might provide care if needed.

Counting and identifying primary and secondary caregivers is a complex enterprise. Primary caregivers, for example, are not all co-equal. A caregiver who is a primary may be so titled if she (or he) helps a parent who needs only shopping and transportation assistance. A primary caregiver in another family may be identified in the same way, but is helping with bathing, toileting, dressing, and walking. Furthermore, a secondary for an extremely disabled older person may be doing much more caregiving than one called primary when the patient for whom the latter is caring is mildly disabled.

To further complicate the picture, in some analyses sons and daughters are grouped together as "children," and in others husbands and wives are combined as "spouses." Similarly, husbands and sons may be grouped as "men," while wives and daughters may be grouped as "women." And some analyses count only spouses and adult children as caregivers, and in general only one individual is counted as the "secondary" although there may be several such additional caregivers. Though each survey may serve a particular purpose, one should be aware of the above differences in interpreting the data and in drawing conclusions.

In their exhaustive search of the literature and thorough scrutiny of studies done between 1990 and 2002 about disability among older Americans, Freedman, Martin, and Schoeni (2002) selected eight surveys from among more than 800 titles. Rating those eight surveys on a variety of criteria, they selected two as being the best: The National Health Interview Survey (Crummins, Saito, & Reynolds, 1997, and Schoeni, Freedman, & Wallace, 2001) and the National Long-Term Care Survey (Manton, Corder, & Stallard, 1997, and Manton & Gu, 2001).

The widely used National Long-Term Care Survey (NLTCS) will be used in presenting the information in this Chapter since it has major advantages for our purposes. First the NLTCS included the institutionalized population. Secondly, the 1984 and 1994 NLTCS were supplemented by what are called Companion Caregiver Surveys. (The NLTC Surveys are conducted every 10 years by the U.S. Department of Health and Human Services). The findings of the 1984 and 1994 Caregiver Surveys as well as the findings about older people's functional capacities are described and trends identified in an excellent article by Spillman and Pezzin (2002), using an analysis of the 1984 data in an article by Stone and Kemper (1989).

Before summarizing the findings of the NLTCS, it is important to recognize that they are not comprehensive in that they do not collect data about all older people who need long term help for various reasons other than ADL or IADL deficits. Once such instance is the group of people who need oversight or supervision because of cognitive or other impairment. Some of those with early Alzheimer's disease, for example, may be functionally capable but may wander off or leave the stove on and therefore require vigilance on the part of family members.

Another segment of the disabled elderly population whose needs are not documented by the NLTCS are those who are "disturbed" because of functional mental illnesses or other reasons. Still another population not surveyed in terms of care needed from families is the "under-65 population of chronically disabled individuals with lifelong mental illness (e.g., schizophrenia), physical impairment, or developmental disability for whom family caregiving remains the primary source of assistance (particularly for mothers whose own aging, in turn, compromises their continuing ability to provide care (Lebowitz, B., May 2001, personal communication).

This chapter will also include some brief information from well-publicized surveys that were carried out for special purposes. One such survey was conducted by the Administration on Aging. A second survey contains some information about the increasing number of Alzheimer's patients, since that ailment is a powerful predictor of caregiver stress. That information was gathered by the 1996 National Caregiver Survey conducted by the National Alliance for Caregiving and American Association for Retired Persons (Wagner, 1997). The latter survey also permits the inclusion of some additional data—for example, about the caregivers' characteristics. A third survey, conducted by the AARP and called "In the Middle" reported on multi-cultural Baby Boomers and aging issues.

First, the data from NLTCS and other surveys will be presented, followed by descriptions of on the various forms of help needed and the allocation of help between formal and informal systems. Then the question will be answered regarding the identity of the particular people in the family who provided the required assistance—primarily adult daughters and daughters-in-law. The latter are characterized here as "proxy primaries." Finally, "secondary" caregivers will also be described as will those in the family who could be called the "back-up system."

THE NATIONAL LONG-TERM CARE SURVEYS (NLTCS)

The NLTCS are of the chronically disabled elderly who are 65 years of age and over and of their active and potential caregivers, both primary and secondary. These surveys have the strictest criteria of all the reports described in that the age criterion for inclusion of the disabled is 65 or over, only spouses and adult children were included as family caregivers unless they lived with the older person or were caregivers, and the elderly had to be experiencing ADL and IADL deficits requiring human assistance for at least three months. The survey did include elderly in institutions as well as those living in the community. Data were collected and reported about help from both the formal (paid workers) and informal (family and friends) systems when the elderly were in the community but did not collect information about family caregivers who help people in institutions.

Based on the 1994 NLTCS, Spillman and Pezzin (2000) updated the estimates of potential and active caregivers reported by Stone and Kemper (1989) that were based on the 1984 NLTCS. Thus, their article speaks to trends—that is, the changes over the decade between 1984 and 1994 in the prevalence of chronic disability and the sources of care in each of those years.

Spillman and Pezzin make many important observations about the changes between 1984 and 1994. First, they note a decline in the prevalence of chronic disability requiring human assistance from 19.7% of the elderly to 16.7%, although the number of disabled individuals remained fairly constant at about 5.5 million. Those figures include institutionalized older people. The decline is notable in light of the fact that the total 65+ population increased from about 28 million to 33.1 million in that time period. The authors point out, however, that the decline occurred primarily among the least disabled. Freedman, Martin, and Schoeni (2002) came to the same conclusion. That is, the prevalence of IADL-only limitations dropped from 7.7% to 5% while the prevalence of any ADL limitation remained constant at about 12%. However, those receiving care were more disabled in 1994 than in 1984, though the percentage of the total disabled aged population declined in both years. About 4.6% of older people were receiving ADL help in institutions. (Institutions included nursing homes, mental health facilities, and chronic disease facilities.) Those in personal care homes without 24-hour health personnel were counted as community residents.

The percentages in the NLTCS should not obscure the fact that the levels of help needed vary greatly within the total disabled population of older persons. Thus, for example, in 1994, within the total of 16.7% of all chronically disabled elderly, 5% received help only with IADLs, 4.6% with two ADLs, and 7.2% with three to six ADLs. As might be expected, the 4.9% of all elderly who were in institutions was made up of 0.4% of the total elderly population receiving only IADL help, 0.9% who had help with one to two ADLs, and 3.7% with three to six ADLs.

In 1984, three fifths of the 7.3 million active, informal caregivers to disabled older people were spouses or children (Stone & Kemper, 1989), a proportion that had increased to two-thirds by 1994. As stated, the NLTCS did not collect information about the informal caregivers of the elderly in institutions, so those percentages are low to that extent. Nor were data collected on other relatives unless they were caregivers or lived with the older person.

It is important to note that at least twice as many chronically disabled elderly were living in the community as were in institutions (11.8% versus 5.9%) (Spillman & Pezzin, 2000). During the same 10-year time span, the number of potential caregivers (spouses and children) increased slightly from 13.9 million to 14.6 million. Moreover, while the proportion of the older people in institutions rose as the number of their disabilities increased, even among the most disabled (three to six ADL deficiencies), almost as many (3.5%) were in the community as were in institutions (3.7%). And it was only at that severe level of disability that the proportions were similar. Of those with one to two ADLs, 3.7% lived in the community compared with 0.9% in institutions. The difference was even greater among those who were IADL disabled only: 4.6% in the community and 0.4% in institutions. In short, the survey once again confirmed that primary caregivers—the women in the middle—surely were not "dumping" their elderly into institutions. In fact, many were maintaining their extremely impaired parents in what long ago were characterized as "one-bed nursing homes." Reasons for placement in nursing homes, in addition to the need for extreme levels of care, will be discussed in chapter 16.

It is reiterated that these surveys did not include older people without functional disabilities but who may have needed oversight or supervision due to early dementia, lifelong psychiatric problems, or developmental disabilities. The inclusion of such older people undoubtedly would have increased the count of older people in need of care and also, of course, increased the numbers of caregivers. Nor were informal caregivers of institutionalized older people included, though, as chapter 16 will show, such caregivers continue to do a great deal.

THE U.S. ADMINISTRATION ON AGING REPORT

The U.S. Administration on Aging report (1998), based on data from the U.S. Bureau of the Census and the National Center for Health Statistics, reported disability rates differently. It stated that in 1995 14% of the 65+ population (4.4 million persons) "had difficulty in carrying out activities of daily living (ADLs) and 21% (6.5 million persons) reported difficulties with IADLs"—that is a total of 37.2% of older people. In reconciling the discrepancies in proportions of disabled people reported in different surveys, language is important. For example, the AOA states that the older people in its survey who were counted as having disabilities "reported difficulties" with the activities, while the NLTC survey based its estimates on chronic disability requiring "human assistance for at least three months" in carrying out the activities.

THE NATIONAL ALLIANCE FOR CAREGIVING AND AARP SURVEY

This telephone survey was carried out in 1996 with respondents capable of answering questions in English (NAC/AARP Survey, 1997). The criteria for inclusion were much less stringent than those of the NLTCS in that the age of recipients of care was set at 50 years or over and they could be free of chronic disability, but had required only temporary help during the year. Households were counted which contained at least one member who was currently caring for a relative or friend (76% of the households) or had provided informal care to a relative or friend within the past 12 months but was not currently doing so (24% of the households). Because of those criteria, the estimate of the caregiving population was much higher than that of the NLTCS. The report concluded that 23% of U.S. households had met the criteria (Wagner, 1997).

Though the use of age 50 and the very broad definition of caregiving have some problems for our focus on women in the middle—that is, daughters and daughters-in-law who are primary caregivers—the National Alliance/AARP report contains some information useful for our purposes. Some conclusions can be inferred from some of the survey data, if we bear in mind that the average age of the care recipients identified in the survey was 77 in 1987 and 78 in 1997—clearly a population that was mainly elderly. Moreover, only 11% and 12% respectively were under age 65 in the two years compared, and 82% of the total had chronic ailments.

The explicit inclusion in the survey of care recipients with dementia or other mental/emotional illnesses is of particular interest here. More than one in five caregivers reported taking care of someone with Alzheimer's disease, confusion, dementia, or forgetfulness as the primary or secondary illness or condition. This finding, states the report, translates into an estimated 5,020,000 caregiving households nationwide that provide care for someone with dementia. In an additional 2.8% of cases, mental or emotional illness was named as the main illness or problem. Not surprisingly, higher percentages of caregivers of dementia patients rated the caregiving demand or intensity as highest of all illnesses or problems.

AARP REPORT ON THE BABY BOOMERS

Baby boomers were redefined by a report of the American Association of Retired Persons (AARP, 2001) as being age 45–55 at the time of a telephone survey in March 2001. The rationale offered by AARP for using a 10-year rather than the usual 20-year age span was that the boomers are the current "sandwich generation"—that is, they are the ones most likely to have both dependent children and aging parents, and, hence, more caregiving responsibilities. The AARP survey found that 44% of their Sandwich Generation had both living parent(s) and children under 21. Twenty-four percent of that group actually helped care for parents, in-laws, or other older adults.

The AARP report is another addition to the long list of studies finding that women still bear most of the burden in providing support. The implications for women in the middle, who have not shirked parent care or lessened their efforts to date, are clear. Unless there are dramatic changes, there will be more and more of them who will be responsible for the enormous group of very old, disabled people. One wonders what the saturation point will be for women in the middle, what the effects on them and their families will be, and what measures are indicated and will actually be taken to deal with their situations.

Despite the increased parent care responsibilities of the baby boomers, the AARP report once again refutes any implication of decreasing filial responsibility. The boomers not only affirmed the importance of family and of caring for their elderly, but also echoed the feelings of their parents that they do not want to impose their own future needs on their children—the familiar, well documented wish "not to be a burden."

It is no surprise, of course, that women in the "sandwich" provided more help than men in activities that consume greater time and energy—for example, talking to doctors, shopping, arranging for aides, and, of course, helping with personal care. As in other studies, the women reported more feelings of stress than the men. Overall, like the generations that preceded them, guilt figured prominently. Almost half of the baby boomers reported feeling somewhat guilty for not doing more!

The report concluded with an injunction concerning the need for government to provide caregiver support for the baby boom generation. It is added here that the need is vital for caregivers in all generations.

MORE ABOUT BABY BOOMERS

Justifiably, baby boomers are attracting an enormous amount of attention at present. As this is being written, each day more and more of them are finding themselves deeply immersed in parent care. This cohort of people who constitute the bump in the otherwise downward slope of the birthrate in this century is generally defined as those 76 million persons born between 1946 and 1964—a 20 year period. By 2010, the first boomers will reach the ranks of old age.

The 1984 LTCS found that 3.6 million men and women were in the Sandwich Generation—that is, having both a disabled elderly parent and one or more children under age 15 (Stone & Kemper, 1989). Spillman and Pezzin (2000) noted that there has been a significant increase in the importance of middle aged, active caregivers between the ages of 45 and 50, both as primaries and secondaries.

A research report on the subject points out that adults in their 50s are particularly vulnerable to being in the "sandwich" between frail elderly parents and their own children (Boaz, Hu, & Ye, 1999). In that study, one-fifth of middle-aged households included at least one elderly parent who could not be left alone and needed ADL help. These were mostly multi-generational households that also included children and even grandchildren. In 29% of the multi-generational households, the adult children provide care, gave money for needed care, and/or shared living space with the disabled parents.

While the baby boomers by no means make up the total population of parent-carers, they claim our attention for a variety of reasons. Looking to the future, they will enter their elderly years beginning in 2010. By the year 2050, the survivors of that group will swell the ranks of the oldest old people (those aged 85 and over), so that they will number 19 million people—24% of all older people and 5% of all Americans (U.S. Bureau of the Census, May 1995). (Contrast those figures with those for 1994 when the "oldest old" numbered 3 million people—10% of the elderly and slightly over 1% of the total population). The Boomers therefore provide a glimpse of what the future will be like for potential care recipients and their caregivers.

Boomers are in double jeopardy. There will be more of them who require care proportionate to the number of adult children available to provide assistance, because their fertility rate was less than two children compared with between 2.4 and 3.6 children for their parents' cohorts (Spillman & Pezzin, 2000). The Bureau of the Census (May, 1995) calculates such changes in terms of the parent-support ratio: (This ratio equals the number of persons aged 85 and over per 100 persons aged 50 to 64). Between 1950 and 1993, the ratio tripled from 3 to 10. Over the next six decades, it could triple yet again to 29.

VARIOUS KINDS OF HELP NEEDED

Though day-to-day functional assistance is a vital and major form of caregiving, it is not the only kind of help needed by older people. Horowitz (1985a) conceptualized family caregiving activities (a conceptualization that is still valid) as falling into four broad categories: the direct services of helping with ADL and IADL, emotional support, mediation with formal organizations and providers (government and social and health agencies), and financial assistance. She pointed out that sharing one's home with a disabled old person is a special form of caregiving that may encompass and facilitate the other kinds of help. The word "caregiving" can describe all help ranging from minimal assistance to total care including assistance with IADL and constant supervision as with Alzheimer's patients, for example.

To that categorization of helping services should be added other forms of assistance that do not occur on a daily basis and almost invariably are provided by the family, such as response and dependability in emergencies, at times of temporary illness or special need, and when convalescent or rehabilitative care is necessary. Those other kinds of help make special demands on caregivers. If such assistance were to be included in counting the numbers of caregivers and care recipients, estimates of the proportion of elderly receiving help and the amounts of help they receive surely would be larger.

Certainly, all people, including older people, who are essentially capable and do not need day-to-day functional assistance may need such special help from time to time. But the disabled elderly undoubtedly have such needs more frequently. They have more medical emergencies, are more often hospitalized, more often need convalescent or rehabilitative care, and may move from one residence to another more often. They may move into specialized housing for the elderly, into an adult child's home, into an assisted living facility, or into a nursing home. Such occasions often constitute a major upheaval with much effort and time required of the helping family members.

Emotional support is the most universal form of family caregiving, the one most wanted by older people from their children and the one the adult children themselves feel is the most important service they can give their disabled parent(s). It is also the kind of help for which no government or paid worker can substitute. The provision of emotional support cannot be quantified and is probably underestimated with respect to the time and effort consumed. Its importance to the elderly cannot be overestimated. It includes being the confidant or the one with whom problems can be talked over; providing social contacts such as phoning, visiting, or taking the elderly person out to family events; and help with decision-making. Most of all, such support means giving the older person the sense of having someone on whom to rely—someone who is interested and concerned, who cares, and who listens. The role of adult daughters in providing this form of support was shown in one study by the responses of elderly women when they were asked to name their main confidant. When the women were married, they most often named their husbands, but widowed women most often named a daughter (Brody, E. M., Johnsen, Fulcomer, & Lang, 1982a). Becoming a widowed parent's main source of emotional support can be the first as well as an ongoing and important filial service.

The effort and difficulties involved in providing emotional support to a parent can be considerable. Some older people need so much support that it can consume many hours a week and be stressful as well. When there have been interpersonal problems between parent and daughter, the increased time spent with each other and opportunities for differences can exacerbate those problems. Although most adult children want to visit and to take the older person on outings, activities of that kind may be difficult to fit into a busy schedule. Or, the notions of the older person and the daughter may not mesh with regard to how frequently such contacts should take place. This in itself may be a strain for the caregiver—that is, the realization that her parent feels that what the daughter is doing is not enough.

Mediation with organizations is a service now called "case management" when it is done by professionals. The real case managers, however, are family members who far outnumber professionals in performing that function. Such mediation or management involves knowing or finding out what entitlements the older person has—for Social Security and Medicare benefits, for example. It involves identifying what services are needed and knowing whether they are available in the community. It involves gaining access to and mobilizing those services—getting in touch with the particular organizations, establishing eligibility, and following through to see that services are actually received and are satisfactory. Such activities are not only time-consuming but may be frustrating as well as step after step must be taken to unravel the red tape involved.

The need to do those things may be new to both the older person and the adult child, neither of whom may have had any previous need to use services from the formal system. Nor is service management a one-time effort. The conditions and needs of older people and their families change and access to different services must be obtained. It is an ongoing task to monitor and orchestrate the various services, as the most careful arrangements break down from time to time. An in-home paid worker may fail to show up on time or to arrive at all, for example, making a flurry of unexpected activity necessary.

Financial support from adult children to their parents has become a much less important pattern nowadays than was true in the early part of the last century. Taking money from one's children is the form of help least wanted by older people and is undoubtedly part of their overarching wish not to be a burden. It is now generally accepted that assuring an income floor for the elderly should be a government responsibility. Through Social Security (1935) and Supplemental Security Income (SSI) (1974), that income floor has been established, though it is low and reductions in benefits are threatened from time to time by proposed changes in social policy.

The change in patterns of financial help is illustrated dramatically by the fact that the proportion of older people who were wholly dependent on their children for economic support dropped after Social Security was enacted from approximately half in 1937 to 1.5% in 1979 (Upp, 1982). Pensions and savings have also helped, of course. Similarly, before Medicare came into being in 1965, an aged person's catastrophic illness could wipe out his or her own savings and impose a severe, even crushing, financial burden on adult children. It was not uncommon in those days for adult children to be compelled to forego sending their own children to college because elderly parents needed support simply to subsist. Total economic dependency is different, however, from not receiving any financial help at all. Nowadays, some adult children do indeed help out with money or by purchasing things needed by the parent. The contributions may be for necessities or for the amenities that make life more comfortable.

There also are costs other than out-of-pocket outlays. Costs that were invisible until the late 1980s are the "opportunity costs" incurred when spouses or adult children quit their jobs, reduce the number of their working hours, refuse job promotions, or take unpaid leaves of absence to take care of the elderly (see chapter 14).

In any case, the complete picture of financial contributions by adult children, whether for amenities or for the purchase of actual care of their disabled parents, has yet to be filled in and, of course changes from time to time. The extent of the burden to those children also varies greatly, depending on their own economic situations.

Shared Households

As Horowitz (1985a) pointed out, shared households are a special form of parent care. Both elderly parents and adult children agree overwhelmingly that it is not desirable for them to co-reside, opinions that are validated by the strains reported by caregivers in such arrangements (see chapter 3). In the main, shared households are formed when the older person is too disabled to live alone or cannot afford to do so. In some situations, however, the adult child lives in the parent's home rather than the reverse. The child may be developmentally disabled, or may never have married and left the parental home, for example. Or, the adult child returns to the parents' home because of economic need or divorce or both, sometimes bringing one or more grandchildren.

Contrary to popular beliefs about the past, the prevalence of households shared by older people and their adult children was low in the late 19th century, as it is now. Widowed older people are much more likely than their married peers to live with a child, particularly in advanced old age when disability precludes independent living.

The proportion of older people living alone increases with age. In 2000, about 30% (9.7 million) of all non-institutionalized older adults lived alone, most of them women (7.4 million), primarily because of the higher rates of widowhood among women. The proportion living with a spouse decreases with age, especially for women. In 1997, 41% of older women and 17% of older men lived alone. The proportion living alone rises with advancing age. At age 85 and over, for example, almost three-fifths of older women lived alone (U.S. Administration on Aging, 1998).

Daughters outnumber sons in a ratio of more than three to one in sharing their households with disabled parents. The ratio rises to four to one when the parent is severely disabled. The most recent data from the NLTCS indicate that more than 48% of the daughters who are the primary caregivers of disabled older people co-reside with those parents (Center on an Aging Society, 1999).

Allocation of Help Between the Formal and Informal Systems of Care

A major issue that has preoccupied gerontologists, government, and all of society is the role that should be played by the "informal system" of family and friends vis-à-vis the role of the "formal system" of government, agencies, and paid workers in helping the disabled aged. The factual evidence about what actually happens is vitally important because, depending on that evidence, different paths may be indicated for social policy and practice approaches. If, for example, the evidence shows that the family has both the capacity and the willingness to meet all the needs of the disabled aged, then little would be needed in the way of formal services, except to provide back-up services for the family. But if the family does not have the capacity to provide all the help needed by the elderly, a responsible society should develop the programs needed to supplement and buttress the family's efforts.

The notion that family values about care of the aged have weakened and that the formal system provides most of the helping services is another expression of the myth of isolation and abandonment. Study after study has found that the vast majority of helping services received by older people comes from family members. That statement deserves emphasis: *The family—not professionals and the bureaucracy—is the main source of assistance to the disabled elderly; only a very small proportion of assistance is provided by the formal system.*

Since the reliability of the family was first documented by research in the 1960s, evidence has continued to accumulate confirming that the family has been steadfast in that respect despite the vastly increased needs for care and the reduction in potentially available family caregivers. It was found that the family provided 80% of the medically-related services (such as bandage changing and injections) needed by the elderly who lived in the community (U.S. Department of HEW, 1972). That the family provides an even larger proportion of household maintenance and other instrumental services (80–90%) was a major finding of the classic study of the Cleveland area carried out by the U.S. General Accounting Office more than a quarter of a century ago (U.S. General Accounting Office, 1977; Laurie, 1978). (Note that those estimates do not include emotional support, dependability in emergencies, negotiations with the formal system, and the mobilization and monitoring of nonfamily services.) The family often provides those kinds of services for long periods of time. And, when older people are bedfast, are housebound, or can no longer live on their own, their families often bring them into their own households.

Over the years, families have sustained their efforts in caregiving. The 1982 Long Term Care Survey found that nearly three-quarters of disabled older people living in the community relied solely on family and friends (the informal system) for the assistance they required; most of the remainder depended on a combination of family care and paid help (Doty, 1986). Only 15% of all "helper days" of care came from non-family sources, and only a very small minority received all their care from paid providers. Such informal care has not diminished. In comparing the years 1984 and 1994, based on the National Long-Term Care Surveys of those years, Spillman and Pezzin (2000) found that only 3.8% of the disabled elderly in 1984, and 4.6% in 1994, depended solely on formal care. In both years, the largest proportions depended on informal care only (51.3% in 1984 and 40.1% in 1994). Some older people depended on a combination of informal and formal care (19.3% and 25.7% in those years respectively). Fears that formal services would encourage families to reduce the amount of help they gave once again proved unfounded. Formal services proved to *supplement* rather than supplant or substitute for family services.

WHO IN THE FAMILY PROVIDES HELP

Families, of course, include many people, male and female, and of all ages and relationships to the older person. Having established the reliability of the family, a next stage of investigation focuses on who in the family provides various kinds of care. A long series of studies beginning in the early 1980s found that there is generally one person in the family who is the main provider—the individual characterized as the "primary" caregiver. Other family members may help out on a regular basis or from time to time, but they play a much smaller role in terms of the amount and intensity of the help they give. Equal sharing of responsibility by two or more family members does occur in a small proportion of families in which there are two adult daughters (Matthews, 1987), but this is the exception rather than the rule.

Within that broad composite picture, some cultural differences exist among various racial/ethnic minorities in the designation of the family members' roles in caregiving, their use of formal services, the number of family members who participate in caregiving, and other factors (Montgomery & Kosloski, 2001). The Administration on Aging report emphasized cultural diversity in caregiving, which will be discussed in chapter 15.

Overall, there is a hierarchy in the relationship of caregiver to care recipient. When a married older person is disabled, the spouse almost invariably becomes the primary caregiver. The vast majority of elderly spouses are extremely loyal to each other. They provide the most comprehensive care and go on doing so even when the husband or wife is severely disabled. Because of the discrepancy in life expectancy between men and women and because men usually marry women younger than they are, most caregiving spouses are women. Those elderly wives are likely to have limited capacities, however, and therefore are often helped in their caregiving efforts by their adult children, most frequently by a daughter if one is available.

Adult children are next in the hierarchy of those in the family who are most likely to become primary caregivers. Recognition of the multiple responsibilities assumed by these adult children for the old and the young (their own children) led to their characterization as the "sandwich" generation (Schwartz, 1979), the term now so widely used.

It soon became clear that just as "family" almost invariably means spouses or adult children, adult children most often means adult daughters. It is adult daughters who help elderly parents care for each other and who are the primary caregivers for those among widowed or divorced older persons who need help. It is those middle-generation women—the women in the middle (Brody, E. M., 1981)—who are the reliable "significant others" who shop, do household tasks, give personal care, fill in when an arranged care program breaks down, and provide a home when necessary.

To emphasize—when the disabled older person has no spouse, a daughter is most likely to become the primary caregiver. As stated above, among primary caregivers, daughters outnumber sons in a ratio of more than three to one; among primary caregivers of the extremely disabled elders, the ratio is four to one (Stone & Kemper, 1989). Women (spouses and daughters together) constitute about three-quarters of primary caregivers (Montgomery & Kosloski, 2001).

The information about daughters' characteristics in the following paragraphs is the most recent available, having been collected in the 1999 NLTCS. It was provided to the author by the Center on an Aging Society (Center on an Aging Society, 1999).

Daughters range widely in age and vary greatly in *stage* of life at which parent care is necessary. Almost two-thirds (65%) of those who are primary caregivers are between the ages of 45 and 64, almost 20% (19.7%) are under the age of 45, and more than 15% (15.3%) are 65 or over. Some daughters (almost one-fourth) still have children under 18 living at home, whereas others have reached the theoretical "empty nest" stage. Those who are over the age of 65 exemplify the growing number of situations in which one generation of older people takes care of members of a still older generation. No matter the caregivers' ages or stages of life, caring for the very oldest segment of the disabled population is no easy task. The levels of disability undoubtedly account for the fact that almost half of the primary caregiving daughters share the same household with the parent, a form of living associated with considerable strains.

Almost three-fifths of the caregiving daughters in the 1999 survey were married; with 11% being widowed, 19% divorced or separated; and 10.3% never-married. (The differences in the experiences of parent-caring women whose marital statuses differ are described in chapters 9 through 13.)

A marked change from the situation a few decades earlier is that almost 48% of the caregiving daughters were in the labor force, up from 43.5% in the 1982 NLTCS. That percentage is deceptively low, however, since it does not reflect the proportions of daughters who had been working but had quit their jobs because of caregiving, or had reduced the number of their working hours, rearranged their work schedules, or taken time off from their jobs without pay (see chapter 14).

Daughters' marital status and work status influence the patterns of help to their elderly parents. There is a tendency for the role of filial caregiver to fall to the daughter with fewer competing roles—that is, to not-married (divorced, widowed, or never-married) daughters, for example (Stoller, 1983). When married and not-married daughters are in comparable positions as primary caregivers, the former provide somewhat less help, with other members of the family offsetting the difference (Lang & Brody, E. M., 1983). Similarly, working daughters tend to provide slightly less care than nonworking daughters, but the elderly parents of the workers receive as much overall care as parents of nonworkers. The difference is made up by services purchased by the family (Brody, E. M. & Schoonover, 1986).

The power of gender in determining who in the family becomes the caregiver extends to other relatives as well. When disabled older people do not have a spouse or an adult child, female relatives—sisters and nieces, for example—predominate over their male counterparts in providing some help (Horowitz & Dobrof, 1982).

Two other factors are straightforward as determinants of being the primary caregiving adult child: geographic proximity and being an only child. Because older people nowadays have fewer adult children and mobility has increased, there often are fewer choices. There may be only one child, or one female child, or only one child who lives close by. There also are psychological factors at work in the selection of a particular daughter as "primary." These determinants of the selection of primary caregiver will be discussed in detail in chapter 6. Whatever situational or psychological factors operate, the particular daughter who becomes the primary caregiver almost invariably provides the bulk of care, with or without help from others in the family.

Daughters often play multiple caregiving roles. For example, when an elderly parent is primary caregiver for her spouse, the daughter may not only assist the latter with care of the disabled person, but often becomes primary caregiver to the caregiving parent who needs help for herself—to be taken to the doctor, the podiatrist, or the dentist, to shop, to arrange any needed services, to say nothing of the considerable emotional support the elderly spouse-caregiver requires.

The Spillman and Pezzin (2000) analysis is of particular value because it examines changes that occurred over the decade from 1984 to 1994. (Again, there is a reminder that the report is limited to spouses and adult children as informal caregivers, and that the NLTCS did not collect information about informal care of institutional residents. Consequently, caregivers to the 1.6 million disabled old people in nursing homes are not included in the analysis.) The report notes that spouses and children are the majority of active informal caregivers to disabled elders. Three-fifths of the 7.3 million active informal caregivers in 1984 were spouses or children of the care recipient, and the proportion had increased to two-thirds by 1994.

In 1984, when the older person received only informal care, 5.9% of that informal care was received from a relative other than a spouse or child, a percentage that dropped slightly to 5.0% in 1994. The comparable percentages for a combination of informal care with formal care were 3.7% and 4.2%.

To emphasize the salient findings reported by Spillman and Pezzin from the perspective of "who helps":

- Between 1984 and 1994, there was a *decline* in the percent of disabled older people receiving any informal care and an *increase* in the proportion using any formal or institutional care.
- None of the reduction in informal care occurred among primary caregivers, whose numbers remained constant at 2.6 million, despite the decline in the number of community care recipients.
- The decline in caregiving occurred among secondary caregivers—that is, the ones who give most help to the primary caregiver.

Spillman and Pezzin suggest the possibility that it was paid helpers who offset the reduction in secondary caregivers, since there was an increase in the use of formal care during the decade. Though the number of older people increased during that time (from about 18 million to 33.1 million), the decline in chronic disability resulted in the number of disabled people remaining constant. However, the decline occurred primarily among the least disabled; the prevalence of ADL limitations remained the same. In short, within the total number of disabled people, there was a shift between 1984 and 1994 toward a *larger* proportion of elderly being more *severely* disabled. The report quoted made it clear, as have many other research reports, that the family has not been reducing the needed care old people receive. *Daughters* continue to predominate as primary caregivers, constituting about 35% of primary caregivers in both years and increasing from about 52% to more than 55% as secondary caregivers. To underline—*children far outnumber spouses as caregivers, and among primary active caregivers, daughters still greatly outnumber sons.*

Spillman and Pezzin (2000) report that there was a "modest" increase between 1984 and 1994 in the proportion of sons who were primary caregivers (from about 10% to 15%). They suggest that the increase may work in the direction of increased use of formal care since, according to Stoller and Cutter (1993), male caregivers are more likely to use formal care.

Sons love their parents, do not neglect them, provide emotional support, and have feelings of responsibility. In general, however, sons tend to do certain tasks reflecting the cultural assignment of gender-appropriate roles such as money management and home repairs, and they often are major participants in making important decisions. But direct, hands-on or personal care of the elderly is almost invariably a woman's role. Sons assume the role of primary caregiver when they have no sisters or none close by. When they do so, however, they are helped by their wives (the daughters-in-law). Sons do less than daughters and experience less strain (Horowitz, 1985b). To emphasize, when sons do become "primaries," they transfer many of the caregiving tasks to their wives and tend to use more formal providers to help than do daughters. Sons help their fathers more than they help their mothers and provide almost no personal care help for mothers (Montgomery & Kosloski, 2001).

Because disabled older people have chronic ailments, caregiving activities must be sustained from day to day, week to week, and year to year. The amount of time spent in caregiving, like the nature of the task involved, changes over time if and when the older person becomes more disabled.

When the parents are extremely disabled, it is necessary for daughter-caregivers to provide help every single day. They are virtually on full-time duty. Others invest an hour or several hours a day. The 1999 NLTCS found that more than 16% had been providing care for 10 or more years! The largest proportion of caregivers—almost 24%—had been enacting the caregiving role for four to seven years, with 18.7% following with two to four years. The remainder had been caregiving from up to six months to nine years (Center on an Aging Society, 1999). Some women report that they have been spending more years in parent care than they had spent in caring for their own children. It is obvious that parent care is not a short-term enterprise. Some of the women will go on caregiving in the future with the tasks becoming ever more demanding. And new recruits will join them as *their* parents begin to need help.

Moreover, parent care is not a one-time episode in a caregiver's life. Many women have *caregiving careers*. In one study, almost half of married daughters caring for widowed mothers had helped their elderly fathers before they died, and one-third of the women had helped other elderly relatives in the past (Brody, E. M., 1985b). Twenty-two percent of the daughters helping their disabled mothers were simultaneously helping another elderly family member(s) who might be a parent-in-law, a grandparent, aunt, cousin, or even a more distant relation. Two-thirds of the women had their own children living at home. Given the discrepancy in life expectancy between men and women, it is inevitable that many of the same women will care for dependent husbands later in their lives.

It is evident that many women in the middle occupy that position more than once. Not only do they do so at different ages and stages, but one woman can have the experience during more than one of her life stages. And each time, psychological issues arise with different variations on the emotional themes.

DAUGHTERS-IN-LAW: THE PROXY PRIMARIES

The increase in the percentage of sons as primary caregivers between 1984 and 1994, though described by Spillman and Pezzin as "modest," nevertheless is of special interest. It calls our attention to an important group of caregivers who rarely appear in survey reports as primary or even as secondary. Though not named as "primary," they often perform the same functions as daughters when the latter are the primary caregivers. When a son is referred to as the "primary," it is likely that his wife does most of the actual, hands-on caregiving. Daughters-in-law are the often-invisible caregivers: the "proxy primaries."

When an older person who has no daughters is asked who serves as the main caregiver or on whom she relies the most, the answer is usually a particular (or only) son. However, as stated above, sons very rarely perform intimate or hands-on helping tasks for a mother. The person who actually does so and often is the main helper in that respect is the son's wife. In terms of tasks they perform and time investment, they could be called "primary." George (1986), in a thoughtful article, reported that in her study of family caregivers for dementia patients, daughters-in-law actually provided major proportions of caregiving. But 90% of them described themselves as "secondary" caregivers!

Another clue to the helping role of daughters-in-law was provided in a study by Horowitz (1985b). When sons were the primary caregivers, they expected and depended upon both emotional and concrete support from their wives. More than three-fourths of the married sons, but less than half of the married daughters who were primary caregivers, reported the involvement of their spouses in care of the elderly parent.

THE BACK-UP SYSTEM: SECONDARY CAREGIVERS, OTHER FAMILY MEMBERS AND FRIENDS

During the half century in which caregiving to older people became a major focus of gerontological research, some of the terminology used has undergone changes. The "informal" system of care continues to refer to the individual or constellation of family members and friends who participate in caregiving. And the "formal" system continues to refer to paid caregivers whether they are paid by the older person, the family, government, or agencies. At some point along the way, the word "secondary" caregivers appeared in our vocabularies and a stream of research—sure to expand in future—has begun about them. Pearlin and his colleagues recently reported on a study of the effects of caregiving on secondary caregivers—in this case, adult children who were assisting an elderly parent who was taking care of a spouse with Alzheimer's disease (Pearlin, Pioli, & McLaughlin, 2001). Since research on spousal caregivers of Alzheimer's patients documents the negative physical health effects they experience, the adult child who is the "secondary" caregiver in such instances is in double jeopardy—that is, she may find herself with two patients.

In the stories of the women in the middle, the roles of others in the family were inescapably revealed. Thus, sons-in-law, siblings, and grandchildren will appear in the vignettes and longer case histories in chapters 6 through 13—that is, as secondary caregivers or part of the "back-up" system of care. They not only assist the disabled older person directly in many instances, but also are helpers to the wife, husband, mother, or grandmother who is "primary."

If we look only at spouses and adult children as primary caregivers, we do not see the complete picture. The NLTCS concentrated on those categories of relatives, and did not deal in detail with other relatives and non-relatives. The small percentages of care reported by Spillman and Pezzin as being received from those other relatives and non-relatives in 1994 represented, to be sure, a small proportion of informal caregivers, but they play an important role for the population of disabled older people. (The 1999 NLTCS did not collect information about secondary caregivers.)

The efforts of such "secondaries" are not often counted when they are sporadic or temporary, but they stand out at times and contribute to the complex mosaic that makes up the caregiving scene. They often will make prominent appearances in the women's stories as when the research that focused on the primary caregivers' siblings is described in chapter 6 (including geographically distant adult children). The sons-in-law themselves speak in chapters 9 and 10, and grandchildren are discussed as well.

Relatively little is known about other family caregivers who fill the caregiving gap when there are no spouses or adult children available—elderly siblings of the disabled person, for example. Nor is much known about caregiving by grandchildren when there is no one available in generation two because the elderly parent has outlived her own children. (A sad consequence of living to advanced old age is that the chances of outliving an adult child increase.) Some of the case histories in chapter 10 will illustrate the roles of grandchildren in helping their grandparents or helping their mothers care for grandparents.

When no closer relative is available, nieces sometimes take some responsibility. While they rarely give as much help as children, they do not abandon the old people and see that somehow care is arranged. Friends and neighbors of the elderly may also provide some help, but do not substitute for family when the older people concerned are significantly disabled, nor does the help they give approach family help in level or duration (Cantor, 1978).

It has become apparent that the characterizations of caregivers as "primary" and "secondary" must be re-thought and re-defined. In particular, the designation as "secondary" is often different from one study to another, without regular or clear criteria for selection of the someone(s) who play that role. But secondaries (notably daughters-in-law) often do not rank second in "doing the most."

If help is measured quantitatively—as in number of hours spent weekly helping—primary caregivers may appear to receive little help from other family members, but that help is often critical and comes at important times, despite being sporadic. Most of the help described is fairly regular and ongoing. But when there is an emergency or a special event (such as a serious illness or a move from one residence to another) even family members who have not been helpers in the past seem to mobilize to meet the needs. At times, their efforts are extraordinary, but are obviously difficult to measure. Such events will appear in the case studies.

How much help does the daughter actually get from other family members—her husband, her own children, and her sibling(s)? A good deal depends, of course, on the size of the family network, the geographic proximity of various family members, whether other family members are male or female, and the kinds of help the older person needs. Although information is not complete about the contributions of other family members, a few studies cast some light on the subject.

In one study (Brody, E. M. & Schoonover, 1986) in which daughters were the primary caregivers to widowed elderly mothers, the daughters provided approximately two-thirds of the help with ADL (personal care) and IADL (such as housework, laundry, shopping, and transportation) as measured by the number of hours each kind of help was received by the mothers. They provided a higher proportion, approximately three-fourths, of meal preparation and help to the mother in using the telephone. They also gave the mother more than half of the emotional support she received and 60% of the help with money management and service arrangements.

As for other family members, the daughters' husbands (the sons-in-law) provided approximately 4–6% of most of those forms of help and 11% of the help with money management, shopping, and transportation. When the caregivers' children still lived at home, they provided just about as much help as the sons-in-law. Other family members (primarily the caregivers' siblings) also provided little help with most tasks except for money management and emotional support, in both instances providing approximately one-fifth of the assistance.

Such statistics do not, however, place a true value on intangibles such as emotional support. Such support cannot be quantified or measured by "time spent." As the case studies of married women will show, the emotional support their husbands provide is often critical in enabling the caregivers to go on. And as the chapter on siblings will demonstrate (chapter 6), their emotional support ranked very high on the caregivers' list of help they received from their sisters and brothers.

The next chapter will document the effects of parent care on women in the middle.

Chapter 3

The Effects of Caregiving

As the preceding chapters have shown, families have responded responsibly—even heroically—to the huge increase in the need for care of the disabled elderly. It is the women in the family—wives, daughters, and daughters-in-law—who provide the vast majority of services for dependent older people, with daughters predominating in helping those who are the most severely disabled. The needs of their disabled elderly family members have exceeded the capacities of many caregiving women. In addition, societal values about women's roles have been changing so that the different values they hold may pull them in opposite directions. This chapter examines the effects of caregiving on parent-caring women and identifies the factors in their situations that affect their well-being.

As professionals and social scientists were becoming aware of the role of the family in caring for older people, so too did the realization grow that caregiving affected the caregivers themselves and the entire family. For a long time, the focus of attention had been solely on the elderly and their needs. When the caregivers were considered at all, it was as the sources of care—as people in the background who might or might not be available to provide services for the disabled aged. In the 1960s, there was some beginning clinical exploration of the experiences of the caregiver and the other members of the family (Brody, E. M. & Spark, 1966; Posner, 1961), and the forerunner of large-scale studies was taking place in the United Kingdom (Grad & Sainsbury, 1966; Sainsbury & Grad, 1966; Sainsbury & Grad de Alercon J., 1970). (It is of interest to note that those seminal British studies concerned family care of mentally disturbed or impaired older people who had been in mental hospitals.) The international symposium mentioned in chapter 2 (Shanas & Streib, 1965) undoubtedly helped to spark the subsequent interest in the family relationships of older people. But important for the concerns of this book was the conferees' acknowledgment that the effects of caregiving on the caregivers were hardly touched upon during the conference. In general, however, caregiving family members received relatively little attention until the mid-1970s. Since then, such studies have proliferated, resulting in a large and remarkably consistent body of information.

To put the matter in perspective, it is emphasized that the vast majority of women want to care for elderly parents and do so willingly. Daughters derive many positive benefits from parent care such as satisfaction from fulfilling what they see as their responsibilities, adhering to religious and cultural values, expressing their affection, seeing to it that the parent is well cared for, reciprocating help the parent had given them in the past, and feeling that they are serving as a good model for their own children to follow. In a study by Kane and Penrod (1995), the positive sources of caregivers' satisfaction were a sense of achievement, pleasure in seeing their family member improve, closer bonds between caregiving family members, affection for the care receiver, and the satisfaction of doing one's duty. (Only 14% reported little or no satisfaction.) At the same time, it is undeniable that many caregivers do indeed experience significant stress effects, though the nature and levels of strains they report vary.

EFFECTS OF PARENT CARE

Parent care often affects women's emotional well-being, physical health, family relationships, lifestyle, work activities, and financial status. In reading this section of the book, there is a caveat about cross-sectional data, as with much other information concerning the aged and their families. Caregivers who report few negative effects or none at all at a particular time may experience increasing strains over time as their caregiving continues—as the older people decline and need heavier care, as the caregivers themselves and other members of their families grow older and encounter health problems, and as their situations change in other ways.

Emotional Strains

Since the studies cited above were done in the 1960s, research on the effects of parent care exploded. In the multitude of reports that resulted, a consistent finding—whether the studies were done in the 70s (e.g., Gurland, Dean, & Cook, 1978; Robinson & Thurnher, 1979; Sainsbury &

Grad, 1970), in the 80s (e.g., Cantor, 1983; Frankfather, Smith, & Caro, 1981), or in the 90s (Yee & Schultz, 2000)—was that *emotional strains are by far the most pervasive and severe negative effects reported by caregivers.* The litany of symptoms identified includes the following:

- Depression
- Anger
- Anxiety
- Frustration
- Guilt
- Demoralization
- Feelings of helplessness
- Irritability
- Lowered morale
- Emotional exhaustion

Related to those effects are restrictions on the caregivers' time and freedom, relationship problems, isolation from being confined to the home, conflict from the competing demands of various responsibilities, and difficulties in setting priorities. Complicating the picture are constraints on lifestyle such as interference with social and recreational activities, disruption of vocational life, and loss of privacy and space if the older person is introduced into the caregiver's household.

The proportion of caregivers who experience moderate to severe negative effects varies from study to study, but generally hovers at approximately half. Two decades ago, the 1982 National Long-Term Care Survey, in reporting the strains of providing help to severely disabled older people (those with ADL deficits), confirmed the findings of many smaller studies in that 40–50% of respondents reported emotional strain, interrupted sleep, and limitations on their social lives; 30% said the older person required constant attention; and 24% reported interferences with privacy.

A thorough and careful review of studies of the psychiatric and physical morbidity effects of caregiving appeared in Schulz, Visintainer, and Williamson (1990). Most but not all of the studies concerned the elderly as care recipients. The authors found that overall, the literature indicates increases in self-reported psychiatric symptomology and increases in psychiatric illness among most caregivers when compared to population norms or appropriate control groups. A decade later in another excellent review of 30 empirical research reports on psychiatric morbidity from 1985 through 1998, Yee and Schulz (2000) concluded that women caregivers (wives and daughters) are at a greater risk for psychiatric morbidity than men caregivers. For example, women have higher levels of depression, anxiety, general psychiatric symptomology, less satisfaction with their home lives, and experience excess psychiatric morbidity attributable to caregiving. The authors of the review noted that women face more caregiving demands, spend more time providing care, and perform more involved day-to-day caregiving tasks. Moreover, men were more likely to get informal assistance and take other measures that can moderate the stress process.

The caregiver's immediate family is also affected by interference with their lifestyles, privacy, patterns of socialization, plans for vacations, and even plans for the future such as retirement or moving to a new location. Her time and energy may be diverted from other family members to the older person. Pre-existing relationship problems can be exacerbated, and interpersonal conflicts may be stimulated among family members—the older person, the caregiver, and the latter's husband, children, and siblings. All of these reactions will be illustrated by case studies in Part II of this book. The Sainsbury and Grad studies proved to have been prescient in their focus on the effects of caregiving on all in the family (Sainsbury & Grad de Alercon, 1970).

The older person's disabilities and decline are often worrisome to those who care for and about her. It is difficult to witness the discomfort, pain, and unhappiness of someone about whom one cares. It is inevitable that the thought comes to mind, "Will this happen to me?" That question, spoken or unspoken, is particularly distressing when a parent suffers from Alzheimer's disease or a related disorder.

Physical Effects

In the past three decades, studies of the effects of caregiving have taken many forms. For example, studies of gender differences in mental health outcomes; the effects of multigenerational households; the effects on caregivers when the older people are in nursing homes; the effects on members of the family other than the primary caregiver; and the effects of the intersection of broad social trends (such as women working and changes in family formation). All of these will be described and discussed later in this book.

One major stream of research concerns the actual physical health effects of caregiving on the caregiver. Various studies estimate that between 15% and 33% of adult children describe detrimental effects on their physical health (e.g., Brody, E. M., Kleban, Johnsen, Hoffman, & Schoonover, 1987a; Horowitz & Dobrof, 1982). Some speak of back problems from lifting and turning helpless older people and of stress-related ailments such as ulcers.

In most such studies, the physical effects of caregiving were self-reports by the caregivers. Studies of actual physical morbidity as effects of caregiving have proliferated. Of the various types of such studies—self-report, health care utilization, and immune function—the last named were primarily of spouse-caregivers of Alzheimer's patients. Such studies undoubtedly rode the rising tide of interest in Alzheimer's disease. (See Katzman & Bick, 2002, for an excellent historical account of professional and scientific interest in Alzheimer's disease.) These kinds of studies will undoubtedly increase rapidly, but the review by Schulz and his colleagues (1990) concluded that the findings of negative physical effects are less conclusive than those of psychiatric morbidity, but do suggest increased vulnerability to physical illness among caregivers.

Many caregivers do indeed perceive that their health suffers from caregiving. In Schulz and colleagues' review of healthcare utilization studies, they found that the studies' findings were inconsistent. Those authors did state that findings of physical health effects are equivocal, but that there are some indications that such stress affects immune functions. One of the earliest of such studies was carried out by Kiecolt-Glaser and her colleagues (Kiecolt-Glaser et al., 1987). That study, too, concerned chronic stress among spousal caregivers of dementia patients. It concluded that the chronic stress results in lower levels of immunological adaptations, which in turn may account for the greater susceptibility of the spouses to physical health problems.

Schulz and his colleagues (1990) concluded their review by stating the importance of documenting morbidity effects in representative populations of caregivers; volunteer samples in most studies were likely to be biased in favor of the more distressed end of the caregiving continuum. Schulz took his own advice and almost a decade later reported about his carefully controlled prospective study, finding that after four years of follow-up, spousal caregivers experiencing caregiver strain had mortality risks that were 63% higher than non-caregiving controls (Schulz & Beach, 1999). (Note that, again, spouses were the caregivers studied.)

Clearly, the evidence is not all in. Certainly, adult children caregivers and particularly daughters should receive research attention as well as spouses in studies of physical morbidity. While spouses obviously are at high risk because of advanced age, their own health problems, and other factors, some daughters also have Alzheimer's patients and other severely impaired elder people in their homes. While adult children presumably have higher energy levels and better heath than elderly spouses, they also have risk factors such as multiple competing demands and, as the vignettes and longer case studies in chapter 10 will show, the women's husbands and children also suffer negative effects at times. Indeed, the repercussions are felt throughout the family—by the caregivers' siblings as well, whether they live close by or are geographically distant.

Some of those family members may be the "secondary" caregivers. The previous chapter referred to the dual role often played by adult children (daughters) who not only help an elderly parent care for an impaired spouse, but also help the caregiving spouse in many ways. And daughters-in-law, while they rarely have the title "primary" caregiver bestowed upon them, often are those who could be characterized as the "proxy primaries" when sons are the designated "primaries" (see chapter 12).

In a recent article, Pearlin, Pioli, and McLaughlin (2001) speak of the "intense and enduring attachments among family members and the lasting devotion one comes to have to the well-being of others" (p. 239). Stating the need for specification of the conditions and mechanisms accounting for taxing the well-being of caregivers, they describe their study of adults having a parent who is primary caregiver to a spouse with Alzheimer's disease—that is, adults who are "secondary" caregivers. The latter were identified by the primary caregiver—that is, the spouse—as the "child most active in providing help." The authors found that the level of involvement of those secondaries is determined mainly by "structural constraints"—in particular, the number of roles played by the adult child, the reduction of commitments to employment, and concerns and insecurities about finances. Those "secondaries" were affected by depression and in their self-rated health. Ample evidence was found that the disruption of people's lives increases significantly with their involvement in the care of an impaired parent, even among family members who are not the primary caregivers. Daughters more than sons tended to express depressive affect, with the extent of caregiving significantly related to depression. It was the caregiver stress due to disruptions in the life domains such as parental or work roles that contributed to depression.

Pearlin and his colleagues concluded that the "demands of caregiving on time and energy have effects that reach into multiple corners of people's lives even among family members who are not the principal caregivers." And they remind us about the powerful bonds that exist among family members and the extension of those bonds across generational lines.

Financial Strains

The financial strains incurred by adult children are extremely variable. As was described in chapter 2, overall, the picture is much different now than it was prior to the Social Security Act (1935) and Medicare and Medicaid (1965). Medicaid and Supplemental Security Income (SSI) (1974) together eliminated compulsory financial support of the old by their adult children. It gives one pause to imagine what the drain on adult children would be nowadays if they had to pay medical and hospital bills for their elderly parents! When cutbacks in Social Security and Medicare are threatened (depending on the political climate), the current generations of parent-carers—including those now called baby boomers—are threatened as well. As matters stand, the gaps in entitlements—notably for long-term care and for payment for medication—cause strain on an unknown number of adult children as well as on the elderly. The same considerations apply when Medicaid beds are not available in nursing homes, or when services such as in-home nursing, daycare, respite care, and other long-term care services cannot be obtained.

Financial strains on different groups of caregivers depend on their own and the parents' incomes and resources, as well as on need and other considerations. Two decades ago, the 1982 Long Term Care Survey reported that 15–20% of adult children had financial problems due to the expenses of the older person's care. In the same vein, according to the most recent national Long Term Care Survey, the cost would be $45–94 billion per year if the work of caregivers had to be replaced by paid home-care (Administration on Aging, Fall 2000). The AOA report notes that each disabled older person who lives with others receives an average of almost 30 hours of unpaid caregiving per week. One review indicates that the annual costs of informal caregiving per patient range from $12,730 to $57,937 (Moore, Zahn, & Clipp, 2001) in addition to any out-of-pocket expenditures. The out-of-pocket expenditures have been estimated to be about $100 monthly to about half of caregivers (Wagner, 1997). Still another survey calculated that the annual cost of care (both paid and unpaid) for an Alzheimer patient at home is $47,083, compared to $47,591 at a nursing home. It quotes Rice et al. (1993) in costing unpaid care as accounting for 12% of the total of nursing homecare, compared to 73% of the total cost of home care.

Some of calculations are made based on the lost earnings of those who quit jobs or reduce work hours (mainly daughters). In one small study for Metropolitan Life by the National Alliance for Caregivers and the National Center for Women and Aging at Brandeis University of how care costs cut into caregivers' earnings, it was estimated that there is an average cost of $659,139 over a lifetime in "opportunity costs"—that is, lost wages, Social Security benefits, and pension benefits (Metlife, 1999).

Information is virtually nonexistent about hidden costs such as that for health care of the caregiver. It is not known how many caregivers need or seek health care as a direct or indirect result of their caregiving activities.

CAUSES OF STRAIN

Identifying the factors that predict or are associated with the strains on those who provide parent care is a complex undertaking. Not only do different caregivers experience different amounts and kinds of strains, but the various factors that produce strain interact with each other in intricate ways. Some are relatively straightforward and objective, such as the type of care needed by the elderly person that may be physically demanding, time-consuming, uncomfortable, or even embarrassing. Other factors are more subtle—the personalities and interactions of the parent and daughter, for example, and the inner, psychological meaning and implications of the need to help a parent. Information that depicts the extraordinarily complicated picture is gradually being filled in. The "objective" causes of strain will be described here. Women's "inner" or subjective experiences appear in Part II of this book and again in the case vignettes and longer case studies in Part III.

Amount and Type of Care

In general, the older elderly people are, the more vulnerable they are to disability; the heavier the care that is needed and the greater is the strain on the caregivers. The latter may begin by giving the little care that is needed at first, but increase their efforts as the older people become more disabled. As disability becomes severe, the older persons are more likely to need help not only with IADL activities such as transportation and shopping but also with ADL such as bathing, dressing, and toileting. When independent living is no longer possible without round-the-clock care, the older person may be introduced into the household of an adult child. More time is consumed in providing an increasing amount of care. Some older people reach a point at which they are incontinent and bedfast. Providing help with intimate tasks is not only difficult physically for daughters and daughters-in-law, but has distressing emotional overtones.

Characteristics of the Elderly Person

Although the functional and physical disabilities of the older person are important in producing strains, mental disabilities—whether functional or organic—are especially stressful and difficult to deal with. In many publications, Lebowitz and his colleagues at the National Institute of Mental Health have emphasized the importance of the aged person's mental health to the well-being of the family (e.g., Lebowitz, 1978; Lebowitz, 1985; Lebowitz & Light, 1993; Lebowitz & Light, 1996).

As noted earlier in this chapter, the forerunner of studies calling attention to the burden on the family of caring for mentally ill older people was carried out by Sainsbury and Grad (1966, 1970) in England. They studied caregiving to mentally ill people of all ages, but found that the burdens on caregivers were much greater when the recipients of care were over the age of 65. Nearly half of the older people demanded excessive attention and companionship. Almost two-thirds of family caregivers ascribed their own emotional symptoms to worrying about the patient, half found their social and leisure activities restricted, and more than one-third described upset in their domestic routines. Three-fifths reported negative effects on their physical health. Smaller proportions (15%) said their income was reduced or that their employment was affected (12%).

Approximately one-third of the caregivers studied by Sainsbury and Grad attributed their insomnia, headaches, and irritability to the patient's behavior. The investigators spoke of the patient being a danger to herself or himself, presenting "odd" behavior, being restless or overtalkative, being troublesome at night, being uncooperative or contrary, and having hypochondriacal complaints. Those early findings preceded subsequent research confirming that disruptive behavior associated with Alzheimer's disease is more distressing than the diagnosis per se.

Older people's mental problems have emerged as predictors of caregiver strain in much other research. In an early study, for example, two-thirds of those caring for the mentally impaired aged reported adverse effects on their households, with the most burdensome problems being heavy physical or nursing care and excessive demands by the patient for companionship (Hoenig & Hamilton, 1966). In another British study, behavioral patterns such as nocturnal disturbances were among the most troublesome problems for more than half of caregivers who reported anxiety, depression, and restrictions on their social activities (Sanford, 1975).

Still other investigations identified mental abnormality, incontinence, immobility, excessive demands, and irritability as particularly bothersome

(Isaacs, 1971). Gurland and his colleagues (1978) found a higher incidence of depression in family members whose household included a depressed older person. They characterized this as the "contagion of depression." A similar reaction occurred in family members of depressed older people who were living in a nursing home and senior housing (Brody, E. M., Dempsey, & Pruchno, 1990). The presence of a mentally impaired older person in the home is more damaging to family relationships than the presence of one who is physically impaired (Cicirelli, 1980; Noelker & Poulshock, 1982; Robinson & Thurnher, 1979).

The problems of caring for older people with Alzheimer's disease (AD) are particularly important because of the increase in the number of elderly afflicted by that or a related disorder. People with such diagnoses may present extraordinary management difficulties. Not only do they inevitably require personal care during the later stages of the disease, but they exhibit many distressing behavioral symptoms—forgetfulness, incontinence, wandering, sleep disturbances, and combativeness, for example. It is those problematic and disruptive behaviors and the impaired social functioning resulting from dementia that are stressful for caregivers (Deimling & Bass, 1986; Gwyther & Blazer, 1984). Studies are consistent in reporting the power of Alzheimer's disease to produce stress. Family members providing home care to AD patients were found to report three times as many stress symptoms as the general population, to take more prescription psychotropic drugs, and to participate in fewer social and recreational activities; women fared worse than men in experiencing such effects (George, 1984). Forty-two percent of the caregivers in an experimental respite project for caregivers of Alzheimer's patients were found to be more depressed than a national sample of adults (Lawton, Brody, E. M., & Saperstein, 1991).

In a recent report, Ory and her colleagues (1999) compared caregivers of dementia patients with those of non-demented patients. Though based on data from the 1996 National Caregiver Survey (National Alliance for Caregiving and AARP, 1997) in which recipients of care were 50 years of age or older, it was clearly an elderly population. The mean age of the demented people was 78.4, and was 75.6 for the non-demented. The dementia caregivers spent more time in caregiving, assisted with more ADL and IADL tasks, and were affected more negatively in terms of strain, mental and physical health problems, employment complications, and family conflict. The negative effects were attributed to difficult behavioral problems exhibited by the afflicted older people.

There are other aspects of the care of demented older people that add to the strains experienced by caregivers. The latter often speak of the distress they feel when the patient is unable to communicate with them or to provide feedback by expressing appreciation for the help and attention they receive. And many caregivers, particularly adult children who have a genetic stake in the matter, are frightened and anxious. They wonder, will this happen to me? Perhaps most poignant is the feeling that they have "lost" the older person. Many state that nursing home placement will take place only when the elderly person no longer recognizes them.

The personality of the older person is probably more important in producing strain than has been emphasized. It is particularly upsetting, for example, when the elderly recipient of care is critical of the caregiver and other family members (Robinson & Thurnher, 1979). This is especially likely to be an issue when the older person lives in the caregiver's household and the latter also has a husband, children, or both, who live at home (Brody, E. M., Kleban, Hoffman, & Schoonover, 1988).

Caregiver Characteristics

Certain characteristics of the caregiver are also associated with the amount and type of strain experienced.

Being a daughter rather than a son is associated with strain. Studies of caregiving invariably find that women experience more stress than men (Cantor, 1983; Cicirelli, 1981; Horowitz, 1985b; Johnson, 1983; Noelker & Poulshock, 1982; Robinson & Thurnher, 1979). To quote the review by Yee and Schultz (2002) of studies from 1985 through 1998: " . . . women caregivers . . . report higher levels of depression, anxiety, and general psychiatric symptomology and lower levels of life satisfaction than men caregivers" (p. 155). This is not surprising since daughters who are the main caregivers provide more help and more help of the kind that requires hands-on care than do sons. But a variety of other suggestions have been made as to why filial care is more stressful to daughters than to sons.

A study by Horowitz (1985b) comparing caregiving daughters and sons illuminated some of the differences between them that hold potential for daughters finding parent care more stressful. She confirmed the findings of others that the men tended to take on the role of main caregiver only in the absence of a female sibling and that daughters were more likely than sons to help with personal care, meal preparation, household chores, and transportation. The lesser involvement of the sons was also shown by the more limited time they devoted to parent care. Sons did talk with the parent regularly, however, and did not differ from daughters in the extent to which they helped to manage the older person's money, provided actual financial help, assisted with dealing with bureaucratic organizations, and gave the parent emotional support.

In addition, sons were more likely than daughters to involve their spouses—the daughters-in-law—in the caregiving situation and to depend on them for help with parent care. They also perceived their wives to have more supportive attitudes towards their caregiving activities than did the daughters in relation to their husbands. For their part, the daughters were appreciative when *their* spouses—the sons-in-law—were neutral toward their involvement in parent care. More than three-fourths of married sons, but half of married daughters, reported involvement of their spouses in care. In short, the sons expected and depended upon both emotional and instrumental support from their wives.

The sons in Horowitz' (1985b) research were less negatively affected emotionally than the daughters. They were more likely than the women to respond "no problems" (34% versus 11%) in relation to parent care. Compared with daughters, sons were less likely to believe they had to give up anything (32% versus 60%), that they had neglected other family responsibilities (9% versus 31%), that their leisure activities were affected (22% versus 56%), that their emotional states had changed for the worse (31% versus 59%), or that their plans for the future had been negatively affected (16% versus 43%).

The vulnerability of daughters to strain also extends to those adult children who are not the primary caregivers. In a study of the local and geographically distant siblings of the daughters who were the primary caregivers, local daughters reported more strain than local sons (Brody, E. M., Hoffman, Kleban, & Schoonover, 1988), and geographically distant daughters reported more strain than geographically distant sons (Schoonover, Brody, E. M., Hoffman, & Kleban, 1989) (see chapter 6 for details). Even when older people are in nursing homes, daughters experience more stress than sons (Brody, E. M., Pruchno, & Dempsey, 1989).

Though caregiving daughters-in-law experience many stress effects similar to those of daughters, their relationships with the older people are different qualitatively and have different historical roots. Townsend (1965) found that when there were poor relationships with a member of the household in which an older person lived, the problem appeared to have been greater with daughters-in-law than with sons-in-law. Similarly, in research by Noelker and Poulshock (1982), when a disabled older person lived in the caregiver's household, it was found that daughters-in-law had more severe stress effects than any other category of relatives. By no means do all daughters-in-law have relationship problems with their parents-in-law, of course, but existing problems may be aggravated when the daughter-in-law provides care. (Qualitative interviews with the daughters-in-law described in chapter 12 illuminate some of their subjective feelings and experiences that lead to their strains.)

Being a woman, then, whether one is a daughter or a daughter-in-law, means experiencing more strain from caring for a disabled older person. As pointed out in chapter 1, many women have roles as daughters-in-law as well as daughters and, therefore, may need to help both their parent(s) and parent(s)-in-law. The number of women who are at risk of simultaneous parent and parent-in-law care will increase in the future due to the falling birth rate. Fewer children means fewer daughters, increasing the odds of a woman being the one to take care of both parents and parents-in-law.

Other Demographic and Health Characteristics

In addition to gender, there are other demographic and health characteristics of caregivers that relate to the strains they experience. Those characteristics are not independent in producing strain, but are interrelated with others of their own and their parents' characteristics. Being an older caregiver, for example, is related to having an older and more disabled parent who needs more difficult care and who has needed that help for a longer period of time. Older caregivers are likely to have more health problems of their own and to be experiencing some age-related decrements such as lower energy levels and problems with vision and hearing. Despite their own health problems, however, caregivers tend to go on providing care as long as they possibly can.

Socioeconomic status is important in determining the kind of care provided. Whether they are rich or poor, caregivers are reliable in seeing to it that older people receive the care they need. Those who can afford to do so are more likely to purchase some services, while those with low socioeconomic status more often find it necessary to provide the hands-on care themselves and to share a household with the disabled older person. The socioemotional costs are greater for those who provide the direct, hands-on care themselves than for those who manage or arrange the care (Archbold, 1983).

Certainly, hands-on heavy care and sharing a household are stressful. But that is not to say that more stress is invariably associated with lower socioeconomic status. It is possible that some daughters who are in better economic circumstances and some of their less affluent peers experience equal amounts of stress, but that their strains derive from different factors in their situations. Horowitz (1985a) suggests, for example, that offspring with high socioeconomic status may have high expectations of leisure time and retirement opportunities; this may create strains when the needs of the elderly relative keep them from realizing those expectations.

Employment Status

In the 1980s, research began to address the effects on women of their employment status when parent care is necessary. The subject is of major importance, because so many women now work outside of the home. This is elaborated in chapter 14. It is noted here, however, that the parents of caregiving working daughters do not receive less care than parents of nonworking women (Brody, E. M. & Schoonover, 1986). The indications are that working and nonworking daughters experience many strains that are similar, but also some that are different. The pressures of fulfilling both the work and parent care roles lead some women to leave the work force, reduce work hours, or rearrange their work schedules; those who continue to work are subject to a variety of work interruptions (Brody, E. M., Kleban, Johnsen, Hoffman, & Schoonover, 1987). Values play a role in the decisions women make. For example, some employed daughters who hold higher level jobs may be conflicted and worried about the increasing care needs of their parents that may interfere with their vocational goals; others may work primarily because they and their families need the money they earn.

Again, when the older person suffers from dementia, it is a strong influence. Caregivers of such parents take more time off from work, more often reduce the number of hours they work, turn down promotions, take early retirement, give up their leisure, have less time for their families, and report mental and physical health problems. In the light of the difficulties of caring for AD patients, it is understandable that such a large proportion of research on the effects of caregiving for older people has focused on caregivers of people with that affliction.

Marital Status

The effects on a daughter of her marital status during the parent-care years is an important issue, particularly in view of the dramatic changes that have occurred in patterns of marriage and divorce. A large survey explored the differential effects of different marital statuses on daughters (Brody, E. M., 1988). The findings of the survey and detailed case histories appear in chapter 10.

Living Arrangements

Contrary to popular notions, the vast majority of older people do not wish to live with their adult children and do so mainly when they become disabled and cannot live alone. When that happens, the older people are approximately four times more likely to live with a daughter than a son.

Every study of caregiving has found that the strains on the caregiver are much greater when the disabled older person lives in the caregiver's household than when the older person lives separately (Horowitz, 1982; Lang & Brody, E. M., 1983; Reece, Walz, & Hageboech, 1983; Sainsbury & Grad de Alercon, 1970). In research in which disabled older people and their caregivers shared households, for example, 22% of caregivers suffered severe multiple stress effects, 50% suffered moderate multiple stress effects; and 28% suffered mild multiple stress effects (Noelker & Poulshock, 1982). (Note that none reported a total absence of stress effects.)

It should not be assumed that simply living under the same roof is stressful in itself, however. It is undeniable that shared households widen the arena for potential interpersonal conflicts; the participants are in enforced contact with each other, and the negative effects on family members stand out in bold relief. But the sharing of a home must be disentangled from other factors. Such living arrangements occur primarily when the older person is severely disabled and can no longer manage independently. It may also be the heavy care that produces strain, and problems may be exacerbated if the home is small or ill-equipped for care, resulting in crowding or loss of privacy.

Intrahousehold caregiving not only is associated with "heavier" care and more caregiver strain, but deters labor-force participation for some people (Soldo & Myllyluoma, 1983), is related to women quitting their jobs for parent care or experiencing negative effects on their occupational activities (Brody, E. M., Kleban, Johnsen, Hoffman, & Schoonover, 1987), and is implicated in strains reported by husbands of caregiving daughters (Kleban, Brody, E. M., Schoonover, & Hoffman, 1989).

Although shared households clearly are more stressful than separate households, there are also differences depending on whether the household contains two or three generations. When three different household configurations were compared (Brody, E. M., Kleban, Hoffman, & Schoonover, 1988) to determine the differential strains on the caregivers, daughters whose elderly mothers lived in separate households fared the best. Their elderly mothers were the most capable functionally and cognitively, and fewer of the daughters experienced caregiving strain, limitations on their privacy or lifestyle, or interference with time and relationships with their immediate families and friends. In fact, there was not one strain variable on which caregivers providing interhousehold help exceeded the strains of daughters in two-generation households (elderly mother, caregiving daughter, and latter's spouse), or three-generational households (when caregivers' children also are present).

In the two-generation households, both mothers and daughters were older than their counterparts in the other two living arrangements. Being in advanced old age was associated with the greater sensory and cognitive impairment of the older women and with their receiving the most help. This undoubtedly accounts to a great extent for the finding that more of their caregiving daughters reported strain than did those living separately. Theoretically, these daughters and their husbands were at the "empty nest" phase of life, but they exemplify the concept of the "empty nest refilled" (Brody, E. M., 1978).

When the "nests" of the caregivers and their husbands contained both their own children and the disabled elderly parent, the daughters had significantly poorer mental health, and more of them reported symptoms of depression, restlessness, and feelings of isolation and missing out on something as effects of care. In addition, compared to the daughters in two-generation households, these daughters were more likely to view their mothers as critical of the sons-in-law and grandchildren, and as more likely to complain. Similar findings about the vulnerability of caregivers in three-generation households were reported by Noelker and Poulshock (1982).

It is obvious that three-generation households hold the potential for problems of space, privacy, and interpersonal conflicts. Such multigenerational living can exacerbate the role strains of the daughter or daughter-in-law in meeting the needs of husband, child(ren), and disabled parent, particularly if the elderly parent complains and is critical of family members.

Living at a geographic distance from a disabled parent may cause different kinds of strain. Because increasing mobility means that more adult children now live at a distance from elderly parents, this has become a significant problem. No matter how concerned and responsible one is, day-to-day care cannot be provided when a parent is far away. In some ways, the strains experienced by such children are similar to those of local children—worry about the parent's decline, for example, and various emotional symptoms. Some strains are specific to the distance between parent and child, however, such as the need to make frequent trips to visit and the feeling that there is no one close at hand on whom the parent can rely. Chapter 6 describes the findings from studies of geographically distant children.

Support from Other Family Members

Virtually all available information indicates that the adult daughter who becomes the primary caregiver provides the bulk of the help needed by the parent, with very little given by the latter's other adult children or other family members. When assistance is forthcoming, it supplements rather than reduces the helping activities of the caregiver (Horowitz & Dobrof, 1982). When the parent lives in the daughter's household, the distribution of services becomes even more unbalanced, with that daughter providing an even greater proportion of help than when the parent lives separately (Brody & Schoonover, 1986).

There is little evidence to support the contention that increasing the caregiving activities of siblings would relieve the main caregiver's strains. In fact, existing data suggest that the actual amount of help the latter receives does not affect her strains. What does seem to result in less burden is her feeling that she has the emotional support of other family members—that they have supportive attitudes and can be depended on at times of need, for example (Horowitz, 1982; Zarit, Reever, & Bach-Peterson, 1980). Such findings were strongly confirmed in a study of caregivers' relationships with their siblings (Brody, E. M., Hoffman, Kleban, & Schoonover, 1989; Schoonover, Brody, E. M., Hoffman, & Kleban, 1988) (see chapter 6).

Quality of Relationships

Any caregiving situation takes place in the context of the qualitative relationships of the family members, relationships that have a long history. Research confirms the logical supposition that it is somewhat less of a strain to help a parent to whom one has always felt close and for whom one has considerable love and affection. Although the presence of good relationships does indeed result in more care being given, adult children feel responsible and provide needed care even when relationships are poor (Horowitz, 1982). In fact, as the case material in chapter 10 shows, daughters often go on giving high levels of care in stormy situations in which there is severe conflict among various members of the family.

Nonfamily Services

The effects on caregivers when "formal" (i.e., nonfamily) services are provided or when they are lacking is an issue that has received considerable attention. There is consensus among professionals and researchers that community services are grossly underdeveloped, and that those that are available are uneven regionally, in short supply, fragmented, and are not funded consistently. Apart from the strains induced by the absence or scarcity of services, caregivers are often confused and frustrated in their attempts to access existing services that are delivered by different organizations, each of which has different eligibility criteria.

Though they are stubbornly persistent, various misconceptions about the effects of formal services have been refuted. As was described in chapter 1, formal services do not encourage family caregivers to reduce the amount of their own care (Horowitz, Sherman, & Durmaskin, 1991), but complement or supplement family services (Lawton, Brody, E. M., & Saperstein, 1991).

Professionals agree that services should have a family focus—that is, they should address the needs of the caregiving families as well as the needs of the older people themselves. Thus, high on the list of service priorities is respite care—such as day care, in-home care, and temporary institutional care—that provide caregivers with opportunities to have some relief and time away from the disabled older person. In a large study of respite service for caregivers of Alzheimer's patients, in-home respite was preferred by families to a much greater extent than other kinds of respite (Lawton et al., 1991).

Controlled studies that determine the actual effects of community services in reducing caregiver stress have been scarce, but a few have been carried out. In the controlled study of respite service for caregivers of Alzheimer's patients, caregivers who received the experimental respite services kept the older people out of a nursing home for a slightly longer time than did the control group caregivers (Lawton et al., 1991). In the large-scale Channelling experiment, the caregivers showed improvements in well-being as measured by the effects on their privacy and social limitations, but did not show reductions in emotional, physical, or financial strains (Corson, Grannemann, Holden, & Thornton, 1986; Kemper and Associates, 1986).

The lack of improvement in caregivers' mental health when formal services are introduced may be due to various factors: the service intervention may be very small as compared with the severity of the strains; the service may not be directed to the most stressful tasks; not all caregivers need the particular service being offered; improvement in one sphere of well-being does not necessarily spill over into another sphere; and some caregivers who may be under severe strain do not avail themselves of enough service, or it may be inadequate to their needs, or they may be too far along in the trajectory of stress (Horowitz, 1985a; Lawton et al., 1991). Another problem in such research is that during the interval between the "before" and "after" evaluations, the elderly patient often becomes more disabled, confounding the effects of the service interventions.

Another way of assessing the effects of a service in reducing caregivers' burdens is to ask for the caregivers' own evaluations. In all reports about respite programs, caregivers are emphatically positive. In the large respite program for caregivers of Alzheimer's patients referenced above, for example, the service was given a resounding endorsement: the caregivers said they had received relief, were satisfied with the program, and wished for respite more than for any other service in the coming year (Lawton et al., 1991).

Stephens, Townsend, Martire, and Druley (2001) studied women who simultaneously occupied four roles—parent care, mother to children at home, wife, and employee. Almost all experienced some conflict among the four roles, and most reported that the most conflict they experienced involved their parent care role. Their stress was due in part to the conflict between parent care and other roles. Women whose parent care situation conflicted with their other roles had the most impaired parents, less education, lower income, and lower status occupations. The authors cautioned that parent care does not necessarily interfere with their perceived ability to carry out the responsibilities of their other three roles.

Institutionalization

It is generally assumed that placement of a disabled older person in a nursing home or other institution signals relief for the caregiver. Professionals who work in such facilities know that this is not so (e.g., Brody, E. M., 1977). Research that examined the question shows that caregiver strains continue after placement (Brody, E. M., Dempsey, & Pruchno, 1990; George, 1984a). Chapter 16 describes in detail the pressures and stress experienced by caregivers when nursing home placement is being considered and after it has taken place.

SUMMARY

There is no question but that the most prevalent and severe strains of caregiving are emotional, though significant minorities of caregivers report physical and financial strains as well. Among the "external" or objective factors that produce strain are characteristics of the older person such as severe disability, mental problems with disruptive behavioral symptoms, and certain personality traits. Caregiver characteristics that relate to strain are gender (being female), being older, work status, role overload, sharing a household with the parent or parent-in-law (particularly if one's own children still live at home), the socioemotional support received from other family members, the quality of past relationships, and help from community services. Having a parent in a nursing home leads to special kinds of strain.

On balance, all information to date shows that some caregivers do so much that they appear to go beyond the limits of human endurance, and often experience a variety of negative effects along the way. The inevitable question that arises is, When is enough enough?

The title of one research paper was, "Why do some caregivers of disabled and frail elderly quit?" (Boaz & Muller, 1991). The authors found an annual attrition rate of about 29% of caregivers who help the most dependent elderly living in the community—that is, those elderly who require help with six or seven ADLs, a level of help that imposes severe physical burden on their caregivers. Half of the elderly relatives of the "quitters" were placed in nursing homes or other institutions; and the others (who remained in the community) had four or more other (paid) caregivers in place. The authors found that the probability of caregivers "quitting" that role was not increased by doing out-of-home work, raising children, having their own health problems, or experiencing caregiving effects in terms of emotional distress. In short, enough was enough not as a result of multiple role demands. But enough became too much when extremely arduous care was needed on a round-the-clock basis—when the sheer physical capabilities of the caregiver were exceeded.

Readers should not infer that the older people in that study were abandoned. To the contrary, though they may have relinquished their hands-on assistance of the care recipients, the data reported by the authors show that the caregivers arranged for ongoing care by others. And, as a number of other studies have shown, nursing home placement does not relieve the caregivers of mental health symptoms, and they continue to enact many caregiving tasks (Brody, E. M. et al., 1990). The sequellae to nursing home placement will be described in chapter 16.

To quote Linda George (1986): " . . . the failure to define acceptable limited leads to unwarranted suffering—both the functional problems that can result from caregiving that is pushed beyond healthful limits and the psychic scars that result from guilt." And she states: " . . . our greatest risk is that family members will not place limits on solidarity such that their own well-being can be sustained" (p. 90).

In short, it appears that at times *enough is enough*. The chapters in Part II will look closely at the subjective aspects of being a caregiving daughter or daughter-in-law that are related to strains.

Chapter 4

Values About Women's Roles and Care of the Aged

Among the qualitative aspects of parent care are intangibles such as values, feelings, and the quality of the relationships among those involved. Values about women's roles and care of the aged evidence change and continuity, values such as those pertaining to family care of the aged and gender-appropriate roles (Brody, E. M., 1995). Some values may remain constant while others may change. The resulting tension between different values may contribute to the strains women experience during the parent care years. A question to be explored is whether values about family care of the aged are affected when they appear to compete with changing values about women's roles.

Values—the "normative expectations [that] serve as guidelines for behavior" (George, 1980)—arise in the context of a particular social environment at a particular time. Though mutable in that they are responsive to changes in the environment, values generally change slowly. Lags may occur, therefore, between conditions that have changed and value changes that respond to the new conditions.

What are often called "traditional" values hold that the provision of help to the disabled elderly is a family responsibility and, in particular, is the role of the women in the family. Those values had developed well before the massive demographic trends described in chapter 1—before the radical change in the number and proportion of older people in the population who lived to advanced old age, before the shift in the nature of their ailments dictated prolonged care, and before the fall in the birth rate. All of those trends combined to increase the demand for parent care while reducing the capacity of adult children to provide that care. Those developments occurred in the context of broad socioenvironmental changes such as urbanization, industrialization, mobility, increasing educational levels, public economic support for the elderly, and inflation. At the same time, values about women's roles were changing. The "new" values hold that it is acceptable, even desirable, for women to have more egalitarian roles with men. The most visible expression of the change has been women's greatly increased participation in the work force, beginning approximately in the middle of the last century (see chapter 14).

Parent-caring women, therefore, have been living in a window of time—a difficult transitional period in which two sets of values have potential for competition, for placing women in the middle.

Women have always been responsive to social values regarding the roles they should play. Indeed, they not only accept, even endorse, the responsibilities assigned to them by society, but often accept the blame when things go wrong. Consider the prime example of women who are now in old age. Through accidents of historical timing, they were buffeted and blamed by a succession of changing values and psychological theories.

When these now-elderly women were in their teens and twenties, the goal instilled in them by society and their families was to marry young, and then to stay at home and perform well (and often exclusively) as wife, homemaker, and mother. The pressures to keep them in those roles have been well described by the leaders of the Women's Movement (Friedan, 1963).

Then, when the women had patterned their lives on the model designed by society, along came the newest pronouncements about childhood development. Mothers were held almost solely responsible for any problems evidenced by their children. Little Johnny's "bad" behavior and little Mary's emotional problems were traced directly to mother's doorstep. Moms were told they had "failed"—they were not being perfect (or even adequate) mothers.

As their children grew, those very same women heard the new message being sent by the Women's Movement: they had consented to being unfulfilled by limiting themselves to the wife/mother role. They should have had careers in order to realize their full potential. Some responded by resuming their education, some entered the work force for the first time, and still others returned to careers that had been interrupted by marriage and motherhood. Some of those who did not, now feel as though somehow they missed out or were out of step with the culture of their times.

Then, in response to the new demography, the need for those women to provide parent care increased exponentially. Though they increased their efforts enormously, yet again they were blamed, this time by the stubborn myth of filial neglect of the old. They were urged by social attitudes and some policymakers to redouble their efforts as an expression of the "old" family values. Again, many had an uneasy feeling that they should be doing more and accepted blame for not doing so.

This was pointed up sharply by a study of parent-caring women in which women were the principal caregivers to their dependent mothers, were in the middle of competing demands on their time and energy, and were experiencing many strains as a result of parent care (Brody, 1985b). Those who had "empty nests" had those nests refilled with elderly disabled mothers—some quite literally, and all in terms of increased responsibilities. For many of the women, care of their parents was but one episode in time-extended "caregiving careers" to more than one older relative. Some of the women had quit their jobs to care for their mothers, and others were considering doing so or had cut back on the number of hours they worked, and many were experiencing problems on the job because of parent care. *Yet three-fifths of those very same women said that "somehow" they felt guilty about not doing enough for their mothers, and three-fourths of them agreed that nowadays children do not take care of their elderly parents as was the case in the "good old days."*

Ironically, now that these women have entered the aging phase of life and some have become disabled themselves, the blame is starting a new cycle. Their daughters—the new women in the middle—are often accused by the very same myth of not fulfilling *their* parent-caring obligations.

Have women's values about family care of the elderly change in response to the enormous pressure exerted by the demographic and socioeconomic trends? Are the "old" values concerning care of the aged being driven out by the "new" values? More specifically, are there value changes among those who are feeling that pressure the most—the women themselves?

The old value is very old indeed. It has been said that "The Fifth Commandment—'Honor your father and mother'—is terse, unambiguous, and powerful in its simplicity. So, too, a parallel form in the Holiness Code: 'A man, his father and mother, must revere' " (Greenberg, 1984, p. 17).

Though it is clear that adult children have always been enjoined to honor, respect, and care for their parents, there is also ambiguity about how "to honor" should be translated into actual filial behavior. In Schorr's classic monograph (1960), he said, "Though there are old and honorable antecedents for the precept to render 'offices of tenderness' to one's parents . . . the *content* of this precept changes with social change" (p. 2).

"Offices of tenderness" may mean intangibles such as respect, affection, and emotional support. The phrase may also be interpreted to mean financial support for day-to-day expenses, payment of medical bills, sharing one's home, and the provision of instrumental and personal care services when one's parents are disabled. Part of the problem in discussions of values about filial responsibility is that such distinctions are not always made. That is, the components of that global concept are blurred rather than sorted out and anchored to particular kinds of tasks or responsibilities.

Undoubtedly, some values have changed regarding the respective roles of the family and the formal support system in providing help of various types to the elderly. S. J. Brody (1987) described societal responses to the aged and their families in this century as having been shaped by the value of avoidance of economic catastrophe. The Social Security Act and its subsequent amendments responded to the catastrophe of widespread poverty. Medicare responded to older people's lack of resources to purchase acute medical care which had resulted in heavy economic burdens on the family. Both responses accepted the new value of societal rather than filial responsibility to meet those economic catastrophes. What S. J. Brody (1987) called the third catastrophe—the need for continuity of long-term care—has received extremely limited response from society, with families still being expected (even exhorted) to meet older people's day-to-day needs for help with personal care and instrumental activities that have gone beyond the adult children's capacities to provide.

Caregiving daughters have continued to feel the impact of that long-term care catastrophe and are a clear expression of the value dilemma. The fundamental question here is whether women's values have changed and if so whether their new lifestyles that responded to value changes have affected or will affect the care of their elderly parents and parents-in-law.

Because there was virtually no information that focused specifically on the intersection of women's changing roles and the increased need for parent care, a research study approached the issue by surveying three generations of Philadelphia-area women in 1977–1978 (a full generation ago) (Brody, E. M., Johnsen, Fulcomer, & Lang, 1983). The women were members of families that included three generations of women—a grandmother, a middle-aged daughter, and a young adult granddaughter. Three generations were studied in order to identify change and continuity in values that bear on caring for disabled older people, particularly values about family care of the aged and about gender appropriate roles. Women were chosen as respondents because they not only are the main caregivers to the old but because the old who are in need of parent care are primarily women.

The relevant issues were examined from several vantage points in order to define and measure the elusive concept of values. Values were operationalized as the women's attitudes, opinions, and preferences that might predict future caregiving. That is, the aims were to discover whether there were differences across the generations; to detect any trends in those differences; and, based on those trends, to determine what they might imply for the future in relation to care of the elderly. Though not identical with behavior, and susceptible to shifts over time, values were seen as significant indicators of the directions that actual behavior might take. In addition, the lives of the middle generation women were compared with the lives of the elderly women when the latter were in their middle years. Finally, some information was collected about actual behavior—that is, the family care that was being given to those of the older women in the families who needed it.

Overall, the findings illustrated, first, that there has been continuity in some values and change in others, but that change that occurred had taken hold unevenly. Second, the global value that favors "filial responsibility" takes on different meanings when linked to specific and different kinds of behavior. Third, the study showed that the values expressed were not always translated into actual behavior. Finally, differences in the filial and parental behavior of the elderly women and the middle generation daughters illustrated the influence of values and environmental change one upon the other.

ATTITUDES: CHANGE AND CONTINUITY

The study found that there had been changes across the generations about the respective roles that should be played by women and men. The women's attitudes with respect to gender-appropriate roles revealed significant trends across the three generations, with progressively more egalitarian attitudes among women of each successively younger generation. Despite these trends—that is, the generational differences—large majorities of all generations endorsed propositions that are consistent with views attributed to the Women's Movement. They favored the sharing of roles by men and women in, for example, traditionally female roles such as child care and parent care. This implies that the attitudes of even the oldest women had changed (though not to the same extent as those of the daughters and granddaughters), as they too had been exposed to the social climate that was encouraging changes in women's roles. The differences among the three generations were greater, however, when the women were asked if sons and daughters should do the same kinds of helping tasks for the elderly parents. The middle generation women were in the middle in that their attitudes about gender-appropriate roles generally were between those of the granddaughters and grandmothers.

Parenthetically, in a telephone survey of the husbands of those middle-generation women, the men generally agreed with their wives' views about egalitarian roles for men and women. The husbands, however, were more likely than their wives to believe that sons should be given more encouragement than daughters to go to college and to feel that a working father should not have to spend as much time bringing up children as a mother does.

Another set of trends was revealed regarding the receptivity of the women to formal (nonfamily) services for the elderly. Surprisingly, the oldest generation was the most receptive to formal services, whereas the youngest was the least in favor of such services. (Note that those "youngest" are the ones who are now at the parent-care stages of life.) At the time, that same young generation of women was the one most in favor of grandchildren helping the elderly. (That attitude was characterized as "grandfilial responsibility.") Here, the oldest women undoubtedly were expressing the well-documented desire of older people not to "be a burden" to their children. The granddaughters may have been responding with the optimism and idealism of their stage of life to hypothetical circumstances which they had not yet experienced at the time of the study, but are now experiencing. The middle generation women (who are now old), on the other hand, again were in the middle; they were divided among themselves about receptivity to formal services. A majority of all generations agreed on one item related to formal versus informal services: that it is better for a working woman to pay someone to care for her elderly mother than to leave her job to do it herself. Nevertheless, some contemporary middle generation women are indeed choosing the latter option. (See chapter 14.)

It is of particular interest that the granddaughters who were the potential caregivers of the future, felt more strongly than the middle generation women (their mothers) and much more strongly than their grandmothers about "grandfilial responsibility" (that older people should expect help from their grandchildren). More than three-fourths of the granddaughters favored such help, in contrast to only approximately one-fifth of the grandmothers; the middle generation (again) were in the middle in that they were evenly divided on the question.

One can only speculate on the meaning of such strong generational differences about the role of grandchildren. Although the young women's attitudes may have reflected their inexperience and life stage, at the least they indicated the vigorous survival of feelings of family responsibility.

We do not know why the middle generation women lacked consensus on that issue. Those who did not expect grandchildren to provide care to the grandparents may not have defined the responsibilities of grandchildren as including such help, or they may have wished to protect their daughters from the excessive responsibilities and strains they themselves were experiencing or were seeing other women experiencing. Those who were in favor of grandfilial responsibility may have been expressing values reflecting strong family cohesion.

Side by side with the trends—that is, the generational differences noted—was *continuity. Values about family care of the aged had not changed from generation to generation.* That is, there were no generational differences in values relating to family responsibility toward the elderly. Regardless of the generation to which they belonged, large majorities of all the women expressed positive attitudes toward family help for the aged and toward intergenerational solidarity and dependability.

It is significant that the traditional value about family care of the old held its ground among the middle generation women even though three-fifths of them were in the labor force (a proportion identical to national data at the time). Moreover, the attitudes of employed women and those who did not work outside the home did not differ. And those attitudes held firm regardless of the amount or type of help needed by their elderly mothers.

But their own endorsement of family help to the elderly did not prevent the women from indicting other families for filial negligence. Nearly four out of five women in each generation believed that adult children nowadays do not take as good care of elderly parents as they did in the past. The vitality of that myth was demonstrated once again!

Continuity as well as *change* were expressed in other responses the women made. Majorities of all three generations were in agreement about what adult children should and should not do to behave responsibly toward a dependent parent. In this, they took into consideration the individual circumstances and competing responsibilities of adult children. They agreed that adult children *should* adjust their family schedules and help to pay for professional care for a disabled widowed mother if need be. But even the oldest women agreed that adult children *should not* be expected to adjust their work schedules or share households with the parent. The three generations also paralleled one another in expecting less financial help but more adjustments in family schedule from a nonworking daughter than a working daughter.

It is important to note that traditional and new values often existed side by side. Despite their general endorsement of egalitarian attitudes toward gender roles, the women also revealed vestiges of the "old" views. For example, all generations were more likely to expect working daughters than working sons to adjust their work schedules to help their mothers. The lack of consistency was apparent in areas other than care of the elderly. Even the youngest women—those most in favor of egalitarian roles for men and women—were divided on the question of whether or not a woman who earns as much as her date should pay her own way when they go out together. Approximately half thought she should do so, one-third thought she should not, and one-fifth were undecided!

PERSONAL PREFERENCES FOR SERVICE PROVIDERS

Another set of questions asked the three generations of women about their personal preferences for the sources of help they preferred (or would prefer) in their own old age.

The preferences expressed also showed both continuity and changes in values. There was continuity in that large majorities of each generation preferred adult children for the intimate functions of confidant and management of their financial affairs in their own old age. But the middle generation women once again were in the middle in that they were least likely to prefer an adult child as provider of housework and personal care services. And they were very much less likely to choose a child for financial help, even though they felt that in principle it is all right for old people to get such help from children.

The preferences of the middle generation women for formal (nonfamily) sources of instrumental help and financial support should be noted, for those women have become the current cohorts of older women. Since the original study was done in 1977–1978, most of them are now in the aging phase of life. The preferences they expressed may mean that they were feeling the pressure of their multiple responsibilities (or were observing such experiences of other family members or friends) and wished to spare their own children similar burdens. They may also have been more sophisticated about government income supports and community services than their mothers. Their responses were striking indications of their dilemma in wanting to be filially responsible as daughters but not wanting to become dependent on their children in their own old age.

In short, it was illustrated that the meaning of needing help may differ with the specific kind of help that is needed (such as housework, emotional support, financial support, personal care), with the source that one turns to (such as formal programs, friends and neighbors, family, even different members of the family), with the stage in one's life when help is needed, and with a variety of other situational factors.

BEHAVIOR

The actual behavior of the women and their families produced even more evidence of continuity, demonstrating once again that attitudes and opinions are not always reflected in actions. Despite their attitudinal acceptance of formal services or many instrumental helping activities, the vast majority of services to the elderly women who needed help was provided by family members. And though there was overall consensus about egalitarian roles for men and women, the adult daughters were the major source of help for parents who needed it. Thus, they behaved in accordance with "traditional" values about women's roles.

The middle-aged daughter's age, her provision of larger amounts of help, and her sharing a household were interrelated—that is, older daughters were more likely to share households with their mothers and to provide more hours of help, illustrating what has been called the peaking of responsibilities as one moves through middle age and the refilling of the empty nest (Brody, 1978). The elderly women who needed more types of care (including personal care) were more likely to be receiving more hours of help, more likely to be living in a daughter's household, and more likely to be older. Daughters who shared households with their mothers provided eight times more help on the average than those who did not, and daughters who were 50 or older provided five times more help than those who were younger. When faced with competing demands on their time, what those women gave up was their own free time and opportunities for recreation and socialization. And some gave up their jobs or reduced working hours (see chapter 14).

Such findings are consistent with the conclusion of Troll and Bengston (1979) that while the rapid pace of social change encourages new ways of expressing old values, it is largely old values that are expressed. But although the data provided behavioral confirmation for the continuity of family values, they also spoke strongly to potential burden on aging caregivers and their families and to possible conflict deriving from competing values.

MIDDLE-GENERATION WOMEN THEN AND NOW

Continuity and *change* again were apparent when the lives of the oldest and middle generation women were compared when each group was between the ages of 30 and 54.

The middle generation women (who are now in old age) had more responsibilities than their mothers had had during their middle years, particularly with respect to helping their own adult children financially and with emotional support. They also were doing more paid work and more volunteer work. These women in the middle also were giving more emotional support to their elderly parents than the latter had given to *their* parents. An area in which the current middle generation women provided less help to parents than their mothers had provided to their parents at comparable ages was financial assistance. This, of course, reflected the improved income position older people had achieved.

The middle generation women seemed to be trying to "do it all." For example, they had already worked many more years than they had expected to as young women and had more responsibilities than did their mothers in *their* middle years.

There was also evidence of the continuity of the quality of family relationships within each family down through the generations—particularly as evidenced in the giving and receiving of emotional support. Those women who had received more emotional support *from* their parents, reciprocated by giving more emotional support *to* those parents. That is, those women who had given and received more emotional support to and from their now elderly parents also provided more emotional support *to* their own adult children and received more *from* them. Those adult children are now the women in the middle—the care-giving generation.

Thus, the family qualitative relationships, whatever their level, continued upward and downward across generations. This finding is consistent with the research and clinical evidence concerning the continuity of individual personality over time (for reviews of this literature, see Neugarten, 1968, 1973) and lends support to the hypothesis that families, too, have "personalities" that often are continuous over time (Brody, E. M., 1974).

WOMEN IN THE MIDDLE—NOW AND IN THE FUTURE

The counterpoint, even tension, in the operation of different values—both between and within generations—is apparent if the findings are reviewed from the perspective of the past and present generations of middle generation women.

The middle generation women, who at the time of the study were in the situation of being both an adult child to an elderly parent and a parent to an adult child, best illustrated the potential conflict of the values they held. The ambiguities associated with that situation undoubtedly accounted for the lack of unanimity among them on some issues. That is, these women may have reacted to the survey questions in their dual roles of adult child and parent. They were the generation least in favor of expecting financial help from children and the least in favor of an impaired parent moving into a child's home. Their multiple roles may account for views that often seem incompatible. For example, though they held egalitarian values, they were the least in favor of married sons adjusting their work schedules or arranging to share a household with their mother. In this, they probably reflected the fact that an elderly woman's son is likely to be a middle-aged woman's husband. That is, the women may have been thinking in their roles as daughters-in-law as well as daughters when they replied to the questions.

The pressures on that past generation of women in the middle are suggested by the data indicating that they have already worked many more years than they had expected to as young women and had more children and more responsibilities than did their mothers in the latter's middle years. And, of courses, "more responsibilities" includes more parent care.

The women who were the granddaughters at the time of the study provided us with a glimpse of what the current picture may be. The potential for conflict in values that was most visible in their mothers was also at work with those young women (who are now in middle age). At an average age of 23 at the time, they were the ones most in favor of equal sharing of roles by men and women, but they were also the generation most in favor of the value of family care of the aged. They were expecting to spend more of their lives in the work force than did their mothers and grandmothers at that age, but they also expected to marry and have as many children as did their mothers and grandmothers. Those young women (now in the middle), even more than their mothers, were expecting in advance to be able to "do it all." Apparently, they have lived up to the expectations they had of themselves when they were young!

To summarize:

- All three generations expressed strong feelings of family and filial responsibility and willingness to be depended on by the elderly parent.

- The fact that attitudes toward gender roles were more egalitarian in each successively younger generation is consistent with popular notions about the impact of women's changing roles and the Women's Movement. The agreement of all three generations that a working daughter need not quit work to care for her elderly mother indicates widespread acceptance of women working. But nowadays many do indeed leave their jobs for parent care (see chapter 14).
- Egalitarian attitudes were diluted by items that specified the sharing of household chores. This suggests that, although women expect more sharing with men, some of them still accept certain tasks as gender appropriate.
- The middle generation women (now old) were more consistently middling and divided in their attitudes toward formal and informal services. Their lack of consensus may have been due to the fact that, being the middle generation, they were thinking in their roles as mothers as well as daughters. Anticipating their own dependency needs in old age, they may have been reacting from the perspective of a care recipient as well as that of a caregiver. Their divergent responses also may have derived from the predicament of many of that generation of women in the middle.

The new values about women's roles apparently had not dispelled old values such as those associated with family care of the elderly. For example, though a majority of the middle generation women were in the labor force (a figure that corresponded to the national average at that time), the strength of their attitudes toward filial responsibility was compelling evidence that the old value (of family care of elderly parents) remained strong despite the new phenomenon of a majority of middle-aged women working. This suggests that most women who work also will continue to be filially responsible and may be particularly vulnerable to the stress and conflicts of role overload. And indeed this has happened (see chapter 14).

The new values seem likely to stimulate changes that have the potential for "role strain" and burden. The information about the lives of elderly mothers and their middle-aged daughters, for example, provided evidence that the latter had more competing responsibilities.

The women of the youngest generation (now the women in the middle) strongly favored shared roles, but at the same time they were even more emphatic than their mothers or grandmothers about filial responsibility. Their emphasis on "grandfilial responsibility" will need to be monitored as the dependent, very old population continues to increase, and as some grandchildren even may become responsible for two generations of elderly—their parents and their grandparents.

Overall, it is clear—contrary to popular misconceptions—that values connected with family care of elderly parents had not eroded and are still powerful, even among women who are overwhelmingly in support of nontraditional roles for both genders.

At the time of the study, the increased help by the middle generation women to their own children was due to the increased educational levels, which prolonged the time during which young people were dependent on their parents. Then, as now, financial assistance generally flowed from parents to children rather than the reverse (Kingson, Hirshorn, & Cornman, 1986), continuing through the early years of the adult child's marriage—that is, until the young couple "gets on their feet." The amount of financial help varies (with socioeconomic status), but the direction is the same. Less financial help to elderly parents nowadays undoubtedly is the result of the better economic position of today's older people who have the benefit of Social Security, Supplemental Security Income (SSI), higher life-time earnings, more pensions and savings, and Medicare.

For some families, the direction of the services and financial help may change when the parent is disabled and in advanced old age. In the main, however, older people are clear about their values: most of them do not want financial help from their children, overwhelmingly confirming their wish not to be a burden. The expectation developed in the United States in this century—the new value—is that basic income for older people should come from governmental programs. In 1935, the Social Security Act was the first major legislative marker expressing this value. Other western developed nations had made the same commitments 50 years earlier. Subsequently, Schorr's (1980) monograph documented the grave negative impact of policies that attempted to compel financial support of old people by their adult children. Medicare, Medicaid, and SSI together and cumulatively signed the death warrant of the destructive and inappropriate Legally Responsible Relatives' provisions that compelled adult children to support their parents. The effect of those pieces of legislation was a precipitous drop in the proportion of old people financially dependent on family (see chapter 2).

Family feeling is not equated with the giving of money. The wish for emotional support and the wish not to need or receive financial help from children exist side by side. Adult children are preferred as providers of emotional support and confidants, but not for day-to-day financial help. It is necessary, therefore, to discriminate between responsibility and emotional bonds on the one hand, and the specific ways in which they are expressed on the other. Financial support is not equivalent to affectional ties, and the study described confirmed that distinction.

The research reaffirmed the need to assess the quality of past family relationships in setting goals for behavior toward elderly family members. Family styles, whether close or distant, often persist over time. Though relatively poor previous relationships do not preclude the provision of a basic level of caregiving, the quality of the affective relationships have been found to determine those who "go beyond the call of duty" for a frail elderly relative (Horowitz & Shindelman, 1981).

In the context of this book, perhaps the most striking implication of the study was that despite egalitarian attitudes of the women in the middle about men's and women's roles in parent care, despite the fact that so many of them were in the labor force, and despite their endorsement in principle that formal services are acceptable for many instrumental helping tasks, those women were providing virtually all the parent care needed. And that is still true today now that their daughters are the new generation of women in the middle.

Moreover, the unevenness with which the "new" values about women's roles take hold implies that the process of sharing parent care between men and women is also likely to be uneven and very slow in developing. Even though more women are in the work force and have less time at home, they are still the vast majority of primary caregivers. Indeed, the evidence in chapter 2 shows unequivocally that families have been steadfast in continuing to provide care for their elderly.

Taken together, the findings suggested that in the future, families will provide their elderly with various instrumental services to the extent that they have the capacity to do so and in response to situational needs. The fear that current and future generations would become cold, unfeeling, and stop doing what they can to help their old appears to have been unfounded. At the same time, the indications are that the pressures on parent-caring women will increase.

What should adult children do?

How can families reconcile the vastly increased need for chronic care for the elderly and their continuing belief in family obligations with women's changing roles? What *should* adult children, and daughters in particular, do to help their parents?

There are extraordinary difficulties involved in establishing values about what constitutes responsible filial behavior. By what yardstick do we measure "normal" or "healthy" or "good" filial behavior? Do we apply the same yardstick to all families? There are as yet no "normative" standards of behavior for families with aged members, as there are for young families in relation to young children, and perhaps there never can be such standards. Setting such standards for aging families is much more complex. It is compounded by the enormous variability in the extent to which older people need services, the nature of the supports they need and their ability to utilize them, and the ages and life stages at which their dependencies occur. In addition, there are variations in family constellations; in the ages, life stages, health, economic situations, and other responsibilities of the adult children who are depended on; in situational factors such as living arrangements, geographic distance; in the quality of past relationships; and in individual and family tolerance for stress.

There is no simple answer to that question of what adult children should do, and it is inappropriate to rely on values developed in earlier periods of time when conditions were vastly different. What is possible now is different because of demography, mobility, women's work force participation, and the much longer overlap in people's obligations to their parents and to their children. (For an excellent discussion of ethical issues about what children "owe" their parents simply because they *are* their parents, see Daniels, 1988.)

Finally, values underlie the judgement of society as to how much and what kind of formal help should be offered through public policy. What should the balance be between individuals' filial responsibility and our collective filial responsibility? The implicit value questions are: How much burden should families be expected to accept before remedies are developed in the form of formal services and facilities? What should the content of filial responsibility be, and what are its limits? How, in fact, do we measure the social and economic cost—to individual, family, and society—of failure to relieve such burdens? And, ultimately, is it not a value judgement as to which type of cost should be the paramount measure?

The 1994 National Long Term Care Survey reported that the degree of caregiver involvement had remained fairly constant for more than a decade, bearing witness to the remarkable resilience of the American family in taking care of its older persons. When values do not accommodate to changing conditions, the lag can add to the strains of caregiving. Apparently, women are still trying to "do it all." The case studies in Part III of the book, in which the subjective aspects of caregiving are illustrated in detailed stories about caregiving, show how the value conflicts experienced by women in the middle affect their well-being and the decisions they make about parent care. The intersection of parent care and employment as it affects women in the middle and care of the elderly is examined in detail in chapter 14.

Part II

Subjective Experiences

Chapter 5

Introduction

Part I of this book summarized the broad demographic and socioeconomic trends that produced the women-in-the-middle phenomenon. It reported quantitative data about some of the consequences of those trends—older people's needs for help, the sources from which that help comes, and the effects of parent care on the daughters and daughters-in-law who provide most of the required assistance. Part I also explored the potential effects of tension between the women's values about family care of the aged and about women's changing roles. Values and trends such as those described interact with subjective processes to influence behavior. With that information as background, Part II and then Part III look more closely at those subjective experiences of some of the real women who appeared earlier as statistics.

Parts II and III are the heart of the book's message. They listen to the voices of women in many diverse circumstances as they tell us of their caregiving careers and their subjective feelings and experiences and the effects on their lives and family relationships. The descriptions of each of the subjective aspects of caregiving are based on thousands of clinical interviews and also on long, verbatim tape-recorded accounts of the caregivers' journeys by the women themselves. The tape recordings were listened to carefully by clinicians and an anthropologist to identify the themes that appeared and reappeared. Not one of the caregivers' words has been altered, though their identities have been carefully disguised.

We now will hear in their own words from women who are the primary caregivers for elderly parents. Some of the main themes apparent in their stories will be identified.

Chapter 6 concerns the daughter's relationships with members of her first family (the family of origin)—her parents and her siblings. Some siblings are characterized as "secondary caregivers" when they help the primary caregiver in her parent care efforts. The approach is first to examine some of the factors that determine how it happens that one member of a sibling set—a particular daughter—becomes and continues to be the primary caregiver. There has been little exploration of the perceptions of her siblings about the caregiving situations, the effects they experience as a result of parent care, or about their relationships with the primary caregiver. Based on a study by the author that concerned the caregivers' siblings, the chapter also examines the roles the siblings play and compares the ways in which caregiving differentially affects the primary caregiver and her sisters and brothers. Some of the problems and rewards in the sibling interactions will be described as they relate to the caregiving situations.

Chapter 7 then will describe six major, fundamental, subjective themes experienced by many of the women in the middle; their experiences in caregiving; and their interpersonal relationships with their elderly parents and parents-in-law, their siblings, and their husbands and children. The chapter ends with a variation on the themes. The variation describes how care of an elderly father appears to differ from care of a mother. The various themes and dynamic processes will be illustrated by many brief case excerpts.

To the extent that available information allows, the perspectives and perceptions of the other family members will be described. Though the main emphasis is on women as caregivers to the elderly mothers and mothers-in-law who constitute the vast majority of care recipients, some of the elderly fathers and fathers-in-law will appear as well. The goal is to advance our understanding of the qualitative aspects of women's parent-care years—the intangible, internal forces that are at work when they assume and continue the caregiving role. The themes in chapters 6 and 7 are not the only ones that are experienced, of course, and others will become apparent in the case studies that follow.

It is, of course, impossible to capture the full range and depth of the subjective aspects of caregiving. Since parent care has become a virtually universal experience, the women come from all walks of life, are rich and poor, highly educated and uneducated. They vary in age and stage of life, in ethnic background, in personality, and in adaptive capacities. The quality of their previous relationships with their parents differs. Their families vary in structure and composition. They are in different stages of their caregiving careers. For some women, those careers may be just beginning as the older people's capacities have begun to decline gradually or were abruptly reduced by a catastrophic illness. Other women have been caring for many years for parents who now are in need of total care. Some of the caregivers share their homes with the older people, whereas in other situations the elderly parents or in-laws live in their own homes. And many women help more than one older person simultaneously or sequentially. All of those factors affect the ways in which the parent-care years are experienced.

The experiences of women do not take place in a vacuum unrelated to the experiences of other close family members—their husbands and children, and their sisters and brothers. Succeeding chapters, therefore, shift the focus to the women's interactions with those close members of their families who constitute a major part of their "social support system."

Consideration of family relationships in the later phases of the family life cycle is a relatively recent development. One of the reasons why later life relationships suffered neglect is that the aged were not much in evidence when psychodynamic formulations about human behavior began. Emphasis therefore was placed on the young nuclear family. Simultaneously, social theorists, impressed with the impact of industrialization, mobility, and urbanization, postulated the isolated nuclear family as the modal, optimal family type in modern society (see chapter 1). As Townsend (1968) pointed out, the last stages in the development of the family were systematically disregarded and only pessimistic predictions of the dissolution of family relationships were made. Stereotypes persisted about the isolation of the aged and their abandonment by families. When, after considerable research, responsible family *behavior* had been thoroughly documented, it was emphasized that it was time to turn to the study of the *quality* and *meaning* of intergenerational relations (Rosow, 1965).

During the family life cycle, there is a constant balancing and rebalancing of dependent relationships. Each change in the capability of each family member necessarily affects every other family member. Change is a constant process in individuals and families in the later stages of the family life cycle as well as in early phases. The chances that the healthy, married 65- or 70-year-old woman or man of today will become disabled, widowed, and dependent on adult children increases with every added year of life, for example. The factor of change applies to the other family members as well. Over time, 40-year-old children became 65- or 70-year-old children. They may retire, develop health problems, and experience losses during the lifetimes of their very old parent(s). The family constellation is constantly being modified by the ebb and flow in family membership as new members are added through marriage and birth while others are lost. Thus, every family experiences continuing processes of change and "periods of adjustment" that never really cease.

At every stage of life, the individual's and family's psychological capacities and relationship patterns are important determinants of how the family manages the various transitions and crises it experiences. Depending on their life experiences and personalities, individuals vary in their capacities to be appropriately dependent and in the extent to which they have the capacity to be depended on by others.

When an older person needs care, reverberations are set up that affect every member of the family. Theoretical understanding of the impact on the entire family has not been fully operationalized in studies of family caregiving, however. Most of the research and clinical literature documents the mental and emotional strains experienced only by the individual characterized as the primary caregiver.

Individual and family behavior at the later phases of the individual and family life cycle is no more uniform than at the early phases. Older families are not exempt from variability along the spectrum from close, warm bonds at one extreme to severe conflict or emotional distance at the other. Any model of ideal behavior at the parent-care stage of life, then, like all models, must be modified by the complexities of each situation. People are diverse in personality, emotional maturity, and stability, and there is wide variability from family to family in the quality of their relationships. Since there are no perfect people or perfect families, it can be expected that residual problems, whether small or large, will be carried forward in time. Similarly, the strengths in the family may come to the fore and facilitate solutions to whatever situation arises.

The relationship between an elderly parent and a caregiving daughter has a long history and is, of course, a central and salient factor. Some ambivalence is virtually omnipresent. Cartoonist Cathy Guisewite captured this concept in her "Cathy" strip in which two middle generation women are chatting. The first woman says to the second, "I'm in this horrible phase with my mother, Charlene." Charlene replies, "Yeah, me too, Cathy." Cathy goes on, "I love her. I need her . . . I think about her all the time . . . but when I'm finally with her, I'm defensive, cranky, and impossible to be with." "Yeah, me too," Charlene agrees. "When did your phase start?" asks Cathy. "Birth," is Charlene's terse answer. "Me too," Cathy says. "No wonder we're so good at it," Charlene concludes.

Whatever the quality of previous family relationships, the need for parent care involves increased amounts of interaction in new and unanticipated forms. What is important here is that parent care does not cause problems in family relationships. Rather, the pressures are such that relationship problems that may have been quiescent are reactivated or exacerbated. The quality of the relationships between caregivers and their parents and parents-in-law, with husbands and children, and among the adult siblings ranges from being close and mutually supportive to being emotionally distant or openly hostile.

The dependency of the parent exerts pressures that compel a rebalancing of roles and relationships, however. The rebalancing may be stimulated by the parent's slow decline that permits a gradual transition. Or, the family may be thrust precipitously into a major upheaval by a parent's catastrophic illness. Whatever the pace of the readjustment, the caregiver's husband or children may compete with the old person for time and attention. New battles may be fought in the old wars among the siblings; old loyalties and alliances as well as old rivalries operate. Even when the family is dispersed geographically, the emotional currents continue to flow and to affect the caring situation. Given the interpersonal and intrapsychic tensions, it is not surprising that the emotional strains of caregiving have been such a consistent theme in research reports.

Though this part of the book is designed to help in understanding the "internals" of care, the "external" factors that relate to the strains of caregiving should be kept in mind as well. Among the objective or external factors that are interwoven with subjective issues are the level and type of the older person's mental and physical disability and the kind of care needed, the living arrangement of the older person (that is, living separately from the adult child or co-residing), and the other roles the daughter plays.

The family situation also interacts with the socioeconomic, physical, and social environment in which caregiving occurs, a context that plays a major role in determining how care is provided and what the effects on all family members may be. Economic status is among those more objective and vitally important factors. The ability to purchase help in caregiving or the availability of services through third-party payors can be of major importance in making the situation more bearable, allowing the caregiver to have some respite and life of her own. Hand in hand with the importance of money is the availability or lack of availability of community services. Caregivers often are unaware of even those services and entitlements that do exist. Even when they are aware of such resources, the difficulties of actually obtaining them can be time consuming, frustrating, and exasperating. In short, caregiving activities take place in and are affected by the social context—the existence and accessibility of services, facilities, and entitlements that could help them or that may be unavailable to those who need them.

The themes that will be described are shared by many caregivers. They vary in intensity from being barely discernable to existing in exaggerated form. Some themes are minor in that they are experienced by smaller groups of women. Even the minor themes are major, however, in the sense that they are prominent in the subjective experiences of those in whom they exist. Many of the themes and processes coexist, and the contrapuntal interplay among them is complex and infinitely varied. This happens not only because of individual and family differences, but because there are many diverse groups of women. Therefore, after this section (chapters 5–7), Part III, "Diversity Among Caregivers" (chapters 8–15) is organized in accordance with four major diverse groups of women. Twenty-five complete case studies are included in order to illuminate the ways in which the various themes in Part II chapters are played out in the stories the women tell about their lives as caregivers.

Chapter 6

On Becoming the Primary Caregiver: Caregiving Daughters and Their Siblings

How does a particular daughter in a sibling set become the one to become the primary caregiver? Among all the subjective processes that exist and interact are those that pertain to that daughter's family of origin—the relationships of all of the adult siblings with each other and their parent(s) as they focus on the caregiving situation. In addition to the effects of parent care on the women in the middle, what reverberations does the caregiving situation have on the other adult children? What are their perspectives? What are the problems and the positive aspects of the siblings' interactions with each other?

Sibling relationships, of course, are significant throughout the life cycle. Their nature and salience in early development is well documented, as are the roles of gender and birth order in, for example, determining personality, intellectual development, and parental attitudes (Lamb & Sutton-Smith, 1982). The literature stresses the uniqueness of the sibling relationship (the shared genetic heritage, cultural milieu, and early experiences) and its long duration (for review, see Cicirelli, 1982).

Relationships among siblings, even among those who have lived relatively separate lives, tend to be renewed when their own children mature and leave home (Manney, 1975) and may become even more important when the siblings grow old. Their relationships with each other are often salient to maintaining morale (Wood & Robertson, 1978). They provide tangible help to each other as well as emotional support (Gold, 1987), notably when the disabled person has no spouse or children to do so, though siblings do less than such relatives. However, in midlife, even siblings who have lived relatively separate lives must interact in unrehearsed ways when the need for parent care arises. The illness of a parent may constitute a "critical event" in the sibling relationship, with the possibility of a positive or negative outcome (Ross & Milgram, 1982).

Though intersibling issues are recurring themes in caregivers' stories, they have received relatively little attention from research. In general, research has had a vertical perspective on family caregiving. That is, studies examine parent/child relationships during the phase of the family life cycle when the parent is elderly and needs help. There has been less consideration of the horizontal relationships—that is, among adult siblings who have a disabled parent.

Another factor contributing to a lack of sufficient attention to siblings is that caregiving situations are seen primarily from the perspectives of the older people concerned and their primary caregivers. When an older person is in contact with a service agency or health professional, it is usually that primary caregiver who accompanies her and whose account of the situation is heard. As a result, most information about the behavior of the various siblings and the family dynamics that operate is not supplemented to a significant extent by reports from other siblings.

As pointed out in chapter 2, the main parent-care pattern is for one daughter to become the primary caregiver and to provide most of the help needed by a disabled parent. The other adult children in the family, who often help to some extent, are referred to as "secondary" caregivers. Typically, the main caregiver sustains her efforts, sometimes for many years, despite any negative effects she and her own family may experience. Even when it becomes necessary to place the parent in a nursing home, the same woman usually remains the steadfast "responsible other" who maintains the closest connection with and does the most for the parent.

The lack of a large body of information about the secondary caregivers leaves a vacuum easily filled by opinions and biases. The siblings may be viewed as having abdicated their responsibilities and allowing their responsible sister to bear the burdens alone. In a related vein, emphasis has been placed on intersibling conflicts about the parent-care situation and the deterioration in their relationships with each other. The many instances in which sisters and brothers collaborate with each other in decision-making, cooperate in caregiving, and give each other emotional support as well as instrumental help go relatively unnoticed.

Though situational factors may play a role in determining who in the family becomes and remains the primary caregiver, there are many subtle forces at work as well. In beginning to unravel this extremely complicated matter, it will be approached from several perspectives:

- The primary caregivers' views about how they happened to occupy that role;
- Reports from caregivers and their local siblings as to the amount of parent care each provides;
- The effects caregivers and their local and geographically distant siblings experience as a result of the parent care situation;
- The accounts of caregivers and their local and geographically distant siblings of the problems they have with each other and the positive side of their interactions.

It is important to keep in mind that family relationships, whether positive or negative (most often there is a mixture), do not arise anew at the parent-care stage of life, but are part of the natural continuum of the family's history. Old loyalties and alliances among siblings as well as old rivalries exist, and the problems and strengths stand out in bold relief when the older person becomes the focal point of their interactions. Among adult siblings, as with all types of family relationships, vestiges of unresolved relationship problems from earlier phases of family life are reactivated and recapitulated during subsequent family crises. The older person's dependency is just such a crisis; it disturbs the family homeostasis and requires a rebalancing of the roles and relationships of all family members.

In exploring questions about how a particular daughter happens to become and to remain the primary caregiver, it is emphasized that there is nothing intrinsically "wrong" when a daughter occupies that role. In many situations, it works out well. Siblings help as much as indicated or as much as they can, and relationships are amicable. Obviously, when the disabled parent can no longer live alone, she cannot live with all of her children and a selection must be made. Serious intersibling problems are by no means inevitable. In most families, sibling relationships fall between the extremes of severe conflict and being "ideal." Moreover, it would be naive to view any human relationship as totally "good" or totally "bad," since both positives and negatives invariably exist simultaneously, though the balance is different in different families and among different sets of siblings in the same families.

When there are serious latent or existing relationship problems, however, the parent may become the storm-center of a chaotic family situation. The stimulation of intersibling tensions that may have been relatively quiescent have been described in reference to situations in which the parent requires assistance or is at risk of institutionalization (Brody & Spark, 1966; Simos, 1973; Spark & Brody, 1970). Helping professionals frequently hear complaints from caregivers about their siblings, much anecdotal material from support groups of adult children highlights sibling conflict, and there are some research reports of widespread deterioration in sibling relationships as an effect of parent care (e.g., Kinnear & Graycar, 1982).

Some patterns will be described that emerged in the course of qualitative interviews with caregiving daughters. Then information will be presented that was elicited directly from the siblings themselves.

BECOMING THE PRIMARY CAREGIVER

A variety of factors may best work in determining the selection of the main person to provide care to an elderly parent.

Gender, Geography, and Being an Only Child

Three powerful determinants of the selection process are relatively straightforward: gender, geography, and being an only child.

The virtually universal acceptance of the proposition that care of elderly people is a woman's role was discussed in detail in chapter 4. The power of gender is determining who becomes a caregiver extends to other relatives as well. When disabled older people do not have a spouse or an adult child, female relatives—sisters and nieces, for example—predominate over their male counterparts (Horowitz & Dobrof, 1982).

Geographic proximity is often a major determinant of becoming the primary caregiver. It is obvious that when an adult child lives at a distance from the parent, she is simply not available to provide day-to-day assistance, no matter how close the emotional bond and no matter how much she wants to help. Though geographically proximate daughters recognize the practical reasons for their caregiving role, there may be an undercurrent of resentment nonetheless.

> I don't mind being the principal caregiver. That's the way it is. I'm up the street from her and that's all there is to it. The main reason I'm the principal caregiver is because I live closest. They all live comfortably away. They can be away and be comfortable because they know I'm here. I think if I wasn't here, they would probably do a little more.

It can be argued, of course, that a parent can be moved to be near a child or that a child can move to bring the parent within caregiving range. This happens at times, particularly if the parent is the one to move closer to a daughter.

> After my mother's heart attack, it seemed logical for my mother and stepfather to move near me since my brother and his wife were both working full-time and I wasn't working.

To adult children who have no siblings, it is self-evident that they should become the caregiver. They invariably say "Who else is there?" or "There wasn't any option." Some only children report that they were aware very early in their lives that parent care would be their responsibility and accordingly prepared themselves for that role.

> Way back when [as a child] . . . I figured I'd have to be responsible for one or another of my parents. I guess I had that in back of my mind all these years. . . . It wasn't as if I was making a huge sacrifice [not getting married] because I like to work. I figured . . . if the day came and the need arose [for parent care], I could probably handle it. . . . That's how it went.

* * *

> It was up to me. I have no siblings. I prepared for this all my life. An ounce of prevention is worth a pound of cure. I'm a preparer. . . . A stitch in time saves nine.

Some caregivers become only children later in their lives because their sibling(s) have died, a situation that is increasing in frequency as more people live to advanced old age and outlive one or more of their children.

> I knew I had to take care of them [parents] and that there would be no one else to help . . . I regret my sister wasn't alive to share the changes.

* * *

> My mother-in-law moved into our house after her stroke because my husband's only brother died.

Beyond gender, geography, and being an only child, no strong patterns of selection have been identified, and there are many subtle forces that operate.

Birth Order

Though birth order (being the youngest or oldest child) is often mentioned as influential, overall it has not emerged as important in the few studies that have been done. Nevertheless, some caregivers do attribute their role to their position in the birth order.

> I'm the oldest, and I always took most of the responsibility.

* * *

> I'm the youngest, so I was still home when Mom starting needing care.

In a small number of situations, the elderly parent and adult daughter have continued to co-reside even after the latter marries, and the caregiving situation is a natural extension of that lifelong arrangement. Co-residence is much more frequent when the adult child had never married or returns to the parental home after divorce.

Some caregivers, when asked, "How did it happen?", offer reasons such as feeling responsible; being better able to provide care; having more appropriate housing, money, or time than a sibling; the elderly mother's preference; or emotional closeness. Since such responses tell us little about the processes at work, further exploration is required.

An intriguing theme is that, whatever the various reasons or combinations of reasons offered, a daughter often votes for herself in the informal election that is held to select the caregiver. (The election is rarely contested.)

It Just Happened That Way

"It just happened," "It just worked out that way," or "That's the way it is" are explanations offered by some caregivers.

> When mother needed a place to stay, I was the only one to offer. It wasn't a conscious decision for me to do it; it just worked out that way. Things happened, and I picked up. When she came to the house, it was for a visit. No one expected it to be permanent. It just worked out that way. Everything just ran together. It all fell into place, and here I've been.

* * *

> We knew we would have to take care of her. Mom trusted us to make decisions about her care; that was how it was. I felt I was home, so I might as well do it. It was a natural thing.

* * *

> It just happened that I made the offer for my mother to come and live with us, and I became the principal caregiver. I don't know if my sister would have made the offer or not. It didn't really enter into my decision.

In many instances, caregivers begin by providing very little help, but the amount of assistance grows incrementally over time as the parent becomes more and more disabled and dependent. Although a catastrophic illness of the parent may initiate the need for care, most situations develop gradually. There is no clear point, therefore, at which the setting of limits is indicated, and the boundaries of care are expanded almost imperceptibly. When parent care expands so that it encroaches on and displaces all other areas of the caregiver's life, other dynamic patterns are at work as well.

Fewer Competing Responsibilities

A selection process may go on in some families so that the role of caregiver falls to the child with fewest competing responsibilities (Ikles, 1983; Stoller, 1983). Thus, daughters who are not married (widowed, never-married, separated, or divorced) are often over-represented as parent carers. This was illustrated in a survey of three generations of women in which all three generations were likely to expect more of not-married daughters than of married daughters or sons—to adjust their work schedules for parent care and to share a household with an elderly parent, for example (Brody, E. M., Johnsen, & Fulcomer, 1984). That expectation was expressed in the women's actual behavior, with married daughters providing less help to their parents than not-married daughters (Lang & Brody, E. M., 1983).

It is not unusual for daughters to offer their siblings' competing responsibilities as the rationale for their own selection as caregiver.

> Being a widow made it easier. I just feel sorry for [caregiving] women who have children or even boyfriends.

* * *

> I felt I was the person to take on her [mother's] care because I was a single person. That was definitely a factor.

* * *

> I don't have any other family obligations per se. I'm not married. I don't have children. And my sister has emotional problems.

* * *

> If I had a family of my own, I would have had to give it a lot more thought. . . . But I felt I was the person to take on her care because I'm divorced.

Although fewer competing responsibilities may indeed be a factor, another influence may also be at work with women who are not married, especially if they are childless as well: the parent fills the universal human need for a close relationship with another.

Burden Bearer

No matter how many siblings there are in a family, it is not unusual for one of them to assume all major family responsibilities, of which parent care is only one. Such individuals have been characterized as the family "burden bearers" (Brody, E. M., & Spark, 1966). This woman's plaint is typical.

> I am always the one who has taken responsibility for my mother. I am the one who shops and takes her to the doctor. I am the one she depends on to take care of her. I am the one she calls late at night if she feels ill.

These women may present themselves as long-suffering, patient, martyred, self-sacrificing, and even oppressed. Sometimes the burden bearer protects and excuses her siblings. "My brother is not well. He cannot be expected to help" or "My sister has emotional problems." Sometimes resentment and bitter envy is expressed, "My sister [and/or brother] does nothing, but is always telling me what to do." Although the behavior of such women may be viewed as admirable, one wonders what gratification they may be obtaining from the very burdens that ostensibly weigh so heavily.

Favored Child and the "Rejected" Child

The child who was favored by the parent or the one who always "got along best" with her may be the one to assume the role of primary caregiver.

> Of all of us [children], I always understood my mother the best.

* * *

> Maybe mother chose to live with me because, growing up, she and I got along the best of the four children.

* * *

> I didn't mind being the principal caregiver. All our lives, my mother was my friend. My one sister and her never got along. My one sister was never a giver, and that was all right. My other sister was willing but couldn't manage mother.

At other times, however, it is the child who feels rejected or the least loved who provides the care in the hope that the parent will come to love her the best. Such daughters yearn to become the favorite child and are constantly trying to win the acceptance or love denied them earlier in their lives. They continue their efforts to do so even when they are "children" in their eighth decade of life, exhausting themselves in a fruitless and never-ending effort to please the parent they are helping.

> I'm the one who does everything for my mother, but my brother is still her favorite child.

* * *

> My mother does nothing but complain and criticize me. When my brother visits, she's a different person.

A variation on the theme is that of daughters who claim to have had their parent's(s') approval early in life, but lost it because of their behavior (an unacceptable marriage or lifestyle, for example). Such a woman may see caregiving as a means of regaining the parent's love or vindicating herself, "I'm a good person [or daughter] after all."

> I remember a lovely relation with my father when we were small. . . . Some of that warmth has come back in taking care of him. It's sort of nice to experience his total acceptance of me after so many years.

Mother/Daughter Enmeshment

Some caregiving daughters say they have been extraordinarily close to their mothers since early childhood. Time has not weakened the powerful bond, and the caregiver seems unable to separate from her parent. In extreme cases, the mother/daughter tie remains central, even superseding the daughter's relationship with her husband and children. These women feel that no one else is satisfactory as caregiver to the mother, or no one else is able to provide care as well.

> I wouldn't be happy if mother didn't live near me. I need her near me. I need to be there and to know what my mother is doing and what kind of care she is getting. So it is good she is here and I can check on her all the time and be there for her. I don't think my mother would have been happy living near my sister. My sister doesn't know what is right for mother.

* * *

> My sister-in-law offered to come over for a few days so we could visit our kids, but I told her that my mother will not let her do what I have to do for her.

* * *

> My husband did not object when I brought my parents to our home, but he withdrew into himself. Now Dad is dead, and Mother is in a nursing home. My husband would like me to turn to him now, but there is still the connection with my mother. I am not free yet.

* * *

> Now that I'm 50 years old, I've decided that I would like to marry. But the man would have to understand in advance that my mother will always come first.

* * *

> Mother said when I was a girl, "You don't want to get married." I did get married, but I never really left her.

Being Worthwhile

Caregiving gives some women a role in life, a sense of competence and of being a responsible individual. Their behavior elicits approval and admiration from those around them, and their sense of adequacy and self-esteem is enhanced: "I'm doing a noble thing" and the doctor tells me 'Nobody gets the care your mother gets.' "

"Professional" Caregivers

Women who might be characterized as "professional" caregivers seem to seek opportunities to enact that role, often providing help to other elderly people in addition to their parents or parents-in-law.

> I also helped my aunt [in addition to both parents]. She had other people to help, but I was the only one around. . . . It just evolved. It started out a little bit and ended up a lot. My father and mother did it, and when my father died it fell on me.

* * *

> I helped my aunt before she moved in here. We would go over every week and take her shopping, and my husband would fix anything that had to be fixed in her apartment. My husband and I decided together to have her live with us. My mother was living with us at that time. The reason we brought my aunt over was because she had tiny strokes. It was when my aunt had a stroke that I quit work. I also have an uncle on my father's side that I help.

Some of these women began to take care of their parent(s) very early in childhood. Caregiving becomes a way of life, and parent care continues that longstanding pattern. The early socialization of these "professional" caregivers sometimes occurs when the parent had a physical or mental disability that was present when the child was very young.

> My parents were born totally deaf, and I began to take care of them when I was a child. I took care of my younger brothers as they came along. You have to be a certain kind of person to deal with deaf people. My brothers are loving and caring but . . . my mother wouldn't be happy except with me. She cares about me, nobody else, just me. Maybe my brothers, but not so much because they aren't with her. Anybody else could do the same things that I do for my mother, but it wouldn't be the same and it wouldn't satisfy her. I took care of my aunt, too, and I have another aunt who is beginning to need my help. I want my house to be the halfway house where all the family gather.

* * *

> Beginning when I was a child, my mother didn't leave the house for 22 years.

She was afraid to go out. We used to do all the errands and bring the stories of our days to her.

* * *

My mother was so sick when I was little that I lived with my grandmother for six years. My father was sick too. For a long time, I thought that's the way things are: You grow up, you get married and have children, and then you get sick.

Deathbed Instructions

The instructions of a dying parent are sometimes offered as a reason for the caregiver's assumption of that role:

Daddy said I should be the one to care for mommy. My sister took mother for a while, but it wasn't right. Daddy said mother should be with me. I'm the only one who could take mom. Daddy wanted most of the care to fall on me. I didn't have a choice. Just before he died, he asked me to take care of mommy. He said I was to be in charge.

Being Responsible and Nurturing

Being responsible, capable, or especially nurturing are traits some caregivers attribute to themselves as accounting for their role.

My sisters think I can handle it better. I'm the backbone of the family. I guess I always acted old for my age.

* * *

When she was dying, my mother-in-law told my father-in-law, "Go to your son's house. That's the place to be." She knew we had a happy household.

Low Expectations

Some women accept the caregiving role because others in the family expect it of them and continue on for years without protest. These women often appear to be unusually passive and to express very low expectations for meeting their own needs. They may attribute severe emotional symptoms or stress-related physical problems to caregiving, but make no effort to extricate themselves or even to obtain family or nonfamily services that would give them temporary relief. Some live extremely restricted lives. When asked what they would like to ameliorate their situations, they reply, "I would like to be able to take a walk by myself once in a while" or "It would be wonderful to have a whole day all to myself."

Transferring the Role to Another

Occasionally, an overburdened caregiver will try to transfer care of the parent to a sibling, usually without success.

> At first, my mother was shuffled around among us sisters, but they wouldn't keep her.

* * *

> When I was breaking down, my sister took my mother. But after a couple of weeks, my brother-in-law put her in a taxi back to us.

* * *

> I asked my sister in Chicago . . . if she could take her. She said she could take her for two months. . . . After three weeks, my sister couldn't wait to get her on the plane to get her back to us.

Equitable Sharing

Sometimes siblings—almost invariably a pair of sisters—collaborate so closely that they have difficulty identifying one or the other as the primary caregiver.

> I don't know which of us is the principal caregiver. My sister lives in Washington, and my mother lives about a mile away from me. Sure, I do the day-to-day things like shopping and taking mother out to dinner and running over if there's an emergency. But my sister comes in regularly, and we save up things for her to do like going to the doctor and the podiatrist and shopping for clothes. She comes in right away if we need her. She takes Mom to Washington for visits. I always know she's there. I count on her and she counts on me.

* * *

> My sister and I are each better at different things. She's more assertive, so she deals with the doctors and the Medicare people and so on. I'm better at dealing with our mother. So we each do our thing, and it works out.

The kind of sharing described in those excerpts is better characterized as amicable and equitable rather than equal. The particular tasks are not divided, but each sibling sees the other as willing to do what she can—a *fair* rather than *equal* share.

SECONDARY CAREGIVERS: THE SIBLINGS' PERSPECTIVES

In turning to the perspectives of the caregivers' siblings, it is reiterated that the data presented derive primarily from quantitative studies; it remains to gain in-depth understanding of those siblings' subjective processes.

Having become the principal caregiver, the daughter provides the bulk of care, with her siblings providing a much lesser amount of help. Reports from those daughters, however, indicate that emotional support from siblings and from other relatives is very important in buffering their strains (George, 1986; Zarit, Reever, & Bach-Peterson, 1980).

In one study, the local (defined as living within 50 miles of the parent) siblings themselves confirmed the imbalance between their own helping contributions and those of their caregiving sisters (Brody, E. M., Hoffman, Kleban, & Schoonover, 1989). The primary caregivers reported they provided an average of more than 24 hours of help weekly (including virtually all the ADL help needed), whereas their local sisters and brothers reported providing eight and less than four hours weekly, respectively.

The lesser amount of help siblings provide should be seen in relation to the mother's living arrangement. Certainly, a daughter whose household includes the mother absorbs many tasks like the mother's shopping and cooking when she does those things for her own family. Nor can personal care such as feeding and toileting be postponed until someone else can visit. In addition, there may be a tendency to view the older person as having become part of the caregiver's immediate family. That being so, other family members assume that the elderly parent's needs are being met. Whatever factors are at work, the net result is that the caregiver's contribution is greater when the parent shares her home; her siblings do less than when the parent lives alone (Brody, E. M., Kleeban, Hoffman, & Schoonover, 1988). Although other members of the caregiver's own household may help a bit more, their help does not offset the reduction in the help from others in the extended family network.

There is another qualification about the roles of the caregivers' siblings. Because estimates of help in surveys are based on day-to-day ongoing assistance with ADL and IADL, certain important forms of help usually go uncounted. Sisters and brothers often rally to provide major services at particularly demanding times or during emergencies—acute illnesses of the older person, the caregiver, or her immediate family, for example, or when the older person moves from one household to another. The sense that siblings can be relied on at such times gives the caregiver a feeling of security and support.

COMPARING THE EFFECTS ON CAREGIVERS AND SIBLINGS

The extensive literature reviewed in chapter 3 shows that approximately one-half to three-fourths of daughters who are primary caregivers report effects such as various emotional strains, negative effects on their physical health, and lifestyle interferences (with privacy, socialization, vacations) and feelings of anger and resentment. When the effects of care experienced by siblings were elicited directly from them in the study of caregiving daughters and their siblings, it was apparent that siblings do not go unscathed, however. Half of them reported experiencing some problems similar to those of the principal caregivers (Brody, E. M., et al., 1989).

It is particularly significant that findings about gender differences in experiencing the effects of parent care proved to be consistent. The daughters who were the primary caregivers experienced the most negative effects of parent care, the local brothers experienced the fewest negative effects, and the local sisters fell in between. To emphasize, though the strains of the siblings were fewer and less severe than those of the caregivers, the latter's sisters, more than the brothers, reported more overall strain and more severe strains; more emotional symptoms such as feeling drained, nervous, frustrated; and more interferences with their family responsibilities.

The brothers' reports that they experienced fewer emotional symptoms than both groups of their sisters may reflect the fact that the men provided the least help. Or, it is possible that as men they are more likely to repress or deny their emotional reactions than women. It is most likely, however, that sisters experience more strain than brothers because they are more involved emotionally and see the responsibility for the care and happiness of their parents as their role as females (see chapter 4).

An effect of care about which the caregivers and their local siblings did not differ significantly is of special interest. Most of the caregivers and their siblings agreed with the statement, "Somehow I feel guilty about not doing more for my mother." The siblings outdid the caregivers in the frequency with which they experienced such guilt, however. Being the one who does most for the parent appears to alleviate (if only slightly) guilt about "not doing more." Some of the adult children felt guilty about other aspects of care as well. Both groups of daughters exceeded their brothers in feeling guilty when they become angry with their mothers. The sisters outdid the caregivers in feeling guilty about not doing more for their mother and in wishing that they were not so busy so that they could assist their mother more.

Nevertheless, one complaint unique to the primary caregiving daughters is particularly poignant. Two-fifths of them said that even though they were the ones who were doing the most for the parent, another sibling was the favorite child.

Sibling Interactions

Other information from the same Brody et al. (1989) study spoke directly to the problematic and the beneficial aspects of the siblings' interactions with each other about the caregiving situation—interactions that were categorized as intersibling "hassles" and "uplifts." As expected, the sibling relationships ranged from those that were close and mutually helpful to those that were extremely problematic, with most falling in between.

Once again, daughters reported more strain than sons. Overall, approximately 30% of the caregivers, 40% of their sisters, and only 6% of the brothers reported a great deal or a fair amount of strain from interactions with their siblings about parent care.

There were many differences between caregivers and their siblings. It was the former who reported the most problems about ways in which their siblings were failing to meet parent-care responsibilities by doing such things as visiting the mother, volunteering to help without waiting to be asked, helping more, or doing a fair share of parent care. The authors of the study characterized such complaints as siblings' "nonfeasance." Other kinds of complaints were called siblings' "malfeasance"—that is, more active negative behaviors such a criticizing the caregiver or trying to make her feel guilty.

The caregivers describe their negative interactions with their siblings:

> My sister took Mother for a period of time but felt very resentful about it. We were not communicating very well.

* * *

> I'm not satisfied with the amount of help they give Mother. They often take turns having her for weekends, but have to be reminded that she sat home for some weekends in a row. With eight of us, it shouldn't be that way.

* * *

> My brother and sister used to help, but when Mother moved in with us, they considered the problems solved.

Again, there was a striking finding about the sisters. They exceeded both the caregivers and the brothers in saying that a sibling had tried to make them feel guilty for not helping more, had complained of doing more than she does, or had said how burdened they felt.

Positive interactions existed side by side with problems in the very same situations, however. The other side of the picture is that the caregivers and both groups of her local siblings reported many rewarding aspects ("uplifts") of their parent-care interactions. The vast majority of all three groups felt that a sibling was dependable about helping their mother and understood their caregiving efforts. *Again, the sisters and brothers differed.* The sisters experienced more rewards from their sibling interactions and felt more benefitted by them than the caregivers. In particular, the sisters were the ones who felt good when permitted to share decisions about the mother.

Many of the rewards reported by the main caregivers were the obverse of the problems they had expressed; specifically, they felt benefitted when socioemotional support was forthcoming from their siblings and felt hassled when it was not. The siblings, too, were benefitted by the same behaviors that caregivers found rewarding and, in addition, appreciated the approval of their siblings and the willingness to share decisions with them.

The caregivers describe rewarding situations:

> Mother had a heart attack, and my father went to a nursing home. My brother went back and forth several times. At a family conference, we arranged for them to move to an apartment in Philadelphia. My brother is very supportive and appreciative. He and his wife come east [from Denver] three or four times a year so we can go away each time for a week, and he calls every week.

* * *

> My sister and I both work. We really tried to share the responsibilities of my mother, and we still share them. We are better at doing different things. I'm better at talking to the staff at the nursing home and getting my mother's needs met because I'm more assertive. My sister was much better at filling out all the forms at the nursing home. We really try to share. There is no resentment that one does more than the other. If there was a difficulty, if one wasn't satisfied or something, we would just talk about it.

Overall, the study of siblings made it apparent that parent care has repercussions not only on principal caregivers, but on their siblings and on the relationships among them. The caregivers and siblings who were most troubled by their interactions were those whose mothers were more difficult to care for because of cognitive impairment and irritability, and whose relationships with their mother and families were not satisfactory. Conversely, those with more positive relationships had mothers needing less help, and better relationships with the mother and the family. This suggests that as the mothers' care needs increase, the pressure felt by her children is expressed in part as increasing tension among them. The caregivers, on whom the burden is greatest, become more aware of the inequity and more sensitive to any failure of their siblings to provide emotional and instrumental support. Close and warm relationships with the mother and among her children, however, appear to mitigate the strains among them.

Overall, an intriguing finding of the study was that, once again, in comparison after comparison, daughters proved to be more vulnerable than sons to emotional strain relating to parent care.

It is understandable that the primary caregivers should feel more strain, but their local sisters are a particularly interesting group. To recapitulate, local sisters fell between the other two groups—caregiving daughters and local brothers—in reporting overall strain and negative emotional and physical consequences of caregiving. They exceeded even the primary caregivers in reporting strain from the intersibling interactions. These sisters were especially sensitive to any implications that they were not meeting their parent-care responsibilities and were appreciative when included in decisions about the mother's care. They were the ones who felt the most guilty about not doing more for their mothers and who most often wished they were not so busy so that they could do more. They joined the caregivers in feeling guilty more often than the brothers when they became angry with the mothers, and they joined the brothers in feeling guilty more often because they were doing less parent care than the principal caregivers. The overall sense conveyed is the discomfort of the local sisters (but not the brothers) about being in the role of secondary, rather than primary, caregiver.

When the siblings who were studied were asked to write briefly about the nature of the problems that may exist among siblings when a parent needs care, their replies spoke to equitable sharing of responsibility, problems of communication, disagreements over the mother's needs and care, and unresolved sibling rivalries.

> Her care is unlikely to be equally shared, which leads to guilt and resentment. Children may have different ideas about what is most important in her care and how she should be treated; those who are not primarily caretakers have little voice in what happens to her.

* * *

> Problems with siblings and rivalry come up with conflicts over who does more for Mother. This creates tension and often hostility and resentment; jealousies emerge.

* * *

> The problem is finding ways to work out an equitable sharing of the help so that old family patterns are not simply reinforced; also, coping with the ways in which different values or different senses of Mother's real needs can create tension and distance rather than cooperation and closeness.

* * *

> The main problems are the unequal degrees to which siblings help (or are perceived to help), the differing extents to which siblings are able to help, and indifference on the part of some siblings.

Geographically Distant Children

Geographically distant children have somewhat different problems than those who live close to the parent. It is probable that more of the children of future cohorts of the elderly will live at a geographic distance. Between 1987 and 1997, there was an increase in the number of caregivers who reported that their care recipient lived more than 20 minutes away: 16%

in 1987 and 24% in 1997 (Wagner, 1997). Although in most cases it is children who move away from parents, the elderly themselves are migrating in increasing numbers.

Geographically distant children are, of course, constrained in their ability to provide regular and sustained instrumental support to an aged parent. In the study described, geographically distant children were compared with their sisters who lived close to the parent and were the primary caregivers (Schoonover, Brody, E. M., Hoffman, & Kleban, 1988). Once again, *women (the caregivers' sisters) proved to be more vulnerable to parent care strains than men (the caregivers' brothers)*. The caregivers' sisters were more likely than their brothers to express feelings of guilt about the mother's situation—in particular, about not doing enough for the mother and the fact that a sibling (the main caregiver) was doing more. In comparison to their brothers, the sisters also felt more guilty about living far away and about getting angry or losing patience with the mother at times. They were more likely to express the desire to spend more time with the mother and to want to live closer so that they could provide more help.

The geographically distant sisters, more frequently than the brothers, report negative emotional effects from the caregiving situation—the now familiar litany of feeling helpless, nervous, frustrated, depressed, drained, overwhelmed, tired, and pulled in different directions by the mother's needs for help. They also reported higher levels of strain deriving from the mother's situation and from living far away from her, and from the intersibling problems that occurred. The sisters were more likely than brothers to say that a sibling had complained of doing more for the mother than they had, had not understood how much help the mother needed, had tried to make them feel guilty about not doing more, had not done his or her fair share, had criticized what they did to help the mother, had complained of doing more, had not visited the mother enough, did not understand how much help the mother needs, and thought he or she knew better what was best for the mother.

Like the local siblings, majorities of both geographically distant brothers and sisters also reported benefits from the social and emotional support provided by their siblings—from their dependability in helping when needed, moral support, reliability in visiting and calling the elderly mother, and understanding of the effort he or she made to help the mother.

Certain themes appeared for sisters and brothers alike in their replies to an open-ended question about the main problems or concerns facing geographically distant children of disabled elderly parents. Their responses included their inability to respond to the mother's needs in a timely fashion or on a regular basis because of family obligations and/or financial restraints; feeling cut off and left out of decision-making and uninformed as to the mother's day-to-day conditions; feelings of guilt for not being able to do more or to relieve the sibling providing the help; and the competing demands of their own families and careers. They wrote:

> I feel sad and guilty both for my mother and my sister's always being "on call." I worry about being unable to get there on time when needed, and I worry a lot about responsibilities of my own here and the stress of not being able to accept a commitment that might be interrupted, or unfulfilled, should I be needed at my mother's side.
>
> * * *
>
> It takes a major effort to visit her, particularly as my children get older. These visits are usually instead of a family vacation. When she is here, we give up our room, as space is limited, and arrange our lives around her. All of this puts a strain on my family, and I feel guilty that I can't please them or help Mother enough. The major problem is not being able to provide help, and not being sure what is really wrong or what is taking place. I never really am able to feel secure about my mother.
>
> * * *
>
> Major problems are finding ways to provide something like a fair share of the help while living at a distance; feeling that I have little right to assert my views of her needs because others are providing most of the care. There is little sense of a sustained relationship that makes a large difference toward her comfort instead of a periodic one that makes little difference on the whole.
>
> * * *
>
> . . . not being able to visit or invite her on a regular basis; helping to make financial decisions when she is not able to do this; the feeling of being almost helpless when certain situations arise.

On another write-in question, the distant siblings were asked if there were any other ways in which the mother's needs affected them and their families. Both sisters and brothers described arrangements whereby they attempted to participate in and relieve their sister's caregiving burden, as well as the ways in which these arrangements affected their and their families lives. In addition, some described the effects of their parent's condition on their own children. For example:

I have developed a pattern of making visits to relieve my sister and brother-in-law several times a year. That is, I take over for a few days and let them get away. This has been very beneficial to me as well as to them.

* * *

We do feel responsible for emotional support and for frequent visits; these visits are wrenching and a strain for the whole family. My children have a pessimistic view of aging and the terrible changes it works on people they love. We often feel caught between the needs of helpless parents and siblings who take the major burden. We feel guilty about taking vacation time for ourselves. Our jobs are often stressful, and we need time for ourselves. It's horrible to see people you love lose too much of their personality and dignity.

The responses of those geographically distant children reinforce other research (Marshall & Rosenthal, 1985; Mercier, Paulson, & Morris, 1987) documenting the persistence and durability of emotional bonds linking parents and their adult children despite the barrier of geographic distance. Though those bonds transcend distance, the degree of social interaction and nature of help such children provide is necessarily different from that of proximate siblings.

ADVICE FOR OTHERS

Still another write-in question in the study asked the siblings if they have any advice to offer others who are in, or anticipate being in, their situations. The dominant themes focused on planning, communication and cooperation, and flexibility among siblings:

Set it up front what is to be shared and include the older person; then all will know what was said. Also, have all meet with the doctor so all hear the same story.

* * *

Be prepared! Understand well in advance what might happen. Attend any and all information meetings, seminars, whatever, concerning older parents and their effects on children.

* * *

Talk to each other. Try to state needs and limits clearly and without placing blame.

* * *

Obtain agreement in advance between siblings as to the sharing of responsibilities.

* * *

Be patient, sympathetic, and permissive towards the other members of the family in terms of their reactions and emotional needs.

Undoubtedly, children whose parents do not have any adult child who lives close by experience more pressing and distressing problems. Anecdotal reports describe their frustration about making arrangements for care at a distance, confusion about service availability and eligibility in a different state, inability to monitor care, financial strain of frequent trips, feelings of helplessness, guilt, and worry. A network of professional case managers has developed to help by providing referral, monitoring, counseling, and coordination of services.

A COMMENT

It hardly needs emphasis that *daughters experience more negative effects than sons in relation to parent care.* Not only do daughters do more and experience more strain than sons when they are in comparable positions as primary caregivers, but also when they are siblings of the caregiver, whether they live close by or at a geographic distance. Gender differences occur consistently, then, in comparisons of strains experienced by sons and daughters of the disabled elderly.

Though this chapter offered a glimpse of some of the themes present among adult children when a parent needs care, those issues are by no means fully understood. Professional and public attitudes often blame the caregivers' siblings for not helping her more, but there is not a great deal of information about why additional help is not forthcoming. Caution must be exercised before critical judgments are made about the behavior of the caregivers' siblings, however. We do know that in some instances, the primary caregiver selects herself for that role and sometimes refuses help, feeling that only she can do the caregiving properly or submitting to the parent's refusal to let anyone else help her. Moreover, though this chapter includes some information elicited directly from the siblings, their views on how it happened that they did not become the primary caregiver are still largely unexplored.

Undoubtedly, there are some situations in which the sharing of care among siblings could be more equitable. But siblings who are "secondary" caregivers are not uninvolved. Sisters in particular experience bothersome strains, though in the main those strains are fewer, less severe, and often stem from different sources than those of the primary providers of care.

In the next chapter, the focus is directly on the primary caregiver. Her subjective feelings during that period of her life are explored.

Chapter 7

Six Major Subjective Themes and a Variation

Beyond the belief that care of the elderly is a family responsibility, there are major "inner" or subjective themes that recur over and over again in the stories daughters and daughters-in-law tell about their caregiving experiences. Those themes cut across the wide diversity in the women's characteristics and situations. Not all caregivers have all of the same subjective experiences, of course, and there are many other themes that may be major or minor for a particular woman or group of women.

The first, most powerful, and over-arching theme, one that appears and reappears for virtually all daughters and daughters-in-law, is their fundamental acceptance that parent care is not only a family responsibility, but more specifically is the role the of the women in the family. Therefore, we begin with that theme—It's a Woman's Role—and discuss several others successively. The next four are: I Have To Make Everyone Happy; Role Reversal and Second Childhood; Dependency/Independence: A Dialectic Tension; and the Struggle for Control: The Psychological Balance of Power. The last of the six themes is the pervasive theme of *guilt* coupled with the feeling that it's *my turn*. Guilt is often expressed in this way: "I know I'm doing all I can, but somehow I still feel guilty." It is intertwined with the feeling that "She took care of me and now it's my turn to take care of her." We leave these two interrelated themes for last in this chapter's discussion of women's feelings because often they encompass and are interwoven with many of the themes that precede them, and are such potent, profound, and punishing forces in the women's lives. Finally, a variation on the themes—Providing Care for Fathers—ends the chapter.

All the themes in this chapter will reappear in the large case studies in chapter 9 and also in chapters 8, 10, and 11 as they are played out in the women's lives.

IT'S A WOMAN'S ROLE

In exploring the reasons why women, rather than men, almost invariably and unquestioningly are the ones to assume the parent-care role, it is not within the purpose of this book to become involved in the perennial and unresolved issue of "nature versus nurture." As Weithorn (1975) noted in her discussion of women's roles in cross-cultural perspective, "Present-day literature is filled with arguments pro and con the question of whether existing relationships are determined by sex-linked biological inheritance or by enculturation" (p. 276). What is basic to our concerns here is that in virtually every culture, the nurturing role belongs to women, no matter how it has come about. That statement, of course, uses a broad brush to paint the overall picture. Differences between the genders are not absolute and mutually exclusive, but a matter of degree. Though men as well as women can be nurturing, however, there is no doubt but that women overwhelmingly are the ones to be the caregivers for anyone in the family who needs help.

Cohler and Grunebaum (1981) pointed out that the sexes are socialized quite differently in early life. Girls are encouraged to identify with and to be dependent on their mothers. As the ones who are taught to be the nurturers and "kinkeepers" in the family, they constantly receive signals that they should be like their mothers. Boys, on the other hand, are encouraged to be instrumental and active like their fathers; they learn early that work is their main role—to be the provider or "breadwinner."

A daughter's identification with her mother is further strengthened when she becomes a mother herself. As one daughter put it,

> I never regret caring for her [mother]. She's the only mother I have. When you have children, you can empathize with your mother.

In that vein, Gilligan (1982) holds that the key difference between men and women stems from the disparate experience children of each gender have of the care they get from their mothers. Girls, whose basic identity is formed from experiencing themselves as like their mothers, therefore develop the inclination to sense other people's needs and feelings as their own. Women, says Gilligan (1982), "judge themselves in terms of their ability to care" (p. 17).

When little girls become women, they are particularly susceptible to demands for assistance from family and friends because they have been educated since childhood into the caregiving role (Cohler, 1983). The widespread, powerful, social value that families are responsible for the care of the old really means that daughters are the ones held responsible.

Such role assignment begins early in life—even as soon as the baby draws her first breath, as the daughter indicates:

> When I was born, my mother thought I was a boy. When the nurse told her she had a girl, she said, "How can that be?" But everyone tried to console her. They said, "She'll be a comfort to you in your old age."

A daughter-in-law explains the process of educating little girls in the caregiving role:

> I guess it falls on women because women have children. As an architect, I always considered myself a professional. Taking care of an old person was the furthest thing from my mind. But when you're growing up, you see your mother doing stuff so you fall into that. Little boys learn from their dads. So that's how it happens.

A divorced daughter, who said she had "divorced" herself from her parents' way of life and had lived a "Bohemian" lifestyle of which they disapproved, said:

> I saw my mother take care of people who needed help. She took care of her own father whom she adored, her father-in-law whom she disliked, and also her mother-in-law. I have divorced myself from many ways of life, but this [parent care] is the right thing to do. You never really change. There are many things that are internalized, even though your thinking has changed.

Caregiving as a female role is so deeply ingrained that most often it does not even occur to daughters that their brothers could have become the main caregivers. They simply assume that when a son provides parent care, it is his wife, the daughter-in-law, who carries out the responsibilities. When, for example, a caregiving daughter was asked whether her brother participated in helping their mother, she replied:

> A daughter-in-law is not the same as a daughter.

In another family, an elderly woman, following a stroke, moved into her daughter's home. The daughter had four siblings, two sisters, and two brothers. Describing how it happened that she became the main caregiver, the daughter said:

> One of my sisters lives in Alaska, and the other is divorced and has to work.

When the interviewer asked, "What about your brothers?" the daughter replied in surprise:

> My brothers? Why would I give my mother to a daughter-in-law when she has daughters?

Caregiving daughters describe their acceptance of the gender assignment of various aspects of parent care:

> I do all the things to take care of my Mom. But my brother is the decision-maker even though he lives far away. He's always on the phone telling me what to do.

* * *

> Caregiving has been my whole life. As women, we're suited for that because we have that nurturing instinct.

* * *

> I'm the one who does almost everything, but my brother is still the favorite. An occasional visit from him is valued more than anything I do.

Even women who in many ways are enacting the new views of women's roles in their lifestyles often behave in accordance with the traditional view.

> My two brothers and I are all busy lawyers. But when my mother got sick—she lives in another state—my brothers just assumed that I would be the one to fly out to her. And you know something? I did it.

A daughter who is a bank executive stated:

> My son is going through a divorce, and he and his child live with my husband and me now. When my grandchild got sick, who stayed home? You guessed it. Me! And who does my mother-in-law's grocery shopping and takes her to the doctor? Don't even guess. We all know the answer.

Daughters-in-law, for their part, also accept the proposition that caregiving is their role when a parent-in-law does not have a daughter. Asked how it happened that they became caregivers for their mothers-in-law, women replied:

> My husband has two brothers, but he was always the one in the family who took the most responsibility.
>
> * * *
>
> My husband is an only child, so there was no one else.

Some women seem genuinely puzzled by the acceptance of the fact that caregiving is a woman's role. They ask "Why *is* that?"

I HAVE TO MAKE EVERYONE HAPPY

The feelings of responsibility of many daughters and daughters-in-law go beyond doing the instrumental and personal-care tasks required by the disabled older people in the family. More than men, women have been socialized to feel responsible for the emotional well being of others. This being so, it is not surprising that women feel a greater responsibility than men not only for helping parents, but for making them happy. In one study, for example, daughters were more involved emotionally with their parents, while sons appeared better able to distance themselves, experienced less guilt, and more readily accepted that they did not have the power to make the parent much happier. Unlike daughters, the sons seldom felt responsible for their parents' emotional well-being (Robinson & Thurnher, 1979). In fact, daughters often feel responsible for the happiness of everyone in the family.

Acceptance of such gender assignment of responsibility for another's emotional support and happiness is further demonstrated by the finding that widowed elderly people generally name daughters rather than sons as their confidants (Brody, E. M., Johnsen, & Fulcomer, 1982b; Horowitz, 1985a, b; Shanas, 1979b).

A divorced woman who is working and raising her two teenage daughters herself does all the shopping and errands for her house-bound widowed mother, who lives 10 miles away. This daughter said:

> On Saturdays, I am like a robot—driving and driving to take the girls and my mother where they have to go and doing the things my mother needs. I make flow charts. I have to decide what comes first, and I don't always succeed. By "succeed," I mean making everyone happy.

After telling about an extraordinarily difficult caregiving situation and her mother's continuing preference for her brother, a caregiving daughter commented:

> I'm glad to be able to do it! It makes her happy.

Explaining why she took her mother into her own home, a daughter says:

> It's important to have her where she's happy . . . I don't think she'd be as happy in a nursing home [as in caregiver's home]. . . . She's happier this way, and I'm happier having her here. I would feel guilty if I put her in a nursing home.

Not infrequently, the boundaries between expressive support and instrumental help are blurred in the perceptions of caregivers. That is, they do not differentiate between caring *about* and caring *for* the parent. Care, then, is interpreted as doing whatever is necessary *for* the parent; if the caregiver does not do it all, she doesn't care enough *about* the parent.

Thus, social values about filial behavior are reinforced by women's expectations of themselves that they perform well in caregiving. Women are under considerable pressure in being held responsible for the care and the well-being of all those in the family who need it. They feel, in effect, "I have to do it all, do it well, and see to it that they are happy." When this does not happen, they experience a sense of failure.

In describing her feeling of responsibility for the happiness of other family members, a daughter said:

> I feel responsible for everyone in the family. I'm the main focus. I keep it all glued together. That's the way it is. That's what I should do. I try very hard to please my mother, but nothing is good enough and then I feel I failed. When my son failed a course in high school, he had to go to summer school. I felt maybe I hadn't done enough. My job is to keep everyone in the family happy. Only I am miserable.

Making people happy is an unrealistic and unachievable goal, of course. Given the human condition, given the fact that some older people's lifelong personalities preclude their being made happy, and given the unhappiness and depression of older people that may accompany their age-related losses (including loss of functional capacity), the expectation of caregivers that they can make the parent happy is often doomed to failure. The failure leads to guilt; that is, guilt about parent care often relates to the failure to make the older person happy as much as to the feeling that one has not provided as much actual concrete help as one should.

The caregiver's guilt is intensified if she tries in any way, no matter how small, to meet her own needs and in so doing perceives that she has failed to make the older person happy. In fact, in setting their priorities, daughters often place themselves last.

Having taken her mother into her household, which also contains her own children, a widowed daughter had no privacy or free time. Occasionally, on her day off from work she wanted to go out for a couple of hours by herself or to curl up in bed with a book. The elderly mother was so disappointed, that the daughter felt she had to give up her outing or put the book away. "She [the mother] has no one but me, and she has looked forward to time with me. It makes me feel so guilty."

Thus, women become women in the middle in the sense that they try to meet the needs (including the emotional needs) of all members of their families and to perform well as caregivers for whomever in the family is in need of care.

The mental health literature is replete with documentation of women's greater vulnerability to emotional stress in general. The fact that daughters experience more strains than sons specifically in response to parent care meshes with Gilligan's (1982) proposition that women's nurturing nature leads them to be more susceptible to experiencing deep stress in the lives of people they love as though it were their own. Strong support for that theory comes from the consistency with which daughters experience more stress than sons when in comparable positions vis-a-vis parent care. Not only primary caregiving daughters, but sisters of those caregivers (both proximate and geographically distant) experience more stress than brothers (see chapter 6), and daughters experience more stress than sons because of parent care even after a parent has been institutionalized (see chapter 14).

Daughters' expectations of themselves may be further heightened when the elderly parent they are helping is the mother. Elderly mothers, by comparison with elderly fathers, tend to have higher expectations of filial support (Seelbach, 1977). Elderly mothers, as well as society in general and daughters themselves, expect daughters, but not sons, to be like themselves—the nurturers and caregivers in the family. That expectation may contribute to the notion that "role reversal" occurs or should occur when an elderly mother becomes dependent on an adult daughter.

ROLE REVERSAL AND SECOND CHILDHOOD

"Role reversal" and "second childhood" are popular but incorrect psychodynamic cliches often used to characterize parent-child relationships in late life. They imply not only an exchange of roles, but that older people go backwards developmentally. These concepts, it is suggested here, are not only inaccurate but intensify the strains for both parent and daughter when the former must become dependent on the latter. Expectations of "reversal" inevitably are disappointed.

Cohler and Grunebaum (1981), in writing about mother/daughter relationships in general, state that "The relationship between adult women and their own mothers is perhaps the most complex and emotionally charged of all the relationships within the family." In their view, various psychological mechanisms encourage a lack of separateness between mother and daughter, and the highly charged relationship that develops is characterized by elderly mothers' high expectations of their daughters.

The "emotional charge"—whether positive or negative (it is sometimes both)—is intensified when the stage of life is reached at which a mother is elderly and needs help from her daughter. Again, mother and daughter need to interact with each other in a caregiving relationship. This time, however, it is the daughter rather than the mother who is the caregiver, and the two women have had no rehearsal for their performances in their changed roles.

As an explanation of the processes that occur when a parent becomes dependent on an adult child, "role reversal" is a simplistic and superficial concept at best. Some elements of caring for another member of the family are similar no matter the relationship of caregiver to care-recipient—whether the dependent individual concerned is a child, spouse, parent, or sibling.

In search of a way to approach this topic, Jarvik (1990) opted to "get away from the concept of role altogether and to look instead at the tasks parents . . . are expected to accomplish" (p. 25). Certainly, some of the tasks the adult child may perform to help the parent are the same kinds of tasks that the parent had performed for the child when the latter was a baby—feeding, bathing, dressing, or changing the diaper, for example. But there the resemblance ends. Though the roles of both parent and adult child undergo change, such change cannot be equated with reversal.

A caregiver experiences very different inner meanings when her young child depends on her and when it is an elderly parent who is dependent. People caring for those who are at opposite stages of life—that is, for a baby and for an old person—have very different reactions to things that are normal and will be dealt with in the normal course of development in the child, but are not normal in the elderly adult. A young mother's feelings about incontinence in her baby, for example, are not in any way similar to an adult child's feelings about incontinence in her elderly parent.

In the main, young parents have chosen to bring a totally dependent being into the world; they expect and accept the baby's need for total care.

In caring for that infant, the future holds promise of a gradual reduction in the child's dependency. The goal is to help the child become more and more independent. Each step along the way is greeted joyfully as a success. Though there may be problems, in the main the direction of the child's growth is towards self-sufficiency, with the parent and child striving for the positive changes that occur.

The contrast with caring for an older person who needs help is sharp. That situation is not expected or chosen by either the adult child or the elderly parent. Caring for the older person presages increasing dependency, rather than increasing independence. Sadness rather than happiness accompanies each change when the trajectory of the parent's dependence is downward. Both the elderly parent and the adult child strive to avoid those changes. Daughter caregivers are aware of the differences:

> I never think of it as a comparison of an older person becoming childish. It's not like having a child in the sense the older person is not getting more exciting or interesting and adventurous everyday but going in the other direction. So it is a downer.

* * *

> It burns me when anyone says this [caregiving to her elderly mother] is like raising a child. Children are malleable, curious, open to learning. They are selectively dependent, and it decreases. Old people do not become like children. Not in any positive ways. I watch my niece and nephew. They display all the positive things about children because they *are* children. Old people bring their own sadnesses with them.

Some daughters do characterize their changed relationships with parents as "role reversal," invariably in connection with illness-induced helplessness and dependency of the parent and most often when the parent is cognitively impaired. Such women are often puzzled, however. They note the differences between caring for a child and an elderly parent, recognizing on some level that reversal is deterioration in the relationship rather than the way things should be:

> My mother is completely helpless. I have no children, so mother is my baby. Our roles are reversed. But it's different. A baby gets better all the time, and an older person gets worse. It's sad.

* * *

> Mother's brain was affected, and she became so dependent that it was a bottomless pit. It wasn't her fault, but our relationship deteriorated. She became the child and I became the mother in terms of role reversal.

Perhaps the most important reason that there can be no true role reversal in the psychological sense lies in the very nature of the parent/child relationship. An older person does not become, and cannot become, the child of the adult child in the feelings of either child or parent after half a century or even more of a parent/child relationship. Although their roles are enacted differently in late life, parents cannot become children to their children and children cannot become parents to their parents. And love for a parent is a different love from the love one experiences for one's child (Brody, E. M., 1990b).

In addressing this subject, Seltzer (1990) took the position that a role reversal orientation is not only inaccurate and inadequate, but is conceptually, ideologically, and therapeutically limiting (p. 5). Gurland (1990) summed up a discussion of the theory by stating that it has probably outlived its usefulness and that "we might do better without an indigenous theory to guide or misguide therapeutic practice and policy. . . . " He concluded by saying: "If daughters and mothers can go on managing without a theory, so for the while can we" (p. 38).

Closely related to the concept of role reversal is the notion that the older person is in a "second childhood." Such a characterization comes from observations of the declining functional capacities and increasing dependency of disabled older people, particularly those with Alzheimer's disease and related disorders. Although the phrase describes some superficial resemblance of behavior and functioning at the two widely separated stages of life—childhood and advanced old age—it does not take note of the very different physiological and psychological processes accounting for that behavior and functioning. Reminiscence about early life experiences, or even failing memory, confusion, and disorientation do not mean that the old person has return emotionally or psychologically to childhood. Eighty or more years of living cannot be erased. The fact that the individual may require services similar to those given to children (such as feeding, dressing, and other personal care) does not make that person a child physiologically.

Nor are other behaviors or personality traits in old age developmental, that is, a "normal" accompaniment to the aging process. They are not regressive in the sense that they represent a return to childhood, though there may be overtones of child-like behavior. Rather, they may be continuations or exaggerations of life-long tendencies that are less masked, become more visible, and are more clearly delineated because the older person is struggling against feelings of loss of control and competence (Goldfarb, 1965). Or, as in the case of patients with Alzheimer's disease, behaviors may be manifestations of actual damage to the brain:

> She fought getting into bed. I tried to encourage her to go to the bathroom like the book says, but she wouldn't listen. Toward the end, she refused to sit on the toilet. It was a fight every night to get her to go to bed. At night I would give her the capsule. But then I realized she wasn't taking them. She was hiding them in the bed.

DEPENDENCY/INDEPENDENCE: A DIALECTIC TENSION

The shift in the balance of dependence/independence is a constant theme that colors thinking about the relationship between disabled elderly parents and their adult children. Much confusion about intergenerational relations is engendered. The goal of parenthood is often misunderstood to mean helping the child from the total dependence of infancy, through childhood and adolescence, to the achievement of total independence and total separation. But over-dependence in any phase of family life is different from normal, healthy *inter*dependence. Psychologically, there never is total separation or total independence. Yet a strong cultural value emphasizes people's independence as the desirable goal.

The psychological issue of the older person's dependency on adult children has its origin in the dependency of the helpless infant on the young parent. The inevitable shift in the longstanding but delicate balance of dependence/independence of the elder parent and adult child is a central issue and reactivates unresolved conflicts about dependency. There is no one moment common to all families at which a shift in that balance begins. For some, it occurs gradually and can be resolved in an orderly manner. For others, it may be precipitated suddenly in the crucible of an acute crisis. That stage may be omitted entirely when premature deaths occur.

The psychological issues that confront the elderly person when dependency begins and progresses are directly relevant to the interaction between parent and child. In the early theory-building days of interest in this subject, the old person's dependency/independence needs were central to much clinical theory and writing about late life (for example, see Goldfarb, 1965; Weinberg, 1976; Butler & Lewis, 1973). The last named co-authors (1973) wrote that the issue of autonomy (self-sufficiency) is as important as that of identity (self-sameness) for old people. Though the sense of self is a continuing issue, the problem of autonomy may become more important as heath problems arise. That is, a critical question then may be, "Can I survive independently without being a burden?" That question speaks to the fear of loss of control over one's own life, of surrendering to the direction of others, and of no longer having the essential sense of mastery.

The individual's previous life-pattern of dependence/independence qualifies adaptation to dependent conditions and situations (Butler & Lewis, 1973). Both the older person who has extreme difficulty being dependent and the one who is overly dependent (these may have been lifelong characteristics) may hamper the efforts of the adult child to behave appropriately in the caregiving role. If successful adaptation is to be made, not only must the adult child have the capacity to permit the parent to be dependent, but the parent must have the capacity to be appropriately dependent so as to permit the adult child to be dependable.

STRUGGLE FOR CONTROL AND THE PSYCHOLOGICAL BALANCE OF POWER

The need to rebalance dependency/independency often sets in motion a struggle between mother and daughter for control of the caregiving situation. A struggle for power is inherent to a lesser or greater degree in all helping relationships.

No one would argue that total control over older people's lives should be transferred to others when they become disabled. Since some sense of control is central to the integrity of the human personality, it follows that it is desirable for the older person to be treated as a dignified adult whose control over her life is supported to the fullest possible extent. It is the loss of that sense of control that so often leads to depression. Thinking of and treating the older person as a child can erode that control prematurely. Maggie Kuhn, the activist who founded the Grey Panthers organization, often exhorted her audiences, "Do not turn us into wrinkled babies!"

In general, therefore, professionals emphasize the importance of permitting the dependent elderly to retain as much control over their own lives as possible—of "empowering" the elderly. Certainly, that is a desirable goal. One must also, however, view caregiving situations from the perspective of the caregivers. Often, the psychological balance of power is held by the elderly parent. Multiple factors contribute to maintaining that balance of power. Culture and religion may reinforce the parent's power. "Honor thy father and thy mother," and even obedience and respect may be invoked. Moreover, in every family's history, it has been the parent who held the power, and vestiges of that relationship remain to a greater or lesser degree. As one caregiving daughter put it, "I'm still intimidated by my mother."

Whatever the dynamics, and whether or not the caregiver is a willing participant, there is insufficient attention on the part of professionals to empowering some caregivers by helping them to extricate themselves from control that sometimes amounts to tyranny.

Shifts in the power relationship when a parent becomes dependent on a child present many difficulties. Early in the family's history, power and control over the helpless infant and the young child were lodged totally in the parent, and there was no question about the parent's "right"—even responsibility—to control the child. As the child grew and his or her independence increased, the parent's power decreased, with the child's adolescence witnessing the classic struggle for independence. Vestiges of this struggle remain throughout adulthood to a greater or lesser degree. Thus, an additional frustration for the elderly parent may be remnants of the unresolved but inevitable loss of control over the child. Similarly, the daughter may have vestiges of her own ambivalent struggle toward independence.

Parenting implies control that is relinquished gradually. It is a generally accepted proposition that it is good and necessary for the young parent to exercise appropriate control over the child. An adult daughter's major prior rehearsal for caregiving is having cared for her own children. Then it was also her parental prerogative to be the decision-maker. When an elderly parent is disabled, some adult children think of themselves as the parent's parent with the same right to power and control (another reason why the notion of role reversal should not be encouraged).

The issue of control can be a source of some confusion to both parent and adult child. Does the child have the right to exercise control over the parent for whom she is caring? Some elderly people readily relinquish control to the child, whereas others fight fiercely to retain control not only over their own lives, but the lives of the adult children. For their part, some adult children continue to accept the right of the parent to control, whereas others strive for their own total control.

> I'm used to my own way. I was never fond of my mother and couldn't wait to leave home when I was old enough. Now, 45 years later she has moved in with me, and I fight with her all the time for control of my own home, my own life.

* * *

> It's so different now. I look at my mother in a certain way. It's hard to cope with when she's childish. I'm the disciplinarian now, but she's still my mother.

* * *

> My role as caretaker for my mother is I feel like a boss. You know, you supervise.

* * *

> She has always felt that she knows best. The control thing—she is the mother and I am the child. She was used to being the mother. Now it's turned around the other way. She can't accept it. She just wouldn't stop telling me what to do. A lot of mothers are that way. They won't let go.

* * *

> My father treats me like a child. He waits up for me at night and asks "Where the hell were you?" If he doesn't like what I do, he says "Why the hell did you do that?" If I hear one more "Why the hell," "How the hell," "Where the hell," "What the hell," I'll go out of my mind.

The situation is further compounded because the elderly mother, though now disabled and dependent on the adult child, psychologically is still parent to the child she has parented and controlled. Being expected to become child to one's child adds insult to the injury of becoming disabled and losing autonomy.

Thus, mother and daughter may each expect to be in control, with the elderly mother wanting her care to be provided in ways that are in accordance with her own preferences. She may resist and resent the daughter's attempt to take over. The daughter may feel that, since she is the one doing the various tasks and the caregiving is arduous, she has the right to do it her way and in a manner that fits in with her lifestyle and other responsibilities.

> No matter what I do, it isn't enough or it isn't right. When I wash her feet, I sort of automatically begin with her [the mother's] left foot. She gets angry and criticizes me. She want me to do her right foot first.

* * *

> She [Mother] calls when I'm in an important meeting and asks me to drop off a pound of coffee on my way home. When I get to her house, she is angry because I bought the coffee in a small store that's on my way instead of going three miles further to the supermarket. She says I could have saved 28 cents.

* * *

> I thought it would be role reversal, but she fights everything I do.

On some level, however, the daughter may have the uneasy feeling that she should provide care in the way the parent wants it. She, therefore, feels guilty if she becomes angry, even when the mother is demanding, controlling, or critical—the more so because the old person, being disabled, is seen as helpless, pitiable, and therefore deserving of patience and kindness. Older people are sensitive to such feelings, and some behave so as to increase the guilt and sympathy of the caregiver.

> My mother gives me "signals of disapproval," and I cry like I did when I was as child.

* * *

> I couldn't bring myself to say no. She was a very old lady, and the older she got, the more pathetic she was. She needed me more . . . I couldn't possibly say no to her now.

* * *

> She [the mother] has her ways of making me feel bad.

This theme was captured by a cartoon in *Punch* (October 21, 1988, p. 16) showing an elderly woman with a cane talking to a middle-aged couple who are dressed to go out. She says, "Now, you young people go out and have a good time. Don't think about me back here, all alone, at the mercy of intruders pushing dope, robbing, raping. I'll be all right."

A common theme in caregivers' reports, and a measure of the parent's power, is that daughters often do not utilizes outside help to relieve even the severe pressures they experience because:

> My mother won't permit any outside help.

* * *

> My mother won't let anyone help her except me.

* * *

> I can't go out for dinner or even to a wedding because my mother is afraid while I'm gone.

* * *

> We don't take vacations because my mother is unhappy when I'm not here.

Although such caregivers express frustration, anger, and feelings of being trapped, some participate fully in avoiding outside help. If they do not provide all the care needed in the instrumental sense, they feel guilty because it implies that they do not care enough. At the same time, providing all the care may also serve the caregivers' own needs:

> No one can take care of my mother the way I can.

* * *

> Mother refuses a babysitter and is very unpleasant about it. She was a miserable patient in the hospital. I was there from 8 a.m. till bedtime. She complains when I'm not here. I'm her security blanket.

* * *

> I'll be able to think I did something for her. I won't feel guilt.

In extreme cases, the older person attempts (sometimes successfully) to control almost every aspect of the caregiver's own life.

Some caregivers keep trying to please the parent, but approval is withheld:

> Whatever my mother wants, I do it. Nothing I do is good enough. I try very hard but I don't please her.

Other members of the family may ally themselves with the mother:

> Should I take charge and fight my mom and my siblings? I'm the one who's doing everything, but I'd be fighting everyone. My brother says, "Don't work. Stay home with mom." My mom makes me feel guilty. She says, "The house is dirty. Wash the windows."

The struggle for control may intensify when the older person has Alzheimer's disease. Now, the caregiver must protect the parent, even insist on doing things to ensure that parent's very survival. The parent, for her part, is struggling against the devastation and panic of losing control—the erosion of her or his autonomy.

At times, the older person's condition reaches the point at which he or she does not have the capacity to exercise control. The long struggle is over. Some daughters state clearly how much easier—even more satisfying—their caregiving then becomes:

> If mother were still herself I couldn't live with her. [Mother has severe Alzheimer's disease.] We didn't get along. It's because she's helpless that I can do it. She's much more childlike now. She was a tough lady. Now she's sweet and gentle. The resentment and anger I used to have toward her have dissipated. As she became more helpless, they dissipated.

* * *

> The more Dad deteriorates, the easier it gets.

* * *

> It's easier now that Mother is on a feeding pump. It makes taking care of her a breeze. I have my routines.

Over-dependence of a parent can be as irksome to caregivers as a parent's assertion of dominance:

> She's so dependent, she even asks me what she should wear. My father turned her into a dependent vegetable.

* * *

> If I could have one thing different, it would be for her to have a couple of friends. Not to be so dependent on me for everything. It makes me feel trapped.

There are, of course, many situations in which the caregiving situation works well, and the parent and daughter are considerate of each other, discuss issues openly, and sustain a good relationship. To the extent that the parent is appropriately dependent and appreciative of the caregiver's efforts, and the latter is sensitive to the parent's need to retain some control and to be involved in decisions, things often go smoothly. Receiving feedback in the form of her parent's appreciation is of major importance to the daughter. One daughter, for example, said that her elderly mother stays in her room as much as possible to give her daughter's family privacy. The older woman is very grateful for the care the family provides and is very supportive of her daughter. The daughter says:

> I take care of mother because I can give her better care [than a nursing home] and I love her. She knows that if she needs 24-hour care and we can't provide it, she may have to go into a nursing home. It's no big secret. We discuss it all with her.

NOW IT'S MY TURN TO TAKE CARE OF HER, AND SOMEHOW I STILL FEEL GUILTY

To recapitulate, a powerful inner experience of caregiving daughters is their deep feeling that they, as women, are responsible for providing care and making dependent parents happy. In the process of attempting to fulfill that goal, they and disabled parents may engage in the struggle for control that is related to the inevitable shift in dependence/independence. The daughters cannot and do not achieve perfection in the caregiving that they see as their obligation. That "failure" contributes to the guilt and other emotional strains experienced by many daughters.

The daughters may have an uneasy sense that the parent wants something more and something different from them than they are able to give. When the mother criticizes aspects of her daughter's caregiving or when either of them refuses to let anyone else help, those behaviors may represent a more fundamental expectation. At some level of awareness, both the mothers and the daughters harbor the expectation that the devotion and care given by the mother to the daughter when the latter was an infant and child—that total, primordial commitment which is the original paradigm for caregiving to those who are dependent and is the basis for women's identity as caregivers—should be reciprocated and the indebtedness repaid in kind when the mother, having grown old, becomes dependent.

It is that expectation—that roles be reversed—that often makes a strong contribution to the caregiver's strain, for the adult daughter cannot and does not provide the same total care for her elderly mother that the mother gave to her in infancy and childhood. This may be the inner, psychological parallel of the social myth that children do not take care of their parents as was the case in the good old days. That is, when people talk of the "good old days," those days may not be an earlier period in our social history (after all, the myth existed then too), but a metaphor for an earlier period in each individual's and family's history to which there can be no return.

There is an inevitable disparity between standards and expectations on the one hand and the unavoidable realities on the other hand. The disparity leads to guilt and other symptoms of stress. The myth persists because the guilt persists, reflecting a universal and deeply rooted human theme. That may be why we hear over and over again from adult daughters, often in these very words: "She took care of me and now it's my turn to take care of her" and "I know I'm doing everything I can for my mother, but somehow I still feel guilty."

Guilt is so pervasive that in one study caregiving women-in-the-middle were not only the primary caregivers to their mothers, but were pulled by competing demands on their time and energy, were experiencing many strains from parent care, were in the midst of extending "caregiving careers" to elderly relatives, and some had quit their jobs for parent care. Yet, as reported in chapter 4, three-fifths of these women said that somehow they "felt guilty about not doing enough" for their mothers! (Brody, E. M., 1985, p. 26).

The fantasy is that "somehow" one could do more and do better in making the parent happy. That may be one reason that so many adult children are overwhelmed with guilt when a parent enters a nursing home. It is experienced as the total surrender of the parent to the care of others—the ultimate failure to meet the parent's dependency needs as that parent met the child's needs in the good old days. These feelings are exacerbated by the parent's spoken or unspoken reproach. The language some caregivers use in talking of potential nursing home placement is striking. They say, "I will not throw her away," "I don't want to give her away," I don't want to warehouse her," and even "I don't want to get rid of her."

Guilt may be a reason that people assert that they and their own families behave responsibly in caring for their old, but that most people do not do so as was the case in the "good old days." Some need to defend against the guilt, and to deny their own negative and unacceptable emotions by feeling that others do not behave as well. Those unacceptable emotions such as resentment, anger, the wish not to be burdened, and even the wish for the parent's death add another dimension to the guilt and may account for the fact that guilt does not seem to lessen as the caregiver increases the intensity of help. By exacerbating the guilt, the myth contributes to the strains of such parent-caring daughters, thus completing the feedback loop. Not only does the myth persist because the guilt persists, but the guilt persists because the myth persists.

That point is emphasized because it is so central to the inner experiences of many daughters. Their strains are intensified by their constant, but fruitless, efforts to close the gap between what they *can and actually do* in caring for their parents and what they and their mothers *think* the daughters *should do*. Surely, their efforts derive in part from oft-cited motivations such as family, religious, and cultural values, a sense of duty, strong bonds with the parent, and affection. (These values are often strongly reinforced by the urging of the clergy and of one's ethnic group.) But it is the inner striving that compels some women to go beyond what appear to be the limits of endurance in caring for their parents and trying to make them happy, doing so for many years at the cost of severe suffering for themselves and their families.

For some women, guilt—that punishing emotion—does not cease with the parent's death, no matter the strenuous caregiving efforts they had exerted. In retrospect, these women remind themselves of other things they could have done or should have done beyond what they had actually done. To quote the late Erma Bombeck, "Guilt is the gift that keeps on giving" (1984).

A VARIATION ON A THEME: CARING FOR ELDERLY FATHERS

Most of the vignettes and case histories in this book are about daughters caring for their mothers, with father-care less in evidence. This reflects the broad caregiving scene in which elderly men in need of assistance more often have a spouse as the primary caregiver because most women marry men somewhat older than themselves and men die at younger ages than women. The result is that most disabled older people who are dependent on parent care are widowed women in advanced old age.

Fathers as well as mothers expect daughters rather than sons to become caregivers. However, virtually nothing is known about how the daughters' subjective experiences differ when they become caregivers for their fathers rather than for their mothers or whether the emotional strains experienced are similar in caring for parents of different sexes.

As seen above, both the elderly mothers and their daughters often expect daughters to repay in kind the nurturance and care the mothers earlier provided to daughters. "She took care of me, so now it's my turn to take care of her." Daughters' stories suggest, however that *elderly fathers and their daughters often expect the daughters to replace their deceased wives/mothers in providing care*, rather than the care being reciprocated or exchanged. That is, daughters maintain their identification with the mother in caring for either parent. But they think of caring for mothers as the way "she took care of me" and think of caring for fathers as the way "mother [as wife] took care of him."

As a result, daughters often define "care" of the father as doing housekeeping, laundry, and cooking, not because the father is disabled, but because he never did those things when his wife was alive. Care of mothers is defined in that way only when the mother no longer has the capacity to do such tasks.

> The day my mother died was the day dad moved into our house. He could have done for himself, but he never did. He was spoiled and used to having everything done for him. So I stepped in, picking up where she left off. I get his breakfast, do his laundry, whatever he wants. He asks, and I do it.

* * *

> I went to work 20 hours a week for my own sanity. Father was resentful. He had to make his own lunch. He's the only one in the house who gets a choice of menu. He's picky with his food. That's what my mother used to do. If I don't, he won't eat. He goes with his nose up in the air. My mother created a monster. She used to say to me, "If anything happens to me, take your father in." I used to say, "I won't pamper him." But here I am doing it.

* * *

> Three times a year I take a train and go to give his house a thorough cleaning and get his clothes in order. I call him in November to tell him to get his coat out—not the raincoat, the wool coat. I don't want him to get pneumonia.

* * *

> I more or less forced the help on him. He didn't need it. But there were certain things my mother [deceased] did for him.

* * *

> When my father became ill, she [the deceased mother] cared for him incredibly well. The best thing I can do for my mother now is to take good care of Daddy.

The last quoted daughter also says that she provides care for her father because:

> Who else is there? And he gave me so much and so caringly, and so completely. There's no way there's too much I could be doing. It's not an exchange. He just deserves it.

Thus, that daughter indicated her wish to reciprocate the father's love and caring ("caring" in the emotional, not instrumental sense of the word) and draws a subtle distinction in saying it's not an exchange, but that her father deserves the care.

Whether the parent is a mother or a father, the fact that the parent has earned the help is often mentioned. That is, in addition to providing care as an obligation or as reciprocity for receiving care as a child, caregivers who have been loved generously and treated kindly by parents talk of the goodness of the parent. “She was a good mother.” “He was a good father.” The parent *deserves* and has *earned* affection and help that goes beyond obligation and the simple call of duty.

Part III

Diversity Among Caregivers

Chapter 8

Diversity in Ages and Stages

Part I of this book focused on how it happened that women are in the middle in so many ways. The needs of older people for help in their daily lives were described. The particular people in their families who provide that assistance were identified, as well as the resultant effects on those helpers. And there was a chapter about the deeply rooted values that emphasize caregiving in general and parent-care in particular as a woman's role.

Part II included some of the subjective experiences of the caregiving daughters and daughters-in-law. It told their stories from the women's own perspectives of how they happened to become the primary caregivers—why, as one of them put it, they were the ones "elected" to that role (often voting for themselves) rather than another of their siblings. There were descriptions of the "inner" or subjective feelings or themes that so many women share as they travel the long roads of parent care.

However, the information in Parts I and II treated the women in the middle as essentially one population, without delineating ways in which major subgroups differ in certain life experiences and problems during the parent-care years. This chapter and the others that follow in Part III of the book address some of some of the diversities which characterize women in the middle. There are, of course, a multitude of ways in which the women are diverse: health status, values, lifestyles, preferences, ages, socioeconomic status, personal resources, ethnic and racial backgrounds, and a host of other aspects of their lives.

Among the extraordinarily complex mosaic of groups, each of which has many subgroups such as religious affiliations, countries of origin, and so on, we have chosen to focus on four forms of diversity: (1) the various ages and stages of life at which women find themselves "in the middle," (2) their marital statuses during the parent care years, (3) their work status at the time, and (4) their ethnic or racial backgrounds. Both the commonalities and the differences in the ways in which the groups of women provide care and the effects they experience will become apparent, with 25 detailed case histories describing the women's journeys through their parent-care years in the women's own words.

We begin with this chapter which addresses the diversity in the parent-care ages and stages of life. Since the need to provide parent care may arise for a daughter when she is 30 or 50 or 70, the chapter speaks to the reciprocal effects of her age and stage of life with the parent care years.

A major theme apparent in the stories of daughters and daughters-in-law who help the disabled elderly was their awareness of their own ages and stages of their lives when parent care takes place. In broad terms, these are the stages of relatively young adulthood, the middle years, and the years during which the caregiving women themselves are approaching or are actually engaged in the aging phase of life.

Those fundamental differences in the life stages at which parent care occurs suggest the question: "Is parent care a normal development stage in life?" Although providing help to disabled parents is normative in the sense that most people have the experience at some time in their lives, the notion that parent care is a normal developmental stage of life is inaccurate. The distinction between "normative" and "normal" relates directly to the strains many filial caregivers experience.

There have been various theoretical formulations about what happens during the life course of individuals and families. The normal, expected life stages have been conceptualized from many different vantage points. Among the most familiar conceptualizations are those with psychodynamic orientations such as Freud's developmental stages, English and Pearson's "normal life crises" (1937), Erikson's eight stages of ego development (1950), and Peck's elaboration of those stages (1968). Sociological conceptualizations of life stages often characterize the last phase of the family life cycle as the "empty nest" stage.

The gerontological literature has given considerable attention to role transitions that occur after the prematurity stages of life: the menopause or climacteric, the empty nest, retirement, widowhood, the processes of aging, and grandparenthood (see George, 1986). Family therapy theory suggested the series of stages as being: launching, postparental, retirement, widowhood, grandparenthood, aging, and illness and dependency (for example, see Turnbull, Summers, & Brotherson, 1984; Walsh, 1980).

None of those theoretical formulations, however, addressed the issue of parent care and its place in individual and family development and the life course.

In the 1960s, when it was observed that a greatly increased number of people were being confronted with the need to help a parent, Blenkner (1965) attempted to place the stage of parent care in people's life course in a developmental framework. In reaching for some criteria of what constitutes "mature" filial behavior, she tried to illuminate what the inner, subjective experiences of adult children might be at such a time. Proposing the idea that parent care is a developmental stage, she characterized it as "filial maturity," defined as the capacity of the adult child to be depended on by the aging parent and to be dependable. If successful, Blenkner hypothesized, filial maturity marks the healthy transition from maturity to old age.

According to Blenkner, in general, the "filial crisis" occurs during one's 40s and 50s when the "individual's parents can no longer be looked to as a rock of support in times of emotional trouble or economic stress but may themselves need their offspring's comfort and support" (p. 57). When filial maturity occurs, she said, the parent is seen in a new light as an individual; this is a way in which the adult children prepare for their own old age as when, in childhood, they prepared for adulthood.

Where there are psychological difficulties in resolving the filial crisis, Blenkner stated, "One of the major roles of the therapeutic professions can be that of helping the middle-aged client or patient accomplish this task to the best of his ability, for it will inevitably determine how successfully he meets the challenge of growing old" (p. 58). (The ways in which adult children resolve their own filial crises may also determine the ways in which their own children will meet *their* filial crises in the future.)

The concept of parent care as "developmental" is not just a theoretical issue, but has very practical implications. If meeting all of a parent's dependencies is the desirable goal, for example, then therapeutic approaches should (as Blenkner stated) aim to help the adult child to accomplish the task of becoming filially mature. If that reasoning is taken a step further, it releases society from any obligation to help the disabled elderly, since the implication is that the adult children should do it all.

Certainly, Blenkner's model illuminated some aspects of how it feels to become the support for a parent on whom one previously depended. However, it is suggested here that parent care is not a developmental stage of life in the same sense that other life stages are developmental. Although parent care is a major transition, it is not a transition in the traditional sense that an individual or a family moves from one stage to another. Accordingly, the transition is not symbolized by what Neugarten (1968a) has called "punctuation marks along the life cycle" (p. 18) as in the case of weddings, christenings, Bar Mitzvahs, and other ceremonies. There are no such punctuation marks to signal the start of parent care.

But the fundamental reason that parent care is not a developmental stage is that developmental stages are specific to age-linked periods of time, whereas parent care is not.

Compare parent care with other stages of life in that respect. The developmental stages or "normal life crises" of earlier life usually occur in a somewhat orderly sequence and progression as people move through more or less well-defined age categories. Those categories (such as infancy, childhood, or adolescence) are linked by age to specific cognitive (intellectual), emotional, and physiological development and capacities. In sharp contrast, the demands of parent care are often incompatible with the psychological, emotional, and physiological capacities of the adult child concerned. For example, the trajectory of the demands on aging children usually goes upward over time (that is, in the direction of providing the increasing amount of help being required by the parent), a direction that may run counter to the declining capacities of an aging child to meet those demands.

Parent care is not a single stage that can be fitted neatly into an orderly sequence of stages in the life course. Among the elderly, age and stage are not the same (Peck, 1968). Young children are programmed developmentally for a gradual reduction of dependency, whereas the dependencies of old age appear with great variability and irregularity, over much wider time spans, and in different sequential patterns. Disability can occur at age 65 or at age 85, for example. In addition, the timing of the marriages and parenthood of both parent and child influence the ages and stages of adult children when their parents need help. If the parent was 35 years old when her child was born, that child may be 30 or 40 years of age when parent care becomes necessary. But if the parent was 18 or 20 years old when the child was born, that child may be 55 or 60 or even 70 years of age when parent care becomes necessary. It is not uncommon nowadays for women in their 70s to be providing help for a parent in his or her 90s.

In the 1999 National Long Term Care Survey (NLTCS), for example, almost 20% of daughters who were primary caregivers of disabled older persons living in the community were under the age of 45, and 15.3% of the daughters were 65 or over (Center on an Aging Society, 1999). Given the older ages at which women have been having children, it is likely that many of those under 45 had their own young children at home. Those daughters who were 65 or over were old themselves.

Parent care, then, can overlay many different ages and stages in different people and different families, occurring as it does in young adulthood, in middle age, or even in old age. Although the largest proportion of parent-caring daughters, for example, are middle-aged, more than one-third are either under 45 or over 65. The caregiver may be a grandmother who is experiencing the processes of aging, or she may have preschool children at home. People who are experiencing the same kinds of other life events may vary widely in age. One filial caregiver may be widowed at age 45, for example, and another at age 70 or even older.

Even when they are in the same age group, the situations of parent-caring adult children are extraordinarily variable. One woman in middle age may be engaged in adapting to the onset of chronic ailments and disabilities; another may be enjoying excellent health and playing tennis regularly. Health, marital and economic status, living arrangements, geographic distance from the parent, personality, adaptive capacities, and the quality of parent-child relationship vary. The caregiver may or may not be employed. She may be working upward on her career, or her retirement (or that of her spouse) may be imminent or already have taken place. Meeting a parent's dependency needs may be concurrent with the "letting go" of one's young adult children. Or, the theoretically empty nest may contain young adult children who have not left it or have returned to it (sometimes with children of their own), a phenomenon that has been increasing.

Because of the different life stages at which parent care occurs, its demands often are not commensurate with the adult child's capacities. In general, the roles played during the life cycle and the social definitions of appropriate behavior in those roles are in synchrony with emotional and physiological developments and capacities. Thus, the child-bearing years are those in which young adults not only may wish for children and have reproductive capacity, but have energy levels equal to the care needs of young children.

Still a further complication is that parent care often is a time-extended process, with some women helping a parent for more than 20 years, years that may span several of the caregiver's age periods or stages. Moreover, for many women, care of a parent at a particular time is only one phase of their "caregiving careers" that may extend well into late middle age and early old age, since many women help several older people in the family simultaneously or sequentially.

"OFF TIME" AND "ON TIME"

Because parent care is not a "developmental stage," the age and stage at which parent care becomes part of the daughter's life may be perceived as being what Neugarten and Hagestad (1976) called "off-time." They wrote:

> . . . social timetables serve to create a normal, predictable life course. Role transitions, while they call for new adaptations, are not ordinarily traumatic if they occur on time because they have been anticipated and rehearsed. Major stresses are caused by events that upset the expected sequences and rhythms of life. . . . To be off-time usually creates problems of adjustment for the individual, either because it upsets his sense of self-worth, or because it causes disruption of social relationships. In either case, the consequences of a role change . . . depend on whether or not the same change is prevalent among one's associates. (p. 51)

Because of the variability in the ages and stages at which women are confronted with the need to provide parent care and because that experience is not "developmental," it is often regarded by caregivers as "off-time." That perception may add to the stress they experience.

Daughters and daughters-in-law in their 30s often mention spontaneously that they are at the "wrong" age and stage for parent care:

> I am doing the same things the people across the street are doing for their parents, and they are in their 50s. Even my boyfriend's mother is taking care of his grandmother. And here I am, my life is on hold.

* * *

> Our group of friends are still not there yet [at the parent-care stage]. My friends don't have to face this. Mostly it's people whose children are grown who have to do it.

When the caregivers are at other ages and stages of life, other considerations may be at work. If, for example, they are married and have young or adolescent children at home or have a strong career commitment (or both), their supply of psychic energy or emotional investment may be overextended. Thus, psychological overload is added to the objective role overload of sheer time and energy. The psychic overload is intensified by internal conflicts over which responsibilities should take priority and whether they have a right to take something for themselves rather than the leftovers after other people's needs have been met.

The pull of having to meet the needs of the older and younger generations is heightened by tension between the daughter's role as child (the historical precedent in the relationship) and her role as caregiver (the historical precedent for which was her role in parenting her own children). Gary Trudeau captured this dilemma in his cartoon strip *Doonesbury,* in which an adult daughter about 40 years of age is talking to her mother on the phone, giving her instructions on how to travel, but the mother is refusing to take advice. The daughter hangs up the phone and says, "God! She can be exasperating sometimes." Her husband says to her, "Joanie, have you noticed you've reached an age where you speak to your parents and your children with almost exactly the same tone of voice?" Joanie, stunned for a moment, then replies, "I don't even want to *think* what that means." The husband replies, "It means don't die. Everyone's counting on you."

When they are further into their middle years, caregiving daughters and daughters-in-law may have the sense that their lives are different from what they had hoped or planned. Particularly striking is the frequency with which women in the "empty-nest" stage say their anticipations of what their lives would be at that time have been disappointed. They say again and again that they had not expected to be taking care of their parents and have had to modify their expectations of freedom and ability to pursue enjoyable activities. The future may seem bleak rather than something to look forward to.

> Our nest was empty, and now it's full. My husband and I had decided to work part time. Neither of us is well—he's had heart attacks and I have ulcers. We decided to spend more time together and to travel. We've always wanted to see California. We've raised our children, and now they're grown and live in different places. But now there is no one else to care for my mother who has gotten forgetful and confused. She can't be left alone. We thought we had seen the light at the end of the tunnel after working hard all our lives.

* * *

> I thought I would be working full time. It was my insurance. I hadn't thought of other options.

* * *

> I have to reevaluate my goals now. I have to reevaluate what I want to accomplish. It's a turning point.

* * *

> I didn't expect I'd be caring for my mother. She said she wouldn't ever live with her children.

* * *

> I looked forward to this time. I expected to be free and to be able to come and go as I pleased.

Equally striking is the frequency with which the women say they had expected to travel. (Is travel a metaphor for freedom from responsibility?)

> Our children are grown and developing. If parents are well, it's a beautiful stage. I wanted to travel. We would like our own lives. The things I'm doing are different from what I expected.
>
> * * *
>
> I wanted to be going on cruises and weekend vacations. I'm bored, and I'm in a rut. I feel lost, sad, everything.
>
> * * *
>
> The main thing I expected to be able to do was travel, be free of regimentation and financial responsibilities.

When the role of caregiver to an extremely disabled, very old person must be assumed in late middle age or early old age, the demands of that role may not be synchronous with the psychological, emotional, and physiological capacities of the caregivers. The physical care of an extremely impaired old person requires strength and stamina. For the adult child whose own beginning processes of aging require major adaptations, the parent's dependency may make too great a demand on the supply of sheer physical energy.

> She [the 91-year-old mother] is so confused that if I take her any place, she wanders off and I have to run, run to catch her. She wakes up two or three times a night, and I never get any rest. I'm exhausted. I'm 71 years old. My back aches from struggling to get her dressed in the morning. I'm too old for this. I simply don't have the strength I used to have.
>
> * * *
>
> I can't leave the house for too long. Physically, I can't do as much as I'd like. I expected a bit more freedom. I expected my health to be better. I didn't expect I'd be caring for Mom. I'm going downhill physically.
>
> * * *
>
> This [caregiving to both elderly parents] has taken a chunk out of me. I looked forward to retiring. At least when I worked for a living, I had a vacation in summer.

* * *

> I'm lonesome and hungry to be with my children at this stage of my life. I feel old. I *am* old. Most of my life is over. I thought I would have a lot of free time—perhaps to be traveling, taking some courses, doing some volunteer work, spending time with the family. The things I'm doing now are different from what I expected. I can't do much. I'm responsible for my mother's care even if I don't do it myself.

Their situations often stimulate caregiving women to think about their own old age and the children who might bear the responsibility for caring for them.

> I don't want to live into my 90s. How can I expect my children to take care of me? When I am 99, I don't want my 75-year-old child taking care of me.

The dissonance between the demands of parent care and the older adult child's physical capacities has its parallel in the psychological factors at work. In Cohler's (1983) thoughtful examination of interdependence in the family of adulthood, he pointed to theories of personality development in late life that show the aging individual's increasing "interiority" or self-absorption (e.g., Neugarten, 1973). He argued that family relationships that are satisfying and appropriate within young and middle adulthood may not be so in later life. Citing the evidence of increased interiority after midlife, he suggested that older people may wish to reduce the time and effort they spend helping other family members. Cohler (1983) reviewed various studies showing that continued family responsibility among older persons may be associated with lower morale and increased psychological distress, particularly among older women. Essentially, he stated that if older adulthood involves increasing interiority—more self absorption—then acknowledging the needs of others can become a source of stress.

In thinking about Cohler's formulation as it might apply in the context of caregiving to the disabled elderly, it may be that an aging daughter's strains are accounted for in part by the tension between her inner developmental processes (increased interiority) and the counterdemand for increased caregiving. That being so, parent-caring children in late middle age and early old age are confronted with increased demands on themselves at the very time of life when, because of personality developments that are part of the processes of aging, they want to reduce the dependency of others on them.

Parenthetically, an unanswered question is the extent to which the disabled elderly are sensitive to the limitations of their children. Are the parents aware of the declining energies and capacities of children who are in late middle age or early aging? People generally think of their children as young and vigorous, and it is natural to deny (in the psychological sense) the aging of the next generation. But some elderly parents are aware that their middle-aged children are experiencing ailments and disabilities that presage old age. That awareness can be extraordinarily painful. It may also signal the risk of not having a "child" with the capacity to meet one's dependency needs in old age.

The evidence shows that the role of caregiver is not a natural developmental stage of life for an adult child, no matter the child's age or stage. It is not an expected "on-time" event. In effect, younger caregivers say, "I'm too young for this"; middle aged caregivers say, "I thought I would be free at this stage of my life"; and older daughters say, "I'm too old; I'm old myself."

A most important consequence of the fact that caregivers do not share a single developmental stage of life is the absence of behavioral norms for this normative life crisis. Since behavior in different people and families cannot be measured by the same yardstick, there is no simple answer to the question that is asked so often: "What *should* adult children do to help their elderly parents?"

Chapter 9

Diversity in Marital Status: Introduction and a Survey

INTRODUCTION

A major and significant source of diversity among caregiving women is their marital status during their parent care years. The 20th century was witness to radical changes, not only in the increase in the aging population and the fall in the birthrate, but also in the patterns of family formation and dissolution. This led to greater diversity in people's marital status: the marriage rate fell, the divorce rate rose steeply, and more women remained unmarried. In addition, the changing demography resulted in many more women than men being widowed. Certainly, the lifestyles of married women, divorced/separated women, widows, and never-married women vary. (We do not have any information as yet about the increased number of same-sex couples.) This chapter and subsequent chapters explore the ways in which those diverse lifestyles interact with and are influenced by women's parent care activities, and, in turn, how their marital statuses influence some of the ways in which they provide care to their disabled parents.

After some background information, the findings of a longitudinal survey of 492 parent-caring daughters will be reported in which the women studied occupied four different marital statuses. The survey, which was at its midpoint when the first edition of this book was published, examined questions such as the effect of their particular marital status on parent caring, how the different groups of women were affected when they co-resided with the elderly person, and how they set priorities among their various responsibilities. There is a note, too, about a subgroup of the not-married women who had a "significant other." The report on the survey is new to this edition, and the chapter summarizes the seven papers that have appeared in professional journals.

Subsequent chapters each focus on women of a particular marital status, including one on daughters-in-law. These chapters include a total of 25 case studies reported in detail. Great care has been taken to disguise the identities of the women and their families, but their words remain accurate as told in their accounts of their caregiving journeys. Though the case study chapters are organized in accordance with the women's marital statuses, other aspects of their lives and diversities will be apparent as well—the mental effects of working and parent care, for example, and their ages and stages of life.

Daughters mature, of course, and form or do not form families of their own. To follow daughters developmentally, we will discuss parent-care themes that derive from the structure of the daughters own nuclear families. When they have husbands and children, women may enjoy considerable emotional and instrumental support, or there may be conflict and competition that make the situation more difficult. Other daughters—who do not have partners, being widowed, divorced, separated, or never married—may feel more alone and lonely during their parent-care years. Some of these are even more alone because they are childless or are only-children.

Since family support is so central to the parent-care experience, the case studies also provide a longitudinal perspective—a view of how the women's situations change over time. The themes many women share will be apparent in the cases, but each chapter will highlight experiences shared by women who are members of a particular marital status subgroup. The case material was collected in a qualitative study of 62 women in which the interviews were tape recorded and transcribed.

The rationale for organizing chapters in accordance with the women's marital status derives not only from the centrality of women's family status during their parent care years, but also because women's lives have been taking increasingly diverse paths. Changing patterns of marriage, divorce, remarriage, and childbearing have resulted in more women being without partners and more women being childless during the parent care years.

In that context, the section on married daughters includes parent-care issues that relate directly to that status—in particular, concerns that pertain to their husbands and children (when the latter are present). There will be information about the perceptions and experiences of those husbands and the roles of children when their wives/mothers are involved in parent caring. It is virtually impossible to describe the subjective experiences of these women without their husbands (the sons-in-law, whom we call the "unsung heroes") and children being included in the picture. Those family members also play active caregiving roles at times and might legitimately be characterized as being among those called "secondary" caregivers.

The married daughters are followed by the stories of those who are widowed, divorced or have never married. Some have family networks and some are relatively alone in caregiving, either because they were only children or their sibling(s) have died, or who are completely alone because they are only children, have no partners, and are childless. In the course of the study, some daughters were identified who were not married, but had "a significant other" in their lives. There is a short discussion about these women, too.

Though many aspects of the care given to older people are similar for daughters and daughters-in-law, there are also striking differences in their subjective experiences that will become apparent. Because it is their husbands—the sons of the disabled parent—who are often named as "primary" caregivers even though their wives do most of the actual caregiving, we call the daughters-in-law the "proxy primaries," and there is a chapter about them that also includes case histories (Chapter 12).

THE MARITAL STATUS RESEARCH SURVEY

The Marital Status Research Survey (Brody, 1988) was carried out between 1988 and 1993. It was prompted by the changing marital patterns that had been occurring. At present, though most caregiving daughters are married, more than 40% are not. In the 1999 Long Term Care Survey, 58.6% of the primary caregiving daughters were married, more than 11% were widowed, 19% were divorced/separated, and 10.3% had never married (Center on an Aging Society, 1999).

Between 1972 and 1983, the marriage rate for women 15 years of age and over had dropped sharply from about 78 per 1,000 to about 60 per 1,000 (National Center for Health Statistics, 1986). Beginning in 1900, the number of divorces rose steadily and almost tripled during the 1960s and 1970s (U.S. National Center for Health Statistics, 1985). During 1996, there were almost half as many divorces as there were marriages (U.S. Bureau of the Census, 2001).

A most significant projection is that in the future, more caregiving women will be widows. Since most disabled elderly are very old, their children, the caregivers, are therefore older and more vulnerable to widowhood. By 1997, almost half of all older women were widows (46%). There were 4 times as many widows (8.5 million) as widowers (2.1 million) (U.S. Administration on Aging, 1998). Although divorced older people represented only 7% of all people 65 or over in 1997, since 1990 their numbers (2.2 million) had increased 5 times as fast as the older population as a whole (2.8 times for men and 7.4 times for women). Equal proportions (4%) of elderly men and women had never married (*Ibid*, p. 4).

Each marital status group of women has unique problems. While the social support married women receive from a husband can buffer caregiver stress, at the same time husbands often present a competing demand for their wives' time and attention. Beginning with the seminal work of Lopata (1973), the strains of widowhood have been well documented. Widows experience desolation, for example, and the loss of a long-standing partner. Divorced women have higher morbidity and mortality rates than people in any other marital status (U.S. Dept. Of Health and Human Services, 1985). They also have been found to have a constellation of other strains such as sharply reduced income, the well-known problems of single parenthood, and family relationship difficulties. Never-married women are characterized as being at higher risk for mental problems by many factors such as lacking an intimate, confiding relationship. Though they do not experience the desolation of widowhood and divorce, among their problems are feelings of rejection. They, too, experience a sharp drop in income.

Thus, each marital status group of women is characterized by special emotional strains and situational problems in addition to those they may share due to parent care. It is ironic that the very problems of those who are not married place them at risk of becoming the ones in the family who become primary caregivers to elderly parents. Wolf and Soldo (1990) hypothesized that not-married daughters are over-represented as caregivers, compared to the general population, because they have fewer competing responsibilities than their married siblings.

The survey of the 492 women referred to above was designed to examine the differential effects of women's marital states on their parent care experiences. Broadly speaking, the questions asked were:

- How did daughters' marital statuses affect their parent-care experiences—that is, what were the advantages and disadvantages of each status?
- How did marital status affect the apportionment of care—that is, the amount of help the daughter provided, the amount provided by various other family members, and the amount provided by paid workers?
- How were the various groups of women affected when their households were shared by an elderly parent?

- How did marital status affect the priorities the women set among their various responsibilities—that is, to the parent, the women's own children, their husbands, their friends, their jobs, and themselves?

How Did Marital Status Affect Women's Parent Care Experiences?

Married women saw themselves as faring better than any of the other groups, a view supported by almost every aspect of the study's findings. The not-married groups of women agreed. They were unanimous in their evaluation that it was better to be married during the parent care years (Brody, E. M., Litvin, Hoffman, & Kleban, 1992).

Overall, the married women exceeded the others on all indicators of well-being. They had more positive affect, were less depressed, more satisfied with family life, received more socioeconomic support, experienced less financial strain (they were in much better financial circumstances than any of the other groups), and worried less about who would care for the elderly parent if something happened to themselves. That is not to say that being married was free of any negative aspects. Though well aware of their advantageous situations, the women were often pulled in different directions by their multiple responsibilities to their husbands and children. (They had more children in their homes than the other groups.) And there were certainly instances of tension. Many husbands were aware of their wives' conflicts. In fact, 40% of the husbands said they thought that their wives felt "caught in the middle" between them and the parents (Kleban, Brody, E. M., Schoonover, & Hoffman, 1989). In general, however, the married women appreciated their husband's support, and the negative effects of being married were more than offset by the positive.

The widowed women fared less well in a number of ways. At least a decade older than all the others, they had the oldest parents and had been providing parent care for the longest time (an average of about eight years). They had lower incomes, less social support, and were more depressed than their married counterparts. Certainly, the widows' depressions may have been related to the loss of their husbands, and most of them undoubtedly had cared for those spouses prior to the latter's deaths. Such women exemplify "caregiving careers": that is, prolonged caregiving to more than one recipient of care until a time when their own decreasing energies and the appearance of ailments make parent care a more difficult enterprise (Brody, E. M., 1985b).

The daughters who were separated/divorced also were more depressed than married women. They and the never-marrieds were less satisfied with their family lives than the other groups. The separated/divorced group also followed the never-marrieds in having fewer family helpers with parent care and in worrying about who would take care of the parent if something should happen to them.

Together with other findings, attention was drawn to the drawbacks of the lack of a close relationship that characterized so many of the never-married women. Such women were in jeopardy in many other ways as well. They spent the most hours each week of any of the groups in helping the parent, even though their parents were not more disabled than the parents of the other groups of women. It may be that they focused more attention on the older person, reflecting the fact that they had fewer other relationships. They not only had the fewest other family helpers, spent more hours in providing care and gave the largest proportion of care compared to their peers in the other groups, but more of them were the parent's *only* helper.

All groups of women without partners placed the lack of emotional support from a close relationship with a partner high on the list of dissatisfactions they experienced (Brody, E. M., 1990, 1992; Litvin, Albert, Brody, E. M., & Hoffman, 1995). But, to some extent, they felt that the absence of competing demands was an advantage.

Patterns of Parent Care: the Apportionment of Help

Though the married women provided somewhat fewer hours of help to the parent than the other groups, they needed to do less because of the participation of other members of their families in the care of the parent (Brody, E. M., Litvin, Albert, & Hoffman, 1994.) An interesting aspect of that help was that their own children (those in their late teens particularly) were of assistance when need be. That "invisible backup system" (Brody, E. M., 1990) not only provided several hours of help weekly but also helped in emergencies, "sitting", and giving their own parent (who almost invariably was the primary caregiver) emotional support. Thus, it seems that the nuclear families of the primary caregiver form a caregiving unit. If the parent lived in a separate household, the caregiver's siblings helped somewhat more (Brody & Schoonover, 1986).

Role Priorities

It is noteworthy that when the caregiving women were asked to rank-order their priorities in responsibilities to husbands, children, self, elderly parent, friends, and work, almost all the viewed responsibilities to immediate family members and to themselves as taking precedence over their jobs. Only the never-married women ranked their elderly parents as their first priority. Apparently, for them the parent was the family—the only family they had (Litvin et at., 1995).

Having a Significant Other

The study discovered that about 30% of all the women who were currently not married had "a special male friend whom they saw exclusively"—that is, a "significant other" (Brody, E. M., Hoffman, & Kleban, 1995). In comparing these women with the not-marrieds who did not have a significant other and with the married women, it was found that those who did not have either a husband or a male friend were the oldest and had the oldest parents who were the most disabled. The married women were significantly less depressed than all the not-marrieds, whether or not the latter had special male friends.

When there were "special male friends," the caregivers saw them as supportive of their roles in helping the elderly parent. But about 30% of those with male friends, and 25% of those who did not, said it was hard to think of getting married while caregiving. (In three instances, the male friend shared the women's households.) In about one-third of the situations, the women said caregiving interfered with seeing their male friends and a similar proportion thought the friend was burdened because of the women's caregiving. On balance, the findings suggested that the "significant others" did provide socio-emotional support, though not to the same extent as husbands. We do not have information about the effects on caregivers of having same-sex partners. At the least, however, the importance of a close relationship is underscored, meriting repetition of the words of Lowenthal and Haven (1968): " . . . the maintenance of closeness with another is the center of existence up to the very end of life" (p. 30).

Co-residence of Daughter and Elderly Parent

An interesting aspect of the study concerned the sharing of households by the parent and caregivers (Brody, E. M., Litvin, Hoffman, & Kleban, 1995a.) Proportionately, the daughters who had never married co-resided with the parent to a much greater extent than the others. In fact, almost half of them had never lived separately, and at the time of the study 90% of them were co-residing with the parent! It was the widowed daughters who had lived in re-formed, shared households the longest, having taken the elderly parents into their own homes.

Women and their parents may share households for a variety of reasons apart from the parent's disability. In some instances, as was particularly true for the never-married women, parent and adult child had never lived apart. Sometimes daughters who were not currently married had lived separately and re-formed shared households because of their own needs (such as divorce or economic considerations) rather than because of the parent(s)' needs. And in the main, such sharing took place not in the child's home, but in the parent's household.

In the survey, even though the parents were all in need of help, many households were shared *before* the parent needed care. Three-quarters of the total sample of women shared households. Of those, almost half had lived separately but had re-formed those households prior to the parent's need for care, and 15% had never lived apart. This information contradicts the common stereotype that co-residence invariably involves an impaired older person moving into a child's home.

In the main, it was the married women who most closely fit the stereotypical view of elderly parent/adult child co-residence involving married women who take into their homes parents who become unable to manage on their own. Indeed, half of the married women had done just that, exceeding the women in the other groups in identifying that reason for re-forming shared households. What is particularly interesting in the light of the high rates of divorce is that more than any other group, the divorced women (40% of them) had moved into the parent's home because of their own separation, divorce, or economic factors! This is consistent with national data showing that, while all groups of not-married women have higher poverty rates than married women, divorced and separated women have the highest poverty rates of all.

Many of the never-married and separated or divorced women in shared households reported retrospectively that at first they had viewed co-residence as temporary. But on an average of seven years later, when they were interviewed for the study, with the passage of time more of them reported their views had changed toward acceptance of the arrangement as permanent. By that time, more than four-fifths of each marital study group viewed co-residence as permanent.

In general, of course, it has been well documented that separate households are preferred by both the elderly and their adult children. As incomes of the elderly improved in the last century due to Social Security and pensions, economic factors played a much smaller role in causing co-residence. But during the same time period, there occurred a large increase in the number of people in advanced old age who have disabilities. Their need for help is often the factor that prompts co-residence. Contrary to general belief, more disabled old people live in the community, most often with their families, than reside in institutions. Data from the 1999 Long Term Care Survey indicate that more than 48% of disabled people 65 or over reside with daughters who are their primary caregivers (Center on an Aging Society, 1999).

When the marital status groups in the study described were compared, it was found that there were no significant differences in the overall amounts of care received by the parents from all sources combined. The daughters saw to the provision of care regardless of their personal situations, and, overall, the women did the bulk of parent care themselves. Some family help was received from siblings by about 20–25% of each marital status group and occasionally from other relatives. Less than 20% of all hours of help came from non-family (i.e., formal) sources, with widowed and never-married women using more such paid assistance.

A caveat is that it is important not to attribute the various problems of the different groups of women solely to the problems they experienced from parent care per se. As pointed out above, each of the different groups of women is known to be at risk in a variety of ways. Their strains during parent care may derive not from parent care alone, but also may reflect long-standing problems that are influenced and expressed in the ways in which parent care is experienced. Nevertheless, the problems that existed prior to parent care can be exacerbated by the additional pressures of a parent who needs help. One aspect of women's changing life styles—the increase in divorce rates and in singlehood—may have had a virtually unnoticed fallout in increasing some of the problems of their parent-care years. In addition, the increase in the number and proportion of very old people means that parent care activities often reach into the caregivers' old age, when decreasing energies and the appearance of ailments make parent care a more difficult enterprise.

The case histories in the following chapters illustrate all of the findings of the survey as they are embedded in the subjective experiences of the women and in their own narratives about their caregiving journeys.

Chapter 10

Married Daughters (and Their Husbands and Children): 10 Case Histories and a Comment

In addition to experiencing many of the themes described in the previous chapters, there are issues for married caregivers that are unique to their marital status. Not only do they have husbands who inevitably affect and are affected by the caregiving situation, but most married women also have children whose ages and stages vary. (Issues concerning children and caregiving are also present in the lives of some caregivers who are widowed, divorced, or separated.)

Since those members of the women's immediate families appear prominently, they, too, are discussed. This chapter also includes the findings from interviews with 150 of the sons-in-law, and discusses the roles of the grandchildren as well. There are 10 detailed case studies of these married women's parent-care experiences, followed by a commentary.

The major themes articulated by women that relate specifically to the intersection of parent care with their status as married women are identified. Available information about their husbands (the sons-in-law) and the couples' children will be summarized as well—their perceptions of the caregiving situations, the effects they experience, and the roles they play. These family members often act as secondary caregivers, though they are not always counted as such in surveys. Brief excerpts will illustrate the themes married daughters share. Then, ten complete case studies will tell the caregiving stories in which the themes and issues are embedded, and the changes over time in caregiving situations.

CAREGIVERS AND THEIR HUSBANDS

A major theme for many married daughters is the emotional support they receive from their husbands. That form of help appears to be more important to them than the instrumental assistance the men provide from time to time. The women emphasize that having a husband provides them with someone to talk to about their parent-care problems—someone who understands and who can share in decision-making. They are quick to point out, however, that such benefits depend on having a supportive husband with whom one has a good relationship. A contrapuntal theme that is apparent even when husbands are supportive is that the latter and the children in the family often represent competing demands for the daughters' time and attention. Those "pulls" may add considerably to her strains.

When competition and interpersonal problems erupt between the husband or children and the elderly parent, the daughter experiences even more stress. Her struggle to mediate the conflicts and to set her priorities is intensified. Whose needs come first? Although, in general, daughters try to honor the loyalty and priority responsibility they see as owing to their husbands and children, it is often a delicate balancing process. A helpless, ill, disabled parent who is unable to survive on her own must take precedence at times—for example, when children are old enough to take care of their own basic needs.

The women themselves are aware of the simultaneous presence of those positive and negative aspects of being married during the parent-care years. One of them, when asked who in her view had the hardest time among women whose marital statuses differ, replied tersely, "Married women." Who has the easiest time? She laughed and again replied, "Married women."

These daughters describe the benefits of having a supportive husband:

> For three years, my husband stopped in every day to check on my parents. He did even more than I did. Finally, he said, "Why don't you move into our home?" Our relationship has not been affected [by caregiving] because it was established long before. We had our ups and downs, but we have weathered it.

* * *

> My husband is the balancing point. When things get on my nerves about the help I give to my mother, I go to him and he calms me. If anything happens to him, I would have no support and I would go crazy.

* * *

> My husband would help her. At night he would care for her completely. It was rough on him, and it's not even his mother. I am very grateful for this.

There are also situations with considerable marital tension:

> Mother was up all night. We weren't sleeping. It was terrible. My husband was working then. I was between the two of them. When I reduced my work hours, my husband was all for whatever would help.

* * *

> My husband moaned, groaned, and complained. He said we should put her in a nursing home. My husband complained about the constant bickering between my mother and me.

THE SONS-IN-LAW (THE UNSUNG HEROES) SPEAK

The above themes and others also emerged in research in which 150 of the sons-in-law themselves were interviewed (Kleban, Brody, E. M. Schoonover, & Hoffman, 1989), confirming the vast body of literature regarding the repercussions throughout the family system of the experiences of individual family members. The men were interviewed by male interviewers, separately from their wives. Half co-resided with their mothers-in-law, and in half of the cases the elderly woman lived separately.

Though most sons-in-law in the study played a minor role in the day-to-day provision of instrumental services to their elderly mothers-in-law (Brody, E. M. & Schoonover, 1986), two-thirds of them said they were under strain because of the caregiving situation, some for many years. Of those, almost 40% had endured the strains for three years or less, almost 30% for 4 to 10 years, and 18% for more than 10 years. The men were troubled by the lifestyle restrictions so often noted by their wives. Substantial minorities of the men reported interferences with time for themselves and with their wives, and with their social lives, privacy, and family vacation plans. Almost one-fourth of them had experienced work interruptions because of the need to help their mothers-in-law, and a small proportion had actually missed work on occasion. Many of the negative effects of parent care on the sons-in-law were associated with the same objective factors that caused their wives' strains—sharing their households with the mothers-in-law, for example, a living arrangement associated with the older people's poor cognitive functioning and severe disability.

The husbands were quite aware of their wives' problems. Approximately two-fifths of them viewed their wives as being "caught in the middle" between their mothers and husbands. Moreover, they viewed the parent-care situations as being more burdensome to their wives than the women did themselves, particularly when the elderly parent lived in the couple's household.

In comparing the perspectives of the daughters and their husbands, the study found both similarities and differences in the views of the marital partners. The spouses agreed about the kinds of disruptions that can be observed with some objectivity—to vacation plans, to the family budget, and to household chores, for example. The wives, however, were much more likely than their husbands to report that caregiving caused problems in the marital relationship, interfered with the time the spouses spent with each other and with the couple's children, and with the relationships with those children. The husbands were more likely to cite interference with relationships with relatives in the extended family. Despite the fact that almost half of the men said they argued with their wives at times about the caregiving situation, very few thought it had driven them apart and most said it had made no difference in their relationship.

The fact that the sons-in-law reported less marital tension than did their wives is consistent with literature to the effect that men are more likely than women to repress or deny their emotional reactions. The sensitivity of the wives in the study may have been heightened because the dependent elderly women were their mothers and the daughters, therefore, felt responsible when problems occurred.

Though the quality of the marital relationships and the interpersonal interaction patterns varied greatly, it deserves emphasis that the vast majority of couples felt that the caregiving situations had not affected their basic relationships with each other. And overall, the support the men give their wives, which is often ignored, justifies their characterization as "unsung heroes" (Brody, E. M., 1985b).

GRANDCHILDREN

An aspect of parent care requiring further exploration is the effects on grandchildren and the roles they may play when an older person receives family help. Yet, most filial caregivers have children of their own, all of whom are witness to the situation and who inevitably are affected themselves. Some of those grandchildren live or have lived under the same roof as the disabled grandparent. Others have not, either because the grandparent maintained her own household or the children had already left the nest when the older person moved in.

Most studies involving three generational family relationships have focused on issues such as the transmission of values (e.g., Bengtson, 1975) or the roles, styles, and meanings of grandparenthood. In the majority of those studies, the grandparents were primarily the younger cohorts of older people, including those who had not yet reached the age of 65. The grandparent's health and functional capacities are rarely addressed, though one study did include the grandparent's health as a variable in the contacts of grandchildren and grandparents (Cherlin & Furstenberg, 1985) and another as it related to the happiness or distress of grandchildren (Troll & Stapley, 1985).

Although grandchildren are often viewed as a "competing responsibility" for their parent-caring mothers, in-depth interviews with such women showed that there is a positive side as well. When they are old enough to do so, grandchildren often become part of what might be described as an invisible back-up system for their mother—"invisible" because the help they give is rarely counted in surveys and may be sporadic. Some grandchildren are important sources of emotional support for their mothers. They may provide some instrumental help on a day-to-day basis, but move closer to center stage when emergencies (such as acute illnesses) arise or special events (such as moving the older person to a new living arrangement) call for added help.

We are not aware of research studies that may have elicited directly from grandchildren what their roles and perspectives are in helping disabled grandparents or the effects they experience for good or ill. However, a study of caregiving women that compared the effects of parent care on women in three different household types offers some insight into the consequences to women of having responsibilities to their own children as well as to an elderly parent (Brody, E. M., Kleban, Hoffman, & Schoonover, 1988). The household types were those shared by the disabled older person, her daughter, and son-in-law (no children present because in the main they had "left the nest"); those shared by the older person, her daughter, son-in-law, and their child(ren) (who ranged in age from preschoolers to young adults in their 20s); and those in which the elderly mother lived in her own separate household.

Households with three generations of people in them not only may have problems of space and privacy, but widen the arena for potential interpersonal conflicts and for women's role strain in meeting the needs of husband, child(ren), and parent. Thus, the daughters whose "nests" contained both their own children and the disabled elderly parent proved to have the poorest mental health. More of them reported symptoms of depression, restlessness, and feelings of isolation and missing out on something because of caregiving. In addition, they were more likely to view their elderly mothers as being critical of the sons-in-law and grandchildren.

The daughters whose mothers lived in separate households fared the best in the effects of care they reported, a finding that supports those of previous studies comparing shared and separate households. As might be expected, the elderly mothers who lived alone were the most capable functionally and cognitively. Of the three groups of daughters, fewer in this type of living arrangement experienced caregiving strain, limitations on space, privacy, and social activities, or interference with time and relationships with their husbands, children, and friends. In fact, there was not one variable on which caregivers providing interhousehold help equaled or exceeded the strains of the two groups who shared their homes with the disabled older people.

When the disabled elderly mothers and their daughters shared two-generation households, both generations of women were older than their counterparts in the other two groups. Theoretically at the "empty nest" phase of life, these daughters and their husbands exemplify the concept of the "empty nest refilled" (Brody, E. M., 1978). More of the older women in this type of living arrangement evidenced symptoms of Alzheimer's disease and impairments of hearing and vision, and they received more hours of help each week. More of the daughters reported strain from caregiving; they felt less in control of their lives, experienced more interference with time for themselves and with the family budget, and reported more problems with their husbands that related to the caregiving situation.

In open-ended interviews, the daughters described their perceptions of some of the effects that grandchildren may experience as well as their roles in caregiving and in contributing to or alleviating the strains of their mothers. The ages and stages of the grandchildren varied greatly, and their roles varied accordingly.

Grandchildren who were in their late teens or young adulthood served as a back-up reserve of assistance. The help they provided was not negligible. Sometimes it was provided directly to the grandparents and sometimes indirectly through assistance to their mothers, ranging from giving advice and emotional support to their mothers to extensive instrumental help. Some cleaned and cooked for the grandparent at times of special need or helped them to move from one home to another. Some did "sitting" to allow their mothers respite to take a vacation or to go to work, or to fill in when she was sick.

The other side of the picture is that grandchildren who were teenagers or young adults often found their social lives disrupted. Sometimes they could not play music or have parties for their friends, or the grandmothers" behavior was irritating or embarrassing when friends came to call. Some were upset by bickering between their mothers and grandmothers, and some resented the burdens their mothers were carrying and the reduction in the time she spent with them.

Some of the caregiving daughters felt they were setting a model of how their children should care for them in their own old age: "I want to set an example." "I hope my children will treat me the same way I treat my mother." Others tried to protect their children from involvement. One of them even sent the granddaughter away to school so that she would not become the "grandparent-care person," and another said "I hope this isn't a turnoff for them."

Daughters in three-generation households are quite literally in the middle in feeling that they must be the ones who mediate conflicts among various family members—not only between elderly parent and husband, but also between elderly parent and grandchildren.

> I was always in the middle, trying to keep grandmother off the kids and the kids off of grandmother.

* * *

> My children [an adolescent son and daughter] are good children, and they help my father a lot. My son gets my father's bed ready at night. My daughter gets the bathroom ready for his shower. They make sure he has his medicine. But he doesn't want them to bring their friends home. But I can't tell my children not to do that. My son is very sloppy. But a 16-year-old boy is supposed to be sloppy. My father doesn't like it. He's a good kid—he doesn't do drugs, he doesn't drink. But my father was angry when he got his ears pierced. My husband says I'm his wife, but my father thinks I'm his daughter and he should take priority. When they fight, I jump in the middle of it. I jump in with my kids, too. I'm the mediator. I'm worn out physically and mentally from trying to keep it all together. I have an ulcer, and it kicks off."

Daughters have varying degrees of difficulties in sorting out the needs of children and parent.

> My mother always sided with her mother, even if she embarrassed me in front of friends I brought home. I won't do that to my children.

* * *

> My son [age 11] would come home from school and try to tell me what happened during the day. My mother would interrupt him and finish his sentences. At

first I told him he had to be polite and then realized . . . I stopped her. My son had to be allowed to talk. That was hard. Telling my mother what to do.

* * *

I knew before my mother moved in that there would be difficult adjustments for all of us. Everyone had always catered to my mother. She was not used to having kids around and objected when my girls [two teenagers] brought their friends home. I said to my daughters, 'We have to tough it out on this one. Bring your friends. This is your home. We have to hang tight and Grandma will come around.' Well, there were some tears and some door-slamming [by grandmother], but she adapted.

Although grandchildren may be involved in care of the elderly when their parents become caregivers, an undetermined number of them find themselves in the role of primary caregiver to grandparents when death or illnesses of their parents leave a gap in the generational caregiving chain. Others become responsible for two generations of disabled older people—their parent(s) and grandparent(s). If the values and attitudes of today's young women are indications of their future behavior, grandchildren will be reliable helpers to older people when need be (for example, see Brody, E. M., Johnsen, Fulcomer, & Lang, 1983; Brody, E. M., Johnsen, & Fulcomer, 1984).

Some of the following case studies of married caregiving daughters illustrate the delicate task they face in balancing the needs of their elderly parents, their husbands, and their children. The daughters' own needs often come last, if at all, in the way they set their priorities.

TEN CASE STUDIES OF MARRIED WOMEN

Mrs. Cooper: "My Mother Wanted Me To Quit My Job."

My mother wanted me to quit

Mrs. Cooper's mother wanted her to quit her job to take care of her. At age 51, Mrs. Cooper is deeply committed to her job as executive vice president of a large hospital. Though she is also deeply committed to the care of her 89-year-old mother, Mrs. Cooper continues to work. She says, "My work is fulfilling." Moreover, quitting her job would have been a financial hardship for her family. Another factor was that the mother was always "difficult," and Mrs. Cooper feared the stress that the care would create between her and her husband. Looking back at the nine years since the problem first arose, Mrs. Cooper says, "It was the right decision. I could not have stayed home and not worked."

It was the right decision to continue to work

Early dementia

Senior housing, assisted living, and two nursing homes

The mother's problems began with signs of dementia that have gotten progressively worse. It was necessary to move her to different living arrangements four times. At first she was moved to a senior housing apartment with services, but with minimal supervision. The next move was to an assisted living facility because of the mother's decline and changing needs. Finally, there were two moves to nursing homes. The first did not provide what Mrs. Cooper felt would be adequate care. Now, in the second nursing home, the elderly woman is severely demented and has a feeding tube.

Continues to help mother despite nursing home placement

Placing her mother in assisted living and later in a nursing home did not mean that Mrs. Cooper was free of responsibility. Rather, she accompanied her mother on all medical appointments by senior transit (Mrs. Cooper doesn't have a car) which she describes as frustrating and stressful due to the unreliability of the system. She has always been involved in her mother's care, spending time with the staff to ensure that her mother receives good treatment. She is vigilant in doing so.

Regular visiting

Mrs. Cooper feels it is most important that she visit at least twice a week. She used to visit several times a week when her mother was more intact mentally. During her visits, she reads to her mother because the older woman seems to enjoy holding the book and hearing her daughter's voice. Mrs. Cooper says, "On the days when my mother remembers my name, I feel like someone has handed me a million dollars."

Emotional strain

No support from sibling

But husband is supportive

Although Mrs. Cooper describes herself today as "not being stressed out and having resolved her feelings," it has not always been so. "It was the emotional parts that were stressful." She describes herself as having been impatient with her mother's behavior in the early stages of her Alzheimer's disease. The ups and downs of her mother's illness, the decisions, the calls in the middle of the night from her mother, the seemingly unending efforts to convince her mother to do what was best, all created considerable stress and strain. To make matters worse, it has been an enormous disappointment that no one else in the family has stepped forward to help or to visit. Mrs. Cooper's only sibling, an older sister who lives in another state, is totally uninvolved despite Mrs. Cooper's best efforts to include her. Only Mrs. Cooper's husband has been there for her.

Despite feeling sad at times "because my mother was a dynamic and vital person," Mrs. Cooper feels that she has done her best and has made good decisions about her mother's care. She is gratified that her mother has expressed appreciation and that their relationship issues have been resolved. She continues to be a caregiver after nursing home placement and appears to have made as good an adaptation as possible.

Mrs. Carter: Total Disruption And Disorder For All Family Members

Mrs. Carter is the youngest of six siblings. Her household includes her second husband, two teenage children from her first marriage, a five-year old from the second, and her mother.

A promise to a dying father

For Mrs. Carter, it started with "doing food shopping, laundry, and going to doctors" for both of her parents. Her father was "definitely senile" so he could not drive a car. Once in a while, one of her sisters would help, but not very often. When her father was on his deathbed, he extracted a promise from Mrs. Carter that she would always take care of "Mommy." "I would have died for Daddy," Mrs. Carter says. The mother had always been a very difficult woman, and Mrs. Carter's siblings strongly advised her against moving the mother into her home. She did so anyway.

Financial problems

When Mr. and Mrs. Carter married, they agreed that she would not work. Mrs. Carter says she had a dream, "I guess everyone has a dream." Hers was to be a "regular" mother. She felt she had neglected her older children because she had to work. But the elderly mother's care strained the family's finances because she must have a diabetic diet and her insulin is expensive. Mr. Carter began to work overtime to pay for these things. Finally, he told his wife reluctantly, "You'll have to go to work. We're drowning. We could lose the house."

Goes to work

Teenagers under pressure

Mrs. Carter worked on the afternoon-evening shift as a waitress so that the younger children could be cared for by the older children after school. The teenagers cared for their grandmother as well, but they complained of all the responsibility. They had no time of their own. "It isn't fair," they said.

The future: mother-in-law care

Mrs. Carter said, "My first husband took no responsibility. I would beg him and say we had to do something with Mom. He would just go and have another drink. Her current husband did not ask her to remove the mother from their home. Mrs. Carter says resignedly, "Someday I'll have his mother here. I know it." When the elderly woman moved into the Carter home, she made the daughter "nuts." At times she was "shuffled around" among the sisters, but they wouldn't keep her.

Total disruption of family life

Someone had to be in the same room with the elderly woman almost all of the time. "I had to leave the door open when taking a bath," says Mrs. Carter. The mother presented extraordinary difficulties that were getting worse. The whole family had to eat diabetic food because she ferreted out and gobbled up anything with sugar in it. She embarrassed her daughter in the supermarket by grabbing sweet things off the shelves, stuffing them into her mouth, and telling the other shoppers that Mrs. Carter was starving her. If the children or the Carters brought friends to the house, she was nasty to them, so they stopped having visitors. She ruined the Carters' sex life by turning night into day. If they shut their bedroom door, she banged on it. Twice, she went out of the house at night and laid down in the roadway. "We are lucky she wasn't run over," says Mrs. Carter.

Granddaughter needs mental health care

The teenage children could not bring friends home because the behavior of their grandmother was disruptive and embarrassing. A granddaughter begged for a high school graduation party. She had never had a party before. Mrs. Carter agreed and planned to send her mother to another daughter's house for the evening. But the elderly mother, in order to thwart the plan, "pulled one of her little tricks." She only pretended to take her insulin for several days before the party and went into shock. There was no party. The granddaughter is now receiving psychiatric care.

Can't be managed in domiciliary care

Sibs can't manage her

At one time, the state social worker found a domiciliary care home, but the elderly woman gave them a terrible time. "She would run away just like she did here, but they weren't used to calling the state police to look for her. They said they couldn't deal with it." The sisters tried to have her with them, but she caused so much trouble they would bring her back to Mrs. Carter. Once, when Mrs. Carter was on the verge of a breakdown, a sister took the mother. After a couple of weeks, the brother-in-law put the elderly women in a taxi and sent her back to the Carters. Mr. Carter started not coming home. "He deserted us mentally. He tuned out."

No Medicaid nursing home bed

Depression

Finally, Mrs. Carter needed psychiatric care. Her older sister said firmly, "This is the end of the road. Mom must go to a nursing home." But it was many long months before a Medicaid bed could be found. The older woman is now in a nursing home, and her daughter says, "It's better without her. It's being able to go in the bathroom and take a shower. It's not have the TV on full blast all day and all night." But she adds despondently, "I think Daddy is looking down and is angry with me. But it ruined my life. I can understand why two of my sisters don't see Mom at all."

The chaotic Carter situation was characterized by disorder and conflict between the extraordinarily difficult elderly mother and everyone else in the family. The caregiver was driven to a "nervous breakdown," both of her marriages suffered, and her adolescent children were experiencing severe emotional problems.

All of this was aggravated by the family's poor economic status. Mr. Carter had to work overtime, and Mrs. Carter had to get a job to pay for things her mother needed but that are not covered by Medicare. Appropriate services and facilities were not available even when Mrs. Carter finally was ready to use them. The domiciliary home sent the mother back to the Carters, and a Medicaid nursing home was not available for many months.

In contrast to the many women who give up their jobs reluctantly when it conflicts with parent care, Mrs. Carter wanted to stay home with her second family. Finances made it necessary for her to work, however, in order to pay for things her mother needed. Although Mrs. Carter's sisters tried to intervene, they were unable to influence her. Mr. Carter does not complain, and his wife hints that he may be anticipating that she will care for his mother in the future. "Someday, I'll have his mother here. I know it."

Ultimately, when nursing home placement was unavoidable, Mrs. Carter's depression deepened. She had failed to fulfill her adored father's stern injunction to take care of her mother.

Mrs. White: "What Would It Be Like To Be Alone In The House With Only My Husband?"

Never alone

Mr. and Mrs. White have not lived alone since the day they were married 35 years ago. First, Mr. White's mother lived with them; then the children were born. An unmarried adult son still lives at home. He lost his job and stays home most of the time. Mrs. White's mother moved in 8 years ago after she broke her leg. Mrs. White feels "torn"—juggling her time between her mother, her retired husband, and her son. The elderly mother usually "wins out," says Mr. White.

A caregiving career

Mrs. White traces her caregiving career: "Ten years ago, my father took sick—he had cancer. Everything fell on my husband and me and the family. After he passed on, we disposed of the house, and my mother moved into an apartment so she could be closer to me. I had an elderly aunt who lived in the same building.

Helps an aunt

It was a little easier for me at that point, for whatever I did for the one, I could do for the other. Then my aunt died and my mother fell. She was in the hospital for a long time, and then she

Mother moves in

went into rehabilitation. I could see from that that there was no way she could go back into her apartment. Her leg was in a brace, and she was on a walker. My husband said, 'Do you think your mother should come and live with us?' We decided we would bring her here for a while. We worked from day to day. We didn't make any firm decision. We felt it was her decision. If she wanted to come here and live, she should make the decision, and if she made it, it was fine with us. Then my other son got married and emptied the room out. It was more or less a mutual agreement between the three of us that she would come to live with us.

Emotionally dependent

"My husband and I have been discussing going away for a couple of days. My daughter asked my mother to stay with her, but my mother hesitated. She went, but I don't think she really wanted to. She is very dependent on me. She has gotten more so since my father died. It is an emotional dependency. She also has this type of dependency on her doctor. She doesn't want to be too far away in case she needs him. I don't think it is good, but I don't know how to get out of it. She transferred this—she was depending on my father, and when he died she transferred all dependency on me. It's the way it is.

"My mother said to me that if my husband and I feel she's too much care, we can put her in a nursing home if we want to go away. I said, 'Yes, I know. Isn't it better to stay with someone you know and love rather than some place that is impersonal?'

Brothers' roles

"My brothers haven't given her much care. After my mother came out of the hospital and rehabilitation, my husband and I wanted to go away, so we left her with one of my brothers for two weeks. The other brother is very impersonal. All she needs is an invitation, but he won't ask. I think I have grown away from my brothers. They don't do much in the way of caring and definitely have no involvement in decisions, though I try. If there is a major decision to be made, I try to include them. I have already told them that if having my mother here affects my own and my husband's health or our marriage, which it could, then she will have to go into a home. If it reaches that point, I won't call and ask them to be in on that decision. It is not theirs to make. Neither one of them offered to take her in. They assumed I would do it.

"When my mother was in the hospital, my older brother came up to see her. She said to him, 'I don't know what I'm going to do if I can't go back to my apartment.' He never answered. I know they would never take her in. My sister-in-law told me that my brother would never take her in—she would have to go into a home. I said it was nice they could be so firm in their plans, so they don't have to make that decision. You should never say 'never.' I said what if something happened to Dan and I? She said they'd put mother in a home. I said what if she doesn't have any money? Are you going to pay? She didn't answer. I hope my kids are different.

Aunt's care

"I helped my aunt because I was the only one around. It just evolved—it started out a little bit and ended up a lot. I helped her with decisions financial and otherwise. For five years I helped both of them with grocery shopping, housekeeping, doctors, and transportation. She and my mother were half sisters, and she was always part of our family activities. My father and mother did it before, and when my father died it fell on me.

It fell on me

"I haven't really thought about using paid help, especially since my husband retired. Now it is the two of us caring. I did think of getting duplicates of some things like walkers for up and downstairs. But since my husband retired and my son is out of work, there are three of us now.

Work was not "just a job"

"I have thought about working again, but I don't really have the desire. I turned down a couple of jobs before my mother came. I felt I didn't want to go all the way into town to work. But I didn't think of my work as just a job. I felt it was very interesting. I worked for a sociologist as a research assistant.

"It's my turn"

"If I didn't take care of my mother, I feel I would not be fulfilling my daughterly duties. My mother cared for me, and it is my turn to care for her. I was the only one around. I did as much as I could for my father, and I'll do as much as I can for her.

Wouldn't it be amazing to be alone?

"Since I've been married, my husband and I have never been by ourselves. We've always had somebody. His mother lived with us. I can't change my life any because I've never had it to change. I said to my husband the other day, 'Wouldn't it be amazing some morning to wake up and have just you and I in the house.'

Separate lives

"My friends ask me how can I stand having a kid still at home. But he has never left, so I never had to adjust to him leaving. He has his life, and we have our life. I don't try to influence him. It is the same with my mother. I try to keep her separate. She is not in our decisions. We have our own life, and we live it.

An understanding husband

"My husband is very understanding. I don't think my mother could have come here to live if he hadn't been. If it hadn't of been for him being so understanding, I wouldn't have been able to say, 'Come and live with us.' Since he is retired, it's made it nicer because he is here to help. He does help. He would do a lot more if she would let him."

Reciprocity in care for elderly in-laws

Mrs. White feels her husband is very supportive of her in her care for her mother because when they were first married, the husband was the sole support of his mother who lived with them for 12 years. "That's why he's like he is."

The Whites' situation illustrates the caregiving careers many women have in that they help several older people in their families. They have helped Mrs. White's mother-in-law, her father, an aunt, and her mother. She is typical, of course, in being the caregiver because she is the only daughter. She feels "it's my turn" to take care of her mother as the mother took care of her as a child.

Mr. White is not unusual in helping with the care of his mother-in-law now that he is retired. Other older daughters, too, mention their husbands' availability and willingness to help when the latter no longer have the demands of a job. Another reason for Mr. White's help is to reciprocate for the help his wife had given to his own mother. This pattern of parent-care reciprocity between husbands and wives will reappear in the stories of daughters-in-law.

Mrs. Anthony: "A Long Haul With Alzheimer's Disease"

A caregiving career

Mrs. Anthony is now 64 years old, and her husband is 68. Their grown children are dispersed in other cities. In a long caregiving career, the daughter took care of her mother for more than six years before the older woman entered a nursing home. Before that, she had helped to take care of her father.

Symptoms of dementia

"I guess we didn't notice a lot of things while my Dad was alive. Soon after he died, the first symptom we noticed was that she didn't know the time. I was working full-time, and I'd ask her to meet me at a certain time and she wouldn't be there. I'd come home and find her, and she would say she waited for me all afternoon. She had no idea what time it was. She would try to go to the bank on Sunday morning or she would pay the same bills three times. We would stop by her house every day. She would come and stay the night with us, and in the morning she would be gone.

Dementia progresses

"Then one of my mother's neighbors called and said she was going out of the house at 2:00 a.m. I knew she was going around to the grocery to check what time it was. When we went to visit our children in Columbus or Washington, we would take her with us. When she came back, she couldn't remember where she had been.

In the middle: husband, mother, and job

"I was beside myself because I didn't know what do with her. I didn't know which way to turn. I saw an ad in the paper about a meeting to help people dealing with the elderly. I couldn't attend the meeting because I was working full-time. But when I called, they suggested that we go to a clinic that diagnosed people like my mother. So I decided we would go there. It was a very stressful time—working full-time and deal with her, going back and forth. Between my job, my mother, and my husband, I was going baloney. I told my husband I couldn't handle everything, so I went part-time in my job.

Reduces work time

Career becomes "just a job"

"I always enjoyed my work. It was an interesting job, a nice job, and very well paid. I think if it hadn't been for my mother, I would have stayed full time. But that was the last straw. The work was very important. I enjoyed it. I just couldn't take it all—work, mother, and husband. I thought I would explode. Before I reduced my hours, I thought of my work as a career. I was good at it. Now that I work part time, it is just a job.

Diagnosis made

"We went to the clinic. They were very lovely. My husband and I went to the final evaluation. It was Alzheimer's disease. They said she wouldn't get better. They don't call it senility anymore. They ruled out all physical problems.

Still in the middle

"She stayed with us more and more after that. Then we took her to our house. She was up all night. We weren't sleeping. It was terrible. My husband was working then. I was between the two of them. He would ask her if she was going to go to bed sometime today. I would try to calm him down. She wouldn't do what you told her. I was in between there, and then it got bad.

Picked up by police

"Prior to this was our first episode with the police. We came home from work, and she wasn't there. When we got home, all the lights were out and the doors were wide open, but she wasn't home. We went to her house, but it was dark. I said to my husband that I bet the police have her. She probably got confused and started walking. They sort of regress to previous years. Maybe she went back to when she walked to my other house and helped me when my children were babies. I called the police. They had found her, but she couldn't remember where she lived. So we went and got her.

Frightened and exhausted

"That did it. I called my sister in Chicago who wasn't working and asked her to take her until we could catch our breath. I was frightened and exhausted. We weren't sleeping, and I had the tension between my husband and my mother. She couldn't be by herself. That's what they told me at the clinic. We couldn't leave her all day because it was dangerous. We didn't know what to do. My sister said she could take her for two months. We put her on the plane. After three weeks, my sister couldn't wait to get her on the plane to get her back to us.

Daycare

"The doctor suggested a daycare center at a nursing home. So that is what we decided to do. Otherwise, we would have to come home to an empty house and the fright. So we applied for daycare, but we had to wait for a few weeks before she could start. I was still working part-time. We got someone to babysit on the days I worked. But my mother was very bad, and the woman quit. We still had one more week before my mother could start daycare. So my brother-in-law and his wife took her for the days I worked. They just did it for one week.

Difficult to manage

"Then she started daycare. She gave them a run-around. They told me she needed some medication. The doctor prescribed some medicine. All the medicine did was make her doze. When she was aware, she was still the same. I told the doctor that one of us needed a prescription. So the doctor tried one medication for the day and one for the night. That worked. She fought getting in bed. It quieted her and made it so that at least we could exist. It helped when she was at the daycare—before she had been very bad and uncooperative. That continued for a while.

Incontinent and resistive

"We tried and gave it our best. I was very afraid they were going to put her out of the daycare. They were really good. Then she started to be incontinent. I tried to encourage her to go to the bathroom like the books say, but she wouldn't listen. I spent my days worrying about the fact she wasn't going to the bathroom. I tried to get her to go to the bathroom, but she refused and invariably would wet the carpet. Towards the end, she refused to sit on the toilet. That was a continuing stress. I was always worried. At the end, I was just satisfied if she would stay in her room. It was a fight every night to get her to go to bed. Sometimes she wouldn't, and I would blow up. That went on for a while. I counted it good if I could get her to her room.

"She was still supposedly taking the medicine. At night, I would give her her capsule. But then I realized she wasn't taking them. She was hiding them in the bed. The woman at the daycare suggested I put the medication in a cookie. I tried it, and it seemed to work.

Severe management problems

"One time we went on a trip, and I fought with her all day to get her to go to the bathroom. I was going bananas. In a restaurant, I finally got her into a stall, but she wet herself. She was soaked. I had a change of clothes with me, but then she fought me when I tried to help her change. She also refused to bathe. But they wouldn't keep her at daycare unless she was clean. We got a home health aide. One time she cooperated, but never again. She couldn't understand. That was the big problem—lack of communication. So the home health aide didn't work out. Every time I tried to give her a bath my stomach would turn over. At the end, my husband had to pick her up and carry her to the tub. This was horrible.

"Our lives revolved around her"

"I was off the wall. I was never myself. I was never me. I was always concerned with her. Our whole lies revolved around her. If she had a decent day, we had one too. At the end, we couldn't take her out. At the shopping center, she wouldn't stay with us. She would take off. It was bad. I was getting to the point where I didn't know what to do. I was concerned that they were going to say "no more daycare," but they didn't complain.

"I didn't care what happened the rest of the week if we could get her in shape for the daycare. That was what we revolved around. At the end, it was a real fight to get her clothes off for bed, and my husband had to hold her.

Sisters can't help

"My sisters must work for a living. My mother visited several times with my sister in Chicago. The other sister is in Baltimore. The sister in Baltimore would occasionally babysit so we could go away. She always said, 'I'll give money, but count me out.' I had suggested we take turns—each caring for Mother for four months. My sister in Baltimore said 'absolutely no.' My sister in Chicago at one point saw I was having a hard time and said I could send Mother out and she would manage somehow. But I knew she couldn't manage. She is really sick. If I sent my mother out there, I would have had to go out and bring her home again. It would have been impossible. That's why that sister never got involved. When my sister in Baltimore cared for her, Mother always got away. The same thing happened in Chicago. Mother got to know the police in both places because they always picked her up.

"The whole thing prevented my husband and me from taking vacations or seeing our friends. But it has made me appreciate my husband ever more. My children really couldn't help because they were married and lived far away, but they were always very good to my mother. They are good children and grandchildren.

"My mother was my friend"

"I didn't mind being the principal caregiver. All our lives, my mother was my friend. She was a nice woman and didn't have much of a life with my father. My other sisters and her never got along. I never faulted them. One of my sisters was never a giver, and that was all right. My other sister was willing but couldn't manage Mother. No one was making me do it. [The brother is not mentioned as a potential caregiver.] I could have put her in a home before. I didn't feel resentful, and here we are. We were always friends beside being mother and daughter. We were able to communicate. That was the worst, when we couldn't communicate anymore. That was the greatest strain.

"My sisters and others said, 'Why don't you put her away?' They said this long before. I said, 'The day she doesn't know me is the day I will put her away.' But our lives became impossible, and I couldn't take care of her. My mother said she hated me.

The time had come

"I felt the time had come. She was unhappy here, and she hated me because I was the one dealing with her. At the end, she wouldn't let me do anything for her. So we started looking around. We were wondering how to go about it and what to do. We were in touch with a social worker. I realized I couldn't handle it. She was fighting me, and I couldn't let go. I could deal with it, but not when she wouldn't let me. That was horrible.

Looking for a nursing home

"Before that I had sent away for some booklets on nursing homes. One booklet gave a listing of nursing homes that were run with the patient in mind and did not make a profit. In the private ones, if you can pay for two years, they take you in, depending on how many people they have on Medicaid. When you run out of funds, they may keep you and put you on Medicaid. I got a lot of feedback from the girls at work who had to place relatives in nursing homes.

"So we sent for some literature on some of these homes, and the three of us visited some of these places. One consideration was financial—how much money Mother had to put down. I tried to look at the places through her eyes.

Accepted and on the waiting list

"I had investigated a nonprofit religious home for my father before he died. I thought it would be a good spot for her. To be a resident, you needed $38,000. We had already filled out forms for another place, but something in me made me want to call the nonprofit home. My husband and I went there, and I said to my husband, "This is it!" My mother has an income, plus $35,000 in cash. They figured she had enough to pay for three years. But they wanted to meet my mother. Thank God—my mother was good. She was Miss Congeniality. My husband and I were saying,

'Thank you, Whoever!' and she was so well behaved. They said she would get the first available space. We were delighted.

Husband uses his vacation time

"But the time wore on and we were having our hassles with bathing and the whole thing. She was still going to daycare. By this time, my husband was retired, so he babysat her. Before when we were both working and she went to daycare, he would get off of work early so he could pick her up. He was wonderful. At the end, so his bosses wouldn't complain, he took it as vacation time.

Admission to the nursing home

"After three months, we got a call and the next day we took her into the nursing home. I didn't know what to do. I wanted to explain it to her. I couldn't tell her because she couldn't understand. My husband and I were there. I asked the Director of Nurses what we should do. I didn't know how long to wait before visiting her. She told me to do whatever I wanted. I stayed away for three days. She was fine.

Worry about care

"But I worried about the care. For anyone to get care, you need one on one, and where are you going to get it? You get it when it's yours, like I gave it to her. I thought she won't get her daily piece of fruit. I wondered what would happen because she can't communicate about anything. That's really hard.

Drugs to quiet her

"One afternoon, the Director of Nursing told me she was fist-fighting with all the attendants. She wouldn't cooperate about anything. They had her on a lot of drugs. She wound up on Thorazine, so she is really spaced out. If I hadn't lived through it, I would be very dissatisfied with that. I know how it is. They have to fight with her to make her do. They are very nice, and she was never alone. I am very satisfied.

"She doesn't know us"

"In the beginning, I went every day. We would walk inside or sit outside. I told my husband I would love to bring her home, but I was afraid it would upset her when I took her back. I didn't know what to do. But I figured I'd chance it. We did it, and she was happy. I took her back, and she didn't say anything, but her face was glum. Since then, I bring her home once a week. It's been fine. She is not as lively because of the medicine. This last Sunday, she didn't know me. I was glad in a way because it lets me off the hook a bit. If she's got complaints it's not me they're directed to as the daughter. One time she confused me with my sister. She must come in and out. This last time, there was no recognition of me or my husband. It will be interesting to see if she knows me next time, but she wasn't antagonistic and she seemed glad to get back to the home. She may be going into another stage.

> "My mother right now has enough money to support herself for three years in the Home. Then, the rest will be covered by Medicaid. The nursing home will take her checks and use them toward the cost of care, and the rest will be paid by Medicaid. This is all arranged now so Mother will not be put out of the home."

The Anthony family is a striking example of a prolonged Odyssey of caregiving to an elderly mother who was deteriorating because of Alzheimer's disease, a situation that went beyond the family's limits of endurance. During their long ordeal, the Anthony's sought and used whatever help was available. Mrs. Anthony was willing and able to secure services: a diagnostic work-up, daycare, an in-home worker, a support group, social work counseling, and education information about management of the parent. But, ultimately, the services did not work because of the mother's incontinence and disordered behavior. As often happens, it was not only the older woman's intractable behavior and the exhaustion of her caregivers that prompted nursing home placement, but, finally, her inability to communicate or even to recognize her daughter. Fortunately, there was enough money so that the elderly woman was accepted by a non-profit home, and both she and her daughter were able to adapt to their new situations.

Mrs. Anthony's story is classic in its description of the development and progression of Alzheimer's disease. It also illustrates many findings from research studies of caregiving. Mrs. Anthony suffered severe stress effects. Parent care competed with her job; she had to reduce her work hours and give up her career. Her husband also was deeply affected and under strain. Though he was "wonderful," at times Mrs. Anthony was "caught in the middle" between him and her mother as well as between her job and her mother. Her mother's premorbid personality and their good relationship were among the reasons why she became the caregiver and endured the situation so long. Despite the horrors caregiving entailed, her long-standing, good relationship with her husband was not damaged.

When caring for her mother was no longer possible, Mrs. Anthony did not "dump" the older woman, but was careful to find a nursing home that she felt would give good care. After placement, she did not abandon her mother but still worried about her, visited faithfully, took her home on visits frequently, and gradually adapted to the situation.

Mrs. Roberts: "My Friends Don't Have To Face This Yet"

Gives up career

Mrs. Roberts is a vivacious, attractive, cheerful, successful professional with a graduate degree. Her marriage is obviously happy and satisfying. The couple does not have children. Mrs. Roberts gave up her job the previous year during her father's terminal illness. After his death, her 75-year-old mother moved into her home. "My group of friends don't have to face this yet. They're not there yet," says Mrs. Roberts. "I'm only 34.

Off-time—"I'm too young for this"

"It's completely changed my life. I stopped working because of my dad's illness. Mother couldn't do it. I had to help her through it. I knew she'd have to come to live with us when he died. They couldn't afford nursing care. My husband and I picked up the tab. But they couldn't adjust to nurses, so I quit my job. Then I had to get her through selling the house. Going to their house after work and sometimes spending the night was too much, so I quit. Now I take Mother to the doctor, write all the checks, do all the paperwork, cook, do all housework, see to it that she eats. She understands English, but doesn't speak it, so she has great trouble making friends. [Her mother was born in South America.] I have to be her therapist and morale booster. Her short-term memory has been poor for about the past six months, and she's very depressed. She resists going to a mental health program and says she wants to join her husband. She had a very hard time adjusting to moving in here, though she has her own bedroom and bath. She had to move in. She could not live on her own, and, besides, her neighborhood was bad and she wasn't safe."

"It's completely changed my life"

Provides much emotional support

Mrs. Roberts describes the curtailment of her lifestyle as going from "total freedom" to being tied down. If she and her husband want to go out, there are always arrangements to be made. She wishes her mother were more independent. The older woman didn't marry until her late 30s, then quit her job as a manicurist and stayed home. "Women weren't expected to claim any responsibility for their lives when she was young," says the independent daughter.

"It's a big change for me and my husband. All of a sudden, there's someone here all the time. That's the biggest adjustment. She tries so hard not to get in the way that she gets in the way. Mother is so dependent, and that's hard, and the time alone that I don't have anymore, and the constant emotional support I have to give me. It's taken almost a year for me to get to being myself again. I still sometimes feel trapped.

There's someone here all the time

"I get really upset with people who say, 'They become like children.' Not in any positive ways. I watch my niece and nephew. They display all the positive things about children because they are children. Old people bring grief, and they're tired of living. It burns me when anyone says this is like raising a child. Children

Not role reversal

are malleable, curious, open to learning. Children are selectively dependent, and it decreases."

A loving mother

Mrs. Roberts' deep affection for her mother is readily apparent. She tells the interviewer, "If you met her, you'd be drawn to her instantly. She is a warm, caring person. She radiates warmth. She has a language barrier, but she's very smart and very sweet. We've always been very close, and I feel responsible and protective towards her. She never meddles." Mrs. Roberts didn't get along as well with her domineering father, who was much older than her mother. He was arrogant, whereas she was submissive. The father never said "thank you," but the mother is very appreciative. "She knows what we've given up and gone through. Dad just expected it."

What do you do?

It was very hard for Mrs. Roberts to give up work. "That's the biggest thing. I had been getting a paycheck for many years. And I was getting recognition from society as a professional person. Now people look at me and say, 'What? What do you do?' " She says she probably will do some consulting work but will not resume full-time employment.

A supportive husband

Mr. Roberts is very supportive of his wife. He is helping her to get over the disappointment about not going back to work and tells her that what she is doing is important. He gets along well with his mother-in-law. The latter tries so hard to stay out of the way that he gets a bit irritated, but the mother's temperament is such that there are no problems.

No options

Mrs. Roberts' one sister has young children and also works. In contrast to the caregiver, the sister cannot afford to quit her job. They have had some words about the fact that the sister does little to help their mother. Mrs. Roberts would appreciate some emotional support and thinks that perhaps the sister should take the mother shopping on a weekend day. As the older sister, Mrs. Roberts has always had more responsibility, so she feels there is no other way and she has no choice. The mother doesn't belong in a nursing home and cannot live alone, and this arrangement is best for her. "I owe my mother to take care of her because she's my mother, not because she took care of me. It's a family responsibility."

I come last

Among the effects of care is the inability of the Roberts to take a vacation. Mrs. Roberts gives her husband and his schedule top priority before her mother, but "I come last," she says. She and her husband have decided to have a baby. If it happens, it will be more important to her than helping her mother.

Women's roles

Mrs. Roberts comments on caregiving to parents. She says, "Women are still responsible for nurturing relationships, for making the home comfortable, for getting the birthday cards out. There are a lot of expectations on women these days." She feels parent care is easier if you're married. Then you are not in it alone and don't have to work for financial reasons. It has opened her eyes to being old, and she has resolved not to be dependent. She feels it's unrealistic to expect old people to change, however, because they probably can't. She is sympathetic. "Don't hold it against the old people. They don't want this situation. As you get older, you lose so much independence, and they've lost this too. It's not their choice."

On being old

Get help! Do it!

She advises other caregivers, "Always go for outside help if you can. I see this in my mother-in-law. She takes care of my husband's grandfather who is in his 90s. She refuses to get outside help. She claims he wouldn't like it. I say 'Do it!' Take as much burden off you as you can if you can afford it." When my mother needs physical care, I'll get someone. I'm not going to be a martyr. I'm a lot more aware now of all these issues, first of all because of the experience with my father. So many things were not covered by Medicare or any third-party pay. Things that would help before they need to move in, to help keep them independent and out of nursing homes."

A women's issue

Mrs. Roberts says, "This is going to be a major issue for women. A lot of people think this is the main issue. Daycare will pop up, but other things are needed. Women, whether daughters or daughters-in-law, will always have the biggest burden of care. The situation will be a major problem. It can sabotage the successes women have had in the past. Unless the funding rules get changed, they will quit their jobs. They need flexible and understanding employers. Not a lot of people have started to address this problem."

One wonders whether in the future many women like Mrs. Roberts will quit their jobs for parent care as she did. Although research findings show that a significant proportion of caregiving women do give up their work lives, they are often the ones in late middle age who have been working many years and who are of low socioeconomic status. Being older, they are less likely to hold the "new" views of women's roles. Because Mrs. Roberts is young ("off-time" for parent care), is highly educated, and holds views associated with the Women's Movement, she may not be typical in having given up her job. She also has a strong positive bond with her mother, excellent financial resources, a devoted husband, and is hoping to have a baby. (Although Mrs. Roberts has given up much already to care for her mother, she is clear about her limits. She will get outside help when it is needed. "I do not plan to be a martyr." She advises women to "Get help! Do it!" She is aware of parent care and the lack of services as a major social issue and suggests what industry should do. Mrs. Roberts also comments thoughtfully on women's socialization to the nurturing role and says that things must be done or the situation will be a major problem.

The elderly mother is part of one of the current minority groups of old people who do not speak English. Combined with her dependent personality, the handicap in communication increases her isolation and places an additional burden on her daughter. The number of such people may increase in the future as those in the new waves of Asian, Hispanic, and other ethnic immigrants grow old (see Chapter 12).

Mrs. Rossman: "Now It's My Turn."

Eleven years of care by an elderly daughter

Sixty-seven-year-old Mrs. Rossman says in an exhausted voice, "How much longer can I do it?" She has been taking care of her 93-year-old mother for 11 years. Although the elderly woman is cognitively intact, she is depressed. Her vision is very poor, and she is almost totally disabled as a result of arthritis and having had several hip fractures. Wheelchair bound, she can maneuver the chair in the house to some extent.

Multiple falls and depression

The Rossmans took the mother into their home a decade ago after her first bad fall. "I was the only daughter," Mrs. Rossman says. Her brother lives in another state, and his house isn't suitable because it has stairs. Each time the elderly woman fell, she became more depressed and more emotionally dependent on her daughter.

Daughter quits her job

When her mother first moved in, Mrs. Rossman was still working full time as a teacher. But when she came home, she never sat down because of the cooking, laundry, and other chores. Then she stopped working full time and did substitute teaching two or three days a week. Finally, six years ago, she stopped altogether when more fractures meant more care for her mother. During the mother's hospitalizations, Mrs. Rossman spent hours at the hospital every day. In addition, Mrs. Rossman was pressing his wife to retire. He felt it wasn't worthwhile financially for her to work, and he was already retired. Mrs. Rossman admits she was having trouble coping. "But I loved the work," she says.

Can't leave Mother alone

Now, the Rossmans lives are so circumscribed that they can hardly go anywhere. Mrs. Rossman does not even attend family functions such as weddings. She sends her husband without her because the elderly mother would not feel comfortable with a paid caregiver. "My children and grandchildren feel bad that I can't come to visit, but it hasn't estranged us," he says. "After all, it's their grandmother, and they love her.

Mother refuses paid help

"I can't use paid help," says Mrs. Rossman, "because my mother resents it. My mother feels she cannot afford to pay for a baby sitter. She thinks in financial terms of way back. Anything over $10 is a lot of money, and she never had a lot of money. I told her before when I worked and had someone come in . . . I told her, 'I have the help not for you but for me, because I don't want to worry abut you, and I don't want my husband to feel he has got to stay home.' But she didn't want it. Now, whenever we go some place, she says, 'You can go. Don't worry about me.' But she know we will only stay two or three hours."

Problems with services

From time to time, some nonfamily help was obtained, "but they only do the minimum, and each time you have to start all over again to tell them what to do. I just got sick of having people around. The physical therapist did a lot. She was excellent, But I was still confined to the house. Medicare didn't give me a penny for outside help. My mother has so little money. Medicare said as long as she lived with the family, she couldn't get anything. I told them I saved them thousands of dollar. We're in the middle—too rich to be given help and too poor to buy it."

Options not feasible

Mrs. Rossman never seems to get out from under, and attributes this to a variety of factors. "I want you to know why my case is different," she told the interviewer. "If Mom did not live with us, it would be easier to send her to a nursing home. Or, if we lived in a smaller city, nursing homes would not be so impersonal." The Rossmans want to move close to their son, but can't find a place even though they yearn to spend more time with their grandchildren.

A husband's advice about nursing home placement

Dr. Rossman resents the restrictions on his life and the fact that his wife can't go places with him. He always respected his mother-in-law and is nice to her. Nevertheless, he often complains to friends and relations that his life is limited because of the elderly woman. He can't go away on vacations or go out with other couples. But when they went to look at a nursing home, he was "wishy washy" about it. Mrs. Rossman didn't have anything against it, but her husband said, "Well, she isn't that bad right now. She wouldn't like it in such a place. I don't know if your mother would be happy there, seeing all those sick people." He thinks too many people place parents in nursing homes nowadays. So they didn't follow it up. "If only he had said 'Enough!'," Mrs. Rossman laments. "If only he had said, 'Your mother must go to a nursing home.' "

Friends' and cousins' advice

Mrs. Rossman's friends told her she had to place her mother in a nursing home. "She might not like it, but she will adjust to it like all the other parents," they said. Mrs. Rossman's cousins told her she would be killing her other if she sent her to a home. "You know how that makes you feel," says Mrs. Rossman.

Mrs. Rossman's brother worries about his sister and the strain she is under. She describes him as a "big man" in Washington and a community leader. He is very busy, very harassed, but he's good about helping with money. Their family relationships are described as close, with considerable visiting back and forth. The sister-in-law even offers to come to Philadelphia when on vacation from her job to stay with the mother, but Mrs. Rossman says to her: "Mom would never let you do for her. She wouldn't be happy with anyone but me."

Brother's advice

The brother thinks his mother should go to a nursing home because he sees what it is doing to the Rossmans. He talked to his mother, and she said "Okay." But when he left, the mother would not mention it. The brother even found a place near his home, but she didn't mention that either. "She wavers in these conflicting feelings," the daughter says.

Professionals' advice

When the Rossmans were in the process of moving to a new home, the mother was about to be discharged from the hospital to convalescent care in a nursing home. It would have been enormously helpful not to have to take care of her temporarily during the chaotic move, but Mrs. Rossman took her home instead. "If only someone had been more forceful with me." She blames the doctor and social worker who said, "If you put her in a nursing home, you'd feel too guilty." She says they should have been forceful in urging nursing home placement. As it was, she didn't have a chance to catch her breath. "If I'd had the luxury of it, I would have had a nervous breakdown."

It's my turn

Mrs. Rossman says she goes on with this caregiving situation because "my mother took care of me. Now I guess it's my turn. I have been brought up with the ethic that you should really take care of your parents. I have a sense of obligation." Besides, her

Mother can't face it

mother is so pathetic. Her mother used to say years ago, "I hope God takes me before I have to go into a home." Mrs. Rossman says the older woman knows logically that she should be in a nursing home, but cannot face it emotionally.

Caregiver's emotional problems

As a result of all this, Mrs. Rossman says she is depressed, sleepless, and nervous, and has headaches. She describes herself as a worrier, and sometimes her hands tremble. She is acutely aware that caregiving frequently interferes with privacy, social activities, vacation plans, and responsibilities to other family members. She claims progressive views about women's roles, but at the same time she does not think sons should take time off from work as a daughter should do to help an elderly parent, nor should sons do household chores. She says she became the caregiver because she's the only daughter and her brother "would have to consider his wife's feelings." She sometimes feels guilty about losing patience with her mother.

"It's changed my life"

Mrs. Rossman says, "It certainly changed my life. I wouldn't stay home even if I wasn't working. I'd take a course or do volunteer work. I'd do something with my mind. My husband and I would travel and spend a lot of time with our children, visit friends, go to see my brother. We would be out more and entertain more. It has changed my life. She is my priority instead of my husband and children. I have to watch about giving her a lot of attention. I make an effort to be more solicitous of my husband. I feel a strain from this.

Competing demands

Son-in-law helps

"My husband has helped a lot with my mother. He has been a moral support in many ways. He has never said we have to get rid of my mother, but I think he feels he has sacrificed."

Not only the immediate family, but members of the extended family, professionals, and friends offer Mrs. Rossman advice. Cousins and professionals are clearly against nursing home placement ("You'll kill her" and "You'll feel too guilty"), whereas friends are for it ("She'd get used to it"). Dr. Rossman sends his wife mixed messages; he complains about the situation, but advises against placement. Mrs. Rossman's brother urges placement, but cannot implement the plan. The elderly mother herself recognizes the detrimental effects of caregiving on her elderly daughter and son-in-law, verbally expresses her willingness to go to a home, but subtly sabotages such a step. Mrs. Rossman cannot bring herself to get some relief. Her values tell her that it's a woman's role to take care of parents (even if it means giving up her job) and that adult children owe it to their parents to care for them. Immobilized, depressed, and unable to go against her mother's resistance to placement, she says, "If only someone had been more forceful with me" and "If only he [her husband] would say 'Enough!.' " Her plea for help has gone unanswered for 11 years.

Mrs. Green: "The Whole Family Cooperated"

A supportive family

Mr. and Mrs. Green have three grown children who have left their nest and have children of their own. Mrs. Green's parents lived in Chicago until 11 years ago. When the mother had a heart attack and the disabled father went to a nursing home. Mrs. Green's brother went back and forth from his home in Detroit several times. At a family conference, it was arranged that the elderly couple would move to an apartment in Philadelphia. Mr. and Mrs. Green both went out to Chicago to get them. A brother-in-law and a friend accompanied them to do the packing and to help manage the move. A granddaughter did all the unpacking and arranged the Harris' furniture to get things ready for them in their new home while they were driven to Philadelphia by the Greens.

The caregiver's husband: an unsung hero

During the next three years, Mr. Green stopped in every day to check on his in-laws. "He did even more than I did," said Mrs. Green. She and her daughter did all the housekeeping, and there was a visiting nurse once weekly. Then both parents began a series of hospitalizations, including several surgeries. When the mother was in the hospital, the elderly father stayed with the Greens. When the father was hospitalized, one of the Green's daughters stayed with her grandmother. Finally, Mr. Green said to his in-laws, "Why don't you move in?" They had deliberately planned their home to accommodate the older people. "We knew it would happen sooner or later." A niece and nephew helped with the move. There was no financial strain because the parents had enough money to support themselves, and the Greens were well off.

Enough money

The elderly couple continued to be in and out of the hospital. When the father was incontinent and comatose, Mrs. Green cared for him. She arranged physical therapy, homemaker service, a visiting nurse, and got all the equipment needed. He improved "amazingly" and was cared for in that way until his death five years ago. Now, the elderly mother is seriously ill. She stays in her room a lot to give the Greens privacy. She is very grateful for the care the family provides and is very supportive of Mrs. Green. The daughter says: "I take care of Mother because I can give her better care [than in a nursing home], and I love her. She knows that if she needs 24-hour care and we can't provide

Many services purchased

it, she may have to go into a nursing home. It's no big secret. We discuss it all with her.

The daughter quits her job

Mrs. Green had given up her job when she had children. "Back then you did what your husband wanted you to do." She went back to work part-time later. "I enjoyed it, it was supplementary income, and the children were proud that I did something besides just being a mother. I was still there for them and could be home." After her parents moved to Philadelphia, Mrs. Green did not return to work. "I felt I was investing my time in them."

Grandchildren help

A helpful brother

Mrs. Green says, "My children have really helped. When I was sick, my eldest daughter took care of things. My youngest daughter would stay with my parents so that we could go out to a movie. Our middle daughter sometimes stays with Mother. My brother is very supportive and appreciative. He visits three or four times a year so we can go away for a week and he calls every week. His daughters visit and call. Even my husband's family is supportive. My husband is a saint, and I try not to slight him. We are very close. Our relationship has not been affected because it was established long before. We have had our ups and downs, but we have weathered it."

Empty Nest refilled

Mrs. Green occasionally feels fatigue, frustration, or being pulled in different directions. She feels it's very important to know what you can and can't do where your parents are concerned. "A lot of it has to do with personality. It's an individual matter. If everyone was complaining, it would have been different. I am very lucky." She adds wistfully, "The only thing is, we are missing out on the Empty Nest syndrome."

In many ways, the story of the Green family is a best-case scenario. There were good interpersonal relationships and cooperative behavior among many members of the nuclear and extended families. Mrs. Green's brother, brother-in-law, nieces and nephews, grandchildren—even family friends helped. Mr. Green is one of the sons-in-law who can be described as "unsung heroes." The elderly mother's personality and understanding of the family's need for privacy and her appreciation of the care she was receiving facilitated caregiving.

The excellent financial situation of both the elderly parents and their children permitted the purchase and mobilization of a battery of supportive services. Equally important, those services were used constructively. The elderly mother did not refuse help from anyone but her daughter, and, for her part, Mrs. Green did not say, "No one can take care of my mother but me." Ample family finances also permitted the creation of an appropriate environment for the elderly people, one that permitted privacy while maintaining closeness so that care could be monitored. At the same time, however, Mrs. Green had reluctantly given up the job she enjoyed and has some emotional symptoms. Like the vast majority of women, she accepts parent care as a woman's role. She allows that role to supersede her wish to work. She is uncomplaining, but she and her husband have given up much of the freedom they had looked forward to as part of their stage of life. "We are missing out on the empty-nest syndrome."

Mrs. Wood: "My Mother Still Intimidates Me"

An only child

She's always with me

No privacy

"My mother still intimidates me," says Mrs. Wood, who is an only child. "She was very strict with me as a child. She always had to know exactly where I was all the time, and she still does it. She keep asking about what I'm doing and whether I plan to go out. If I'm on the porch, she looks out the window to see what I'm doing. I have no privacy. If I close the door to have a telephone conversation, she walks right in. She'll even walk in when I'm in the bathroom. That's the most strain—no privacy. Sometimes I take a walk even if it's raining, just to be alone. I'd like to do some things without her. I do crafts upstairs, but I can't do it when I want to. She keeps asking what I'm doing.

Cannot take a regular job

Mrs. Wood is 58 years old, and her mother is 84. Mr. Wood, age 67, is a retired corporation executive. The couple has been married for 40 years. Mrs. Wood works one week a month as a switchboard operator. She says that "anyone could do" the work she does, and she does it to get out of the house a little. She would like to have a regular job that uses her skills, but she can't be away that much.

Mother moves in

Signs of Alzheimer's disease?

Mrs. Wood had been going back and forth from her own home to her mother's to help and found it very stressful. The mother was not functioning properly, but moved to her daughter's home reluctantly. She was forgetful, her personal hygiene (formerly meticulous) was very poor, her house was dirty, and she was not eating. In addition, her arthritis was getting worse. At first, Mrs. Wood was relieved to have her in her own home, but now she says there are days when she'd gladly put her in a nursing home.

Behavior problems

The elderly woman causes many problems. She's sarcastic with visitors. She's "spoiled." She, like her daughter, was an "only" child, and her husband "did it all her way." Sometimes, if the Woods have guests and sit on the porch, the mother slams the door and locks them all out.

Elderly grandmother competes with grandchildren

Mrs. Wood and her husband have five children, all married and living close by. Her mother had objected to the daughter's pregnancies. "She would make me feel bad. She would go through all the reasons I shouldn't be pregnant." Now when Mrs. Wood's grandchildren visit, the elderly woman resents the attention Mrs. Wood gives them. "I'm her only child, and she doesn't like to share me. She's jealous. But I don't let her get on the kids."

Guilt

If Mrs. Wood talks back to her mother, she goes on a "guilt trip." Once the Woods went away for a week's vacation and put the older woman in a nursing home just for the week. One of the grandchildren stopped in every day, but she was very angry. "I felt so guilty. I can't have help in during the day because I don't think she'd react well. I talked to her about it and she said, "I wouldn't like that."

Daughter not permitted to leave her

Mental health symptoms

Mrs. Wood has many mental health symptoms. "Some days I can't handle it, so I go out for a bit and my neighbor looks in on her. I can't just go away for a weekend. I get headaches. I don't have the get-up-and-go I used to have. I worry. Is this the way I'm going to be? I don't want my children to have this. I'd want them to put me in a nursing home. I tell them to do it even if I complain. Jut because I'm a good mother, I don't feel they have to take care of me when I'm old. My mother does feel that way.

"That's the way it is"

"I take care of her because there's no one else. That's the way it is. I'm resentful because she always said, 'You have to do this because I'm your mother.' It would have been different with my father. He was more understanding of the way I felt."

Care of father-in-law

This is not the first time Mrs. Wood has taken care of an older person. Her father-in-law had lived in the Woods' home for several years when her children were preadolescent. But he was easy. He enjoyed the kids, and they could discuss things with him. Also, the Woods were at a different stage of life. Mrs. Wood had to be home a lot anyway with the kids. Now that they are grown, she feels she should have more freedom. "I always thought I'd be traveling at this age."

Off-time; the empty nest refilled

"It's going to be me someday"

Mrs. Wood concludes her interview by saying her situation is getting more and more prevalent. She says, "I'm the generation that's going to be involved. It's going to be me someday. We need to understand what to do."

In some ways, Mrs. Wood has made her life separate from that of her mother. The older woman tried to avoid sharing her daughter with others—objecting to Mrs. Wood's pregnancies, for example. But the daughter had five children anyway and protects her grandchildren from her mother's criticisms. She even works part time to get away from the situation at home. The elderly parent, however, apparently sees no boundaries between her daughter and herself, intrudes intolerably on the caregiver's privacy, and acts out by locking her daughter and son-in-law out of the house when they have guests. Mrs. Wood submits to her intimidating mother by not having outside help and not going on vacations. Her strains are evidenced in mental health symptoms, and she does not want to do to her own children what her mother is doing to her.

Dr. Marcus: "Our Lives Have Been Pushed To The Back Burner"

Adopts a child

Dr. Ellen Marcus (her patients call her "Dr. Ellen") is a 40-year-old clinical psychologist. She and her husband adopted a child from another county two years ago. It was an arduous process involving two trips to the child's country of origin and a visit of the child to their home in Harrisburg. But it was more than worth it, the couple says. At that time, Dr. Ellen reduced her work hours from full time to half time. Since she was self-employed, she feels lucky that she was able to do so and planned to be full time again when the child was old enough to go to day school.

Moves to a retirement community

Before the plan could be implemented, Dr. Ellen's father died. He and his wife had lived in Boston. The 80-year-old widow needs some help in shopping, cooking, travelling, and money management. When she fractured her arm in a fall, Dr. Ellen and a son (who lives in Washington) decided that the elderly woman should move to a retirement community in Philadelphia. Though Dr. Ellen's husband invited his mother-in-law to live in his home, she and Dr. Ellen both were adamant in saying no!

A son-in-law who is "always there."

The son-in-law is "wonderful." He is very involved and, in Dr. Ellen's words, "He's always there." He helps with shopping, finances, is active in helping in emergencies, and takes care of the couple's child, to free Dr. Ellen for caregiving activities.

A supportive brother

The older woman's son, too, is very supportive. He visits regularly and talks to the mother and his sister often on the phone. Dr. Ellen says her brother "really listens" to her—even all the "minutiae." He also takes on special projects such as managing his mother's move to Philadelphia.

Ups and downs

Dr. Ellen is candid about experiencing "ups and downs." She is a bit surprised at how alone she feels despite the excellent support given to her by her husband and brother. She says, "Our friends are not there yet"—that is, not at this stage of life. When there are bad time, she tries to control her worries, "It comes in phases." She feels good when things are stable, but thinks, "How is it going to be?"

Juggling and balancing

Dr. Ellen's child is a joy, but there is also the tension of balancing, as when the elderly mother's medical appointment conflicts with the child's pre-school schedule. Sometimes it's exhausting.

Work is third priority

Social life affected

Her work is now her third priority. She cannot increase her professional work time as planned because of her mother. It is very important to Dr. Ellen that her mother gets good care. Dr. Ellen and her husband have felt the effects of caregiving on their social life. In fact, they no longer have any social life to speak of and get behind on everything at home.

Grandmother loves child

On the positive side, Dr. Ellen says her own health has not been affected, family relationships are good, and there are no financial problems. In addition, her own relationship with her mother, which had been "distant" in the past, is now much closer, and that is "really nice." Dr. Ellen says, "It's wonderful how Mother loves my child."

Living for two people

Our lives are on back burner

Dr. Ellen feel that sons and daughters should share equally, but "it depends" and they should work it out. She is shocked by the idea that she is really living for two people. She had felt that way at first when her child was adopted. Her husband is "incredibly understanding," but "it feels like our lives have been pushed to the back burner."

Dr. Ellen is an unusually sensitive, loving, and conscientious person and is fortunate to have such a supportive husband and reliable, involved brother. Yet her strong sense of responsibility keeps her fully occupied. While she says work now takes third priority, it is obvious that she puts herself at the very bottom of the priority list. Though this highly educated woman enjoys and wants her career, even young women who grew up in the context of the women's movement often adhere to the "old" values about women's roles when parent care is needed. And Dr. Ellen also illustrates the feeling of being "off time" in what she had expected life to be like at this stage.

Mrs. Rossi: "I'm Living My Mother's Life."

"I was going to be a career woman," says Mrs. Rossi, who is now

Gave up her career

51 and feels that time is running out. A social worker, she had planned to go back to school to take a doctorate so that she could teach at a graduate school. But her mother was her priority, so she took a lower level job with less pressure. It meant less money, and she and her husband will need the money in the future. "No one is going to take care of us," she says. "We have no children, and my husband is not a bank president." Mr. Rossi is a psychologist who works in a state hospital. "I didn't know whether I should be home or at work. I was torn. People [her family and her husband's family] said I should be home. Work is therapy for me. But I had to choose between a human being—my mother—and money. The hardest thing is the loss of freedom, not the physical things. There's no break. Going to work is like getting out."

No one is going to take care of us

Work as respite

Parent care is your job; it's a woman's role

When she was 12 years old, Mrs. Rossi's father died. When he was dying, he told her, "Now you have to take care of your mother and brother [who then was six]; that's your job." "My mother and I saw to it that he had education to start him off," says Mrs. Rossi. "It's clear to me that caring for my mother is my job. It was instilled in me. It's my duty. It becomes your own idea."

Caregiving since childhood

The elderly mother, now 79, has always been sick. Mrs. Rossi cannot imagine having healthy parents. Her mother was so sick when Mrs. Rossi was a child that she lived with her grandparents for six years after her father's death. Mrs. Rossi wept as she recalled the loving grandmother who cared for her. "I've never known a time when I wasn't taking care of someone. As a child, I thought that's the way it should be." When Mrs. Rossi married, her mother came to live with her at once. They have never lived apart.

Almost total care

The elderly mother is now in a wheelchair because she has rheumatoid arthritis. She needs help with everything except eating. Mrs. Rossi bathes, dresses, and transfers her. The home has been fully equipped for care. There is even a chair-glide for the steps.

Unacceptable feelings

Guilty

Mrs. Rossi says, "I'm thinking about this a lot lately. I think it'll be one of us next. I guess I'm getting older. I think, Why me? Why didn't I put Mother in a nursing home like other people? I wouldn't do it, but why not? Why didn't my mother die? Then I think, My God, I don't want that. The house would be empty. I wonder, Why? I have these terrible feelings. My husband says it's normal. I say, 'Why didn't God take her and give me a little break?' And he says, 'It's normal. You're tired.' I feel guilty about my thoughts.

"But she devoted her life to me and my brother; she thought only of us when she was widowed. So how can I throw her away now? I would only put her in a nursing home if it were not humanly possible to have her here. I don't know what I'd do if she got worse. If I went part time, I wouldn't get any benefits. I'm worried about money. We'll need it when we're old. Sometimes I think families take advantage of one person. Like me. My mother always has some problem. Now she has a decubitis ulcer. It's frustrating. No matter what I do, it's not getting better. I've tried everything the doctor says. It's like going around in circles. And ulcers on her toes. I have to bandage them when I come home from work. I feel consumed by it. It's terrible. Do I have to wait for my mother to die before I begin to live? I'm living my mother's life, not my own."

I'm living my mother's life

Mrs. Rossi calls her husband her "saving grace." He takes care of Mom as though she were his own mother. His family would be angry if they thought we might put her in a nursing home." She takes care of her mother, she says, because in their ethnic group the daughter is always left with the mother. Also, her mother took care of the children when her dad died. She never even looked to marry again. I guess it was her duty. I ask myself, Is it my duty to take care of her?"

The pressure of culture

The son-in-law takes his mother-in-law to the bathroom in the middle of the night and gets up in the morning. He's a comfort to his wife and helps her in relation to the rest of the family. They used to say to Mrs. Rossi, "It's your job. You have to take care of your mother." He sets them straight. "He told my brother, 'You have to be there when a decision has to be made.' My brother is wonderful, but he sees it as my job. I get angry at him sometimes. Why doesn't he take her off my hands once in a while? He's so involved with his wife and daughter and his job that he's unavailable. It has brought my husband and me closer. Maybe it's not good. The emotional bond is so tight. We don't do anything without each other. We're very close, in some ways like a newly married couple. I look at him and think, Why isn't he complaining more?"

Why doesn't husband complain?

Mrs. Rossi is getting tired. She and her husband haven't had a vacation in five years. They need to get away. She was so energetic, but now she's tired and recently had a bad case of shingles. When she was sick, everyone worried about who would take care of the mother. The daughter is depressed, resentful, and angry. "I'm at the helm all the time. I have to manage." She would like to have 1 day all to herself or go out to dinner or go to a movie or go away for a weekend.

Fatigue and depression

Is it my duty?

"My mother took care of me, but she had me. I didn't have her in that way, but I do want to take care of her." Her mother is "a good person," and they are good friends. "If she were a difficult person, I don't think we'd put up with it." Mrs. Rossi asks, "When do I get what I want? My whole life is around my mother." But "it could be worse," she says, "Mother could be senile." She advises other people in her situation to look for help and asks, "What's going to be done?"

Unlike the couples in the previous cases, the Rossis are childless. They, therefore, have a worry that is shared by other childless caregivers: Who will take care of them when they are old?

Mrs. Rossi, pressed by both her own personal history as a life-long caregiver and a powerful cultural injunction, which reinforce each other, has given up the career she had hoped for. Her father, her siblings, her husband's family, and her husband all see caregiving as her role. Even in her childhood, she was socialized to giving precedence to males; it was up to her to take care of her brother and see to it that he was educated. She still works, but has curtailed her vocational goals. She has unacceptable thoughts about her mother, but feels guilty about them because the mother is a "good person." But she has no life of her own and wonders why her husband doesn't complain. Why doesn't he?

COMMENTARY

The ten women whose stories appear in this chapter illustrate many of the themes described in earlier chapters. Their reasons for taking care of their mothers varied. Some felt "it's my turn" while others felt a deep sense of obligation ("It's a family responsibility"). Some daughters loved their mothers deeply; these daughters cared for the older women because they cared about them. Others had poor relationships with their mothers, but provided care for them anyway. Factors were apparent that affected the situations for good or ill—the quality of their relationships with parents, siblings, and husbands and the personalities of the elderly mothers. In particular, mothers who were nonintrusive, appreciative of the care they were being given, and who had been "good" mothers at earlier stages in the family life earned the devotion of their daughters. But even when the mothers did not have those qualities, even when the struggle for control was bitter, the daughters were steadfast in fulfilling what they perceived as their filial obligations.

The daughters' guilt and ambivalent feelings related not only to the nature of their relationships with the mothers, but were reinforced by powerful cultural, social, and religious values. The intense pressure of those values reinforced the daughters' commitment that they must be the ones to provide care, no matter how long or how arduous, even if it meant that they themselves were deprived of opportunities to grow and develop through education and employment. Some daughters, however, like the one who said she did not plan to become a martyr and those who were able to seek and use services, were able to strike a balance that was comfortable for them and their families.

The cases showed that the roles of services and of money are not to be underestimated. They may not alleviate all of the distressing emotional symptoms, but they can ease the paths these women are following. The Carters, for example, needed an array of supports: counseling, a thorough assessment of the elderly woman, economic support, resources and services to supplement or substitute for family help, professional case management to mobilize and monitor those services, and education in techniques of managing the resistive parent.

Many of those issues will also be apparent in the stories to follow that are told by not-married women. Unique to the married women in this chapter is the salience of the support they receive from their husbands and children and their appreciation of that support. Not all husbands were their wives' "balancing points" or "saving graces," of course. But at the least, the behavior of many as seen through the eyes of their wives justifies their characterization as "unsung heroes." At the same time, however, the pulls exerted on the women in the middle by the competing needs of husbands, children, and mothers were also apparent.

Chapter 11

Daughters Without Partners

We now turn to daughters who do not have partners during their parent-care years. Members of each group—the widowed, divorced, and never-marrieds—tell their stories in their own words. Overall, their stories indicate that they are aware of the benefits and problems their married counterparts experience—the emotional support that husbands provide on the one hand and the difficulties of trying to meet competing demands on the other hand. The women without husbands also are aware, however, that the quality of the spousal relationships are important for their married peers. The main themes for those who are not married are often the obverse of those described by married women. They may feel the absence of a supportive husband or "significant other" keenly but, at the same time, point out the benefits of not having competing demands on their time and energy. As one of them said, "I couldn't bear it if I had people pulling on me saying 'You're spending more time with her than with me.' "

The subjective experiences of these women may have some positive aspects as well. Some indicate that parent care gives them a sense that they have a role in life; for some, the presence of the parent provides a feeling that they are not alone. As we listen to the parent-caring women who are widowed, divorced or separated, or have never married, the special problems of each group will be apparent. The women come from diverse situations socially and educationally. But the advantages some have enjoyed in the past often are no protection against the miseries some of them now experience.

I. WIDOWED DAUGHTERS

Mrs. Levy: "There's No One To Talk To About Little Things"

Working at age 70 A jovial 70-year-old woman with a good sense of humor, Mrs. Levy has her father in her household but is still working as a hairdresser. She enjoys the young people who work in the beauty salon. She was widowed a few months ago after being married for 50 years to a man she obviously loved dearly. The couple experienced no conflict about parent caring. Mrs. Levy's own parents had loved each other, she says. "It was a comfortable house."

A happy household

When Mrs. Levy's father and mother moved in 25 years ago, her father-in-law had already been in her household for two years. Her mother-in-law had told her husband, "When I'm not here, go to your son's house. That's the place to be." The older woman had known that the Levys had a very happy household and that Mrs. Levy would be compassionate and caring. Though the mother-in-law also had a daughter, she didn't think the son-in-law would like it if the elderly man moved in.

Two dads and a mom

Mrs. Levy nursed her mother before she died. For many years afterwards, both fathers lived there amicably. The father-in-law then died, and her own father, now 97 years old, is getting weaker. Until just a year ago, he played cards at the senior center all the time. Occasionally, he got dizzy, and then his granddaughter would pick him up. Now he is deaf and has trouble walking. He has begun to pick up his food with his hands and is a bit confused as to the day and the time. Sometimes he forgets to turn the stove off. He no longer can make his bed or cook and needs help with taking a shower. Mrs. Levy takes him to the barber and puts his clothes away.

Getting weaker and confused

Mental well-being has not suffered

Though she says she is never tired, Mrs. Levy does feel helpless when her father is not feeling well. He complains of feeling very cold, and she doesn't know what to do. As a widow, she now has all the responsibility. Her husband had been retired and had helped a lot. She feels lonely and angry sometimes, but knows its "normal." Occasionally, she feels emotionally drained and depressed. Though she feels some strain, on the whole she does not feel her mental or physical health has suffered because of parent care. Right now, her concern is not to leave her father alone too long. She likes her father and "wouldn't have it any other way." Her parents lived with her because she is more tolerant and patient than her siblings. Her father gives her emotional support, but she is pretty much alone in parent caring. "It's all up to me," she says.

It's all up to me

Compassion as a tradition

Mrs. Levy's two daughters are kind and considerate. One of them lives in Philadelphia and gives her mother respite. She stays for a few days and lets her mother go to a wedding or another event. The other daughter is in California and is supportive as she can be. Mrs. Levy praises her daughters. They give her a lot of emotional support. She feels her own parent caring has helped her girls to see how things should be and to be compassionate.

Her husband was her best friend.

Mrs. Levy's widowhood is recent. She is grieving and having to adapt to being without her husband. She has had to learn to do the things her husband used to do. She feels alone. "Married friends don't treat you the same. Your social equity has changed. You're a single person to them. My friends are nice to me, but there's a difference. You feel that you're alone when you're out with couples. There's no one to talk to about little things—what channel to watch, what restaurants to go to. And my income has dropped. My daughters are wonderful, but your husband is your best friend. You can say anything."

Dad is a reason to come home

As for caring for a parent when you're widowed, "You can't talk about it to your husband and turn to each other when you're frustrated." But there's a positive aspect to having a parent at such a time. "If you have someone to care for, you're not living alone. I have a reason to come home, a reason to be." She wishes she could afford to have someone stay with her father in the afternoon.

Get help

Mrs. Levy advises other women: "You have to care to do it. If you can't do it, that's different. If you can afford help, get it."

Though she has some problems, Mrs. Levy is not overwhelmed and her mental and physical health has not suffered. She has a history of warm, loving family relationships—with her parents, her husband, her in-laws, and with her daughters, of whom she is proud and whose support she appreciates. In addition to that tradition, she is transmitting another tradition—caregiving. She has had a caregiving career; she cared for three disabled older people in her home while she was raising her own children. Though Mrs. Levy is feeling the effects of being a widow during her caregiving years, she remains essentially optimistic and enjoys joking with her young fellow workers at the beauty shop. She is a self-described "plain woman" who had a solid, loving marriage. She thinks parent care is easiest for a "plain married couple; they have each other." As with some other caregivers without husbands, she gets emotional support from her very old parent. Caring gives her a "reason to be, a reason to come home."

Mrs. Levy is managing well right now. As her father deteriorates, she may face a dilemma because she cannot afford to purchase help.

Mrs. Gordon: "Mother Wanted Me For Herself"

Doing a noble thing

"I'm content," says Mrs. Gordon, "I'm doing a noble thing." At age 73, Mrs. Gordon is a childless widow caring for her

Spouse care

Brother helps

helpless 93-year-old mother in their large suburban home. She had nursed her husband through several severe strokes before he died 13 years ago. During the subsequent two years, Mrs. Gordon traveled extensively and loved it. It was her "reward." Then her mother began to need care and has gotten progressively worse during the past 11 years so that now she is bed-bound. Recently, Mrs. Gordon's only sibling, an unmarried brother, joined the household. He helps by lifting the mother and doing other chores. Mrs. Gordon can now go food shopping without anxiety.

Attuned to mother's needs

A feeling of well-being

Though Mrs. Gordon had worked for 30 years and enjoyed her job, she finds caregiving more satisfying. It is much easier with her mother than it had been with her husband. "I always know what she wants. I have always known even if she doesn't speak. I wasn't as successful with my husband but am attuned to Mother. Mother complains when I'm not here. I am her security blanket. It's not an obligation. I'm glad to do it. It's my job, and I take pride in doing it well. I get a feeling of well-being—wholeness. It's a natural female function. There isn't any other way. I never considered fighting it."

A set routine

Mrs. Gordon has her household organized and has a set routine. The first floor of her home has been converted to a hospital-like setting. She is in complete control every moment of the day. Caregiving is even easier now that her mother has a feeding tube, she says. "It's a breeze." When the older woman was able to walk, Mrs. Gordon was always worried about her falling.

Only daughter-care is good

"There's no other way," says Mrs. Gordon. "Mother would be miserable in a nursing home. She wouldn't last two months. She was very uncooperative in the hospital, and I stayed there from 8 a.m. till bedtime." When Mother came home from the hospital, nurses came in, but the daughter was eager to terminate their services and get into her own routine. "I'm a do-it-yourself-er. I'm better off doing it myself." The doctor who attends her mother praises Mrs. Gordon. He says "no one gets the care your mother gets."

"She never lost me"

Mrs. Gordon and her mother have always been very close. "We were like sisters. I would have taken care of her no matter how many children there were." They've lived together all their lives except for a few years after Mrs. Gordon married. "Mother didn't want me to get married; she wanted me for herself. She used to say 'You don't want to get married.' She didn't want to lose me. She never lost me. We were always together anyway." The mother never pampered her daughter. If the latter got into a fight as a child, "Mother would say "It's your fault. You must have done something.' It made me more self-reliant." Even when Mrs. Gordon was widowed, the mother offered no sympathy. "Help comes from inside," says the daughter.

Once was enough

Mrs. Gordon points out the advantages of her situation. "It's safe and secure," she says, and protects her from establishing a relationship with a man, which wouldn't have worked out. This way she leads a healthy life. "I'm better off for not having met anyone. Once was enough." Being widowed and childless make it easier. There is no "tug of war." She feels sorry for parent-caring women who have children or husbands.

No tug-of-war

Misses some things

Asked about disadvantages of parent care, Mrs. Gordon says she misses playing the piano (she gave it up because it disturbed her mother) and taking trips. Her social life and community activities have dwindled, but "I'm not a lonely person. I'm not really social. I'm self-reliant." She says she used to feel stressed and that she was giving things up, but no longer. She has a hankering for a smaller house as the big one is a financial hardship. On balance, Mrs. Gordon is content. She says "it's a heroic thing to take care of someone."

Despite the fact that she is old herself, Mrs. Gordon's relative lack of strain and satisfaction she takes in caregiving are striking aspects of this situation. The current picture is part of the continuation of 73 years during which the enmeshed relationship of the two women has been the central feature of their lives. Apparently, the relationship of the two women always superseded Mrs. Gordon's relationship with her husband. Although Mrs. Gordon says it's "sad" to see an old person deteriorate, she finds caregiving easier, as her mother's care comes more and more under her control. Being in control of the situation fits perfectly with Mrs. Gordon's personality, and her self-esteem comes from doing her job well. She points out the advantages of not having competing demands and has systematically stripped her life of potential diversions from caregiving—dating and hobbies, for example. "I'm better off this way." Caregiving provides her with an important role in life, one that enhances her sense of doing something worthwhile and that earns her the admiration of the doctor and others.

II. DIVORCED AND SEPARATED DAUGHTERS

Divorced Daughters

Mrs. Harris: "I Saw My Mother Do It"

"What do poor people do?"

Fifty-seven years old and divorced for 32 years, Mrs. Harris is now caring for her 80-year-old mother who has Alzheimer's disease. Her father had taken care of his wife for many years. When he died, Mrs. Harris moved into the mother's home. The

As an executive, she continues to work

daughter asks, "What do poor people do? It must be terrible for those who cannot afford help. *You must have help!*" She is in the midst of a successful career as an executive of a professional organization. Considerable paid help aids her in caregiving. She employees someone full time during the week, and a second person comes in on weekends to supervise the elderly woman.

Paid help

Both are "gems." Nevertheless, she has reduced her workday by one half hour at the end of the day so she can get home earlier. Though Mrs. Harris does no housework, she does the cooking and dishes and bathes and dresses the mother. She and the workers she employs share the shopping. The expense is worrisome, and her savings are being depleted. The mother has some money, and she hopes it lasts.

"I'm the logical person"

Mrs. Harris' sister works and has children—a full life. She says, "I was the logical person. The demands are different for my sister and me," but she doesn't mention her brother as a possible caregiver. Being divorced and childless was a major factor in becoming the main caregiver. She feels her sister does as much as she can.

"I saw my mother do it"

"I saw my mother do it," says Mrs. Harris of caregiving. "It's the way I grew up. When people needed help, she did it. Mother took care of her own father and both of her parents-in-law." Mrs. Harris comments, "When I was divorced, I divorced myself

Old values and new

from many ways of life, but this is the right thing to do." She is referring to the very different and freer lifestyle she had adopted and lived for many years in an artistic community. Her mother was not supportive. "I think you're crazy," she told her daughter, but later accepted it. But, Mrs. Harris says, "You never really change. Many things are internalized even though your thinking has changed."

A prisoner

She goes on. "I have an obligation. I was free as a bird and could do whatever I pleased. I can't do that now. I'm a sort of prisoner. That's the thing I mind the most." Her emotional wellbeing has been affected. She is often angry, always tired, depressed, and so drained that sometimes she doesn't feel much.

Easier because of Alzheimer's

The mother is helpless now and much more childlike. She thinks she's 40 years old and her father is still alive. She was a "tough lady" in the past, but now she's very sweet, gentle, and friendly. "If she were still herself, I couldn't live with her," Mrs. Harris says. "We didn't get along." On an "elemental level," she says she gets some emotional support from her mother. Nevertheless, at times the older woman drives her crazy because she repeats the same things, asks the same questions, and cannot follow the simplest instructions. Still, the resentment and anger she once felt toward her mother have dissipated.

Being divorced makes it easier

The fact that she's divorced makes parent care easier, Mrs. Harris thinks. She adds that if she were younger, it would have had a major effect on the course of her life. Now she has no responsibilities to anyone else, and at her age, life is not "unrolling" before her.

Mrs. Harris continues to work and does not mention the possibility that she might do otherwise. Nevertheless, she described the conflict in values that many women experience nowadays. She had lived for many years in accordance with "new" values about women's freedom and chose a lifestyle that was not traditional. When parent care became necessary, she found that she still held a powerful traditional value—the care of a disabled parent is a daughter's responsibility. She refers to the role model her mother had been in that respect.

Mrs. Harris also illustrates what some other caregivers relate. When her mother became relatively helpless, she also became "sweet." The tension between the two women eased, and despite the Alzheimer's disease, the older woman provides some emotional support to the daughter.

Like other daughters, Mrs. Harris sees the differences in the experiences of married and unmarried caregivers. There are no competing pulls for her because she is divorced and childless. She also points out the importance of services which, fortunately, she is able to purchase.

Mrs. Jackson: "My father is 96 and my uncle is 97. I have a toddler and a diaper baby."

"I may as well open a center for senior citizens"

Mrs. Jackson has two elderly men living with her, both of whom require considerable care: her father, age 96, and her uncle [her father's older brother], age 97. "I may as well open a day center for senior citizens," she says. Mrs. Jackson means that literally and is now in the process of establishing such a center. She has already purchased a building, hired staff, and arranged for a doctor, a dentist, and a podiatrist to visit the center. The building is named for her father.

Divorced

Now 51 years old, Mrs. Jackson has been divorced for many years. She raised her three sons by herself, experiencing many of the problems of a single-parent family along the way. The two older boys, in their 20s, are living on their own now. The third, 16 years old, goes to boarding school.

Mom care

Mrs. Jackson cared for her mother before her death because her father couldn't manage. At that time, her children were young. She had to quit her job and solved her problem by opening a

Quits job

daycare center for children. In that way, she was able to care for her mother, be with her children, and earn a living. It was a good decision, she says.

Moved to Dad's house

After her mother died, Mrs. Jackson went back to work. Her father lived on his own until five years ago. Mrs. Jackson then moved from a neighboring state into her father's home because he needed care and was refusing to leave his house. First, there was a conference in which Mrs. Jackson, her sister, and her brother participated. They would have put their father in a nursing home. Mrs. Jackson was the only one willing to move to their father's house, so she was "elected" to take care of their father. "I voted for myself," she says. The siblings felt it was easier for her because she had no husband. But Mrs. Jackson doesn't blame them, since she made the choice. The siblings don't help, though lately her brother takes their father to church and the sister once took him on a visit for one week.

"Dad didn't put me in an orphanage"

An adopted child

"I owe him"

Mrs. Jackson explains why she will not put her father in a nursing home: "That's where the guilt comes in. He didn't put me in an orphanage. I owe him. He's not really my biological father. He's my biological father's cousin. My parents gave me away, and he adopted me. I think of him as my father. His wife I thought of as my mother. She was so sweet. My biological father and mother had six other children. This dad always treated me like a daughter, and his wife treated me like she had given birth to me. I have such gratitude. That's why I do this. They didn't put me in an orphanage. I do get tired, but I don't complain. Getting tired is the hardest part. But I have a responsibility. The people I call my sister and brother are his biological children. But I feel more of a bond with him. I know my biological parents and siblings. They are sarcastic about my dad. They say "She just loves him to death.

"I'm grateful, grateful"

"I grew up grateful to those two people. I'm just grateful that they let me share their lives. It's repaying a debt. Doing for them what they did for me. I'm a helping person. I'm always trying to help, even though sometimes I can't help myself. My minister says, 'Just accept it.' "

Uncle arrives

Her uncle lived in New York, and her father used to talk about him a lot. Then Mrs. Jackson had a phone call from a hospital in New York. Her uncle was in the hospital, and they were refusing to discharge him to go home alone. Mrs. Jackson said, "I'll come and get him," and she did. "That was a bad decision" she now feels, "but he's here, and he didn't have anyone else."

Dad confused and cooperative

Both elderly men are confused. Her father is forgetful. He forgets to eat and bathe, and his clothes are dirty. He opens the door for strangers and once was mugged by an intruder. After being awake for a couple of hours, he dozes. He calls Mrs. Jackson by her mother's name. His personality, however, is kind and sweet, as it always had been.

Uncle confused and grouchy

Her uncle, on the other hand, is grouchy and complaining. He cannot see well, can barely walk, and has to be fed, bathed, dressed, and taken to the bathroom. He doesn't like anyone, not even himself. His mind is back in the 1950s and 1960s.

A toddler and a diaper baby

Mrs. Jackson quit her job a month ago to devote her time to planning the day center. She has a strict routine, and times all her activities. She breaks her neck to do it all. It reminds her of how she did things when her own two older boys were small children. Again, she now has a "toddler and a diaper baby." She cooks and freezes meals so her father can put them in the microwave when she's not there, but lately he forgets to do it.

Like a TV sitcom

Mrs. Jackson's sense of humor comes to her rescue at times. She says the two old men are like a television sitcom. She comes home and finds the meals uneaten. She says, "Why didn't you eat?" Her father says to her uncle, "Didn't we eat breakfast, Tom?", and Uncle replies, "Maybe." Her father takes her uncle's medicine and gives her uncle his own medicine. The crotchety uncle calls to his deceased wife when he's upset, "Here I come, Anna!"

Stressed out

One night her father was upstairs, and she heard a thud and ran up. He had fallen asleep and tumbled from chair to floor without awakening. Her uncle thought her father was dead and began calling "Here I come, Anna." Mrs. Jackson says, "I thought 'Oh no.' I put my dad on the bed and said 'Uncle, what's wrong?' Uncle was jealous of the attention I was giving Dad. Then when it was over, I began to cry. I guess I was just tired and stressed out."

The teenager had to go to boarding school

Caregiving has made major changes in Mrs. Jackson's life. She told her 16-year-old son there was no room for him. Jokingly, she says, "I threw him out." On his own, the boy found a fine boarding school where he is doing extremely well. "It's really better for him" says Mrs. Jackson. The boy "had to accept it." At first he was disappointed, says his mother; then he understood. Mrs. Jackson told him, "I have to do it. It's the only thing I can do." She could have put her uncle in a nursing home but figured if she had to take care of her father, she might as well keep her uncle too. She says, "My son said the other day that when he wants to see me, he has to make an appointment. But I have to take care of my Dad. My son can do other things. When I told him I was going to have a day center, my son said, 'Oh, no. Now I won't even be able to bring my friends home. It will be smelling like urine.' "

Effects of care

No homemaker service

Exhaustion and sleeping pills

Mrs. Jackson says caregiving is not as hard physically as it is mentally and emotionally. "I don't sleep well. I'm listening for them with one ear. I gave up my social life. We've been on the waiting list for a homemaker for a year. After I get them dinner and to bed, I can't do anything but shower and go to bed. Uncle was turning day into night so the doctor gave him sleeping medicine. He was hallucinating and running through the house. I've been so stressed that I've been taking their medicine. That's so easy to do. I try to practice not being upset and drained. I have to exclude other things from my life. I have to say 'no' when men ask me for dates. It's too much trouble. A month ago, I met someone and he's being very supportive, but I don't know how long it will last."

"You have to rearrange your life"

Plans for the day center

She hopes the daycare center she plans will make it better. "I'm going to hire an assistant and a cook and an aide so I'll be able to get away at times. And I won't be away at work worrying about them. I got phone calls at work. I still have to figure out what to do at night. Maybe my assistant will have to work one night a week. Maybe I can get away for a few hours, even if I only read a book. You have to rearrange your life. When you take care of an older person, you have to sacrifice some things. Sometimes I take a deep breath and say to myself, 'Take it easy. It's not that hard.' Once I called a support group. I saw the phone number on TV. But it was far away. I called Philadelphia Corporation for the Aging [the local Area Agency on Aging agency], and they said I wasn't in the right location. Frustration gave me an idea. I'm going to start my own support group when I open the center. I'm going to have a nice place. I've arranged a doctor to come and a dentist and a podiatrist. It's going to be like I'd like for my own two old people. Not take them to the doctor and wait all day like I have to do now. I'll have little outings for the people. The real reason I'm opening the daycare center is because I identify with the caregivers. I want them to have a place to bring their old people. There's not a place available in the area where I live for me to take my old people."

Lonely

Mrs. Jackson is lonely. "I'd rather go out with someone than put my uncle in the bath tub. Then it passes. You just have to grin and bear it. The first year, I thought I'd have a breakdown. Then I developed supports. My minister. He'd send someone from the church to spell me for a bit. I wish my sister and brother would offer to spell me a bit, but I won't ask. I have too much pride. Dad deserves to receive my care. It's different with Uncle. But I have to do it. I'd like to spend more time with my children. But I have to turn down their invitations."

Divorce and parent care

As for parent care and being divorced, Mrs. Jackson says, "I was divorced before my Dad needed help. But being divorced gave me the freedom to do it. Your time isn't divided. A supportive husband would help, but it would have been harder if I had a husband. My other boyfriend said that taking care of my father and uncle was a great idea, but then we broke up because I wasn't able to spend time with him. This boyfriend cares for me and that makes it easier for me to care for them. He'll let me take a nap or bring dinner. It lessens the burden. Little things. But I don't know how he'll react when things are bad. Like when there are emergencies when I am stressed out and cry."

A lack of services

Mrs. Jackson says there should be more help for caregivers. "Certain services aren't available. Or if they are available, there's a long waiting list. You're limited by your economic situation. The alternatives are a nursing home, or a homemaker, or staying home and doing it yourself. If you choose homemaker, their wages are too high. Your own salary doesn't really take care of it. That's not very fair. Senior citizens have paid their dues, and they don't get much in return. We've been on the waiting list to get a homemaker. Medical service is OK. Medicare pays for that."

Mrs. Jackson describes her situation and the powerful need to care for her "Dad" so well that little comment is necessary. That need is so great that not only all of her own needs are superseded, but her own son must leave her home. Generalizations cannot be made, of course, but for this particular woman, her adoption appears to have intensified to the ultimate degree her feelings that she must pay back what her "Mom" and "Dad" did for her.

Mrs. Hill: "There Was No Love In My Family"

"I was not loved"

Beaten with a strap

"There was no love in my family," says 61-year-old Mrs. Hill. "My mother was not the type who was warm and loving to me when I was a child. When my own children came along, she said 'You had them, you take care of them.' I can't remember any hugging or kissing. My father was violent. He beat my mother, and he beat me. I was not loved. I was afraid to death of him. I hated my father till the day he died. I never would have cared for him. No, never! Maybe that's why I try to do for her. She had such a rough life. If she didn't get anything, how could she give anything? I was 14 the last time he beat me, and I quit school at 16 to go to work so I could get away. But my mother went to the authorities and had me brought home. She wanted my board money. So I got married at 17 and got out of the house."

Mother two hours away

An apartment like a garbage dump

Mrs. Hill does indeed try to "do for" her mother who is now 84. Divorced for 20 years, Mrs. Hill lives with her son and daughter-in-law, who had invited her to move in when she came back to Philadelphia from Pittsburgh. She works as a cashier in a restaurant. The elderly mother lives in senior housing located a two-hour drive away. Until the housing manager threatened to put her out unless Mrs. Hill kept the place clean, the latter had been unaware of what was going on. The mother's apartment was like a "garbage dump—full of sacks of newspapers, garbage, maggots, and roaches, and with spoiled food in the refrigerator."

Mother refuses paid help

Women's roles

Guilt

Mrs. Hill now drives to see her mother every week on her day off. She cleans the apartment, bathes her mother, dresses her in clean clothes, changes the dressings on the older woman's legs, and does the banking. Her mother refuses to have any paid help, has no idea how exhausted the daughter is, and complains that she doesn't come to see her on both of her days off. Mrs. Hill has a brother. She says to her mother, "Why can't he help and spell me once in a while?" The mother replies, "He's a man and you're a daughter. You should do it. You're supposed to do that stuff." The brother laughs and tells Mrs. Hill, "Keep up the good work." She says, "I have no life of my own. It's work and go to Mother's. If I don't go, the dressings on her legs don't get changed, and I feel guilty."

A doctor's advice

Support group

Mrs. Hill discussed the situation with her mother's doctor and told him how Mother will not even permit Meals on Wheels or any other service. She refuses to allow anyone into the apartment. The doctor told the daughter, "Do not put her in a home. They don't last long when they go into a home." She went to a support group. The other participants said, "You have to change your feelings." They didn't give her support. They didn't understand what she goes through. "They just sit there and tell each other stories. They say you can't change the old people. You have to change. They have no suggestions."

Takes anti-depressants

Mrs. Hill raised her five children by herself and has no money. Her four other children live far away. She is alone most of the time, having been unable to make friends when she moved to Philadelphia because going to see her mother uses all her spare

On being divorced

time. She hates the long drives, feels guilty and nervous, and has been taking antidepressants. Her arthritis is painful. She won't do it when she's 65 or 70 years old, she says. She won't be able to drive back and forth. She thinks being divorced makes it harder. She feels alone and has no one to do things with. But on the other hand, she feels at least she doesn't have to worry "Am I giving enough time to people? Married women have to deal with a husband, a job, and children," she says.

Mom preferred son

Makes Mom happy

Mrs. Hill worked all of her life. When she was raising her children as a divorced woman, she worked two jobs, and she had to do the washing and ironing on weekends. "I never got any help from my mother. I don't ever remember her asking if I needed any help. Her son was more important to her. Even today, her face lights up when she talks about him. He never visits her. Now she kisses me when I leave. She does it out of need—she needs me." Summing up the caregiving situation, Mrs. Hill says, "I'm glad I'm able to do it. It makes her happy."

Having received so little from her mother all her life, one wonders why Mrs. Hill is exerting such strenuous efforts to help her at this time. Perhaps she is still seeking the affection and approval that she had been denied as a child and through the years. She gets no help from her brother, her mother's physician, or a support group. Like some other daughters, Mrs. Hill accedes to her mother's refusal to allow any formal services. Also, like some other caregivers, her protests about her brother not helping are feeble. Her mother tells her, "You're my daughter. You do it." Though Mrs. Hill is overburdened, depressed, guilty, and taking antidepressants, she says she is glad she is able to do it and wants to make her mother "happy."

Separated Daughter

Mrs. Stern: "I'm Caught In A Web That Goes Down Deeper And Deeper"

Mrs. Stern's 95-year-old father has been totally helpless for 22 years. Her 26-year-old daughter has multiple sclerosis. She is separated from her husband and in the midst of bitter divorce negotiations. She had cared for her mother through a long illness. She had helped her mother-in-law who had Alzheimer's disease.

Plunged in deep problems

Mrs. Stern says, "I've been plunged in deep problems for 22 years." She feels "caught in a web that goes down deeper and deeper." She is struggling to extricate herself from the web and from her depression and is intensely anxious about the future.

She describes a long list of symptoms including exhaustion, sadness, resentment, and feelings of helplessness.

Wanted to work

"What I know best is catastrophic illness"

Something had to go

A suburban housewife from a highly educated and successful family, Mrs. Stern is verbal and articulate. Her father was a judge, and her mother a physician. She has no siblings. She holds an advanced degree in art history. Dr. Stern, her husband, is a well-known surgeon. As the Sterns' children moved toward adolescence, she wanted to work, but there was no market for her skills. Mrs. Stern, therefore, decided to take another degree—this time in computer science—and started back to school. Things were fairly stable at that time. Her father had been paralyzed from a stroke for many years and was totally aphasic, but was being cared for by her mother and nurses, with help from Mrs. Stern. Then when her children were in their teens, her mother became ill and went downhill steadily for two years before her death. In the meantime, Dr. Stern's father died, and his mother showed signs of Alzheimer's disease. Mrs. Stern had to assume responsibility for her mother-in-law's care as well. Dr. Stern's brother took no responsibility. Immediately after her mother-in-law's death, Mrs. Stern's daughter, then 20 years old, showed the first symptoms of the progressive disease from which she suffers. "What I know best is catastrophic illness," Mrs. Stern says. She dropped out of school. "It got too crazy. Something had to go. My husband and children couldn't go. The parents couldn't go. So school had to go."

Her husband leaves her

Then Dr. Stern announced that he was leaving his family. He had never been home a lot, not even during his daughter's illness, but his wife had attributed his absences to his busy surgical practice and professional meetings. When he left, she was in shock—"a basket case."

An uncertain future

Mrs. Stern is alone in facing all these serious problems. Her income has plummeted as Dr. Stern has now stopped giving her money. She had trusted him and knew nothing of their financial affairs. She is ill equipped to earn a living. Though she is looking for a job, her father and daughter require considerable time and effort. The divorce negotiations are ugly and stressful. She is extremely worried about finances and does not even know whether she will be able to keep her home. Her disabled father's money is running out as well, and she is frightened about what will happen to him if he outlives his resources.

Caring for Dad

Mrs. Stern's daughter is now in remission, but her elderly father is in a continuing decline. There are constant crises, and he often is in a hospital. He lives in an apartment with round-the-clock attendants since he can do absolutely nothing for himself and cannot communicate. Mrs. Stern runs that household and manages her father's financial affairs. Keeping nurses on hand is a major problem. Sometimes they don't show up or quit without notice. She constantly has to "soothe their feathers" and has a sense of desperation about keeping the ball rolling.

Dad is indomitable

Despite her problems, Mrs. Stern refuses to consider nursing home placement for her father. She would do so only if his mind goes. "I'd rather go into debt first." The daughter describes her father as a "model of surmounting adversity. He's indomitable." She is proud of him. He reads, listens to music, and is interested in politics. He bears his terrible situation with dignity, grace, and cheerfulness, and tries to make it as easy as possible for his daughter. "We were always very close," says Mrs. Stern. "He was always a good guy. He taught me to be open and honest, but now I'm deceiving him." She is referring to the fact that she has not told him about Dr. Stern leaving her because she does not want to add to his anxiety or worry about his own care. "I'm hiding something major that affects his welfare, but I'm doing it to protect him." The deception bothers her. She knows that if she told him about her separation, she would feel emotionally supported by him, but "I have to look out for his emotional well-being as much as possible."

There are pluses and minuses about caring for her father, Mrs. Stern says. "The way he has dealt with it makes me proud of him, and I've learned from it, but it is a drain. I don't know whether the pluses and minuses neutralize each other. There's that duality."

She cares for and about him

He deserves it

Why does she provide care for her father? "Who else is there? And he gave to me so much and so caringly and so completely. There's no way there's too much I could be doing. It's not an exchange. He just deserves it. Sure my mental health has suffered, but in a way, it's been enhanced by helping Dad. I'm doing something." She hints of having her own health problems and jokingly says, "If I became disabled, I'd move in and let Daddy take care of me."

A good wife and mother

Dependency a bottomless pit

Mrs. Stern was close to her mother too. Though her mother was a physician, she always made time for her daughter. When her husband became ill, she cared for him "incredibly well." The best thing I can do for my mother now," says Mrs. Stern, "is to take good care of Daddy." Unfortunately, during the last year of Mother's life, her brain was affected, and she became so dependent that it was "a bottomless pit. It wasn't her fault, but our relationship deteriorated. She became the child and I became the mother in terms of role reversal."

Laying on the "guilt trip"

How was it different to care for her mother and mother-in-law? Mrs. Stern replies, "One loved me. The other did not. Guess which was which? One rejected me all the way. It was difficult to be kind and respectful, but she was weak and frail, and I had to try regardless of the past. I didn't want to let my negative feelings take over and take advantage of the fact that she was weak now. I owed her something. She was my husband's mother." The mother-in-law had played her two sons off against each other and made them compete for the "golden apple" of who was best to Mom. "She was laying on the guilt trip. Which son was going to be the kindest? Which daughter-in-law?"

Parent care and being separated

Mrs. Stern does not really think taking care of all the parents caused her husband to leave. She understands that there was much stress, and the tension may have put additional pressure on the marriage, just as their daughter's illness added stress. However, "The stresses should have made us closer rather than driven us apart. His psychopathology would have done this even without the parents."

I'm without a support network

Surely parent care and being separated at the same time make things harder. "Now I have to face things alone. I'm alone in the world. I'm without a support network. I have friends, but people turn away from misfortune. Couples turn away. You're a fifth wheel. Your friends don't want to hear it. And there's no longer a couple, so social relationships have fallen by the wayside. One of the hardest things is the financial problems and realizing that my earning capacity is limited. The children wish they could mend the parental relationship. They're hurt and resentful and feel vulnerable. We're trying to be mutually supportive. I guess I haven't set too good an example in how to cope."

No light at the end of the tunnel

"I just want to do things normal people do. Vacations are out of the question. I feel bitter and pessimistic. I don't see light at the end of the tunnel. I guess you have to rise to it."

"I fit into this slot"

Asked why she was willing to be interviewed, Mrs. Stern replied, "I don't fit into many slots in my job hunt. I saw the notice about the research and thought 'I sure fit into this slot.' "

Mrs. Stern has indeed had "deep problems" for more than two decades. Still involved in her long caregiving career, she is now experiencing two very serious additional problems—her daughter's illness and the trauma of her husband leaving her. Each of the problems has an impact on the others. The sharp drop in income creates anxiety, not only about her own future and that of her children, but also about future care of her father whose money is running out. The father's care creates an additional problem for this beleaguered woman. Being separated has reduced the support network she needs badly. Not only has she lost what support her husband could have given her, but since she is "no longer a couple," her friends are less in evidence.

It is particularly poignant that her father, though unable to move or speak, still represents emotional support for Mrs. Stern. She wishes she could have a full measure of that support, but is denied it because in order to protect him she hasn't told him about her separation from her husband. Her wish is also apparent in her sad little joke: "If I become disabled, I'd move in and let Daddy take care of me."

Mrs. Stern illustrates some of the themes that are common to many other caregivers. She would place her father in a nursing home only "if his mind goes." Helpless as he is and overburdened as she is, she still sees a "plus" in caregiving—she is proud of her "indomitable" father, and by helping him she's "doing something." That is one area in which she can feel good about herself. She feels responsible for her parent's emotional as well as physical wellbeing. She cares *for* him as well as *about* him.

It is interesting that Mrs. Stern used the phrase "role reversal" in relation to her mother, but not in relation to her father or mother-in-law. The context in which she used that phrase is suggestive. The mother's brain was affected, and the relationship "deteriorated" into role reversal. In so saying, Mrs. Stern implies that "role reversal" is not desirable or healthy.

Mrs. Stern's mental health surely has suffered from the multiple assaults she has experienced. She is in an uncertain limbo because she doesn't know what the divorce settlement will be or what her life will be like "at the end of the tunnel." She may exemplify the anxious transitional state of other separated women who are neither here nor there but has multiplicity of other really serious problems. It is not only in relation to her search for a job that Mrs. Stern feels she does not "fit into many slots."

III. NEVER-MARRIED DAUGHTERS

Ms. Collins: "She'll Be A Comfort To You In Your Old Age"

"My life is on hold"

"My life is on hold," says Ms. Collins. "I'm 32, I'm not married, I have no children. It'll be too late for me." Ms. Collins lives in her 67-year-old mother's home. The mother has severe emphysema, is arthritic, and has some memory problems. She needs some help with grooming, bathing, and toileting. The youngest of three siblings by 12 years, Ms. Collins attributes the fact that she is the main caregiver to being a woman, to being the youngest child, to her

Brother makes decisions

sister's mental illness, and to her brother's geographic distance. The brother makes all the decisions, but Ms. Collins feels that's fine. "After all, he's a policeman and has even saved people's lives." Her siblings and her mother put her in the role of a child and tell her what to do. She quit her job when her mother was acutely ill. Now, the brother tells her, "Stay home with Mom." The mother expects her to keep house and take orders. "Wash the windows," she says, and complains about how the housework is done.

Quit her job

Ms. Collins says, "When I was born, my mother was 35. That was old in those days. My Mom thought I was a boy, but the nurse said no. Mom was disappointed. People consoled her and said 'She'll be a comfort to you in your old age.' But she got more than she bargained for. We fight all the time. She does things to make me feel guilty. I take care of her because I owe her. I feel like I was a little spoiled in being the youngest and coming along later."

A baby girl: "a comfort in your old age"

Because Ms. Collins is not working, she has no money and cannot be independent. She has a boyfriend who also lives in the same house. Her family does not approve of her lifestyle but has accepted it. She and her boyfriend would like to take a place together but cannot. A previous relationship with a man ended because the latter did not understand about Ms. Collins' need to take care of her mother. He wanted her to move with him to Pittsburgh. Jim (the current boyfriend) is more understanding. His own mother is taking care of his grandmother. But, Ms. Collins says she's doing things like a 50 year old. The neighbors across the street care for elderly parents, but their own children are in the same age bracket as Ms. Collins.

A sympathetic "live-in" boyfriend

Care is "off time"

Ms. Collins is disconsolate. "My self-esteem is down. I should make a list of things to do—a schedule—and save some time for myself. In this hot weather, the beer in the frig looks better and better, and I drink it. My sister gets to go away. I don't. I should put my foot down more. I get Jim off to work. I get breakfast, do the laundry and the dishes. Then I sit down and argue with Mom. I have no energy left. I watch TV. All the things I should do seem overwhelming—paying bills, getting the car fixed. I'm lonely. If I didn't have Jim, I wouldn't have anyone. I feel I'm losing my identity, abandoning my life. No one admits I'm doing it all. I have problems. Do I get married? Do I have children? Do I abandon her? Should I take charge

Depressed and immobilized

"I need counseling"

and fight my siblings and Mom? I'd be fighting everyone. I need counseling. But I can't afford it. If I wasn't single, I might be forced to say 'I can't stop my life because of you.' "

Clearly, Ms. Collins is depressed and immobilized. Everyone in her life exerts pressure to keep her in the caregiving role. Even her current boyfriend is "understanding." She is not struggling to extricate herself from the virtual isolation in which she lives. She does not look for a job though her mother can be left alone during the day, and she is beginning to drink. She complains, but she thinks it's right for her brother to make decisions. The question here is how to reach Ms. Collins with the counseling help she knows she needs before, as she puts it, it is too late for her to move in a positive direction and get her life off "hold."

ONLY AND ALONE

Some parent-caring daughters have been only children all their lives, whereas others become "only" children when a sibling (or siblings) dies. A major theme for such women is their intense sense of being alone in caregiving. Those who have always been only children often say they had expected and anticipated eventually being the only caregiver to their parent(s); they wish in advance for someone with whom to share filial care when the time comes. Those who had sibling(s) who died also wish for a sibling who could share and provide emotional support, but, in addition, they experience a sense of desolation and loss.

When women without husbands or children are also without siblings, they are totally alone during their parent-care years. They often have unusually close bonds with the parent for whom they care and are burdened by the sense that it's all up to them. There simply isn't anyone else at all on whom to rely.

Two questions are part of the inner experiences of these women: "What will happen to my parent if something should happen to me? And "Who will take care of me when I am old?"

Ms. Brown: "It's An Awesome Responsibility"

It's an awesome responsibility

Ms. Brown, who had never married, has always lived together with her mother, now 84. The mother, a former school teacher, is intact mentally but needs considerable personal care because of severe arthritis. Ms. Brown had a brother who died suddenly of a heart attack 12 years ago and a sister who was killed in an automobile accident four years ago. Ms. Brown said, "I never ever thought of sharing my mother's care. My sister and brother just shared. But now I realize I'm alone in caring for my mother. It's an awesome responsibility."

What would happen to mother?

Ms. Brown has stopped working as a secretary because of a back injury. She sings in the church choir and teaches music to the children at the church. She occasionally feels depressed, overwhelmed, or tired, but says it passes and she becomes "normal." She referred often to the loss of her siblings and her feelings of being solely responsible for her mother. "It's scary to think what would happen to Mother if anything happened to me."

No competing responsibilities

Ms. Brown notes that being single has some advantages when parent care is necessary. "When people are married, they have to take time from their families and children. I don't have those problems. Being single never bothered me. I have a busy and productive life. You don't have five or six people to worry about. My biggest problem is being the only child. And I don't have children to help. I was put into it because my sister was taken. Before that, she would come whenever. It makes a big difference. If there is no one to do it, you have to do it. It's a big responsibility."

Life stages and parent-care

As for the problems experienced by parent-caring women of various marital statuses, Ms. Brown says it depends as well on factors other than marital status. "You can't put a label on who has it the hardest. First in importance is how much care is needed. Then marital status. If you're married, it takes away attention if a parent is severely ill. But mental capacity is important. If my mother were senile, that would be different. It also depends on the individual and their capacity and how they look at life. One person is stressed out at something, and another one not. And there are different stages for different people. A woman may have raised her children and planned to go back to work. Freedom, that's it. Are they mentally prepared? You can't pinpoint things and say this is good and this bad."

Ms. Fox: "Nobody Cares About Us. Who Will Take Care Of Me?"

Unmarried and an only child

Ms. Fox's elderly mother has Alzheimer's disease. Unmarried and an only child, she has lived together with the 86-year-old widowed woman for four years. Ms. Fox has a degree from a respected university and works for a large industrial firm as an accountant.

A compliant mother

The elderly mother has two brothers, both of whom also suffer from Alzheimer's disease. One is in a nursing home and the other is cared for at home by his wife. By contrast with Ms. Fox's mother, those elderly men wander, their behavior is aggressive, and sometimes they are "nasty." Ms. Fox's mother is "sweet; she doesn't complain or argue." The mother enjoys going places, and Ms. Fox takes her every place she goes. At home, the mother wants to help and does so, with instruction. She cleans, dusts, and washes the dishes after dinner.

Will I get that way, too?

Ms. Fox describes her mother as having been a pleasant, efficient person in earlier life—outgoing, very social, and having lots of friends. Now she can't do anything on her own. "I wonder if I'll get that way, too," says Ms. Fox, "but my father was very alert. I don't know which one I'll take after. I have to put her clothes out and tell her what to wear. She can't put her clothes away. She's even lost one shoe. I have to cook everything. I have to buy her clothes. She wants to look nice so she cooperates."

Planning for the future

As insurance for the future, Ms. Fox has registered her mother at a sectarian nursing home where she is at the top of the waiting list. Ms. Fox says, "I'll keep her as long as I can. Why should I be alone? I even take her on group day trips. She looks fine. I buy her nice clothes. Other people don't even know she has Alzheimer's. She's a companion for me. I have no other family. Even though we can't carry on a conversation, she is a companion. She loves to go out. I say to her, 'Do you want to go out?' and she says, 'Sure.' I take her to New York all the time. I guess it sounds weird. But I'm not alone."

A companion

Daycare

The elderly woman goes to daycare so that Ms. Fox can go to work. The daycare center is located at a hospital, so the mother gets her medical care there—"doctor, x-rays, even a foot doctor. That's a tremendous load off me. I don't have to take time off from work. Now I only have to take her to the dentist."

I have no one

Ms. Fox describes crises during which her feelings of being alone were acute. "I had a scare when we had an automobile accident, but she did get better. She doesn't give up and get depressed. She keeps pushing. I get depressed, but she doesn't. I get depressed mostly about being alone. I have no one to call on. I had a mastectomy three and one-half years ago, and I have a bad heart. I think 'What would happen to us if I become an invalid?' After the auto accident, I was in the hospital, and I was almost hysterical. However, I've put my mother's money in trust, and there's a trust officer if anything happens to me. They could even put her in a nursing home. I think I've done very well to do all that. But I still have not taken care of myself. I don't even

Some counseling

have anyone to talk to. I go to a counselor three or four times a year. My job pays for five sessions a year. But now my firm has been bought out. There are constant layoffs, and another one is coming up. People over 59 have been asked to take voluntary retirement, but I'd get a very small pension, and at my age I'd have trouble getting another job. So I'll stay as long as they'll keep me. I get depressed and upset, but there are a lot of people worse off."

No respite

Ms. Fox says her worst caregiving problem is her inability to go out occasionally in the evening. Teenagers don't want to "baby sit" as they get upset. The homemakers charge too much, and sometimes they come late or leave early. "I can't go to a club meeting or even a retirement party. I can't go away for a weekend. I haven't had a vacation in years."

Nobody cares about us

Ms. Fox compared herself with other caregivers who have family support. "My mother's brother has a wife and children and grandchildren. She's like a general. She tells them all what to do to help. I don't have anyone. I even went to a support group, but it only made me feel bad. All they talk about is to tell their families to do this and that. Well, I don't have any family. I feel as though nobody cares. Nobody cares about us. It's true. I don't even go to support groups anymore. They don't *know*. There aren't too many people all alone, but they exist. It's best for caregivers who have family. When I had surgery, I had to go to the hospital myself. When I came out of the anesthesia, there was no one there."

A heavy schedule

Ms. Fox feels very tired. She never gets to bed before 1 or 2 a.m. because she has housekeeping and things to do, and gets up at 5 a.m. to get things ready before she goes to work. She loves to cook and spends a lot of time doing that in the evening. She sometimes feels frustrated and angry and is often depressed and worried. She attributes all of those feelings to her situation of being alone in caregiving. Even when she had the accident, she had to take care of everything herself—car repairs, insurance, taking care of her mother, taking care of herself after her hospitalization. On holidays, she and her mother are alone. She thinks people should be more caring and invite them. She wonders if its her own personality. She says in a low voice, "Maybe it's my mother. Maybe they don't want my mother." She's even given up inviting people to her home. "They don't come. They don't realize what it's like to be alone. Even at Christmas. We used to do it. When we met people at church and they were alone, we always invited them. I can't understand it. Maybe I take things too seriously. Maybe someone else would handle things better.

No friends

I guess there's people in worse situations. At least she's not an invalid in bed."

It's my duty

As for why she keeps on caregiving despite her multiple strains, she says, "All my life I remember my parents saying that children have to take care of their parents. It's my duty. My parents were very strict. I was brought up that way."

Care for both parents

Ms. Fox had also helped her father, who was practically blind, before he died. He had his own business, and she helped him with the accounting work. At that time, Ms. Fox cared for both parents. She was tied down. But her father was alert even though he got very depressed. He would sit in a chair and cry and get irritable. "But at least I could tell him something, and he would remember. With my mother, it doesn't go through to her brain. She's been getting worse during the last eight years."

It isn't fair!

"If I came from a big family, there would be lots of demands and fights, so maybe this is better. But some families do get along. It isn't fair that I was an only child. But she was always a good mother—caring and thoughtful and understanding. I was brought up to do unto others as they do unto you. But even if she had not been good to me, I would take care of her. In lots of ways, I have no choice."

Work life affected

There are many limits on Ms. Fox's life. Not only can't she go out in evenings, but she can't have people in. Her social network has shrunk. Her work life is affected. Her boss is not understanding. On a couple of occasions, she had to miss work to go home, and he resented it. It affects the ratings he gives her.

"I come last"

Her priorities are clear, Ms. Fox says—"My mother comes first, my job comes second, the house and my three dogs come next, and I come last."

Being alone the most strain

On balance, Ms. Fox says, "My mother does what I tell her to, so I have some control," and the older woman's income covers her expenses. "If I were unhappily married, it would be worse. I have friends who are married, and some of them are unhappy. In some ways, I'm better off. Nothing is perfect. I will take care of my mother until I can't do it. Then she'll have to go to a nursing home. If I had a cooperative husband and children, it might make it easier. Being alone is the most strain. It really depends on the situation. Some widowed women are helpless because their husbands did everything. It depends on the relationship."

Trying hard to look at the positives in her life and in her situation, Ms. Fox says, "When I was young, I always wanted to go around the world. I did it. I've been in 50 countries and lived in some faraway places. [She used to work for the State Department.] Its made me a stronger person." At this point, Ms. Fox wept, then said "Being stronger makes me able to do the caregiving. I have to take care of myself, and I might as well take care of her too."

Do your best

As for the future, when her mother is gone, she'll sell her house and go to a retirement community. She advises others like her, "Do your best."

The theme expressed by Mrs. Brown as well as Ms. Fox is, of course, the feeling of being alone. "I don't have anyone. "I feel as though nobody cares." "I don't have anyone to help." "What will happen to my parent if something happens to me?" "What will happen to me when I am old?" "It's scary."

It is striking that for both women, their elderly mothers provide their only sense of having someone, having family. Ms. Brown's mother is mentally intact, and the daughter respects and loves her. But Ms. Fox says of her cognitively impaired parent, "Even though we can't carry on a conversation, she is a companion. I guess it sounds weird, but I'm not alone."

Ms. Brown, though alone, manages to live an active life. Because her mother is intact mentally, she can be left alone while the daughter pursues her outside interests. Mother and daughter get along well. Ms. Brown is perceptive in assessing the pros and cons of being a not-married caregiver. She notes the absence of competing demands but also that she has no children to help her. Overall, the strain Ms. Brown is experiencing at present is mild, but she worries about the future.

Ms. Fox's life is much more restricted than that of Ms. Brown because of her mother's Alzheimer's disease. Ms. Fox does go to work, thanks to the daycare program. But like many other caregivers, she cannot locate satisfactory helpers so that she can have some diversionary activities. Her social life has been shrinking. She cannot even go to a "retirement party," let alone take a vacation. She is fortunate that daycare is available in her community. Ms. Fox has planned as well as she can for her mother's future and for her own by locating a nursing home and a retirement community, again underlining the importance of adequate financial resources. But what can be done to alleviate the painful sense of aloneness and loneliness with which people such as Ms. Brown and Ms. Fox live?

Chapter 12

Caregiving Daughters-in-Law: (The Proxy Primaries): 7 Case Histories and a Comment

When a son is identified as a parent's primary caregiver, it is likely that his wife is the one who does most of the day-to-day care. Thus, though daughters-in-law are named as primary caregivers much less frequently than biological children, they probably serve in that role more often and provide more care than they are generally given credit for. For that reason, we call them "Proxy Primaries." At the same time, there undoubtedly are many daughters-in-law who do not assume the role of primary caregiver. Existing information suggests that daughters-in-law in general may not be as willing as daughters to provide the high levels of personal care needed by extremely disabled older people. For example, old people without daughters enter nursing homes at lower levels of disability (Soldo, 1982b).

Whatever the prevalence of daughters-in-law as primary or "secondary" caregivers at present, their experiences are important to understand not only in their own right, but because the continuing fall in the birth rate means that in the future even fewer daughters will be available for parent care. Fewer daughters, in turn, may result in more daughters-in-law becoming involved in care of their parents-in-law. Moreover, when there are fewer adult children, it is more likely that couples have more than one older parent between them who may need care. In the future, a woman will have increased chances of becoming a caregiver in both roles—as daughter and as daughter-in-law.

Little is known about the qualitative aspects of daughter-in-law care—about such women's subjective experiences and how they differ from those of daughters. As noted in Chapter 4, acceptance of caregiving to the elderly as a woman's role is so deeply ingrained that some daughters-in-law simply assume that they should provide the care when their husbands, the sons, become the ones in the family responsible for seeing to it that an elderly parent receives help. Though this usually happens when a daughter is not available, some daughters-in-law become the caregivers even when there is a daughter if such behavior is culturally dictated or there is some special circumstance. Some daughters-in-law accept caregiving as their role so completely that they even are grateful for the help their husbands—the elderly parents' own sons—give them in the caregiving enterprise. Though sometimes resentful, daughters-in-law on occasion mention the positive side of caregiving, such as making someone "happy" or doing so because it fits in with her religious beliefs.

There are, of course, similarities in caregiving by daughters and daughters-in-law—particularly in the "externals" of care—that is, in the nature of the concrete caregiving tasks performed (e.g., see Peters-Davis, Moss, & Pruchno, 1989). Emotional strains are caused by such factors as "heavy" care, the sharing of a household with the dependent older person, the disturbed behavior of Alzheimer's patients or those who are mentally ill, and lifestyle disruptions. But the subjective experiences of the two groups of women differ in significant ways, and there are some qualitative differences in the nature of their strains. These will be illustrated in the case studies in this chapter.

Some daughters-in-law are relatively uninvolved in providing services either because someone else is the primary caregiver and the daughters-in-law's own help is truly secondary or minimal. Sometimes the son provides much of the help the elderly parent(s) needs. Some sons go beyond their traditionally assigned tasks of decision-making, money management, home repairs, and chores to do things like shopping and transportation. It is extremely rare for sons to provide personal care to their mothers, however, although they may do certain personal things for a father such as shaving and bathing. When their mothers need personal care, they enlist the aid of their wives. Daughters-in-law who are relatively uninvolved may experience little emotional strain, though there are exceptions

When a mother-in-law actually lives in the daughter-in-law's household, the stress can be extraordinarily severe, particularly if the older woman requires a good deal of help or the previous relationship of the two women had been poor. In the Noelker and Poulshock (1982, p. 47) report of shared households, the daughters-in-law experienced more severe stress effects than any other category of relative. Some of the themes and issues that will appear in the cases to be presented are not experienced by all daughters-in-law, of course, but recur often in the caregiving stories they tell.

One theme is the clear distinction the women make between the quality of their emotional involvement with parents-in-law and with their own parents. Some report more detachment and less strain in relation to their in-laws. Those who are having or who have had caregiving experience in both roles—that is, as daughter *and* as a daughter-in-law—describe this well.

> There is less emotional involvement [with a mother-in-law]. One is your mother, and the other isn't. I can deal with it much easier when it's my mother-in-law. I don't get upset as much. Maybe you have less guilt.

* * *

> You don't carry the emotional baggage into the situation [with a mother-in-law] that you do with your mother.

The sense of responsibility they feel is related to the intensity of their emotional involvement.

> I never have the feeling that I have to be "in charge" with my mother-in-law. It's my husband. With my mother, it's *my* responsibility.

* * *

> I don't feel the same sense of responsibility for my mother-in-law that I do for my father.

In a related vein, elderly parents-in-law are sometimes perceived by daughters-in-law as being less demanding of them than their own parents are because there is no biological link. The elderly in-laws may be more cautious and feel less entitled to help from daughters-in-law. One said, "My mother-in-law is a 'lady of control.' Her daughters feel it, but as a daughter-in-law, I do not."

Because the sense of obligation to parents is different from that to parents-in-law, daughters-in-law do not say (as daughters do), "She took care of me so now it's my turn to take care of her." They do not have the powerful motivation of reciprocity for the care they received as children, or the feelings of love (albeit ambivalent) and biological connection. They say such things as "Blood is thicker than water," and "One is your mother. The other is not. There is a bond."

A different kind of obligation often exists, however. Some daughters-in-law see care of their parents-in-law as having been an implicit part of the marriage contract: "It's part of the deal," and "I owe her because she's my husband's mother."

Reciprocity with one's husband also plays a role, in that care of the parent-in-law may be viewed as repayment for the husband's help with the caregiver's own parent in the past or even in anticipation of the future.

> My husband was patient and understanding when my father was ill and was kind to him.
>
> * * *
>
> My husband doesn't complain about my mother. I'll have his mother here some day. I know it.

The qualitative relationships between older people and their daughters-in-law are extremely variable, of course. They may be close and warm at one extreme or actively, openly hostile and conflicted at the other extreme. There are instances of extreme devotion to a parent-in-law, sometimes even after the husband of the caregiving daughter-in-law is no longer in the picture.

A woman who is divorced from the son of the elderly man for whom she has provided care for seven years says: "He [the father-in-law] is 92 years old, and he and I always had an excellent relationship. If I didn't take care of him, who would?"

A widowed daughter-in-law continues to tend to the needs of her mother-in-law: "She lives in senior housing, but she needs someone to do her laundry and shop for her and take her to the doctor. We always got on well. I see it as my responsibility."

The ultimate example of devotion, of course, appears in the biblical story of Ruth and her mother-in-law Naomi. Ruth says to Naomi, "Intreat me not to leave thee, or to return from following after thee: for whither thou goest, I will go; and where thou lodgest, I will lodge" (Book of Ruth).

There also can be extreme conflict, antipathy, hostility, and resentment.

> When she [the mother-in-law] is in the room, I put my magazine or newspaper high in front of my face so I don't have to see her.
>
> * * *
>
> She never accepted me. She tries to control our lives completely and criticizes me to my husband.

A major and pervasive issue that is almost invariably present, though it may be barely discernible or overt and dominant, is the competition that sometimes erupts into a bitter struggle between wife and mother-in-law for the man who is husband to the one and son to the other. Conventional wisdom has it that the mother-in-law/daughter-in-law relationship is often characterized by tension and conflict. An elderly mother-in-law's need for care, particularly her presence in the same household, may exacerbate the situation so that the emotional currents are intense. In such instances, there is no respite from day-to-day contact that provokes those feelings. The shared household becomes like a pressure cooker without an escape valve.

Narratives told by daughters-in-law provide some clues to the reasons they suffer more stress effects than other relations when households are shared. The competition between mother-in-law and daughter-in-law and resentment at needing to help someone who is not even their own parent add an extra edge of bitterness to their stories of caregiving. Such feelings are heightened if the mother-in-law had "rejected" them from the outset and there were relationship problems along the way.

All of those inner feelings and others as well appear in the seven case studies that follow. In two of the situations, the daughters-in-law became the caregivers because their husbands were "only" children and in two because their husbands became only children when sibling(s) died. In the fifth case, the husband had no sisters. In the last two cases, the husbands did indeed have sisters, but there were special circumstances.

Mrs. Chase: "She's Sitting In My *Chair."*

Alzheimer's disease

Mrs. Chase, age 36, lives with her husband, three preschool children, and her 78-year-old mother-in-law who suffers from Alzheimer's disease. Although confused and in need of help with all instrumental and personal care tasks, the older woman is still ambulatory, knows where she is, and recognizes her family members.

Husband an only child

Mr. Chase is an only child. His mother had lived in a rural area in Massachusetts and was widowed one and one-half years ago. The elderly woman then had several fainting spells, and became unable to drive, shop, or manage her affairs. She called her lawyer repeatedly about tax reports that had already been done. She had approximately 15 kinds of pills, which she took indiscriminately; her apartment was a mess; and her son found "enough cleaning supplies to open a store." Finally, when the rescue squad took the elderly woman to a hospital, the doctor refused to discharge her to go back to her apartment alone. At that point, the Chases considered various options such as a nursing home and a housekeeper, but decided to bring her to their home because she lived too far away for them to manage her care effectively.

A career woman

Mrs. Chase had been married for five years when her mother-in-law joined the household. She holds a master's degree in computer science, had enjoyed a successful career for 10 years, and had continued to work, taking her two children to a babysitter during the day. She had stopped working eight months prior to the interview. At that time, she was pregnant with her third child, who is now three months old.

The career is interrupted

When Mrs. Chase stopped working, she became a full-time caregiver to her own children and to her mother-in-law, who could no longer stay alone in the house. Mrs. Chase is thoughtful and candid about her decision to quit her job. She said, "I would not have quit just to take care of my mother-in-law, but I could do it for my kids. It's not like I turned my back on my career. I'm still doing some consulting, and I'll work again eventually." Another factor determining her decision was that she had been passed over for a promotion she had earned and for which she was well qualified. A man had received the promotion. Mrs. Chase feels that her pregnancies and caregiving responsibilities made the male employee more desirable in the eyes of her employer.

Behavioral symptoms

Mrs. Chase does all the household and childcare tasks. She gives her mother-in-law her medicines, washes her hair, and takes her on all errands such as grocery shopping. Mr. Chase manages his mother's money. The mother's behavioral symptoms are getting worse. She put paper on the stove when it was lit and hides her money. Her personal hygiene is poor, and she has an unpleasant odor.

Mental health "being challenged"

Off-time and on-time

Mrs. Chase has been trying hard. She says she is not normally a nervous person and even now knows how to set priorities. She does what has to be done first. However, the situation is wearing her out mentally; she is often upset and occasionally depressed, feels emotionally drained and overwhelmed. She says, with humor that her mental health is okay, but "it's being challenged." The family privacy has been "invaded," and Mrs. Chase is never alone with her husband and children. The couple cannot do certain things, but at the same time, Mrs. Chase says that the needs of her children and mother-in-law coincide in some ways—that is, in requiring a constant presence in the household. She thinks it might be worse for caregivers whose own children are grown. They would be deprived of the freedom to go out. However, Mrs. Chase says, "She is always with me." The Chases had to buy a larger car and are looking for a more spacious home.

Husband helps

There is no paid help except an occasional sitter. Mr. Chase cuts the grass and cooks Sunday dinner. The caregiver feels he is a great help psychologically. On one occasion, Mr. Chase's cousin took the mother-in-law for a two-week visit at the same time the latter's sister was visiting. It was "a great rest" for the Chases, but the cousin said, "Never again." Daycare is too costly. If the mother-in-law gets to the point of not even recognizing her family members, Mrs. Chase says nursing home placement will be made. Then, "It won't make any difference."

Making everyone happy

Mrs. Chase attributes her stress to her relationship with her mother-in-law and to the behavioral symptoms of Alzheimer's disease. Despite the many problems, Mrs. Chase feels that the positive side is that they are helping someone. "We're making her happy. That's a good feeling. It's a juggling act, a balancing act—to make everybody happy. You do what has to be done at the moment. It's crisis management, that's what it is." Her role as wife is constantly being "squeezed." It is a constant effort to find time with her husband.

The mother/son ties

Now she's the queen

She's sitting in my chair

Mrs. Chase is well aware of her own inner feelings and is candid in saying she is jealous of the bond between her mother-in-law and her husband. "When he comes in, he hands *her* the newspaper. He's a gentleman, and I was the queen of the house. Now *she's* the queen. At dinner, he serves her first. Even on my child's birthday, she got the first piece of cake. She's taken over. I know it's not rational. All of a sudden it's like the mother/son ties are there again. It makes me feel like he's not really married to me. I know it's not the case. But that's why having her here is so psychologically trying. We bought a new car because she couldn't get into the back seat in a two-door. The front seat was mine, and all of a sudden she was in my seat. I thought 'She's sitting in *my chair*.' I tell my husband 'She is not a full voting member of this family.' Decisions must be between my husband and me. She cannot be a third member of this adult family. She is here because she needs care or she wouldn't be here."

"I do what I should"

Mrs. Chase says: "I do what I should for her. I do for my children because I love them." She and her mother-in-law "got off on the wrong foot" because the older woman did not want her son to marry Mrs. Chase. "A parent should never do that. I think it's a big hurt. It's hard to get over. Maybe I'm beginning to get over it. It's a big struggle in my life. I try not to let her presence affect my relationship with my children. I don't let her discipline them, though she tries. I try not to let my feelings spill over onto the children. Once I was vacuuming the rug and she was sitting in a chair. When I approached the chair, she lifted her feet for the vacuum. I said, 'I'm not your servant.' I do it because I'm a human being and a Christian."

An appreciative husband

Mrs. Chase feels that her relationship with her husband has been strengthened by the caregiving. Her husband appreciates it. He knows that if he hadn't married her, he couldn't do it. "I try to give my mother-in-law respect because she is the mother of my husband. Maybe I could be more patient. I try to do my best. I could do better, and I could do worse." But sometimes she explodes. She understands that it is hard for Mr. Chase to see his mother going downhill. He thinks of her as she used to be. Mrs. Chase says, "It's a stress to see an intelligent parent degenerate."

It's different for a daughter-in-law

Mrs. Chase is thoughtful about how it is different for a daughter or a daughter-in-law. "There is less past baggage." In some ways, it is harder. "How much do you love her? Respect her? A daughter-in-law can be more detached, like running a nursing home." Mrs. Chase imitates a nurse's cheery voice saying, "Here's your medicine. Here's your juice." You wonder why this role is falling on me; I'm a professional women?" She answers her own question: "When you're growing up, you see your mother doing stuff, so you fall into that. Little boys learn from their dads. So that's the way it happens."

Women's role

Plans return to work

Mrs. Chase's plans for the future are to raise her children and go back to her career. "I hope my mother-in-law can live out the rest of her days with us, but I hope it's not 20 years." When asked if she has any advice for other women in her situation, she advises them to go to support group meetings, get whatever help they need, and try to be patient and understanding. "Rely on other people to get whatever you need in the way of emotional support." She tells the interviewer, "Even talking to you today has helped me. I read the article about the research, and I said 'This is me.' A lot of people are facing it. I've learned a good deal and can learn more. If I can help others, I want to and I thought it could help me."

Mrs. Chase was open in her description of her problems and acutely, even painfully, aware of her own inner feelings—feelings that arise to some degree in most daughters-in-law—the underlying struggle between mother and wife for primacy with the son/husband. Such competition often begins early in the relationship. Mrs. Chase also states clearly one of the main differences between caregiving daughters and caregiving daughters-in-law—namely, the quality of the emotional investment and problems, but says she does not carry the "emotional baggage" into the situation that a daughter might.

Though she is highly educated and espouses the new views of women's roles with respect to employment, Mrs. Chase does not challenge the notion that she should do the day-to-day care. She states that she became the caregiver because she is a woman and was socialized into the caregiving role. Her husband was an only child, so there were no siblings to step in or to share. She sees it as her role not only to provide the actual care, but (as daughters do) to make her mother-in-law happy.

Like some other working women, Mrs. Chase quit her job due to a combination of circumstances that included the need to care for an elderly person. She and her husband share the parent-care tasks in traditional "gender-appropriate" ways. Mrs. Chase does the actual care, whereas he manages the money. She is grateful to her husband for helping. He cuts the grass and cooks Sunday dinner.

The difficulties of caring for an Alzheimer's patient are well described—the distressing behavior, poor hygiene, and the need for constant surveillance. Yet, like many daughters, Mrs. Chase says she will not consider nursing home placement until the older woman no longer recognizes family members.

In caring for an elderly person while there are also preschool children in the family, Mrs. Chase is "off time" (see chapter 9). She points out, however, that there is an on-time aspect to the situation in that the lifestyle restrictions attendant on caring for the young children are similar to those of caring for the older person.

Mrs. Chase experiences and describes the negative emotional and lifestyle effects of caregiving that are shared by many caregivers. Nevertheless, like so many women, she sees her role as going beyond caregiving to making people happy. She also expresses the gratification derived from helping someone and living up to one's religious beliefs.

On a practical level, it is apparent that Mrs. Chase could use services such as respite care and case management, particularly since her mother-in-law's condition will inevitably worsen.

Mrs. Blum: Empty Nest Refilled With Old And Young

The empty nest refilled with young and old

Mrs. Blum, age 58, works part time as a substitute teacher in a private school. Her husband, a college professor, is semi-retired due to three heart attacks and open heart surgery. Mrs. Blum says, "We were an empty nest, and now we're filled." Living in the household are her mother-in-law and two of the Blum's grown daughters. A son has moved out, but both daughters returned home after completing graduate school and are looking for jobs.

Suddenly a new person is in their home

Mr. Blum is now the only child. His mother moved in three months ago when her other son, in whose home she had lived for 32 years, died after a short illness. The widowed daughter-in-law immediately said she could no longer keep her mother-in-law in her home. With her husband gone, she felt she no longer had an obligation, and the Blums had to make room for the elderly woman. "Suddenly, there's a new person in the household," says Mrs. Blum. She was devastated and is deeply angry. Her own widowed father had died one month previously at age 92, but he had been fiercely independent and was still living alone. Mrs. Blum contrasts her father with her very dependent mother-in-law.

Symptoms of mental decline

The elderly woman is extremely depressed due to her son's death, eats very little, is losing weight rapidly, and is "losing her faculties." Mrs. Blum too is depressed. "Our whole life has been disrupted." The mother-in-law hides things, accuses her granddaughters of taking her possessions, is very forgetful, lives in the past, and only gets bits and pieces of what people say to her. She turns night into day, and her personal hygiene is poor. The granddaughters try to give her emotional support.

A difficult adjustment

The change in the mother-in-law has been dramatic since her son's death. She had memory loss before, but in her familiar environment she had bustled about doing the cooking and household tasks. Now, the Blums have to see to it that she eats something.

The mother-in-law had always been a controlling person and still is. She doesn't like Mr. and Mrs. Blum to go out, and if they do she stands at the window and watches for them. She forgets to eat. The Blums have absolutely no privacy and have to make sure there is someone at home at all times. They can't travel or take a short vacation. What makes matters worse is Mr. Blum's attentiveness to his mother. He sits with her even after his wife has gone up to bed.

One kitchen, two women

When the mother-in-law first moved in, she tried to continue the pattern of living developed when she lived with her other son and daughter-in-law. Then, she had done all the shopping and cooking. Here she wanted to make her son's breakfast, and Mrs. Blum had to make it clear that it was *her* kitchen. At times, Mrs. Blum tries to let her help with cooking, but it doesn't work because the older woman criticizes the daughter-in-law's style of food preparation. She does let her set the table and help with the dishes, but all of these readjustments are very hard.

Mrs. Blum has colitis and gets very upset. She tries to "detach" herself from too much involvement with her mother-in-law. She is always worried about her husband and had been hoping for a few peaceful years. She was deeply devoted to her own father, was very proud of him, and is grieving profoundly about his death.

An old-fashioned woman

Mrs. Blum thought of day care, but her mother-in-law would not accept it. The older woman's whole life had been housework and family. "She's very old-fashioned and was never involved in activities outside the home. She's a relic," says Mrs. Blum. "Women nowadays are different." She points out that her sister-in-law, whose widowhood occurred at the same age as the mother-in-law's, did not move in with her son and try to control the household. Rather, the new widow is trying to make a new life—taking courses, traveling, working part-time, and going to exercise class.

"I never expected this"

"I never ever expected this," Mrs. Blum says. "My father would never have moved here. When my mother was ill, we had nurses and my sisters came in from out of town, but most of it fell on me. My parents had cared for their parents, but my parents always said they would never do that to their children."

Work as respite

Mrs. Blum gets tired, is depressed and very angry, and doesn't sleep well, but working is a great help to her. So far, the mother-in-law can stay alone for a few hours during the day, but "we are keeping our fingers crossed." Mrs. Blum is resentful because she has her mother-in-law to care for, particularly because her husband had never been very willing to help her parents, who needed very little. Mr. Blum is, however, trying to share his mother's care by taking her to the doctor and supervising her medications. Nursing home placement would be a last resort.

Women have to be everything to everybody

The Blums are again involved in many lives—not only because of the mother-in-law, but also because of the daughters who returned home. Mrs. Blum had thought that once her three children had finished college, it would be a time for herself and her husband. "Women have to be everything to everybody," she says. She adds wistfully that she likes to take courses and learn and had tried very hard to be independent. But women of her generation, she says, were not encouraged to be independent, but rather to be appendages of their husbands. It has been a struggle for her to achieve some feeling of being her own person.

Different lifestyles

The lifestyles of mother and daughter-in-law are very different. To the older woman, "You're not a woman unless you are married." She was interested only in home and family. Mrs. Blum always went to school, took courses, and wanted to work.

"I'm a woman of the '50s and we're living in the '80s. In my generation, the woman took care of the children, and you were the woman behind the man. You helped your husband in his work. But I got cabin fever. After I had my children, I just had to get out, and I went back to work. I was home when the children got home from school. The money helped to educate the children, to do special things, and to build up my social security. She feels that she and her husband have "paid their dues" by raising their children and so on. "That's life."

Blood is thicker than water

Mrs. Blum had given personal care to her own parents and would do it for her mother-in-law if it became necessary, but says she would be resentful. It would be a struggle. "Blood is thicker than water. We're friends, but we're not deep close buddies. Superficial."

Pulled between wife and mother

The Blums worry about the future, particularly if the mother-in-law should get worse. Mr. Blum feels the pressure, his wife says. It has caused some marital problems. There is a pull between his mother and his wife. Mrs. Blum's work has been affected. She calls home to see if the older woman is all right, but can't get a straight answer about what's going on.

Mrs. Blum says, "I see myself in her. That's what will happen to us if we live long enough." It is very painful to Mr. Blum to see his formerly strong mother age and decline. Mrs. Blum tries to escape the situation by going to her own room to read or by going out for a while. The whole family is trying hard. She hopes taking care of the elderly woman means that her husband will never have to feel guilty.

The story of my life

"Caregiving is the story of my life," Mrs. Blum says. "Maybe women have a nurturing instinct." She advises women in her situation to try to take time out for themselves. "Women of today understand that better than we did. We weren't allowed to have careers." She hopes this research in which she is participating will help to do something about the plight of women.

Again, in the Blum situation, the theme of competition between mother-in-law and daughter-in-law is apparent. Mrs. Blum asserts her own control over the kitchen, but her husband stays with his mother after the wife goes to bed. Mr. Blum is another man in the middle.

The daughter-in-law describes the pull of different values in her life very clearly, and she contrasts herself with her mother-in-law. The older woman's whole life was household and children, whereas the younger woman had tried to educate and assert herself. She is caught between the "old" traditional values and the new values about women's lifestyles. Though angry about it, she lives her life largely in conformance to the old values.

The Blums' situation also illustrates the predicament of many middle-generation couples nowadays whose nests have been refilled with their young adult children as well as with an elderly person.

Although the daughters-in-law in the situations described so far were articulate in expressing whatever anger, resentment, and upset they felt, the two women whose stories will be told below do not appear to protest their situations. These two women differ from the others, too, in that their husbands have siblings, but they are the main caregivers to their mothers-in-law nonetheless. The reasons for their assumption of that responsibility are very different, however.

Mrs. Parker: "I Have a 40-Year-Old Retarded Son and a 94-Year-Old Teenage Daughter"

A career of caregiving

Sixty-four-year-old Mrs. Parker has had a long caregiving career. Married for 45 years, she has cared for many people simultaneously and sequentially. For all of his life, she has taken care of her retarded son, who is now 40 years old. The Parkers also have a normal 30-year-old son who is now on his own. The retarded son goes to a day-time "workshop," but he cannot read or write. He requires direction to dress and bathe himself, and needs skin care and supervision of his diet.

A retarded son

Twenty years ago, when her father-in-law died, Mrs. Parker's mother-in-law moved into the Parker home. The two grandsons had to share a room in order to accommodate her. In the past few years, the older woman has needed more care because of a variety of chronic and acute ailments. During the same period, Mr. Parker had several bad heart attacks, and his wife quit her job to care for him. "It was too much," she says, "with three people to care for." She misses her job. "I could turn off things that happened in the house when I went to work. Now I can only turn off when I go to market."

Mother-in-law moved in

Husband has heart attacks

The elderly mother-in-law is very demanding and critical. "The emotional strain is the worse part of it," says Mrs. Parker. "After all, I married my husband, not my mother-in-law." Her mother-

A demanding mother-in-law

in-law doesn't hesitate to speak her mind. "She has a heart as big as an elephant and a mouth to match." The older woman complains about the house and the neighborhood. The family would like to move, but it would mean a year's waiting list for the son to get into a workshop in the new catchment area. The mother-in-law wants the family to have a fancier car, she complained bitterly because the dress she wore to a family wedding was not the most expensive one there, and her main worry is what to wear and how she looks. "I have a 94-year-old teenage daughter," says Mrs. Parker. The older woman refuses all nonfamily services—even transportation. She came from an affluent and sophisticated family. Mrs. Parker stands in awe of that background as she herself came from an immigrant family.

One person does the most

No vacation

The mother-in-law tries to control everything. "It's competition," says Mrs. Parker. "It's always been that way, but it was better when she could go out by herself and I was working. My husband shares that now that he's retired. His brothers take no responsibility. I guess it's that way in most families. One person does the most." Mrs. Parker says jokingly, "There's not much I can do except run away." She and her husband would like to take a short vacation, even a weekend, she says wistfully, but the mother-in-law would "sabotage" it. "Ten years ago, we had a two-week vacation. My younger son was there at night, and my brother-in-law during the day. It was wonderful. But my mother-in-law wouldn't let it happen now. I guess I resent it. She has a lot of fears and is afraid to be left alone. She keeps us from going out."

Restricted lives

Mrs. Parker became caregiver to her mother-in-law, she says, because her husband had always assumed responsibility in his family, though he has two older brothers who are now in their 70s. Also, Mrs. Parker's own family was a close one and had a tradition of caring for older people in the home. She thinks her brothers-in-law should help more. The Parkers can't go out at night unless their younger son comes to stay or they take the older son and mother-in-law with them. Their social life is virtually nonexistent and their budget squeezed. As for privacy, Mrs. Parker asks, "What privacy?" She says sadly that her own father went to live in Senior Housing because she had no room for him. He would have been easier to have in the home than her mother-in-law is. "He wouldn't interfere."

Competition

Mr. Parker has always shared equally in caring for their son. There was mutual support. But there are things he can't do for his mother. He is often torn between his wife and mother, but takes his wife's part when his mother is critical. "It's more stressful for him," says his wife.

"It could be worse"

Mrs. Parker tries to be philosophical. She wishes she could have a little time for herself. Even a whole day. "I'm getting older, and I have more responsibility than ever. But I know people worse off," she says, "I know single parents who have retarded children."

What will happen to our son?

"It's lucky we have a good marriage. This caregiving. That's my life. I read. That's my outlet. But what would I do if my husband should die before my mother-in-law? What will happen to our son when we're not here?"

The Parkers are caring for two disabled people of different generations simultaneously—their son and Mr. Parker's mother. The poignancy of the Parkers' worry about the future of their son need not be underlined. That worry is shared by all such parents. Mrs. Parker's story illustrates a situation that is growing more and more common as more developmentally disabled people have been enabled to live longer lives. It is not unusual nowadays, for example, to see elderly women even in their 80s still caring for their "children." The prevalence of "double dependency" situation such as that of the Parkers is not known, but a clue is provided in a study done by Soldo and Myllyluoma (1983). They found that when an older couple lived with others in caregiving households, approximately one in nine of the caregivers provided assistance to two or more disabled persons, one of whom is an elderly person and the other most often being an impaired adult child of the older couple.

The Parkers' lives and experiences reflect many of the themes already described: the caregiving careers many women have, the difficulties of shared households, employment as respite for caregivers, the struggle for control between daughter-in-law and mother-in-law with the husband/son caught in the middle, and the family's severe lifestyle restrictions.

The sadness of the Parkers' story is overwhelming. But surely it could be alleviated, if only a little, if they could they could obtain some respite and if the mental health system permitted the family to move without having the retarded son wait for a year in the new catchment areas until he could attend the "workshop." An overarching question, of course, is why Mrs. Parker permits her mother-in-law to control her life. The mother-in-law doesn't let them go out, doesn't let them take a vacation, and refuses Senior Citizen's transportation. Mrs. Parker allows that to happen. Her only respite is going to market; her only outlet is reading. She jokes about running away, but continues on without even the day off for which she longs.

Mrs. Cohen: "It's Like A Cloud Over Our Heads"

A mother and a mother-in-law need help

At age 62, Mrs. Cohen has an 83-year-old mother and an 89-year-old mother-in-law, both in need of help. Her mother is in a care facility following a hospitalization, and it is not known whether she will be able to return to independent living. The mother-in-law lives in senior housing, and Mrs. Cohen wants her to go to a nursing home, but the mother-in-law refuses. Though she provides very little help to her mother-in-law, Mrs. Cohen defines herself as caregiver because her husband's only brother had died. Thus, there is no other woman in the picture. As for help with caring for her own mother, her two sisters live too far away.

According to Mrs. Cohen, she and her husband agree on issues concerning both mothers, but are now "obsessed" with the problems. "It's all we talk about. It's like a cloud over our heads." The couple's sons are grown and out of the house, but Mrs. Cohen's small business is being neglected.

A rejecting mother-in-law

Mrs. Cohen describes her mother-in-law as controlling, domineering, unpleasant, and rejecting. She had not wanted her son to marry Mrs. Cohen. Mrs. Cohen's intense dislike of her mother-in-law was readily apparent. She attributes the strains she and her husband are experiencing to her mother-in-law, not to her mother. The mother appreciates the things done for her, but the mother-in-law does not. The latter had lived with the Cohens for one year many years ago, but it was an impossible situation. The day after she moved out, Mr. Cohen had a heart attack. It happened on Mother's Day.

A heart attack on Mother's Day

"It has taken my husband away"

Mrs. Cohen's severe strains do not relate to providing instrumental help to her mother-in-law, since it is Mr. Cohen who helps his mother with shopping and anything else she needs. However, Mrs. Cohen resents the situation. "It has taken my husband away" and "She treats me like I'm an outsider." She attributes her very frequent fatigue and resentment to her mother-in-law (only occasionally do such feelings arise because of her own mother, and they are mild) as well as her frequent feelings of frustration, being emotionally drained, and overwhelmed. Another clue to her feelings is her description of her own mother as being acquiescent, whereas her mother-in-law refuses to be controlled in any way. Mr. Cohen has become seriously depressed and appears to be caught in the middle between two strong women.

Like Mrs. Chase and Mrs. Austin, Mrs. Cohen's husband has no sister to assume responsibility, nor is there another daughter-in-law. Because

Mrs. Cohen has both a disabled mother and a disabled mother-in-law, she highlights some of the qualitative differences in those relationships. She is actively and openly hostile to her mother-in-law, attributing all problems to the latter's personality and behavior. The "externals" of care are also different for Mrs. Cohen and the daughters-in-law in the first two cases in that Mrs. Cohen is providing virtually no instrumental help or personal care to either mother. Yet Mrs. Cohen reports experiencing much more stress. The theme of competition with her mother-in-law for her husband is strong, and Mrs. Cohen's feelings about her mother-in-law combine with her inability to control the older woman to result in fury and frustration. Mr. Cohen too is showing signs of severe stress. He has become a man in the middle between his wife and his mother.

Mrs. Austin: "Women Like Me Are Dinosaurs"

Stopped working

Now 48 years old, Mrs. Austin had worked as a young woman, but stopped 25 years ago when she married. She then worked as her husband's unpaid secretary and bookkeeper, putting in more than 40 hours weekly. Her career caring for her parents-in-law had begun 15 years previously. Mrs. Austin stopped working 4 years ago because by then the elderly couple needed so much attention.

A long siege with two parents-in-law

Mrs. Austin says it's been a "very long siege." Since Mr. Austin is an only child, there are no siblings to help with parent care. The parents-in-law lived a few minutes away from the Austins until the elderly man died 10 years ago. He had suffered from Alzheimer's disease and was violent. They often were called in the middle of the night to pick him up from various parts of the city. Eventually, he had to be tied to a chair. The family did not put him in a nursing home because they needed to conserve his funds for his wife.

Difficult behavior

Mrs. Austin's mother-in-law went to a retirement community after her husband died. The daughter-in-law used to take the elderly woman out several times a week, do her shopping and banking, and take her to the doctor. She spent several hours daily with the older woman. The mother-in-law entered a nursing home three months ago at age 87. She had been in the hospital, fell out of bed, suffered multiple fractures, and became mentally disturbed. The elderly woman then caused her son and daughter-in-law much anguish. She was verbally abusive to them, phoned them every few minutes, and also called her bank dozens of times accusing everyone of stealing her money. She called her son at work. "She'd have my husband weeping, and he was such a good son. She turned on him."

Mrs. Austin feels very angry about caring for her mother-in-law. Her husband is not as involved in helping his mother as he was in helping his father, and it is a terrible strain on the marriage.

"The woman is in the middle"

Mrs. Austin says, "The woman is in the middle, taking care of older people and children." She describes taking her mother-in-law for routine visits to the doctor and sitting for hours, and "all they do is take her blood pressure." My life revolves around my mother-in-law," she says. Taking the older woman to the dentist, podiatrist, and physicians consumed considerable time. She has read whole books while waiting in doctors' offices and had to learn to give her mother-in-law enemas. "There was no one else to do it." Mrs. Austin does an imitation of the doctor talking to her as though the older woman was not present. "He treated my mother-in-law like she was a jerk. She never complained, but it's degrading to an older woman. She wasn't deaf or blind. I felt angry. The doctor said to me 'Take her home and give her an enema.' It never occurred to him that I didn't know how and didn't want to. So I did it. The female gets the brunt of it."

A doctor's attitude

"My husband's an only child, so what's the alternative?" She says wryly, "My husband would take care of big things such as picking a doctor when she was hospitalized. He'd find the best hip surgeon around. My job was going to the supermarket, buying her stockings—the dirt work, the day-to-day stuff. They presume because you're a woman, there's no reason why you can't do it."

The dirt work

"My mother-in-law was never satisfied. I made sure she had the right shoes, that there were no cords for her to trip over. Nothing was quite good enough no matter how hard we tried. There were days I could strangle her and days when I felt so sorry for her I would weep."

Nothing was good enough

The constant stress caused marital problems. "It wears you down. You get nuts." As for why she did it, she says, "Someone has to do it, and he can't. What are you going to do? I felt trapped. My husband tried a little harder to do things for her, and I tried to stop feeling martyred and to make a positive thing of it. I'd take her out to lunch to make it pleasant when I had to be with her. I made him take her to the doctor sometimes. But there's no way out. It's part of the deal when you get married."

Trapped

Mrs. Austin's own parents died young. "I don't know how I would have managed four old people." This has been her only experience with old people. "At least with a two-year-old, you

Not like child care

put them down for a nap and they wake up better. We probably spent more time caring for them than for our children. Children grow up and become less dependent on you. It's different with children."

"She's my husband's mother"

The two women had always gotten along well on a superficial level. "We were civil. We never had words, but I don't feel toward her like she was my mother. She's my husband's mother. But crying for a mother-in-law is not like caring for a mother. "It's different with your mother just because she's your mother. It's a bond. She's been a very good loving grandmother to my children. They're very attentive to her."

Then the mother-in-law became calmer but was living in the past. She wanted her mother, who's been dead for 70 years. When told her mother's dead, she wept and said, "Where was I when it happened?"

Then, very recently, the mother-in-law died. "It's been bad," says Mrs. Austin, "but I'm starting to heal. I have no one to take care of for the first time in my life. There's no one sucking at me. I don't even want to take care of a goldfish. I feel liberated.

Hard for older people

"It was hard on me. I'm not the nurse type, but I had to give her enemas." Mrs. Austin empathizes with old people. "It must be awful to have to rely on another person for everything."

"It's my turn"

Mrs. Austin referred to her stage of life and sums things up. "In a way, I'm lucky. It's over. Now it's my turn. Most women are older when they do this. I did it because it was expected of me. She was my husband's mother. I like me. I did a good job. I tried. I'm a better person for it. I really did it for him [her husband]. I couldn't have done anything more."

Look for help

She advises other women in her situation to try not to feel martyred by it and to maintain a sense of humor. "Look for help! That's important. There must be something out there to help. Services. Facilities." She and her husband recently had a big conversation. They want to make the most of the years they have left. For the first time ever, Mr. and Mrs. Austin have no one else living in their home. Their children are out of the nest. "It's made us sit back and say, 'Let's change our lives. Our responsibilities are over. Let's not keep the pace up.' He's worn out.

People don't know

"I think I'm the last generation of women available. Women like me are becoming dinosaurs," said Mrs. Austin. She tells the young interviewer, "Your generation of women won't do it because you're working." She responded to the call for research participants because "I saw the little thing in the paper, and I thought 'My God. There are other people out there like me.' Maybe people can learn from this. People don't know."

In saying that women like herself are dinosaurs, Mrs. Austin is referring to women's changing lifestyles, in particular their participation in the labor force and the increased assertiveness associated with the Women's Movement. She is also expressing her deep resentment and anger at how totally her life and her husband's life had been disrupted by care of the elderly in-laws—feelings that are more intense because it is not her own parents for whom the care was provided. She points out that the bond is different when it's your own mother. She did it not because of her own indebtedness to her in-laws but for her husband. "It's part of the deal when you get married."

Like so many other women—daughters and daughters-in-law—Mrs. Austin has had a "long siege," a career of caregiving to more than one older person. The disturbed and disturbing behavior of both parents-in-law undoubtedly intensified the stress. Like other caregivers, she advises people like herself to look for help. "There must be something out there."

Mrs. Austin's critique of the doctor's attitude was pointed and caustic. He not only talked about the mother-in-law as though she were not in the room, but was totally insensitive to the caregiver's feelings and needs. Despite her anger, she did what he ordered. She is rebelling against the traditional gender-role assignment, and her anger no doubt is due (at least in part) to her own compliance with injustice.

Mrs. De Lisi: "I Would Like To Be Able To Take a Walk"

"I was here"

At age 48, Mrs. De Lisi provides her 95-year-old mother-in-law with virtually total care. Mrs. De Lisi had moved into her parents-in-law's household as a bride. Her husband had fallen in love with her photograph, shown to him by a cousin, and went to Italy to marry her and bring her to the United States. The elderly woman's other sons and her daughter had already married and moved out of the parental home. The De Lisi's have three sons (young adults) still at home. Asked how it happened that she became the main caregiver, the daughter-in-law replied simply, "I was here."

A good marriage

Though the other siblings do nothing to help with caregiving, Mrs. De Lisi is uncomplaining. "I do not hold it against them." She voices no resentment and appears to accept her role as caregiver. It had never occurred to her to work outside the home. The De Lisis are devoted to one another. Mrs. De Lisi speaks of her husband lovingly and describes with appreciation his willing help around the house and with his mother's care.

This is the way it should be

This daughter-in-law does not make any effort to change her situation. "This is the way it should be. Its just something that you do." In her view, this is the role she should play. When asked directly, she admits to feeling very tired and having some emotional symptoms. She attributes her "nervous stomach" to the caregiving situation and says she gets hurt "real easily" when criticized by her unappreciative mother-in-law. She and her husband can't go out in the evening, but their friends visit them, and she has "a bunch of rain checks." The only time there is any respite is when they get a sitter for a truly important occasion such as when a son was graduated from college.

"I'd like to take a walk"

What would Mrs. De Lisi want for herself? She thinks for a minute and then says, "I would like to be able to take a walk once in a while." As for the future, she says wistfully that she'd like to visit her family in Italy.

A critical mother-in-law

Mrs. De Lisi thinks it might be easier to take care of her own mother. The mother-in-law is critical of her at times, and the older woman is very different with her own daughter. Mrs. De Lisi can't feel close to her mother-in-law though she had been close to her father-in-law before he died. "He was more modern." She feels her caregiving is made possible because she and her husband have such a loving relationship.

Mrs. De Lisi advises others in her situation to "have a ton of patience" and to "keep in mind that you'll get old someday, and you'll want someone to do for you what you did for her. They suffer so much to bring you up, you have to repay them. You never really can repay."

In Mrs. De Lisi's culture, sons (therefore, daughters-in-law) are often groomed to take the responsibility for parents. She does not protest. Women like Mrs. De Lisi probably will not disappear from the scene in the near future because of the large immigration into the United States of people from Asian and Hispanic countries who have similar values about women's roles and care of the elderly. Though accepting of her role, Mrs. De Lisi pays for her passivity with her "nervous stomach." Her low expectations of what she herself could do to fulfill her own needs epitomize the low expectations so many women hold: "I would like to be able to take a walk once in a while." The theme of repayment of care from one generation to another appears, but on the collective level—"You have to repay *them*"—

rather than on the personal level, as with the daughters who say "It's my turn to care for *her*."

Mrs. Holden: "I'm Not Really Passive"

Trays to three elderly in-laws

"I've watched trays go up and down the steps to the third floor for 35 years," says Mr. Holden sadly while the interviewer is waiting to see his wife. Mrs. Holden is upstairs bringing a tray to her mother-in-law, age 95. When she comes down, Mrs. Holden describes her caregiving history in a matter of fact way. As a young couple, the Holdens moved into the parents-in-law's home with their one-year-old baby. Mr. Holden's sister had recently married and moved out. Mr. Holden had been in the Navy during World War II, and when he was discharged he and his wife came home to help care for his disabled grandfather. Before the elderly man died, his grandmother had a bad stroke and needed care and was on the third floor for three years until her death. Then, Mrs. Holden's mother-in-law, the current recipient of the trays, became ill. For two years, she was in a coma from an undiagnosed illness, and her devoted daughter-in-law worked hard day and night to bring her back. A miracle happened. She had been "really out of it," and then she got her mind back.

A career in caregiving

During her caregiving career, Mrs. Holden gave birth to a second daughter. (Both are now married.) Over the years, Mrs. Holden moved into and out of the workforce (she is a stenotypist) as the care needs of the various family members dictated. She finally retired two years ago when her mother-in-law could not be left alone at all

Into and out of the labor force

Mrs. Holden does not complain. "It all worked out well," she said several times. "We never lacked for a babysitter, and the old people enjoyed the children. No problems." Her mother-in-law is "great fun to be with," she says, though the older woman does get upset and nervous, and she's harder to take care of when she's not feeling well. Mr. Holden, who had been listening to the interview from another room, has another opinion. "She wants to be waited on hand and foot," he says of his mother.

"No problems"

Mrs. Holden praised the help her husband gives her. He rigged up buzzers so that his wife could respond whenever his mother needed her. "It's real handy," Mrs. Holden said. She also praises her sister-in-law for keeping her mother supplied with books from the library. "She never ever forgets and brings the same one again," Mrs. Holden said admiringly.

It all works out

I'm not passive

"I don't mean that I'm passive," Mrs. Holden repeats, "It all works out." She tells of a time when she asserted herself. She wanted to go to her own daughter who was having a baby, so her sister-in-law came to stay temporarily. But "things were a mess" when she returned.

The day after the interview, Mrs. Holden phoned the interviewer to emphasize the fact that she's not really passive.

Mrs. Holden, who is providing total care for her mother-in-law and had done so for two grandparents-in-law as well, is deeply appreciative of her husband's help in caring for his three elderly relatives. She tells herself and others "It's all worked out." Why, then, does she need to reiterate, "I'm not passive"?

A COMMENT ON CAREGIVING DAUGHTERS-IN-LAW

In some ways, the reactions of daughters-in-law to care of the elderly parent-in-law resemble those of daughters to their mothers. The two groups of women react to the pressure with similar emotional symptoms, and many strive to make the older people "happy." The women also have in common their awareness of their stages of life during the parent care years. Some daughters-in-law as well as some daughters (and their husbands) still enact the "traditional" gender assignment of roles, despite the "new" roles enacted by many women nowadays. And both groups are grateful to their husbands for any help they receive in caregiving. The daughters-in-law are appreciative even when the older person involved is the husband's mother.

The stress on women who care for their mothers-in-law (particularly when they live in the same households) appears to have several unique sources, however. The competition between the two women for the man they share may be minimal or fierce, but has potential for strain. There is more than a hint in the stories of the daughters-in-law of the strains their husbands experience even though their wives do most of the parent-care work. Certainly, as the case studies showed, the emotional ties to a mother have much deeper roots than the bonds to a mother-in-law, and there is a genetic link to a mother. Although daughters often feel that they should reciprocate the care their mothers gave to them in childhood (see Chapter 7), daughters-in-law have no such histories with their husbands' mothers.

Some daughters-in-law are deeply angry at finding themselves in the caregiving situations. And, given the fact that they provide care as a matter of obligation, they may also be harboring resentment against their husbands for expecting it of them. At the same time, some of them do it to earn their husbands' appreciation. Some express their anger, whereas others seem to accept their situations passively as "the way it should be." What is striking is that even the women who are explicitly angry provide care for their parents-in-law. They complain of their own severe problems, of the disruption of their marriages, lifestyles, and personal ambitions, and comment that they are "dinosaurs." But they do it nonetheless.

The women who responded to the research call for participants are, of course, the ones who did assume the caregiving role. Information is simply not available at present about daughters-in-law who do not do so. Obtaining such information is another item on the agenda for research exploration.

Chapter 13

Commentary on the Marital Status Case Studies

The themes described in Chapter 7 were played out in the lives of the women who told their stories in the case studies of women who occupy different marital statuses. The full impact of the demographic changes was seen, as many of the daughters and daughters-in-law enacted long careers of caregiving, often to several older people in their families. Most suffered negative effects on their own well-being and put themselves at the bottom of their priority lists as they tried to meet the needs of all the people in their families. The women often articulated their sense that parent care was "off-time" in their lives—they were too young or too old, or had envisioned their middle years differently. Some of those whose nests had been emptied found those nests refilled with elderly parents, and sometimes refilled as well with their children who had grown, left the nest, but then returned to the parental home. Also illustrated were nests that contained both young and old because the caregiver had a developmentally disabled adult child. The compelling force exerted by the value that care of the elderly is a woman's responsibility often drove out the new values about women's roles. Some of the women, for example, even gave up their own opportunities and jobs that they needed or enjoyed when work and parent care competed. (This will be further illustrated and discussed in detail in Chapter 14.)

Those and additional themes in the lives of parent-caring women appeared in the case studies. It was apparent that older people themselves and other people in the family know intuitively and from experience who is accessible for the role of primary caregiver, whatever the reasons may be. (Listening to the subjective experiences of those adult children who do not become the primary caregivers is another item on the research agenda of the unfinished business of parent care.) Potent influences in either producing strain or easing the situation for the caregiving women are the quality of their long-standing relationships with the dependent older person and the latter's personality. When the older person was appreciative, accepting of her care needs, and considerate of the caregiver and her family, the strains of the daughters and daughters-in-law were eased. But women went on providing the needed help even for parents or parents-in-law who were controlling and critical or with whom relationships were problematic historically. Some caregivers yielded when the older people refused to accept any help from other members of the family or from nonfamily sources. In such cases, the elderly parent or parent-in-law held the psychological balance of power.

Some of the cases of difficult older people offer an important reminder. Specifically, functional deficits (in ADL and IADL) are not the only conditions that cause strain and disruption. Alzheimer's disease has been receiving considerable attention in that respect—and rightfully so. But other mental, emotional, or both problems of elderly care-recipients have been relatively under-attended. Look, for example, at the Carters' situation. Though functionally capable (she would not have been counted in the NLTC Survey), the older woman has produced total chaos in the family, with severe emotional problems occurring in each of the three generations in the household. And what of the problems in another of the case histories when the daughter, her husband, and their guests are chatting on the porch and the elderly mother actually locks them out of their own house? The studies cited in Chapter 3 are clear in pointing to such disturbed behavior as a powerful source of strain. And those seminal studies in the U.K. (e.g., Sainsbury & Grad de Alercon, 1970) were unequivocal in their documentation of the burden on the family. But for some reason, the problems have not been given their due as have problems caused by functionally disabled and Alzheimer's patients.

The impact of the caregiving situation on all members of the family was described graphically by the women. Their husbands, children, siblings, and even more distant relations affected and were affected by the caregiving process. Not only were the historical relationships between parent and daughter recapitulated and elaborated, but also those among siblings, and between the daughter and her own family members. The women showed the double pull of their own nuclear families on the one hand and the families of origin from whence they had moved developmentally. In this, they were "in the middle" in still another sense of that phrase.

One of the potent inner experiences of the women was their wish to provide care for their parents and parents-in-law and to make them happy—a wish that exited side by side with strong negative feelings as well, which, in turn, contributed to their feelings of guilt. Daughters had long-standing, enduring bonds with their parents, for example, but at the same time may have wished to be free of their crushing burdens. Ties between daughters-in-law and their elderly in-laws began later in the women's lives, and initial attitudes of their parents-in-law towards them when they first entered the family colored their feelings even many years later. Though the nature of the bonds was quite different from mother/daughter ties, positive and negative emotions existed side by side in daughters-in-law too—dislike and compassion, for example, and resentment and a sense of obligation.

The sense of obligation and duty took another form as well—that of reciprocity in parent care between husbands and wives. Some daughters caring for one of their own parents pointed out that they had helped their husbands' mothers in the past or might need to do so in the future. Similarly, some daughters-in-law felt that they were reciprocating for help to their parents that their husbands had given or would be expected to give in the future. Many marital partners apparently see helping each other's parents as an unspoken part of the marriage contract.

A central and major theme that emerged clearly is the social support women have or that is lacking during their parent-care years. Some have rich networks of family members—husbands, children, grandchildren, siblings, and other relatives as well. At the other extreme are those who quite literally have no one—who are not married, who are childless, who are "only" children, and who have no other relatives.

Some of the problems and rewards women experience derive from the composition of their families. Those with many relatives often received much emotional and instrumental support; some also may have had a unique source of stress due to family conflict and a sense of inequity in caregiving. Women without husbands and children did not have the feeling that they were being pulled by competing responsibilities, but felt lonely and alone, feelings that were especially intense when they were also without siblings.

Regardless of the quality of their relationships with siblings, women who do have sisters or brothers seem to have some sense of security about their parents. Such daughters do not ask, "Who will take care of my parent if something happens to me?" There may be severe problems in sibling relationships, or the siblings may be emotionally or geographically distant from the parent and virtually uninvolved in providing instrumental help, but at some level the primary caregiver knows that if something should happen to her, in most cases her sibling(s) would not abandon the frail elderly parent.

In a similar vein, women who have children know that the latter would not abandon their grandparent(s). Indeed, even other relatives—aunts and uncles (the elderly siblings of the elderly parents), nieces, nephews, and children-in-law—behave with a sense of family responsibility when there is no adult child in the picture. The amount and type of help they would provide in the eventuality that "something" happened to the daughter probably would be much less extensive and intensive than that given by women in the middle, but they would see to it that the older person did not go without care. (The experiences of those relatives in care of the elderly is another item on the unfinished agenda of research about caregiving.)

When, in addition to the lack of potential caregivers for the elderly parent, the women are childless and therefore have no potential caregivers for themselves, still another theme appeared: "Who will take care of me when I am old?"

The challenge is to understand the problems unique to each caregiver and to each family situation and to design appropriate interventions. The needs of the large, but conflicted family, for example, differ in many ways from the needs of daughters who are all alone.

At the least, the case studies justify two conclusions about family support in caring for the elderly. First, they bear out the implicit assumption daughters make that other family members will come forward to help if need be. The sense of family responsibility is powerful indeed, and those relatives constitute a backup system of care.

Second, there is no question but that parent-caring women need and want social support. Those who have family support are aware of their need and are deeply appreciative when it is forthcoming. Husbands head the list of those family supports. Those men are the ones closest to their wives' situations and the ones whose lives are most directly affected by the women's care of the elderly people. They are their wives' "stabilizers" or "balancing points," who actually help with care of their in-laws and to whom the women "can say anything." One cannot help but be impressed by the efforts and contributions of so many sons-in-law. (An intriguing side light of that support is the extra help those men provide when they have retired from work.) At the same time, however, in some cases there are hints of the need for skilled exploration of the husband/wife interactions about the parent-care situation. For example, one daughter who is moving in the direction of nursing home placement for her mother laments "if only someone [the husband] would be more forceful with me"—that is, in encouraging placement. Why *does* he discourage placement while simultaneously complaining bitterly of the negative effects of parent care on his lifestyle?

Also important are those siblings who understand the primary caregivers' efforts and problems, who phone and visit, provide some instrumental help and respite at times, and share important decisions. Still another source of social support comes from grandchildren who "sit" with their grandparents to let their parents go out occasionally, who take their grandparents to their homes for a weekend once in a while to give the caregiver respite or when there is illness in the family, who help with residential moves, and who are understanding about their mothers' problems.

The family supports of daughters-in-law include their husbands—the sons of the elderly people being cared for. The women are even grateful to those husbands for helping with care of the men's own parents. (Such is the depth of women's socialization to the nurturing role and the social, cultural, and religious values that exert powerful pressures in defining and keeping them in that role.)

The most poignant expression of the need for social support comes from the women who do not have it—who do not have anyone to meet that universal human need. Their deprivation is such that even a parent who cannot speak or whose Alzheimer's disease has progressed to the point that she doesn't recognize the daughter becomes a source of support. In the words of Lowenthal and Haven (1968), "the maintenance of closeness with another is the center of existence up to the very end of life" (p. 30).

Support of a different order comes from the "formal" system—the complex of organizations and agencies that provide entitlements for the older people and services designed to help them and their caregiving families. When they are available and are utilized, they ease the women's burdens. Unfortunately, however, as the case studies showed, obtaining entitlements is often confusing, even baffling. Services are not always available, available in timely fashion, affordable, or accessible, and not all caregivers know of their existence. Undoubtedly, readers were aware of instances in which supports were indicated—daycare, respite service, home care, nursing home care, and others that should be available in long-term care system.

Even when services are available, there are barriers to utilization such as the caregivers' reluctance to use their own and the older people's financial resources until they "really need it" (perhaps when the time comes for nursing home placement), resistance to accepting "charity," not wanting to disclose income and be subjected to demeaning means testing and to poor quality services. As one daughter noted, they may be too rich to be eligible for subsidized services and at the same time too poor to pay for the services themselves. Some cases illustrated the benefits of adapting the physical environment of the home that is the context of care, but not all caregivers have the economic capability to do so.

There are also psychological barriers to the use of services. In addition to deep-seated relationship problems between them and the parents that shape the ways in which the caregiving role is enacted, other barriers are the women's feelings that it is their responsibility alone to provide care (and society's reinforcement of this notion); that only they can provide good care; that people in their particular ethnic, racial, or religious group "take care of their own"; and that the acceptance of help or nursing home placement of the older person is a loss of social status. Unfortunately, as the case studies showed, some professionals reinforce the women's reluctance to accept some relief. In any case, when psychological barriers exist so that severe strains are incurred by caregivers and other family members, counseling is clearly indicated.

Surely, services must be developed and designed so as to reach women in the middle who need them, regardless of their family status. An additional challenge, more difficult to accomplish, is to be creative in reaching out to caregivers who have no one. Although no bureaucratic organization can substitute for the intimacy and comfort of having a close family member, ways must be found to give such women the sense that *somebody does care*. As one of them phrased it, "There aren't many of us, but we exist."

It is reiterated that no judgements are made about the health or pathology of the caregivers' behaviors. Certainly, the answer to the question, "When is enough enough?" lies to some extent in their capacities to set limits, and to avoid such extreme enmeshment with the parents that their own self-preservation is jeopardized. And in turn, that capacity has its roots in relationships that developed much earlier in the family history.

The interviews recorded were not designed to identify "pathology" or to delve deeply into the historical relationship patterns and psychodynamic processes that were at work. The purpose of identifying the themes and patterns is to stimulate professionals to a more complete understanding of the various processes, to think about some of the solutions to any problems that may exist, and to explore relatively unexplored frontiers in order to point the way to helping approaches that could alleviate much suffering.

It is inescapable, however, that some women will be seen as doing well, while the severe strains others experience will be obvious. Some families mobilize their own and their families' resources and community resources that may exist in a relatively orderly fashion, and the various family members help each other along the way. Other family scenes are chaotic and characterized by conflict.

It will be apparent that some daughters and daughters-in-law are able to set limits on what they do, whereas others are not able to do so. Some of the latter provide arduous care for many long years, going beyond what appear to be the limits of endurance. They may do so at the cost of their own well-being and with severe deprivation and suffering to their own families. Some such women appear to be subject to compelling and powerful forces; they fail to make any attempt to free themselves and their families from parent-caring burdens that are oppressive even when options to relieve them are available and are offered. What returns do they get from their efforts that outweigh the burdens?

Thus, a fundamental question concerns the value judgments made by professionals and society. When is continued caregiving viewed as "good" and "normal"? At what point are these women judged to need help in *reducing* their caregiving activities? Are women to be applauded because, as one of them put it (repeating this after recounting each of many crises in her long caregiving career), "I persevered"? Are the women to be criticized when placement of a parent in a nursing home occurs as soon as a parent can no longer live alone or if such placement is made after 3 or 6 or 19 years of arduous caregiving by women in the middle? Readers will make their own evaluations about which women should be urged to redouble their caregiving efforts, which ones are managing well, which need help to ameliorate their situations, and the kinds of interventions that may be indicated for the latter.

Professionals need to examine their own attitudes. The caregivers are well aware of those attitudes. One daughter-in-law said the doctor talked as though the older woman was not present. He treated her "like a jerk." She said, "It's degrading to an older woman." The daughter-in-law sardonically quotes the doctor who says, "Take her home and give her an enema." The caregiver says, "It never occurred to him that I didn't know how and didn't want to. So I did it." Still another physician tells a daughter not to put her mother in a nursing home. "They die there," he says.

A final comment: the positive side of parent care should not be obscured by the emphasis on burdens and problems. Many caregivers receive considerable satisfaction from a sense of fulfilling an obligation, or repaying a loved parent for the love and attention received in the past. Sometimes the parent is a strong resource for the daughter as when separated/divorced women re-enter the parental home in their time of need and economic problems. Though the caregiving literature has tended to emphasize the strains so many women experience, some do not complain of emotional problems. We should not forget the admirable qualities many women exhibit that enable them to deal with their situations. We see some of them in a different light when we observe their humor, resourcefulness, creativity, and generosity.

Chapter 14

Diversity in Work Status

A major source of diversity among parent-caring women is their work status. That status is subject to change from time to time. Some women work full-time, some part-time, some leave their jobs or change the number of hours they work, some have never been in the workforce, and some move in and out of the work force as their needs and those of their families dictate.

The enormous increase in the need for parent care and the rapid entry of women into the workforce occurred almost concurrently in the last century. The proportion of employed women rose from about one quarter of working-age women in 1930 to about three-fifths in 1998. Yet interest in the reciprocal effects of those trends each upon the other began only about a quarter of a century ago.

The burst of interest in parent care, which began in the 1960s, resulted in major surveys by government and national organizations and a steady flow of research articles by gerontologists. But the interface of adult daughters doing out-of-home work and parent care was not a major focus of interest until the late 1980s (Brody, E. M., 1985; Brody, E. M., Kleban, Johnsen, Hoffman, & Schoonover, 1987a). About that time, the business community became aware of issues that arose because so many of their workers were involved in parent care. The influential Conference Board therefore began to examine the situation and to report about it (most recently in 1997 and 1999) based on surveys it conducted. Their publications include information about what steps business firms are taking to respond to problems and to make recommendations for additional activities. (The Conference Board is the world's leading business membership organization, and includes 3,300 enterprises in 63 countries.)

After some background information is presented, this chapter will discuss various aspects of the subject of women, work, and parent care.

Among them are the effects of women working on care of their parents and parents-in-law; the differential experiences of parent-caring daughters and their families when those daughters are in the labor force and when they are not; the actions women take when parent-care and out-of-home work compete, and some of the activities of the business community in response to what it now calls a global issue.

BACKGROUND

Chapter 1 included the data on the vast increase in women's labor force participation and the reasons that influential change occurred. In brief, in 1950 one in three women worked, compared to about 60% now. The U.S. has the highest percentage of women in any country who work full time (Wisensale, 2001). It is projected that by the year 2008, about 62% of women will be in the work force (U.S. Department of Labor, Bureau of Labor Statistics, Winter 1999).

Most relevant to our subject is that a large proportion of the increase in women's labor force participation was attributable to the entry of *middle-aged* women into the workforce—women most likely to be in the parent-care years. Between 1920 and 1974, for example, the number of women workers between the ages of 18 and 34 increased 115%, by 143% for those 35–44, by 266% for those 45–54, and by 352% for those 55–64 (Lingg, 1975). By 1998, 76% of women 45–54 were working! While young and single women used to predominate in the workforce, now the largest age category of working women is middle-aged married women.

Whatever the reasons that so many women now work, many of them are also helping disabled parents. Thus, two major new roles—parent care and work—were added to the multiple roles women play. Not all caregiving daughters and daughters-in-law are in the labor force, of course, and not all of those who work have parents or parents-in-law in need of their help. However, in the early 1980s, approximately 44% of daughters who were providing considerable help (that is, personal care) to their parent(s) were also doing out-of-home work (Stone, Cafferata, & Sangl, 1987). Business firms estimated at the time that at any given time between 20% and 30% of all working people were helping a disabled older person and that most of those caregivers were daughters (Travelers, 1985; AARP, 1987). Such cross-sectional data do not reveal the number of working women who had parent-care responsibilities in the past or who would do so subsequently. Nor do they include women who may have left their jobs or reduced their working hours because of parent care.

The relatively little attention that was paid to the problems of middle-aged working women at the time contrasts sharply with the considerable interest that was focused on young working women. Though concerns about young women who juggle work and family life were well founded, middle-aged women also were subject to multiple pressures. The specifics of their situations were different, however. The need to provide parent care often arose when middle-aged and aging women—and their husbands and brothers—were experiencing age-related changes such as lower energy levels, the onset of chronic ailments, retirement, and interpersonal losses. This, in the light of the congressional report on *Mid-life Women* (U.S. House of Representatives, 1979) that emphasized the importance of the middle years as preparation for the prevention of severe problems in old age. The report discussed problems such as widowhood, being a displaced homemaker, low income, and the need for educational and occupational opportunities for women between the ages of 45 and 64.

The need to focus on parent-caring women who work is reinforced by an analysis of data from the 1989 National Long-Term Care Survey and its companion Informal Caregivers Survey (Doty, Jackson, & Crown, 1998). The authors reported that working-age male primary caregivers were rare and employed male caregivers even more rare. As copious and consistent data show, female relatives are much more likely to become primary caregivers of older people. Moreover, primary female caregivers were only slightly less likely to be out of the labor force than their age peers among women in the general population. This suggests, Doty and her colleagues stated, that while not-employed women may be more likely to take on the role of primary caregiver, employment is only a weak influence, and other factors may limit or affect the choice of primary caregiver (p. 340).

DO PARENTS OF WORKING DAUGHTERS RECEIVE LESS CARE?

Prior to the early 1980s, it was often assumed that women's parent-care activities were necessarily reduced when they were employed. Early research findings were sparse, tentative, and sometimes contradictory. However, overall, scattered reports indicated that working women continued to help their elderly family members while continuing to meet their responsibilities by maintaining rigid schedules, negotiating parent-care tasks around their work schedules, and giving up their own free time (Cantor, 1983; Horowitz et al., 1983; Lang & Brody, E. M., 1983). Being employed was found to significantly decrease the hours of assistance provided by sons to their parents but not to have a significant impact on the hours of assistance provided by daughters (Stoller, 1983).

Predictors of caregiving involvement found to be more significant than the daughter's employment status, were geographic proximity, the level of the parent's impairment, responsibilities other than work (such as being married), and sharing a household with the dependent elderly person (Horowitz, 1982; Lang & Brody, E. M., 1983). Sharing a household with an older person was not only associated with more caregiving (Lang & Brody, E. M., 1983) but deterred labor-force participation for some people (Soldo & Myllyluoma, 1983). And very few significant differences were found between working and nonworking daughters in the types of tasks they performed for the elderly (Horowitz et al., 1983).

In the study described in Chapter 4 of the attitudes of three generations of women about women's roles and filial care, majorities of all generations agreed that it is better for a working woman to pay someone to care for her elderly parent than to leave her job to do so. Most of the women in all three generations stated that adult children should not adjust work schedules for parent care, but were more likely to expect working married daughters rather than working married sons to do so. Although the women were strongly in favor of sons and daughters providing equal amounts of parent care, in practice, the daughters were doing virtually all of it (Brody, E. M., Johnsen et al., 1984; Lang & Brody, E. M., 1983).

Research designed to compare working and nonworking daughters, all of whom were helping a disabled mother, showed that older people whose caregiving daughters were employed did not receive fewer hours of service-provision from all sources than those whose daughters did not work (Brody, E. M. & Schoonover, 1986). Families provided the vast majority of helping services, and the daughters were the ones in the family who provided most of that help, even when employed.

In that study, the work status of the daughters was, however, associated with variations in the sources of some kinds of assistance. Those variations occurred both in the apportionment of help among the various members of the informal network and in the overall balance between the informal and formal systems. Working daughters provided as much emotional support as their nonworking counterparts and somehow managed to do as much housework, laundry, transportation, grocery shopping, money management, and service arrangement for their mothers. However, when the daughters were in the labor force, the provision of help with personal care and meal preparation was more often shared by other providers. Notably, helpers paid by the family and, to a much lesser extent, the women's husbands and other family members, were more involved. For the most part, it was the services of paid helpers that offset the reduction in the hours of help provided by the daughters themselves.

The fact that the working women in the study described were of higher socioeconomic status than the nonworking women may account in part for the larger amount of purchased care for their mothers. That supposition was supported by other reports to the effect that caregivers of lower socioeconomic status tended to provide more services themselves, whereas those of higher socioeconomic status tended to purchase more care (Archbold, 1983; Kinnear & Graycar, 1984; Noelker & Poulshock, 1982).

Such findings were consistent with women's personal preferences as to who various providers of services should be in their old age (Brody, E. M., Johnsen, et al., 1984). Personal care and household help were the kinds of assistance most were willing to accept from nonfamily members. The forms of help that most women preferred their children (rather than other people) to provide were emotional support and financial management. Daughters, whether or not they worked, provided the overwhelming majority of services with those very tasks—a level of assistance that was stable regardless of the daughter's work status. When formal services were utilized, most of them were purchased by the older person or family, with very few being subsidized by government or community agencies. In fact, in the national 1982 Long Term Care Survey, all formal services together accounted for less than 15% of all "helper days of care" in the community (including such services as home health, homemaker/chore services, and adult daycare programs) (Doty, Liu, & Wiener, 1985).

In short, as the research accumulated, it became apparent that the dependent elderly were not suffering neglect because of the increased workforce participation of the daughters who were their primary caregivers. Moreover, the concern that was expressed to the effect that women's employment increases the taxpayers' burden by substituting subsidized community services for the women's own help to their parents proved to be unfounded. The fact that employed daughters continued to provide most of the help received by their dependent mothers deserves emphasis. When it was necessary for the daughters to reallocate some of the care to nonfamily providers, services were purchased rather than shifting the economic costs to the community. The caregiving workers themselves were found to accommodate work by rearranging work schedules, taking time off without pay, or reducing work hours (Stone & Short, 1990).

The many surveys and studies agree on several major finding:

With respect to the effect of women working on care of the elderly, *there is no evidence at all that the latter receive less care because of the increase in women's labor force participation.* To quote the meticulous analysis by Spillman and Pezzin (2000) that compared data from the 1984 and 1994 National Long-Term Care Surveys: "A much larger group of both men and women faces the competing demands of potential caregiving responsibility and full time work, and workers make up an increasing proportion of primary active caregivers." They also reported that: "About eight million persons, 56% of all spouses and children of disabled elderly persons, worked 30 hours or more per week in 1994, the same proportion as in 1984 [p. 10]. . . . They accounted for 27% of primary caregivers in 1994, up from 22% in 1984." Over that 10-year period, the proportion of women (wives and daughters grouped together) who were full time workers (i.e., 30 or more hours weekly) and had a disabled spouse or parent increased about 4.4%.

Doty, Jackson, and Crown (1998), in their excellent article about the impact of female caregivers' employment status on patterns of formal and informal eldercare, came to similar conclusions. (They, too, grouped wives and daughters together.) Those investigators used data from the 1989 National Long-Term Care Survey for their analysis and concluded that, "Overall, increased female labor force participation is having less of an effect on the availability of informal eldercare than many experts predicted" (p. 340). A most important finding was that " . . . disabled elders with employed female primary caregivers tend to use more hours of help from other sources than disabled elders with nonemployed female caregivers." That finding, the researchers state, suggests that others in the informal network may supply more help when women who are primary caregivers work, and that reduced-caregiving by those women is offset by paid workers as well. Their conclusion is similar to Brody, E. M. and Schoonover's (1986) finding that when primary caregiving daughters in their study were in the labor force, others in the family and workers paid by the family offset the slight reduction in help from those daughters. On balance, the evidence led Doty and her colleagues to conclude that women still enact the powerful injunction that *caregiving is a women's role* (see chapter 7).

Confirmation of caregivers' steadfast, responsible, parent-care behavior comes from still another analysis that compared the 1982 and 1989 National Informal Caregiver Surveys to determine any change over time in the effect of full time employment on informal caregiving (Boaz, 1996). This analysis was limited to primary caregivers whose care-recipients were disabled in performing ADLS. While it found that full-time employment reduces caregiving time, the effect of full-time employment on informal caregiving by primary caregivers of ADL disabled elderly (the most disabled) did not change during the 1980s.

EFFECTS OF CAREGIVING ON WORKING AND NONWORKING DAUGHTERS

Studies of caregivers that did not differentiate between those who worked and those who did not were consistent in reporting that large proportions of all parent-caring women experienced negative effects on their emotional well-being and on their family lifestyles, and smaller proportions experienced physical or economic strain (see chapter 3). Early workplace surveys identified similar strains and also estimated that the average duration of care was approximately five to six years (Travelers, 1985; AARP, 1987). Many families reported that they had additional expenses related to caring for an elderly person.

In another study, differences emerged in the patterns of strains that working and nonworking women attributed to parent care—differences that suggest somewhat different sources of strain for the two groups. In one study, interference with privacy was of relatively greater importance among nonworkers, especially in shared households (Kleban, Brody, E. M., Schoonover, & Hoffman, 1989). Such co-residence was associated with depression among nonworkers but not among workers, even though the two groups contained equal proportions of families in such households. It is known that severely impaired older people tend to live with families and that co-residence predicts larger amounts of care, as well as more caregiver strain than when the older person lives separately. But the depression of the working daughters in the study cited did not relate strongly to shared living arrangements or to lack of privacy. This suggested that work itself offers respite from the caregiving situation and that some caregivers may require relief from sustained intrahousehold caregiving efforts. Depression among nonworkers was also associated with their dissatisfaction with the mother/daughter relationship and to lower family income. Again, this implied a lack of relief from the ongoing caregiving situation as well as an economic inability to purchase help that would provide some respite.

In the same survey, employed daughters' reports of depression and feelings of being upset related as well to their worries about meeting their mothers' future needs and with the mothers' cognitive deficits and negative personality traits. It is understandable that cognitive deficits signaling dementia are a special source of concern when the caregiver is not at home to monitor the older person's behavior. For working daughters, such symptoms may have been particularly distressing in that they augured increased caregiving demands and additional changes in lifestyle, and raised questions as to the women's future ability to juggle these multiple responsibilities. The working daughters' emotional reactions suggested the uncertainty of being in such potentially transitional states, a supposition supported by their anxiety about the future.

Disagreements between women and their mothers about the amounts of help the latter required also related to the depressions reported by employed daughters. Work responsibilities may have imposed constraints on daughters' attentiveness to the older people, or created a dissonance between mothers and daughters in their expectations about the nature, extent, or timing of the help given.

The findings of that research should not obscure the fact that, whether or not they were in the labor force, a substantial proportion of the women studied did *not* report depression and other strains related to their caregiving roles. Nevertheless, the data offered a glimpse of the unique problems associated with the work status of parent-caring daughters. It became apparent that there must be concern not only about the effects of women's work on parent care, but also about the effects of parent care on women's work-force participation and on their own well being.

One finding in particular that is of major importance to parent-caring women alerts us to what happens when work and parent care compete. Specifically, depressions of some nonworking women were related to having given up their jobs to take care of their mothers.

WHEN WORK AND PARENT CARE COMPETE

Though it is well known that many women enter and leave the work force in response to family needs such as childcare, there had been virtually no information about such patterns in relation to parent care. The study that compared working and nonworking women providing parent care found that 12% of all of the women studied, or 28% of the nonworking women, had left the labor force in order to take care of their disabled mothers. In addition, 26% of the working women were considering quitting or had already reduced their work schedules for the same reason (Brody, E. M., 1985b; Brody, E. M. et al., 1987a).

Results from the caregivers study of 1982 Long Term Care Survey were strikingly similar to those findings about the effects of parent care on women's workforce participation. In that national representative sample, 11.6% of all caregiving daughters had left their jobs to take care of an elderly parent, and 23% of working daughters had reduced their working hours (Stone et al., 1987). In the Long Term Care Survey, 35% of working daughters had rearranged their work schedules and 25% had taken time off without pay, again confirming the findings of the Brody study.

Similar reports were also emerging from British studies showing that the most common reason for women to quit jobs before retirement was to look after a sick relative (Rossiter & Wicks, 1982). Moreover, approximately one-fifth of female part-time workers worked part time for the same reason. Hunt (1978) found that one working woman in eight was responsible for the care of at least one elderly or infirm person. And Land (1978) commented that daughters are more vulnerable than sons to potential conflict between work and parent care; sons are much less likely to stop working because of an elderly parent, having been socialized to work as their major role.

In a study of the competing demands of employment and informal caregiving to disabled elders, Stone and Short (1990) found that primary caregivers and those whose elders had greater care needs were more likely to take unpaid leave, reduce work hours, or rearrange their work schedules to assume caregiving responsibilities.

The study conducted by E. M. Brody and her colleagues offers the most complete information available about the interaction between parent care and daughters' labor force participation (Brody, E. M. et al., 1987a; Brody, E. M. & Schoonover, 1986). The sample was divided into four groups characterized as follows: In the *quit-work* group were the women who had left the labor force in order to take care of their mothers. A second group, comprised of the other non-working women in the study, were called the *traditional* women because they were not working at the time of the study and had not been working when the need for parent care arose. In the third group, called *conflicted,* were the working women who were considering quitting their jobs or had already reduced the number of hours they worked because of the parents' need for help. The fourth group, the *persevering* women were so named because they were working and had not considered reducing their working hours or quitting their jobs because of parent care.

The strong contrasts that were found among these four groups of women highlighted the differential interaction between socioeconomic trends and situational factors in the lives of daughters and their disabled mothers. They also pointed to potential conflicts in the values influencing women's decisions about parent-care and work force participation.

The women who had quit work and those who were working but were conflicted had the most severe parent-care problems, problems that resulted from work-related pressures in combination with time-extended processes of caring for a severely disabled parent. The women who had left their jobs had the oldest and most disabled mothers (four-fifths of the mothers were over 80, and 25% were 90 or over), had been helping the longest, and were the most likely to have their mothers living in their households. More of the women in the quit-work and conflicted groups reported problems and lifestyle disruptions, and they were more likely to be their mothers' sole helpers. Similar findings were reported by another study (Enright & Friss, 1987) in that caregivers who had quit their jobs and part-time workers experienced the most stress and spent more time giving care to relatives who had the most severe behavioral problems.

Socioeconomic status and values also appeared to play roles in the decisions the women in the Brody study made when parent care and work competed. The women who had left their jobs had less education and lower family incomes than any of the daughters in the other groups, and their mothers received the least paid help. They had held lower status jobs than the two groups of women who were still in the labor force. In addition, these non-working women who had left their jobs more often thought of their previous employment as "just a job" rather than as part of a career, and held less egalitarian views of women's roles than did either group of working women.

Although many women in all four groups reported competing demands and difficulties in setting priorities, it was the conflicted working women who allowed us to see the competition between parent care and work most clearly. The pull was strong between their feelings of obligation to take care of their parents and their new views of women's roles (Brody, E. M., 1981). For example, they had been helping almost as long and reported strain comparable to that of the women who had quit work. Furthermore, they experienced the most interference with time for themselves and with their husbands. They held the highest level jobs, were the most career-oriented, had the highest family incomes, and their new views about women's roles were similar to those of the persevering working women. Although the mothers of those conflicted workers received the most paid help, these daughters were the ones who most often felt tied down and that they had missed out on something. They also reported more negative effects on their occupational activities than the other working women.

The "persevering" workers (those who were not considering quitting or reducing their work time) and the traditional nonworking women appeared to be faring relatively better than the others. The former reported the best health status, felt more in control of their own lives, and had the most capable mothers. The traditional nonworkers, whose views about women's role were less egalitarian than those of either group of working women, reported the least strain. Nonetheless, those traditional women and the group of women who had quit (that is, the two groups of nonworking women) had poorer mental health than both groups of working women—again suggesting that being employed may offer some beneficial respite from parent care.

Taken together, the findings of the study suggested that many of the women who had quit their jobs had worked because they and their families needed the money they earned. Whatever processes were involved in their decisions to leave the work force, their family incomes were much lower than those of the other groups of women. As one reviewer (Allen, 1983) of British studies had pointed out, women do not work for pin money now. It is obvious that the juggling of multiple responsibilities and role overload are not the exclusive province of "career" women.

In the study, women described the pressures of having "two jobs" that precipitated their decisions to leave the work force:

> I didn't want to juggle two jobs anymore. I wanted to pick one job over the other. If mother wasn't living with us, I would have picked work. But I really didn't have much choice. I would return to work if I had the means to care for my mother. I would love to return to work.

* * *

> I began to worry about mother at work when she began to do dangerous things. When she became irrational, I decided to quit. But I had enjoyed my career.

* * *

> When we first noticed the change in mother, it was very stressful working full-time and going back and forth. I told my husband I couldn't handle everything, so I went part-time. It was no big deal. I didn't feel I was forced into it. It was the last straw. I was glad to be away from the pressure.

* * *

> The job was a lot of fun for me because it was intellectually very demanding. But it got to be a strain because I was torn with the home situation. So I quit.

* * *

> When my Mom fell and broke her hip, I had trouble coping. I considered quitting. Then she fell and broke her arm. The doctor said don't be shocked if she falls

again. At that point, I realized I probably wouldn't be able to work again, so I told my boss to find somebody else. But I loved the work and felt great there, and my boss and I had a wonderful relationship. I miss the interplay between people and the stimulation.

* * *

I was working when my mother moved in with us. Then it got to the point where I couldn't handle it, and she couldn't handle it. I had to be here. It was emotional strain and stress. When I quit my job, I missed the people.

* * *

After she lived with me, I would come home and find the water running. It wasn't a hard decision to quit. I don't know how I'd feel if I was making big money.

Some women worked part time rather than full time because of parent care:

Mom started being picked up by the police, and we had to move her in here with us. I went part-time in my job. I couldn't handle everything. If it hadn't been for Mom, I would have stayed full-time. Before I thought of my work as a career. Now it's just a job.

* * *

My boss said I had to work full time if he promoted me, but I couldn't. I had to have the time to take care of Mom.

Other working women left their jobs because they could not afford to purchase services for their mothers:

I hired a girl to come in while I went to work. She ended up with more money than I made.

* * *

There wasn't enough finances to hire people to do the things my husband and I did for Mother.

* * *

I never considered using paid help because I couldn't afford it. It never crossed our minds.

Purchased services or help from other family members often did not help enough:

> The nurse's aide was some help but you still have a lot—meals, laundry, etc. But that's only a few days. You still have the rest of the week and the weekend. You begin to wear down.

* * *

> My husband took off from work early to pick Mom up at daycare. He used his vacation time. But you can't keep that up forever.

The attitudes of the elderly mothers towards paid help also influenced daughters' decisions to leave their jobs:

> Mother resents paid help.

* * *

> Having paid help would be an admission of dependency to Mother. She would have objected terribly.

* * *

> Mother needed someone to live with her, but she was not cooperative.

* * *

> My mother wouldn't like paid help. She is used to being catered to and taken care of. When push comes to shove, it's not a thing she will be pleasant about.

Needing the money earned at work is a reason that some daughters work despite the demands of parent care:

> I have to work because my husband was killed in an auto accident, and I have two children to support.

* * *

> I went back to work so my oldest child could go to private school.

* * *

> I've considered changing my schedule since my mother's stroke. I don't know if going part-time will affect my retirement benefits. I've also thought of giving

up work altogether till mother dies. I don't know if emotionally I could handle that. You have to be a financial wizard to figure out what the best deal is.

* * *

I had to go to work to pay for my mother's insulin and diabetic diet. My husband said I had to or we'd lose the house.

The daughters often spoke to the value of work as respite:

Sometimes my work had really helped me to cope. Other times, it's just been another thing on my mind. But sometimes it has helped me to forget things. You become all absorbed with what you're doing at work and forget the personal things in your life.

* * *

When my mother's condition began to deteriorate, I never considered reducing my hours or quitting my job. I needed to get out—it saved me.

* * *

When I'm at work, I usually blank out what's going on at home.

Work is important to women for other reasons:

I'm not the kind of person who wants a super-career. At the same time, work is important to me. I feel I contribute and make a difference.

* * *

I wanted to be a doctor from the time I was eight years old. What I do is important to me and to my patients. I'm having trouble juggling things, but fortunately I can afford help at home.

* * *

My mother had a stroke just as I was about to be made a partner in the firm. I never considered quitting. Help is hard to get, and there are always emergencies. I stop in to see her every day and to see to it that she's okay. I'd be too resentful if I quit. And I'm not the nurse type.

Even when women are true "career" women, have never considered giving up their work, and can afford to hire as much nonfamily help as is necessary, they say the juggling of priorities is a strain. As one such woman put it, her parent-care responsibility is "a constant presence in my life."

A major theme apparent in the case excerpts is that work is important to the women, though it has different meanings for different women. Although some feel relief at resolving the conflict between work and parent care by leaving the workforce or reducing their work time, most of those who did so were regretful. They missed the people and the activity on the jobs they held, were wistful in recalling the gratification they received from working, and felt badly about having to forego promotions and further their personal development. The women had derived benefits from feeling that they were making a contribution in their jobs and that what they were doing was important.

Among the compelling factors when women quit their jobs were financial barriers to purchasing nonfamily care or to purchasing enough such help. At the same time, some women entered the work force or held onto their jobs because they needed the money. Some daughters acceded to their elderly parents' refusal to accept nonfamily help. Accordingly, they left their jobs, putting the elderly person's wishes above their own. Financial worries accompanied decision to quit in some instances, since those decisions meant they would have lower retirement benefits.

There was an undercurrent of sadness among the women who gave up their work. Whatever values or situational factors were operating, many of them had given up something they valued and that was important to their self-esteem. Again, it is apparent that for such women, the old values about parent care being *their* responsibility had not been driven out by "new" values concerning women's roles.

Because the women who had quit work were interviewed after they had left their jobs, it is not known whether doing so had relieved, intensified, or otherwise changed the nature of the pressures they experienced. Nor can it be assumed that the women had made their final decisions. As the capacities of the mothers declined over time, their daughters may have experienced more pressure and may have chosen other options concerning both work status and the care of their mothers. Some of them may have decided to stop work, and some may have decided to return to work or to redistribute parent-care responsibilities in a different manner. Indeed, when followed up within two years after they had first been interviewed, one-fourth of all the women in the study had changed their work status. Some of the nonworkers had entered or reentered the workforce, most because they needed the respite from parent care that work provided or because they needed the money. And some of the working women had increased or decreased their working hours or were no longer working.

Although studies of the shifts in women's roles generally had been focused on the earlier stages of the life-course, it became apparent that a process of role change also occurs in response to the needs of disabled elderly people in the family. Obviously, patterns of parent care, work, and other role performance must be viewed as long-term processes about which information can best be gathered by longitudinal studies. As yet, we have no knowledge about this extraordinarily diverse and complex mosaic depicting responses to parent care over the individual and family life-course. Little is known about the processes by which different options are selected—processes that have profound implications for practice approaches and social policy, and for employees as well. And little is known about other options chosen such as nursing home placement of the parent or the redistribution of care in other ways along the informal and formal support systems.

Given the increasing diversity in women's life courses, we do not know what choices will be made by future cohorts of women as they move into the parent-care years, nor is it known how the old behavioral borders that have been measured by research will respond to lifestyle changes, to possible changes in family structure and size, or to economic changes, for example.

Moreover, it cannot be assumed that differential socialization of men and women will be a constant. In the main, the cohorts of middle-generation daughters studied in the 1980s were socialized to being wife, mother, and homemaker. But as Lopata and Norr (1980) had pointed out, it is no longer accurate to speak of women's "typical" work cycle or life course, given the increasing diversity in the patterns of women's lives. Accordingly, later cohorts of caregivers may make different decisions and the future may again witness changes.

There were hints from the study, however, that women who are more highly educated and more committed to careers will tend more than others to continue in the labor force. A similar pattern was observed some years later in that higher rates of labor force participation among women with newborn children were reported by more highly educated women. Sixty-three percent of women who had a birth in the previous year and who had four or more years of college were working in 1987, as compared with 38% of those who had less than 12 years of schooling (U.S. Department of Commerce, 1982b).

THE DOLLAR COSTS AND THE RESPONSE OF THE BUSINESS COMMUNITY

Considerable activity was generated in the business community as it became aware of the problems and actions of employed caregivers. An article titled "Elder care: the employee benefit of the 1990s?" (Friedman, 1986) appeared in *Across the Board*, the publication of the Conference Board. It called elder care a "bottom-line business concern." Based on surveys of their employees, some companies were reporting problems such as absenteeism, lateness, the use of unscheduled days off, excessive phone use by employees and negative effects on their work, excessive stress and physical complaints, and a decrease in productivity and the quality of work. The article suggested that high-level executives are likely to endorse dependent-care benefits (everything from counseling to subsidies), since senior level decision-makers are more likely to be caring for elderly parents than for preschoolers and that solutions may follow for others throughout the organization.

Though the issue of caregiving employees captured the attention of some of the leadership in the business community, a February 1987 article in a newsletter published by The Center for Corporate Community Relations pointed out that most companies were hardly aware of the problems (*Community Relations Letter*, 1987) and that the employees who quit or adjust their work hours are likely to be experienced, well-trained workers who are difficult and expensive to replace. It commented that companies' concern for eldercare speaks both to social responsibility and to good business practice.

Some firms took a variety of steps such as evaluating elder daycare as an employee benefit; surveying employees and planning to test support programs (such as a telephone line to the local Center of Aging, on-site support groups, and respite care); caregiving fairs to inform employees about community services; referral services to connect employees with resources; and lunch-time seminars.

The business community's interest in working caregivers accelerated in the 1990s, as the dimensions of the situation and the effect on all levels of employees became apparent. The Conference Board has been monitoring the effects of working caregivers on the women themselves and on business. A Work-Family Research and Advisory Panel survey was conducted in 1997, called *Juggling the Demands of Dependent Care* (Conference Board, 1997). It is important to note that this report concerns childcare as well as eldercare and focuses on "baby boomers" whom they define as the 77 million individuals born between 1946 and 1964. Though the information developed cannot be compared with other surveys because of differences in sampling, definitions, survey questions, and so on, some of their findings and observations are reported here nonetheless. The report states that eldercare and childcare differ in many ways, but that eldercare issues generate greater stress levels and absenteeism. In addition, they point out that eldercare often encompasses long distance, deteriorating health, and increased needs.

To quote the report, "The biggest problems facing those with [both] child and elder responsibilities [i.e., the sandwich generation] are emotional and psychological in nature. While time and stress is a problem, caregivers experience a great deal of guilt and anxiety about their inability to be there for parents and still emotionally support their children" (p. 6). They identify the competing pulls plus contributing forces such as geographic distance, fewer siblings to share the care, a lack of affordable child and eldercare, and greater work demands. About a dozen beneficial programs are suggested including flextime, family and medical leave, referral to resources, employee assistance programs, and part time/job sharing.

Another Conference Board conference in 1999, Work-Life Initiatives in a Global Context, noted the future increase of the problems and advocated "flex firms" as part of the solution (i.e., "flexible ways of connecting and disconnecting people 24 hours a day, flexible time arrangements, and flexible staffing" (p. 38).

The Conference Board report described a study funded by Met Life that is being conducted by the National Alliance for Caregiving and the Center on Women and Aging at Brandies University. That study, too, combined males and females, but was focused on eldercare. It estimates the length of time caregivers provide care is an average of 11 years for nonworkers and 18 years for workers. In addition, the caregivers' heath is affected negatively due to stress, lack of focus, and no time to exercise. The average amount of money caregivers contribute over the lifetime of the older person that would have gone into savings is estimated at about $30,000. This does not speak to the opportunity costs incurred (primarily by women) who reduce their hours or quit their jobs. The Metlife Juggling Act Study (1999) estimated that caregiving costs individuals as much as $659,000 over their lifetimes in lost wages, social security, and pension contributions not made.

At work, these caregivers pass up training and promotions, and the quality of their work diminishes. There is a heavy toll on their work: 87% used the phone about eldercare, came in late, or left early; 71% took time off; 64% used sick leave or vacation time; 42% decreased their work hours; 20% switched to part time; 20% took leave of absence; and 15% quit. In the same vein, the AARP Sandwich Generation report found that slightly less than 20% had reduced the amount of time they work because of eldercare, nearly 3 in 10 changed the timing of their vacations, and nearly 2 in 10 changed where they plan to live or readjusted their own savings for retirement.

Nor is the business community unaware of its own dollar costs. One study estimated the loss to U.S. employers to be between $11.4 and $29 billion per year (Metropolitan Life Insurance Co., 1997). This includes replacement costs for employees who quit work because of caregiving, absenteeism, and extra time off and workday interruptions.

A comprehensive report (Wagner, 2000), funded by Metlife Mature Market Institute, traced the activities of the business community and the programs it has created to help workers involved in eldercare. Responses are categorized by policies, benefits, and services. The report summarizes how workers use various programs and states that little is known about how productivity is affected. An increase in elder care among workers is foreseen and suggestions made for dealing with the situation.

THE FUTURE

It has become obvious that the work/parent care situation affects virtually the entire work force. It is inevitable that many people in the labor force who are not helping an elderly parent now may be doing so tomorrow or next year. Those providing only shopping help today, tomorrow may need to see to it that the parent is bathed, dressed, and fed. Workers at all levels and both sexes are affected, from maintenance staff to corporation presidents and chairpersons of the board.

And various socioeconomic trends are occurring that will increase the difficulties for working women in particular. A *New York Times* headline read "Now a Majority: Families With Two Parents Who Work" (Lewin, October 24, 2000). It noted, "For the first time since the Census Bureau began tracking the numbers, families in which both parents are working have become the majority, even among the most traditional families: married couples with children." The proportion went up from 33% in 1976 to 51% in 2000, and it was expected that the trend for working mothers of even very young children would grow.

Other aspects of the situation have also captured the attention of the media. The *New York Times* also reported that the numbers of working women will increase due to the fact that, lacking pensions, older divorced women remain at work (Uchitelle, June 26, 2001). That article points out that thousands of women in their 60s, part of the surge to the workforce that started a generation ago, continue to work because they lack enough money to retire. For the first time, the article continues, divorced women outnumber widows in falling into poverty. The percentage of divorced women 55 to 64 years of age has risen since the mid-1960s, from less than 5% to almost 15%, while the proportion of 65–74-year-old women who are divorced rose from about 2.5% to about 8%.

It is apparent that women in the middle are being subjected to ever increasing pressures.

Chapter 15

Racial & Ethnic Diversity

*Avalie R. Saperstein**

Ethnic and racial diversity is increasing rapidly in the United States and therefore in the elderly population and their caregivers. Most of the discussion in previous chapters is based on American daughter caregivers collectively, without differentiating among those of diverse racial/ethnic origins. Such diversity is projected to increase in the future. A question to be asked is: Do adult children in different racial/ethnic groups provide care for their parents differently from each other?

In 1990, there were 28 million people in the White elderly population; 2.5 million African Americans; 1.1 million of Hispanic origin; and 5 million of "Other" races. "Other" includes Asians, Pacific Islanders, American Indians, Eskimos, and Aleuts. It is projected that by 2050, the White population 65 years of age or older will grow to 65 million, and there will be 8.4 million African Americans, 12.5 Hispanic Americans, and 6.7 million Other (Hobbs, 1996). Looking at the data from another perspective, the

---

*Avalie R. Saperstein is a consultant specializing in organizational development and evaluation for not-for-profit organizations and foundations and program and environmental design for elderly persons. She participates in major aging-related research projects at the Polisher Research Institute. Ms. Saperstein has over 27 years of long-term care experience in operations, strategic planning, development, facility design, and research and evaluation. Prior to becoming a consultant in 2001, Ms. Saperstein was the Senior Vice President of the Philadelphia Geriatric Center. She has been key in creating innovative community programs that are integrated into long term care continuums of care, dementia services for older persons and their caregivers in institutional and community settings, and housing programs for the elderly. The Counseling for Caregiving Program which she created in the early 1980s has been widely replicated. Ms. Saperstein has published in peer-reviewed journals on a variety of aging topics, has written book chapters, co-authored one book, and has delivered more than 50 presentations at national conferences.

proportion of non-Hispanic White elderly therefore will decline from 87% in 1990 to 67% in 2050. Among the elderly in 2050, 16% will be Hispanic; 10% African American; 7% Asian and Pacific Islander; and less than 1% American Indian, Eskimo, and Aleut (Hobbs, 1996). In other words, by 2050, the African American elderly will quadruple, the Hispanic elderly will increase sevenfold, and the Asian/Pacific Islander elderly will increase 6.5 times (Dilworth-Anderson, Williams, & Gibson, 2002). Among the factors contributing to this dramatic increase in diversity are decades of falling fertility rates among Whites and lower immigration rates of Whites than of other groups, particularly of Hispanics and Asians.

In some respects, there appear to be few differences among different cultural groups in caring for their elderly. Basic family emotional ties and instrumental forms of help to family members in need are universal, and all cultures are committed to caring for their vulnerable family members. Daughters in all groups struggle with the same basic conflicts, issues, and stresses, and they experience similar "uplifts" in caring for their elderly parents (NAC & AARP, 1997).

At the same time, certain differences do exist in the ways in which families enact their caregiving roles. Culture—a set of learned values, rules, behaviors, traditions and sometimes, language—is an important determinant of how people perceive their world, behave, and derive meaning from their lives. Cultural variation is particularly salient in the norms that are attached to familial roles. For example, the roles of daughters and sons can be very different in different cultures. Thus, daughters-in-law in Asian cultures have had strictly-prescribed roles in caring for their husbands' parents. Along with cultural differences in family organization and in role norms, these are likely to translate to variations in styles of caregiving (Montgomery & Kosloski, 2001). Perceptions about and meanings assigned to disease also reflect different cultural groups' values and norms. Further, these perceptions and meanings help those groups to understand and interpret their caregiving experiences (Dilworth-Anderson et al., 2002). (In this chapter, the phrase "ethnic/racial identity" will be used as a proxy for cultural values, beliefs, and norms.)

Those views are not antithetical, however. That is, caregivers from different ethnic/racial groups share the same basic commitment to providing care for their elderly, but do have unique situations, culturally influenced attitudes, challenges, and responses to caregiving situations. The uniqueness of each group is mediated by numerous factors such as socioeconomic and educational status and the extent of acculturation to the dominant culture. These and other mediating factors influence choices of caregivers in a given group—factors such as sufficient income to buy services or the availability of services in the community in which they live. Thus, although racial/ethnic differences may be operationalized somewhat differently for different groups, their value differences are significantly confounded by cross cutting factors.

In general, available data confirming cultural differences are derived from large national data sets that reflect large groupings of people such as those in the NAC and AARP sample and census data. We therefore must direct our attention to those larger groupings including White, African Americans, Asian Americans, and Hispanic Americans. While these categories account for the gross differences between groups, they do not reflect the multiple diversities within each group. There are many subgroups in each of the ethnic/racial groups, and each has its own cultural traditions that reflect their country of origin (for example, Russians, Mexicans, Puerto Ricans, Japanese, and Koreans), religious preferences (such as Judaism and Catholicism), urban and rural residence, and so on. The many differences that exist within each large group are not reflected in the following discussion. Caution must be exercised, therefore, about generalizing the findings reported.

RACIAL/ETHNIC DIFFERENCES IN THE ELDERLY POPULATIONS

There are differences among racial/ethnic elderly that have a significant impact on caregiving. For example, the rates of severe functional impairment among minority elderly are higher than among non-minority elderly (U.S. Department of Health and Human Services, 1991). Among the contributory factors are differential access to health care, attitudes about using such care, income, and educational status. Another difference is that rates of institutionalization are lower for minority elderly than for Whites. Again, a combination of factors are at work such as adequate income to pay for nursing home care, an insufficient number of Medicaid beds, and reluctance to institutionalize the older person because of cultural and language barriers in the facilities to which their elderly would go. These factors combined suggest that minority caregivers may be caring for more severely impaired, non-institutionalized elderly than White caregivers. Further, some studies indicate that minorities, especially African-Americans and Native Americans, use formal services at lower rates than their White counterparts (Dilworth-Anderson et al., 2002). This may be true in areas that do not have caregiving services affordable for low income groups or appropriate culturally sensitive programs. Philadelphia is an example of an urban center that does have a rich array of services for low income elderly and some culturally sensitive services as well.

Overall, it is clear from these findings that minority caregivers may be the most challenged of all, caring for the most dependent family members, and with little or no formal help in some areas of the country.

The NAC/AARP Survey (1977) reports higher incidences of households caring for people 50 years and older among Asian Americans (31.7%), African Americans (29.4%), and Hispanics (26.8%) than in the general population. The modified and larger families of African Americans and Hispanics may account for the larger amounts of informal care in these two groups (Chatters, Taylor, & Jackson, 1985).

One can't help but wonder what will happen to these caregiving networks as the number and proportion of older racial/ethnic elderly increases in the future. The proportion of older people within each racial/ethnic group will increase. In 1990, African American elderly were 8% of the African American population, and Hispanic elderly were 5% of the population of Hispanic origin. By 2050, 14% of African Americans and Hispanics could be 65 or older (Hobbs, 1996). In 1990, about 1 in 5 elderly care recipients were 80 years or older in the African American and Hispanic population, but by 2050, those proportions could increase to 30% for African Americans and 38% for Hispanics (*ibid*). Those projected increases, particularly in the older old cohorts, will pose a challenge to their caregivers to provide care. Meeting the challenge could result in patterns of caregiving that differ from those that operate today.

WHO ARE THE CAREGIVERS?

Caregivers of the racial/ethnic minority elderly vary considerably in their ages, marital status, education, and income, and in their relationships to the care recipients. Overall, in the total population of dependent people in the U.S., adult children provide 42% and spouses 25% of the care. Whites are more likely to receive assistance from a spouse (28%), a result of longevity and therefore marital status. Asians and African Americans are least likely to be caring for a spouse. Though African American caregivers are somewhat older (mean age of 45 years old) than Asian caregivers (mean age 39) and Hispanic caregivers (mean age of 40), they are the least likely racial/ethnic group to be married or living with a partner (51%) (NAC & AARP, 1997). Their caregivers tend to rely on their children for assistance (42%) and, compared to other groups, are the ones most likely to depend on adult grandchildren (10%) and other informal caregivers (neighbors and friends) in addition to family members for care (33%). Four percent of Whites and 6% of Hispanics depend on adult grandchildren (National Academy on an Aging Society, 2001). This may reflect the wider caregiving networks that characterize African Americans.

Hispanic elderly rely most heavily on their adult children (52%) (National Academy on an Aging Society, 2000). Although all racial/ethnic cultures strongly imbue children with the value of filial responsibility, Latino children hear a common phrase from childhood on: *el dereche de los hijos son los padres*. This phrase emphasizes that adult children should care for their parents. Respect for informal care also has strong religious roots. Religious faith, or *fe*, helps Latinos to trust that family, community, and a superior being will care for them in time of need (OWL 2001 Mothers Day Report).

Asian and Hispanic caregivers are significantly younger than Whites and African Americans, with average ages of 39 and 40 respectively. Thus, based on age, Asian and Hispanic caregivers are likely to have children under the age of 18 living at home (NAC and AARP, 1997). (This survey was conducted by telephone and only interviewed English-speaking respondents. The findings, therefore, under-represent persons who are not English speaking and those without telephones. Another limitation of that survey is that a care recipient was defined as 50 years of age or older, though a large majority was over 65.)

Despite the older age of African American caregivers, they have children under the age of 18 living in their homes to the same extent as Asian and Hispanic caregivers (50%). These children are often their grandchildren. According to an Older Women's League (OWL) report, nearly 12% of African American children reside only with their grandparents, primarily grandmothers (OWL, 2001). These three groups—Asians, African Americans, and Hispanics—are more likely than Whites to be women-in-the-middle caregivers, therefore, in the sense that they are sandwiched between generations of dependents.

The OWL 2001 Mothers Day Report indicates that Asian American men and women share caregiving tasks more frequently than the national average. Of Asian American caregivers, 48% are men and 52% are women, while among all caregivers nationally, 72.5% are women. One of the reasons may be that Asian caregivers are more likely to be employed (77%), both full and part time, than caregivers of other groups. The comparable percentages are 65% for Whites, 66% for African Americans, and 65% for Hispanics.

Whites and African American caregivers are more likely to be retired than Asians (NAC & AARP, 1997). Another possible explanation for the more equal sharing of men and women is that daughters-in-law may actually be providing the care rather than sons. There is a stronger tendency within the Asian culture to identify a son as the caregiver, despite the powerful custom that daughters-in-law do the actual tasks.

Asian caregivers are better educated and earn higher incomes than any other group, perhaps because of the high value various Asian groups place on education. African Americans have the lowest educational attainment and lowest incomes, followed in both categories by Hispanics. The numbers may be somewhat inflated for Asians and Hispanics due to language barriers that may have caused recent immigrants, who are poorer and less well educated, to be excluded from the study (NAC & AARP, 1977).

Bengtson and Silverstein (1993) state that there is little consensus about the relative importance of culture and poverty in structuring support networks in older minority families. Some of the literature they reviewed suggests that the family is more responsive to the support needs of older African Americans, while other research has shown that the latter have few advantages, and are occasionally disadvantaged when compared with Whites.

TYPES AND AMOUNTS OF CARE

African American caregivers provide some of the most difficult kinds of care—caring for family or friends with dementia (28%), for example. As seen in chapter 3, the behavioral symptoms of dementia are strong predictors of burden and stress for the caregiver. Together with Asians, African Americans are more likely to be caring for more than one elderly person at a time, and are also more likely to be caring for grandchildren as well (NAC & AARP, 1997).

African Americans spend more time than other groups in caregiving tasks (20.6 hours weekly), followed by Hispanics (19.8) (NAC/AARP, 1997). Two theories suggested as the reasons are cultural differences (e.g., greater familial reciprocity) and increased disability of minority elders. However, Tennstedt and Chang (1998) found that even when controlling for disability, African American and Hispanic caregivers provided more care than Whites.

Asian caregivers spend significantly less time per week in caregiving tasks than other caregivers (15.1 hours weekly). It may be that, in general, they encounter fewer demands for their caregiving services. For example, Asians provide care to elders who are the ones least likely to be 85 years of age or over and the least likely to be demented (3%). In addition, since Asian care recipients are more likely to live in the homes of caregivers than other groups (36%) (NAC & AARP, 1997), caregiving tasks may be less differentiated from general household responsibilities and tasks.

Although employment status has no impact on the incidence of assisting with IADLs, income does make a difference. Caregivers with household incomes under $15,000, no matter their ethnic backgrounds, are more likely than those with high-incomes ($50,000 or more) to provide assistance with housework and meal preparation. Similarly, high-income households are more likely than low-income households to arrange for or supervise outside services and to manage finances.

FAMILY RELATIONSHIPS AND CAREGIVING

Chapter 2 showed that, in general, among all Americans, caregiving is not generally shared equally or even equitably among family members, but that one person tends to provide most of the informal care, usually the daughter of the elderly person. Although all research findings do not agree (Tennstedt, 1999), it appears that racial/ethnic groups have more diverse informal networks than their White counterparts. Minority elders have more caregivers due to the greater involvement of extended families and modified extended families. Drawing on their larger caregiving networks, African American caregivers have been shown to share the care with secondary helpers to a greater extent than White caregivers. They do, however, remain involved in most activities (Dilworth-Anderson et al., 2002; Tennstedt, 1999).

Three-quarters of all caregivers report that other helpers—mostly family members—assist them, though African American caregivers more often identify friends as important helpers. A higher percentage of African American rather than of Asian caregivers report that they themselves do most of the care (49% vs. 36%), and a higher proportion of Asians than any other group report that daughters-in-law also provide care (NAC & AARP, 1997).

Asian and Hispanic caregivers are more likely to feel satisfied that other family members are doing their fair share (61% and 54%) than African American (43%) and Whites (49%). In general, as care needs increase, all groups report less satisfaction with relatives' contributions to caregiving (NAC & AARP, 1997).

No differences among racial/ethnic groups have been identified with respect to family conflict about caregiving. Where differences do occur, it is the age of the caregiver, the level of care needed, and the employment status (employed caregivers report more family conflict) that account for differences (NAC & AARP, 1997).

IMPACT OF CAREGIVING ON RACIAL/ETHNIC GROUPS OF CAREGIVERS

One summary of research findings about depression and burden among racial/ethnic caregivers indicates mixed results due to such factors as differences in sample sizes, control variables, and recruitment strategies (Dilworth-Anderson et al., 2002). Some studies report no differences between African American and White caregivers on depression and burden scales, while others report more depression and burden among White caregivers. It may be that cultural differences that relate to positive appraisal of one's caregiving situation increase the stress ratings of Whites and decrease those of African Americans. Further, it is suggested by various studies that cultural values, norms, expectations, and feelings of obligation and reciprocity may encourage positive appraisal of caregiving experiences for caregivers of racial/ethnic groups.

Lawton and his colleagues reported that greater burden was associated with depression, and suggested that burden mediated the relationships between depression and caregiver physical health, amount of time spent caregiving, and caregiver satisfaction for African American caregivers (Lawton, Rajagopol, Brody, E. M., & Kleban, 1992). S. Tennstedt (1999) agrees that no clear relationships can be found with respect to racial/ethnic differences and psychological and physical distress. Since minority elders are more disabled and receive more care from African American and Hispanic caregivers who in general have lower financial means, it is possible that they experience more burden and stress. Tennstedt suggests that it may be erroneous to assume that cultural differences such as increased familism or reciprocity are mitigating factors, but rather that lower levels of burden found in minorities may be due to measures that are not culturally sensitive. Her previous work suggests that minority caregivers express their distress differently than do White caregivers.

Survey findings as well as research studies about emotional and physical health consequences of caregiving sometimes contradict each other. In the NAC/AARP study (1997), a higher proportion of African American than

Asian caregivers report having suffered mental health problems as a result of caregiving (19% versus 10%). In addition, a higher proportion of African Americans report experiencing physical strain (19%) than either Whites or Asians (10% each). Although this finding intuitively makes sense in light of African American caregivers' more advanced ages and the larger number of caregiving hours they provide weekly, as well as the higher likelihood that they care for more than one elderly person, it is not supported by other sources. Moreover, the NAC/AARP study reports that Asian caregivers report the least amount of emotional stress. This may be contradicted by AARP's In the Middle survey (2001) that studied caregivers only between the ages of 45 and 55 years old. Those findings indicated that Asian Americans express more stress caused by pressures of caring for family members than do other minorities. The same report found that although all groups report that they are dealing relatively well with the responsibilities of caregiving, African Americans report feeling more stressed about needing to handle all of their family responsibilities.

As for guilt—that distressing feeling that figured so prominently as the subjective theme that plagued so many of the women in the middle (see Chapter 7)—all ethnic/racial minorities reported that feeling. It has not dissipated over time as each new generation enters the parent care years. Overall, nearly half of the Baby Boomers reported feeling guilty about not doing enough for their parents! The proportions varied from group to group, however, with 72% of Asian caregivers expressing such feelings compared with 65% of Hispanic Americans, 54% of African Americans, and 44% of Whites.

Not surprisingly, because of their lower incomes, African American and Hispanic caregivers are more likely than Whites or Asians to state that caregiving is a financial hardship—13% and 11% respectively, compared with 6% of White and Asian caregivers. Expectedly, reports of financial hardship correlate with lower income and lower educational status. (NAC & AARP, 1997).

Most studies on caregiving and employment indicate that the caregivers' employment has no impact on the total amount of care provided to dependent elders. Rather, employed caregivers make accommodations in their work schedules to continue to meet their caregiving responsibilities or purchase some care. The only noted difference among racial/ethnic caregivers in this respect is that Hispanics and Asians are more likely to take a leave of absence from work (18% and 22%) than similarly employed Whites (10%) (NAC & AARP, 1997). Since Hispanics are one of the poorer groups of caregivers, it is self-evident that loss of wages can have a negative impact on their financial well-being.

COPING MECHANISMS

The NAC/AARP Survey (1999) identified the following common methods caregivers use to help them cope: prayer (74%), talking with friends or relatives (66%), exercise (38%), and hobbies (36%). African Americans caregivers use prayer (88%) more than any other group. Whites and African Americans are more likely than Hispanics or Asians to talk with friends and relatives to relieve stress. Asian caregivers are less likely to seek help from a professional than either Whites or African Americans (6% versus 17% and 14%). Coping methods were used more frequently when the patient suffered from dementia or required heavier levels of care.

USE OF FORMAL CARE

Increased involvement of family and friend caregivers is associated with lower use of formal services (Tennstedt, 1999). Since most racial/ethnic groups are more involved (hours spent) with caregiving than their White counterparts, one would expect that they have a lower utilization of formal services. This indeed is the case. Both African American and Hispanic caregivers use more informal and fewer formal services than do White caregivers. Dilworth-Anderson et al. (2002) offer three possible explanations based on a thorough review of research studies. Caregivers may avoid seeking outside help because of feelings of shame, feelings of obligation to provide care themselves, and feeling that outside help is not culturally sensitive. Studies by Levkoff, Levy, and Weitzman (1999) also support the concept that racial/ethnic groups may avoid formal services because those services lack cultural sensitivity. Asian and Hispanic language barriers may lead these caregivers to seek assistance from organizations with an ethnic orientation. Though African Americans used formal services, they expressed dissatisfaction due to cultural misunderstandings.

Asian caregivers are significantly less likely to use the traditional community based services (e.g., homemaker, home delivered meals) than all other groups. The reason for this under utilization of formal services is not clear (NAC & AARP, 1997). Again, language barriers and cultural factors may be at work (e.g., meals programs do not provide the type of food that older Asians eat).

Utilization of formal services is also inhibited by the unavailability of low cost or free services, with African American and Hispanic caregivers being particularly disadvantaged in that respect. In some areas, affordable services may not exist, whereas in other areas, services may not exist in the types and quantities needed. This is particularly true of social services such as homemakers, meals, and transportation, rather than medically linked services such as home health care aides who are typically paid for through Medicare. Expectably, caregivers with higher incomes are more likely to purchase services than those with low incomes (NAC & AARP, 1997).

The NAC & AARP survey (1997) reports some interesting findings about the reasons caregivers do not use formal services. The primary reason offered by caregivers—most frequently by African Americans (29%) and Hispanics (26%), compared to Whites (15%)—is that they have no need for services. The second most frequent reason given is they are not aware of the existence of services—again mentioned more by African Americans (27%) and Hispanics (29%) than by Whites (17%). The third reason was that caregivers were too busy to use a formal service, reported more frequently by Hispanics (21%) than the other groups (10–11%). At the same time, daughters of minority elderly who provide more household and personal care tasks for their elders expressed a need for formal services (Montgomery & Kosloski, 2001).

Parenthetically, it is ironic that the very groups who constitute the vast majority of paid caregivers to the disabled elderly—ethnic/racial minorities—are the ones who themselves use paid services the least. As Olson (2000) has pointed out, both institutional and home-based personal care attendants are increasingly women of color, especially immigrants. In nursing homes, these low-paid aides are the primary caregivers, delivering almost all direct patient services.

PROBLEMS AND UPLIFTS

Despite the differences in racial/ethnic groups described in this chapter, the similarities among the groups demonstrate the universal characteristics of family relationships. There are no differences among the various groups in identifying the most difficult aspects of providing care. The most frequent problem is demands on time, followed by watching or worrying about care recipients' deteriorating conditions, followed in turn by care recipients' uncooperative or demanding attitude. One exception is that more African Americans than Whites identify the physical demands of caregiving as their biggest difficulty in providing care, which is consistent with their provision of more care and often more difficult care to their elders than Whites (NAC & AARP, 1997).

Similarly, there were no differences among the groups in identifying the uplifts from their involvement in caregiving. The most important rewards were knowing that the care recipient was well-cared for, personal satisfaction in knowing that one is doing a good deed, and the care recipient's expressions of happiness or appreciation. Caregivers noted that watching the care recipient's health improve, family loyalty, "giving back," fulfilling family obligations, and spending time together were significant rewards (NAC & AARP, *op. cit.*).

The strains, the uplifts, and the familial responsibility are the constants that operate regardless of ethnicity or race. Despite modest variations across ethnic/racial groups in service—utilization, size, and composition of caregiving networks and so on—there are no indications in the various studies and surveys that any of the groups was remiss in caring for its disabled elderly. In fact, the most recent and most diverse cohort of caregivers, the Baby Boomers (defined by AARP as those between the ages of 45 and 55), are reported to welcome the opportunity to be involved in caring for their elderly.

Though this chapter did not deal with cross-national research (that in itself would be another book), that body of research, too, confirms the strength and durability of human bonds. As Wenger and Jingming (2000) suggest in their studies of family caregiver support in Liverpool and Beijing, "family involvement and care for older members is more likely to be a human universal than a culturally defined trait" (p. 90). So, too, are the human reactions to the stresses of elder care. When Patterson and his colleagues compared Alzheimer's caregivers in Shanghai and San Diego, caregivers from both cultures reported more depressive symptoms than non-caregivers. They concluded that the negative health consequences of caregiving appear to be similar in both countries (Patterson et al., 1998). It is well to remember that the cultural differences noted in this chapter are not immutable and may be blurred as acculturation takes place among those who have immigrated more recently.

A striking example of change is the shifting attitudes and behavior regarding the individual in the family who is responsible for care of the old in Japan. Philadelphia research about three generations of women toward gender-appropriate roles and filial responsibility studied elderly grandmothers, their middle-aged daughters, and young adult granddaughters (Brody, E. M., Johnsen, Fulcomer, & Lang, 1983). However, when Campbell and the Tokyo Metropolitan Institute of Gerontology replicated that study in Tokyo, the middle-generation women studied were predominantly daughters-in-law, reflecting the widespread custom in Japan that elderly parents live with a son whose wife is responsible for caring for her mother-in-law (Campbell & Brody, E. M., 1985). But that powerful injunction is changing. A *New York Times* article headed "On the Rise in Japan: Assertive Daughters-in-Law" describes what amounts to a full-scale rebellion of daughters-in-law who are refusing to be totally obedient and subservient to their mothers-in-law (Strom, April 22, 2001, p. 3). As different ethnic/racial groups are acculturated in the United States, their values too may be subject to change.

In summary, this glance at ethnic/racial similarities and differences confirms our general thesis that *change, continuity,* and *diversity* are omnipresent in caregiving to older people. Despite the diversities and inevitable changes in some of the ways in which care is provided, family loyalty and caregiving to the old is a constant and continues over time and across ethnic/racial differences. Most differences found are a question of *degree* rather than of *direction.*

Finally, the excellent recent review by Dilworth-Anderson and her colleagues of studies concerning issues of race, ethnicity, and culture in caregiving examined 59 articles published between 1980 and 2000 (Dilworth-Anderson et al., 2002). The article spells out methods and issues important for future research. It is to be hoped that the tide of research studies in future that will explore this vast subject will heed their advice and suggestions.

Part IV

Nursing Homes, Community Services, and Living Arrangements for Older People

Chapter 16

Nursing Home Placement: A Painful Decision

Discussions about appropriate living arrangements for the disabled elderly too often take the form of institutionalization versus community care. The controversy is frequently framed in terms of dollar cost, with community living advocated as being less costly. Studies, however, beginning with the landmark Cleveland study by the GAO (U.S. General Accounting Office, 1977), have shown that for extremely disabled older people, community care is more expensive. The sanctimonious value often used as the rationale for advocating community care is that it is the family's obligation to take care of its elderly. This attitude disregards the large and consistent body of research and clinical evidence showing that institutionalization is the very last resort of families.

Though few would argue that to live in a nursing home is an arrangement preferred by the older person and family, the reality is that at time it is a necessary arrangement. The sad fact is that congregate facilities are often the only "alternative" for those who have no families and for those who are extremely disabled and, after caregiver's long and arduous efforts, have exceeded the latter's capacities. The recent report by the Administration on Aging states that 50% of the elderly with long term care needs but without a family network are in nursing homes, compared to only 7% of those who have family caregivers (U.S. Department of Health & Human Services, Administration on Aging, Fall 2000, p. 1). The chances of being in a nursing home increase with advancing age. At age 85 or over, 21% of older people reside in nursing homes.

Despite the harsh realities that dictate nursing home placement, the process is often described by adult children as the most painful decision they ever had to make, even as the worst moment in their lives. That such placement is unavoidable does not alleviate those children's distressing emotions, such as feelings of guilt, depression, worry, sadness, and failure at needing to take this step (Brody, E. M., 1977).

As the previous chapters have shown, considerable attention has been paid to the effects on the well-being of families when they care for the noninstitutionalized aged. That interest has not been matched by concern with the effects on families as a result of their decision to move an elderly family member into a long-term care facility and the effects they experience during the period of residence. The well-being of older people and their family members continues to be interlocked no matter where they reside, each affecting the other in reciprocal fashion (Brody, E. M., 1985a; Brody, E. M., & Contributors, 1974).

The notion that older people are dumped into nursing homes by uncaring family members is the most virulent expression of the myth that children nowadays do not care for their elderly parents as was done in the "good old days." In addition, it is widely assumed that once such placement is made, children are relieved of responsibility and of the stress they have endured. To the contrary, adult children continue to be vitally interested in their parents, behave accordingly, and may experience a whole new set of strains.

This chapter describes the extent of the need for nursing home care, the growth in the number of nursing home beds, and the characteristics of institutionalized older people. Caregiving daughters and their families will then be followed through the process of placement: their feelings about nursing home care prior to the parent's admission, the decision-making process, and the effects they experience during the parent's residence in a nursing home. Case excerpts illustrate the steps in that sad journey. The question will be answered: Does nursing home placement of a parent relieve daughters from the position of being in the middle and reduce the strains they experience? The chapter will end with a brief summary of some of the problems that exist with nursing home care, some of the needed measures that could alleviate those problems, and some positive developments that have occurred.

NEED FOR NURSING HOME CARE

The effects on adult children of having an institutionalized parent is of particular importance in the context of demographic projections. The most rapid increase in the elderly population will continue to be among the very old—those who are most vulnerable to the chronic disabling ailments that characterize nursing home residents.

In the following section, unpublished data from the 1999 National Nursing Home Survey was supplied by the National Center for Health Statistics.

The National Long Term Care Surveys (NLTCS) of 1984 and 1994 found that about 5% of all older people (about 1½ million individuals) were in nursing homes for both years (Spillman & Pezzin, 2000). The number of institutionalized older people had increased during that decade because the total number of older people had increased, but the percentage remained essentially the same. The percentage represented a rise from approximately 4% in the late 1960s which then leveled off at about 5%. The 1999 National Nursing Home Survey reported 1,879,600 beds containing 1,628,300 people (an occupancy rate of 86.6%).

There was consensus in the 1980s that the number of older people in need of long-term care would continue to increase for at least the next two decades, but that the proportion might not increase (Brody, S. J., 1985; Fries, 1984; Schneider & Brody, J. A., 1983). One possible scenario suggested was that the nursing home populations would increase 80% to 2.2 million people by the year 2000 (U.S. Department of Commerce, Bureau of Census, 1982a). Another possibility suggested was that dramatic scientific discoveries could prevent or cure one or more of the major disabling ailments—Alzheimer's disease, for example—and cause a sharp drop in the nursing home population.

The absence of the sharp rise in nursing home use that had been predicted may have had multiple determinants. Apart from declines in disability rates (among those with only IADL deficiencies), contributants may have been the increase in Medicare home health use from 5% to 9% between 1985 and 1995 and the increased use of assisted living as a substitute for nursing home placement (Stone, 2000). Occupancy rates declined from 92.3% in 1987 to 86.6% in 1999 as more people sought care in alternative settings (their own homes, ALs, personal care homes). As a result, nursing home residents are older and more functionally disabled (Williams & Hawes, 2000).

Regardless of the absolute number or percentage of nursing home residents at any given time, a longitudinal perspective presents a different picture. Because of turnover—that is, new admissions and discharges—many more older people spend some time in a nursing home in the course of a year. Admission for many is not the first or even the last admission to a care facility. In 1999, the largest proportion—46%—of those admitted came directly from a hospital (not necessarily the first admission); 30% from a residence; 11% from another nursing home; and almost 7% from a retirement home, board and care, or residential care facility (National Center for Health Statistics, 1999; U.S. Department of Health & Human Services, National Nursing Home Survey unpublished data, Table 3, 1999). About 4 out of every 10 people 65 or over will use a nursing home at some point in their lives (AHCPR Research on Long-Term Care, 2002).

Though nursing home care is usually thought to be a permanent plan lasting until the residents death, long-stay residents constitute only one of several different populations in those facilities. Several other resident populations are those admitted for relatively short stays (that is, for less than 90 days); those who are admitted for rehabilitation or convalescence, subsequently returning to the community; those who are admitted for terminal care; and those who are discharged to a general hospital or to another nursing home. Of those discharged alive, some return to their own homes or the homes of relatives, and some go to another health facility (most to a hospital and some to another nursing home or mental facility). The 1997 National Nursing Home Survey found that in the year between October 1996 and September 1977, 2.4 million people were discharged from nursing homes. Admission to a hospital (29%) and death (25%) were the most frequent reasons for discharge. Two-thirds of those discharged required help in three or four ADLs—that is, they constituted an extremely impaired population (U.S. Department of Health & Human Services, *The National Nursing Home Survey: 1997*, 2000, p. 2). New residents were being admitted to those emptied beds, of course, swelling the total number of individuals who spend some time in a nursing home in the course of a year, and therefore increasing the number of families affected.

The overall picture, then, is one of considerable movement of these disabled older people, who not only move back and forth between community and hospital, but circulate among institutions of various types. Many moves may be made before they become permanent residents of long-stay facilities and eventually die there or are moved back to a hospital for terminal care.

This constant movement has major implications not only for the repeatedly relocated elderly, but for their families. Family caregivers, too, are subjected to the attendant disruption, disorganization, frustration, and emotional strains that are overlaid on their concern and upset about their older family members. The effects on family members when the older person is relocated or becomes a long-stay resident in a nursing home should be seen against that background.

GROWTH IN NURSING HOMES

The existence of a large number of nursing homes is a 20th century phenomenon. The growth in number is evidenced by the fact that in 1939 the Bureau of the Census estimated 25,000 nursing home beds in approximately 1,200 homes in the United States; by 1954 there were approximately 450,000 beds. By 1970 that number had almost doubled to 1 million. By 1973, there were 1,075,800 residents (almost 1.2 million beds) in 15,033 nursing homes (U.S. NCHS, 1975); and by 1977 there was an increase to 18,300 nursing homes containing a total of 1,287,400 residents (1,383,600 beds), of whom 1,097,900 were 65 or over (U.S. NCHS, 1978, 1973). By 1983 there were approximately 1,315,800 people in nursing homes (U.S. NCHS, 1985), of whom 20% were under 65 years of age. At the time of the 1997 report of the National Nursing Home Survey, there were 17,000 facilities containing 1.6 million residents (U.S. Department of Health and Human Services, *National Nursing Home Survey: 1997,* July 2000). The latest (unpublished) data from the 1999 survey show 18,000 facilities with 1.6 million residents (National Center for Health Statistics, 1999; U.S. Department of Health & Human Services, National Nursing Home Survey unpublished data, Table 3, 1999).

The major factor accounting for the phenomenal increase in nursing home beds was, of course, the rapid increase in the number of vulnerable older people who reach advanced old age, as well as the use of nursing home beds for retarded persons under 65 years of age. The rise in the number of nursing homes was made possible by developments such as federal programs making funds available to purchase long-term care (Old Age, Survivors, and Disability Insurance; Kerr-Mills; Medicare and Medicaid). Perhaps even more important were federal grants and loans enabling sponsors to construct, equip, and rehabilitate facilities—for example, the Hill-Burton Act, Small Business Act and Small Business Investment Act (1958), and the National Housing Act (1959).

Large-scale programs to discharge elderly mental patients from state hospitals to the community, spurred by the Mental Health and Retardation acts of 1963 and 1965, also played a major role in the growth of the nursing home industry. Many of those discharged simply went from one institution to another. That is, institutional beds were redistributed among facilities that were under different auspices, with the major drop being in state psychiatric facilities and the major rise being in proprietary (i.e., profit-making) homes. Voluntary (non-profit) homes for the aged also dropped in the proportion of all beds they contained. In 1960, for example, most of the institutionalized aged (92%) were distributed in roughly equal proportions among psychiatric hospitals (29%), nursing homes (35%), and domiciliary homes (primarily homes for the aged) (35%). The major shift in institutional auspices for older people is dramatized by data from the 1999 National Nursing Home Survey. Of the 18,000 facilities, 66.5% were proprietary (for profit), 26.7% were voluntary (non-profit), and 6.7% were government (Table 3). Nursing homes have become a large for-profit industry.

CHARACTERISTICS OF OLDER PEOPLE IN NURSING HOMES

The characteristics of older people in nursing homes indicate some of the reasons they have entered those facilities. Comparing them with noninstitutionalized elderly reveals that the two populations are very different:

- Older people in nursing homes are in advanced old age—much older than the total population of elderly. About 46% of nursing home residents are 85 years and over, compared with between 8–9% of all older people. The chances of being in a nursing home rise steadily with advancing age, from 12% of those 65–74 to 32% of those 75–84 (NLTCS, 1999).
- Most nursing home residents (more than 80%) do not have a spouse. About 17.6% are married, about 57.4% are widowed, 8.4% are divorced or separated, and 15% have never married (National Center for Health Statistics, 1999; U.S. Department of Health & Human Services, National Nursing Home Survey unpublished data, Table 24, 1999). The comparable percentages for all older people are that about 74% of men and 42% of women are married, 16% of men and 46% of women are widowed, 4% of both sexes had never married, and 6% and 7% of men and women respectively are divorced. Note that women greatly outnumber men in being widowed (AOA, 1998, Profile of Older Americans).
- Women predominate in nursing homes. About 72% of residents are women, compared with more than three out of five of all older people. One factor contributing to the over-representation of women is their longer life span. Thus, there are more of them who are vulnerable to the social, physical, and mental disabilities associated with advanced old age. Another factor is the tendency of men to marry women younger than themselves. Thus, a disabled elderly man is more likely

to have a "young" wife to provide care for him at home, whereas a disabled elderly woman is likely to be widowed.

- Nursing home residents are markedly more disabled mentally and physically than older people in general. The salient fact about their multiple problems is that they are chronic and result in functional disability, leading to dependence on others to help them in day-to-day living. Almost 40% have four or more deficiencies in ADL such as bathing, dressing, toileting, eating, and transferring; another 50% have two or three such deficiencies. These proportions are immense when residents are compared with the noninstitutionalized older people. Most residents have some kind of mental problem. Although estimates vary, it is safe to say that from one-third to one-half suffer from some form of dementia. Thus such people are enormously overrepresented in nursing homes, since about 4% of all Americans are estimated to suffer from such ailments (*National Academy on Aging Society*, No. 11, September 2000; *2000 Progress Report on Alzheimer's Disease*, National Institute on Aging). Depression is also a prevalent problem among long-stay residents. One careful study found that approximately 17% of residents of a large facility suffered from major depression and another 40% from minor depression (some of both groups were cognitively impaired as well, but those whose impairment precluded responses were excluded from the study) (Parmelee et al., 1989). And still other residents have other mental disorders.

Most relevant to the concerns of this book is the family status of elderly nursing home residents. As indicated above, the vast majority do not have a spouse to care for them. One of the contributants to the increase of the number of residents in recent years has been the smaller number of children available to older people because of the falling birth rate (Crystal, 1982). The absence of at least one daughter in the family may indicate a greater risk of institutionalization at a lower level of disability, underlining the role of daughters (Soldo, 1982b).

Thus, social support in the form of family is a critical factor in avoiding nursing home placement. The sheer existence of family does not invariably preclude such placement, of course. Other considerations operate as well, such as the characteristics of the family members themselves. People in advanced old age are likely to have children who themselves are approaching or already in the aging phase of life. Institutionalization of a parent is often precipitated by deaths or incapacities among the caregiving adult children (Brody, E. M., 1966a). Thus, that proportion of increased institutionalization that is attributed to the increase in the very old is due not only to the functional incapacities that accompany advanced old age, but to the absence of social supports and social losses that are age-related.

Undoubtedly, the increase in the number of very old people and therefore in the number of those with dementia (rates rise sharply with advancing age) contributed to the increase in nursing homes. It is extremely difficult for families to cope with behavioral disturbances such patients often exhibit. The case histories in this book illustrate those difficulties. Wandering, incontinence, disruptive behaviors, aggression, agitation, and even violence may make it impossible for families to continue to provide care. The same behavioral symptoms undoubtedly contributed to the sharp rise in the creation of special care units for this population. The first such unit, the Weiss Institute, was created at the Philadelphia Geriatric Center in 1974 after a decade of careful research and planning.

HOW CAREGIVERS VIEW NURSING HOME PLACEMENT

Though most adult children want to continue home care for their parents, their capacities to provide help to severely disabled people are qualified by their own age-related problems such as the appearance of chronic disabilities, lowered energy levels, interpersonal losses, retirement, and lowered income. They and children who are younger may have other limitations such as competing responsibilities to other family members and employment. In the overwhelming majority of cases, however, nursing home placement occurs only after caregivers have endured prolonged, unrelenting strain (often for years) and can no longer continue their efforts.

More subtle factors also are at work. There often is an accumulation or clustering of stresses. The older person's personality, the quality of family relationships, the capacity of individual and family to tolerate stress and their coping abilities, and socioeconomic factors play their roles (Brody, E. M., 1969; Brody, E. M., & Gummer, 1967).

In short, there is no one "reason" for institutionalization; it is multiply determined. But the accumulated evidence is definitive: admissions are due to varied social/health problems, and nursing home care is a social/ health solution for which in most instances there is no other option.

Caregivers who are providing home care for their parents or parents-in-law almost invariably express deep aversion to nursing home placement, even when they are far along the path and are experiencing severe strains. Participants in the case studies made comments such as: "I can't throw her away," "I can't warehouse her," and "I don't want to give her away." Subjectively, surrendering the parent's care to others is experienced as a total abdication of their own responsibility. They see admission as a dreaded, ultimate solution to be used only if they no longer have the capacity to provide the care needed. When the parent has Alzheimer's disease or a related disorder, most caregiving daughters and other relatives indicate that they would place the parent only when the latter no longer recognizes them—when, in effect, the person they knew and with whom they had a relationship is no longer there. A similar observation was made by George (1986). She noted that family members often describe their demented patients in the past tense, e.g., "He was a wonderful man." They apparently see the demented person as "someone different" from the person who used to occupy that body (p. 83).

The following excerpts from interviews with caregiving daughters illustrate their feelings about the prospect of nursing home placement. Their parents' attitudes and those of other family members are also apparent.

> It's a rule of the house, we don't talk about going into nursing homes. My feelings are based on her [the mother's] feelings. This is the one thing in her life that she's been terrified of. All of her life. Her condition would have to deteriorate or have to be pretty bad.

* * *

> I hope I never have to do that [nursing home placement]. I really do. If it was absolutely to the point where she became totally senile and it was a danger, then it would have to be done. I'd do almost anything before that. Unless there was a danger somewhere—if I worried about her wandering the streets. I would have her move in here if her situation deteriorated.

* * *

> My mother is with me, and this is her home. I felt like I was taking her out of her home. I think if my mother had been living in her own apartment, I would have told her that she couldn't live alone anymore and she should go into a home. But she was with me, so to her there was no reason why. Mother wavered in those conflicting emotional feelings that she is hemming me in, that she's done this to me and my husband. But at the same time, she couldn't face going into a home. I don't know about the future; who knows how much longer I can take it.

* * *

> I would only consider putting my mother into an institution if she became a vegetable and I couldn't physically take care of her. Otherwise, I would never

put her into an institution. I couldn't do that. My father was very sick and I cared for him in my home till he died. My emotions wouldn't let me put them in an institution.

* * *

I visited one home with my mother. She got very upset. I felt such a crunch.

* * *

My mother is depressed and angry about the possibility of going into a nursing home.

Some daughters recognize that the need for placement may be inevitable and try to face that prospect:

I've always told her that I'll keep her as long as I can. I never promised we'd keep her forever. She knows that if she needs 24-hour care and we can't provide it, that she may have to. It's no big secret. We discuss it all with her.

* * *

I have told my brothers that if it comes down to it, if having my mother here affects our health or our marriage, which it could, then she would have to go into a home.

THE DECISION-MAKING PROCESS

When placement of an older person becomes an imminent reality, it is a critical psychological experience for the elderly individual and all family members. Families rarely are prepared psychologically, and the prospect may precipitate an emotional crisis for all concerned (Brody, E. M., & Contributors, 1974; Brody, E. M., & Spark, 1966). Feelings of guilt, conflict, and shame may coexist with the conscious or unconscious but very human desire of caregivers to be relieved of the severe and unrelenting burdens they have carried.

Early studies of the paths leading to institutional care showed that placing an elderly relative was the last, rather than the first, resort of families, and that in general they had exhausted all other alternatives, enduring severe personal, social, and economic stress in the process, before making the final decision with the utmost reluctance (Brody, E. M., 1977;

Lowenthal, 1964; Tobin & Lieberman, 1976; Townsend, 1965). Some of the case studies in Part II of this book illustrate the long road some caregiving families travel that ultimately lead to placement.

When institutional care is being considered, the degree or intensity of stress may vary, but family relationship patterns are revealed vividly. Although the historical quality of the interpersonal relations between the generations and among adult siblings is a most important component in the complex of psychological reactions, it would be unrealistic to suggest a simplistic model of "good" relationships in which there is no residuum of unresolved conflict.

The elderly person may be in state of intense anxiety and fear. Even if family relations are basically warm and the necessity of placement is recognized on a reality level, some feelings of abandonment and rejection are still experienced. The feelings of all family members are communicated to each other, and the distress of each increases that of the others. The placement in psychological terms is a separation that stimulates the reactions associated with all separations from those in whom there is an emotional investment. Coming at this phase of life, when the total family is confronted with the fact that this may be the final plan for the old person, it carries overtones of the ultimate separation. Moreover, there still exist strong, deeply internalized, guilt-inducing cultural injunctions against placing an elderly parent, regardless of the most reality-based determinants of that placement. Exacerbating the reactions of all concerned is the perception that nursing homes are cold, dehumanizing environments.

Family behavior during the placement process reflects and is part of the natural continuity of past relationships from which it flows. In some families, family members—husbands, wives, adult siblings, and the older person concerned—are mutually supportive and cooperative. This enables them to move forward constructively in the placement process. When there is a history of unresolved relationship problems, however, they are often reactivated, intensified, and acted out at this time. Bitter sibling rivalries may flare up that focus on financial planning or opposing attitudes towards what constitutes the best plan for the parent. Powerful ties between the elderly parent and adult child may intensify the suffering at placement, or even sabotage it entirely.

At best, the decision-making process is never easy. As the following case excerpts will show, there are several major themes in the caregivers' feelings and experiences: They feel guilty, they are careful about selecting a nursing home, and they worry about the quality of care the parent will receive. Some sets of siblings agree about what to do and help each other.

Or, the daughter who has been the primary caregiver may receive mixed messages from other family members when some of them support the decision and others oppose it.

This daughter describes her mixed feelings and struggle to make the right decision:

> I don't think I could, from the perspective of my personality or looking at it from her perspective, put her in a nursing home. If I had four kids, I don't think I would want to end up in a nursing home or retirement home if that need not be the case. During one of her illnesses, they told me I might have to consider putting her into a nursing home. That was a hard decision once they are with you and under your care. I had mixed emotions. In one way, you think it would be a big relief; it would be an easier burden if she was elsewhere. I also had to come to terms with the fact that from a medical aspect, if she was as bad as we thought, then I really couldn't care for her. In another way, I wasn't too thrilled from what I knew about nursing homes. As far as that goes, some of it was guilt, in letting her go from here to there. There is something about having to let go and put her into something like that. My siblings were encouraging me that that would be the probable step. My husband agreed with them. They agreed that from a physical, emotional, and medical aspect, we couldn't take care of her at that point. They have also said recently that if Mother gets worse and with me and the newborn, that there may come a time when we can no longer care for her here. So that is still in the back of my mind.

Daughters are acutely aware of their parents' feelings:

> When my sister and I picked a place for Mother, we looked at it from her perspective. Originally, we never told Mother that her placement in the nursing home was a permanent thing. Now, I've had to tell her. She realized that that's where she should be. My sister and I didn't know how to approach Mother about the nursing home. If this is what she had to do, she would do it. It was hard for me because it was such a negative thing. My mother wanted to die rather than go into a nursing home. A nursing home is like the last stop. We didn't want her to go. It's so impersonal. You give up everything; you have to rely on people for everything. It's scary.

Sometimes an inexorable progression of events goes beyond the caregiver's control:

> I feel I didn't make the decision because somehow events fell into place. From the hospital, yes, she should be in rehabilitation. From hospital, yes, she should be in the nursing home for a while.

* * *

> We really didn't consider a nursing home. We thought she would die here. When she got the bladder infection, she became so disoriented, confused, combative in the hospital. I couldn't bring somebody like that home.

Efforts may be made to postpone placement in the hope that things will improve:

> We didn't want to put her in a nursing home, but unfortunately there really weren't any alternatives because she needed 24-hour-a-day care. We were hoping she would come around. For a long time, we kept her apartment. We were hoping she would come out. But she just got worse and worse.

Caregivers often involve their siblings in making this important decision:

> My sister and I made the decision about where to place Mother. I wasn't going to make that decision on my own. No way was I going to carry that load.

Family members may have different views:

> My husband thinks it's time for a nursing home. My son said when she began to go downhill to put her in a nursing home. My daughter says I can't put her in a nursing home. She said it would be better if she fell over dead at home.

* * *

> My brother was all for putting Mother in a nursing home. My cousins told me I would kill her if I sent her to a home. You know how that makes you feel.

* * *

> My husband was torn about the nursing home decision because then we wouldn't be doing what was expected of us. Two of my sisters were relieved because Mother wouldn't be coming to them. Then one of them said we couldn't do it. All of a sudden she was concerned.

When professionals are looked to for advice, their recommendations may be received with relief by the family as permission to make the placement and in placement being in the older person's best interest. Contrast two different professional approaches. One is exemplified by the doctor who told the exhausted daughter of an elderly Alzheimer's patient, "Don't put her in a nursing home. They don't last long there." Another is the doctor who wrote, "It quickly became evident that institutionalization was necessary . . . but feelings of deep affection and nagging guilt had made a realistic decision . . . difficult. My role, as I saw it, was to assuage guilt sufficiently so that the son or daughter could pursue the course that he or she had finally come to recognize appropriate. . . . The physician's 'orders' can alleviate guilt and resolve the . . . relative's problems regarding difficult decisions in institutionalization" (Hollender, 1988, pp. 105–106).

These daughters describe the role of the professionals in the decision-making process:

> Both my parents were in the hospital, and the doctors said they should be transferred to a nursing home. The doctors made the decision.

* * *

> After Mother's third stroke, the doctor said to put her in a nursing home because she was ready for that. I called my sister and told her what the doctor recommended. I told her I needed her to come help me find a nursing home for Mother. At first she said she wouldn't come. She finally decided to come for two weeks. The doctor felt Mother might not recover and might need constant care.

* * *

> My sister and I went to a caretakers meeting [support group]. The speaker was a woman who for a fee helps families decide how to care for parents. We hired this woman to help us. We had been debating about whether a live-in companion or a nursing home situation would be best for Mother. The woman told Mother she couldn't afford a live-in companion. She gave us guidelines when looking for nursing homes. It took somebody from the outside. We feel the Lord led us down the path. It wasn't coincidence. It all just worked out. She was going to have to go cause she needed what they offered.

Counseling and referral is often helpful:

> After my mother was in the hospital for three months, the nurses told us they had to release her. Thank God in a hospital like that two social workers became involved. They had to make sure we had a placement for her. That was very helpful.

* * *

> A geriatric consultant has given me some leads and advice. In other words, you are thinking of a nursing home type of situation. I don't think she could come

back. I don't think she could live in anybody's home or our family's. I think that our family has bent our lives around enough, and I think that we, with the help of my brother and sister, have given her the best care that we could, and I don't think we have to try to extend it in any way.

Considerations such as quality and range of services, costs, proximity, the physical environment, and sheer availability determine the choice of a nursing home:

The things we considered were proximity to our homes, the quality of the physical therapy department, physical attractiveness, the staff, and the type of funding they required. We had to look for a facility that accepted Medicaid.

* * *

My sister and I went to a number of nursing homes and checked things out. We would talk about the pros and cons of each one afterwards. Towards the end, it came down to a gut feeling. I don't know if we made the right decision.

* * *

First, I considered the cost. I wanted a simple place that was kept well. I had to feel right about the place. These were the things that helped me decide: simplicity, cleanliness. I try not to think about the food.

* * *

I would want to know that there was good care and that the place was reasonably well run. I would want to be sure the attendants would give her as tender and as good care as possible. I would want it to be somewhere I could visit routinely.

* * *

While she was in the hospital, I tried to get her into a decent facility, but there were no beds. So a social worker called this convalescent home, and I took her there. It was a brand new home, but the food and the care she got was bad. It was like she was there to die. She didn't know who I was and who my brother was. Finally, there was a bed available at another place. She came around beautifully.

In some instances, the older person and daughter adapt well to nursing home placement and are satisfied with the care.

It took Mother a long time to relax and enjoy the nursing home. She kept thinking back to her bad experience in the temporary placement where she fell

> and fractured her hip the first night. I had to help her with that. It took her 6 months to adjust. Now she feels she is there for a purpose. The staff at the nursing home are wonderful.

Some daughters, however, have severe negative reactions to placement:

> I'm 75 years old. I took care of Mom for 10 years. My husband had an operation, a stroke, and a heart attack. He kept saying we should put Mother in a nursing home. I said I didn't think she was ready yet, that it would be worse on me. If she was senile then maybe it would help out. I told him I couldn't force someone in there. . . . A year ago I put an application to a nursing home. I was very desperate. I was sick and lost a lot of weight. I hated to do what I did. I tried to prepare her as best I could. But it was a disgrace as far as the neighbors were concerned. Mom said, "All right. You don't want me anymore." She said she wouldn't forget. She was really sarcastic. The day after I put Mother in a nursing home I was sick. I couldn't eat or sleep. I did a terrible thing.

The distress affects other members of the family as well. An article on the Op-Ed page of the *New York Times* written by the granddaughter of a women being placed in a nursing home expressed the feelings of many of the family members poignantly. She described the agony the family members experienced and the torment of the grandmother who suffered from Alzheimer's disease. The old woman pleads, "You can just kill me if you want, but I won't stay here." The granddaughter ends her article, " . . . it feels like the most violent act in which I have ever participated. I would take it back if I could" (Kaplan, February 1, 1999).

WHILE THE PARENT IS IN A NURSING HOME

Family concern, interest, and contacts do not stop suddenly after institutionalization of the older person. Ties between the elderly parents and their adult children remain strong and viable, and most of the caregiving children continue their caring efforts, though some of the specifics of their activities may be different (Brody, E. M., 1985a; Brody, E. M., & Contributors, 1974a). The belief that children abandon their parents to the institution has been refuted.

Most elderly nursing home residents have a "next-of-kin" who most often is an adult child. As with community care of the aged, daughters continue to outnumber sons in being the one to take most responsibility for and to do more for the parent after placement (Brody, E. M., Dempsey, &

Pruchno, 1990). The individual who was primary caregiver prior to placement almost invariably continues in that role afterwards as well.

The National Long Term Care Survey of 1994 did not collect information on whether any informal care was provided to nursing home residents, but there is considerable other evidence to affirm the families' continuing efforts. Relatives provide many services such as grooming, bringing things (food, clothes, spending money, flowers), straightening bureau drawers, taking care of laundry, taking the resident for a walk, cheering him or her up, making special visits on the resident's birthday, managing the resident's money, and talking to staff abut the older person's care and needs. Though family members continue to be involved and to visit regularly, visits are progressively shorter and less enjoyable if the elderly person has Alzheimer's disease and the impairment deepens (Moss & Kurland, 1979; York & Caslyn, 1977). In general, the frequency of contacts between newly admitted residents and family and friends does decrease by half. Kinship closeness, proximity to the nursing home, and non-demented status of the resident are positively related to more frequent contacts (Port et al., 2001).

Such data do not tell us about the qualitative aspects of family members' activities, however—about the content of their visits to the older people or their contacts with staff, the effects they experience from having institutionalized relatives and from visiting them, or how they perceive their roles.

The continuity of family relationships with elderly nursing home residents and their caregivers' emotional strains have been described by clinical and research reports (e.g., Brody, E. M., 1977; Lewis, 1980; Brody, E. M., Hoffman, & Winter, 1987; George, 1984a). Adult children may experience guilt and even shame about having made the placement, sadness and worry about the parent's decline, depression, and frustration. Anxiety about their own aging processes is stimulated. Some have negative emotional reactions to visiting the older person, and some continue to experience competing demands on their time and energy. When interpersonal conflicts among adult siblings have existed, they may continue to focus on the now-institutionalized older person.

Although some strains family members experienced prior to placement continue, other strains are often different. Families attribute some of their strains to what they perceive as poor care of the parent in the nursing home, negative staff attitudes towards the elderly person and the family, the physical environment, the presence of other deteriorated patients, reluctance to "complain" about care or staff because they fear retaliation on the helpless parent, and ambiguity about their own roles vis-a-vis staff. When the older person is on Medicaid, their families often fear that the nursing home will not continue to keep them because the reimbursement is low.

The characteristics and adjustment of the older person also affect family members. When the parent is complaining or unhappy about being in the nursing home, for example, or evidences the same kinds of disordered behavior as prior to placement, there often are negative emotional effects on their family caregivers. And there is evidence that caregivers' depression is linked to how well the resident and caregiver adjust to the nursing home environment (Whitlatch et al., 2001). At the same time, placement may indeed afford the caregiver some relief. In one study, daughters were more likely than wives to place the care recipient in an institution, and experienced increased social participation and decreased subjective burden after doing so (Seltzer & Li, 2000).

The relationships of the institutionalized elderly and their family members have potential for positive change even at this late stage of the family life cycle. Some relationships improve and close family ties continue following institutionalization, perhaps because the care needs of the parent had been stressful and there is now some relief (Smith & Bengtson, 1979). In an intervention study focused on cognitively impaired older people in an institution, the family relationships of the treatment group improved significantly as compared with those of the control group (Brody, E. M., et al., 1971). And in another study, the importance of the physical environment of the facility in encouraging family visiting was underlined. Visiting increased when older people with brain impairment were moved from a traditional older building to a new, experimentally designed facility (Lawton, 1978).

Even severely impaired residents can continue to serve a positive role for family members. In one study, for example, more than one-fifth of the relatives of old people with Alzheimer's disease reported that the residents were helpful to them when they visited—cheering them up at times, giving them advice (e.g., "to take it easy"), telling them about the family's past history, and sharing recipes (Moss & Kurland, 1979). The residents often initiated conversations about family events, the past, and the institutional milieu. Interestingly, they were more likely than their family visitors to bring up disturbing topics (such as family ill-health or deaths, relationship problems, or financial difficulties). For their part, many family members were protective and had not told the residents about most of such problems or events that had occurred during the past year. Most family members said they frequently talked about the resident with other relatives and worried about her, primarily because of her poor health and deterioration.

The well-being of residents in nursing and old-age homes is vitally and beneficially affected by their receiving attention and assistance from preferred members of the family or devoted friends (Harel & Noelker, 1978). The elderly people's emotional bonds with family members often become relatively more important to them than during their middle years, perhaps because of the reduction in their other roles and associations that occurred as they aged and were institutionalized (Kleban, Brody, E. M., & Lawton, 1971).

There has long been some controversy on the subject of "integration versus segregation" of cognitively impaired residents and those who are mentally intact. The overwhelming number of expert opinions of most professionals to the effect that demented residents should be segregated from those who are cognitively intact was reflected in a study that elicited in the opinions of family members. The vast majority prefer separate living quarters for the two groups (Liebowitz, Lawton, & Waldman, 1979).

FAMILY ROLE CHANGES

Some family roles change dramatically when the old person enters a nursing home. Family members no longer share their homes with the older people, lift and turn the bedfast, bathe and dress the disabled, shop, cook, and clean for those who cannot do so, nor protect the confused from setting fires or wandering away from home. Some roles continue, however, and some new ones are added.

The provision of affective support is a major family role that continues and that is critical to the well-being of older people. Though families have been relieved of many arduous personal care and instrumental tasks, the emotional support and socialization they provide may become even more important to the old people. They care, visit, phone, are present during illness, and provide linkage to the larger family and the outside world. The family continues to be "the someone who cares," to meet the needs for affection and concern that are shared by all human beings.

This does not mean, however, that the expression of this role is free of problems. Family behavior, like the behavior of the older people, may be maladaptive to the nursing home situation. Moreover, the past relationships of older people and their families continue. Institutional personnel are familiar with family members who make a multitude of angry complaints and unrealistic demands, as well as with those who are fearful of "bothering" staff. Some "visit" by arriving daily at the nursing home at dawn and staying until the resident goes to bed (no one else can take proper care of the old person). At the other extreme, some family members distance themselves ("I can't bear to see the way my mother is now"). Anecdotal reports (Locker, 1976, 1981) suggest that individual and group counseling/therapy can improve such situations and provide an opportunity to resolve some of the psychological problems. (Not all "difficult" family behavior is unjustified, of course, as instances of abuse and poor care in some nursing homes do happen and often are reported in the media.)

Family members also continue to play a major role that is accepted as legitimate when an elderly relative is not in an institution but is ambiguous when nursing home admission has taken place—the role of advocate and mediator with the "formal" system. Now, however, the formal system is the microsystem of the nursing home rather than the social/health macrosystem in the community. But families are uncertain about how to enact the role of mediator/advocate in the nursing home. They often are reluctant to complain about the resident's care, fearing that staff will retaliate to the disadvantage of the resident who is "in their power." The uncertainty of family members about their roles is compounded by differing perceptions and attitudes on the part of the facilities' personnel who may send mixed messages. On the one hand, some staff assume that the family has no legitimate role once the care of the old person becomes the responsibility of the nursing home and they have "taken over." Family involvement—that is, asking questions about the elderly nursing home resident's condition, "complaints" about various aspects of care, and so on—may be viewed as "interference" and criticism. But if family members are not visible and articulate in expressing their concerns, their behavior is interpreted as evidence of "dumping"; they may be considered to be hard-hearted and to have abdicated their responsibility. Thus, family members often are caught in a classic "Catch-22" bind.

Another role—participation in decision-making—is equally ambiguous. A multitude of decisions are constantly being made about the lives of the residents. Some are necessarily the prerogative of nursing home staff—when, for example, a room change is necessary because the resident's changed condition indicates a move to a different level of care. But when the resident does not have the capacity to make certain decisions for herself, who has the right to make those decisions? Who decides, for example, whether the Alzheimer's patient who is unsteady on her feet should be restrained or permitted to walk and risk falling?

Not only the differing perceptions of staff and family about the latter's roles, but the different perceptions of family and the residents themselves may be a source of difficulties. For example, are the expectations and wishes of the old people with respect to family visiting congruent with the family's perceptions of what constitutes appropriate frequency of visits?

EFFECTS ON FAMILY CAREGIVERS

When an older person has been placed in a nursing home, it would seem that family caregivers should experience considerable relief from strains. They no longer need to provide the most arduous instrumental and personal caregiving tasks, no longer are giving up privacy and space in their homes, and no longer constantly witness disturbed behavior the older person may exhibit on a minute-to-minute basis.

The belief that nursing home placement of an aging parent eases the family caregiver's burden is not borne out by clinical observation or by research, however. In one study, there were no significant differences in mental health, stress symptoms, and physical health between caregivers whose patients resided in long-term care facilities and those whose patients lived with them (George, 1984). Families of nursing home residents spent almost as much time with the patient as if they were caring for the patient at home. The researcher observed that the emotional stress of watching the deterioration of a loved one continues regardless of living arrangement. Moreover, while nursing home placement may solve some problems, it causes new ones. It was concluded that institutionalization brings only limited relief from caregiver burden. A recent review of the burden on family caregivers when a relative with Alzheimer's disease is in a nursing home showed that burden continues after placement because most families continue their commitment to the caregiving role (Tornatore & Grant, 2002).

Other studies cast additional light on the problems of families. In one investigation, the patients' behaviors were identified as the most salient factor predicting the relatives' well-being—even more salient than interactions between caregiver and staff and the practical aspects of the caregiving role (Stephens & Townsend, A., 1988). The most frequent sources of stress affecting three-fifths of adult children were dealing with the older person's mental state and problems relating to balancing time for the resident with other commitments (Townsend, A., Deimling, & Noelker, 1988). Significant proportions of the children (roughly between one-third and one-half) were concerned about the cost of care, problems such as getting parents to eat properly and their complaints about food and other people in the nursing home, and staff not listening to them.

There were some particularly cogent findings in the Townsend, A. et al. (1988) study about adult children's strains. First, the children who reported greater difficulty coping with the parent's placement were the ones who perceived their parents as having more trouble adjusting. This serves as a reminder of the impact on the entire family when one member experiences a problem. It is reminiscent of Gurland's (1978) concept of the "contagion of depression" between depressed older people and the family members in whose homes the depressed people live (Gurland, B., Dean, Gurland, R., & Cook, 1978). A similar phenomenon was revealed in another study in that relatives of depressed older people in nursing homes and senior housing were found to be more depressed than relatives of the nondepressed older people (Brody, E. M., Hoffman, & Winter, 1987). Relatives of depressed residents felt more burdened, worried more, had the poorest relationships with the elderly people, and had the poorest mental health. Nevertheless, the depressed residents' relatives visited them regularly. Apparently, depression is not only "contagious" when caregiver and an older person share a household in the community. The "contagion" appears to operate even when the elderly and the relatives are separated by the walls of congregate facilities.

Among other problems experienced by family members in the Townsend study was getting other family members to visit the nursing home. Adult children who had greater difficulty coping with the placement had significantly more trouble with the institutional environment—different expectations than staff and uncertainty about their new roles. Cost and quality of care also created difficulties. Finally, it was found that children's sources of stress were significantly correlated with their mental health. The investigator commented that children need "to feel that their parent is happy there." Guilt loomed large, characterizing nearly three-fifths of the adult children. The researchers wrote:

> . . . greater guilt was significantly associated with nearly all the sources of stress, including greater difficulties coping, balancing multiple demands, the parent reportedly not adjusting well to placement, dealing with the parent's mental state, getting family to visit, and the facility's environment. . . .

In that study, adult children were compared with spouses. Significantly greater proportions of children than spouses experienced stress due to dealing with the older person's mental state (Alzheimer's disease), not being able to visit enough or having time to devote to the elderly resident, and being torn between the competing demands. (Elderly spouses, of course, usually have fewer competing demands on their time and energy.)

Though the study did not differentiate between the effects on adult sons and on daughters, the majority of the children were daughters. Obviously, daughters continue to be pulled in multiple directions even after a parent is placed and to predominate in caregiving, though the nature of the caregiving is different.

In a study that compared sons and daughters of the institutionalized aged (Brody, E. M., Dempsey, & Pruchno, 1990), predictors of depression and negative reactions to their parents' situations were the adult children's poor heath, time-pressures, viewing the parent as demanding, lack of involvement with IADL tasks, upsetting visits, negative perceptions of nursing home staff, and being female and young. Perhaps being young when a parent is in a nursing home is experienced as unexpected (off time) and therefore less synchronous with one's stage in life (see chapter 9). Daughters reported more health problems, time pressures, emotional symptoms, and depression than sons. Health was strongly predictive of depression for both sons and daughters, and indeed was the *only* predictor for the sons.

The study confirmed the continuing negative emotional effects on adult children, with large proportions of them feeling frustrated, angry, guilty, upset, worried, sad, overwhelmed, or emotionally drained as a result of having the parent in a nursing home. Particularly relevant in the context of this book is the finding that daughters experienced all of those symptoms to a significant extent more than sons, and daughters were also more depressed (Brody, E. M., Pruchno, & Dempsy, 1989).

To emphasize, *just as with caregivers providing home care, daughters of nursing home residents experience more stress than sons*. And, as is consistent in all caregiving literature, daughters continue to outnumber sons as caregivers and to provide more help even when the parent is in a nursing home. Apparently, daughters continue to be women in the middle even after the parent is in a nursing home. Like daughters providing home care, they may feel that "somehow" they have failed to meet their responsibility to provide care. Such feelings are present even though on a reality level they had recognized that nursing home care was unavoidable.

The daughters' guilt may be exacerbated by the parent's feeling of having been rejected, a feeling experienced even when the older person, too, knows there was no other option. The parent may intensify the child's guilt by complaining about the care received in the nursing home ("They don't take care of me the way you did"), by being dissatisfied with the amount of visiting, or by simply looking reproachful.

The sadness and worry of family members about the parent's decline is not relieved by nursing home placement. Since a downward trajectory in the health and functioning of the old person inevitably continues, the adult child continues to experience such painful feelings and to witness the parent's emotional reactions. In addition, the child may be silently asking the question, "Will this happen to me?"

The quality of care in a particular nursing home also affects the emotional well-being of family members. Although there are, of course, many good nursing homes, there are also many in which the quality of care is questionable or poor. Children want their parents to receive good care and to be treated well by the staff. When the parent has Alzheimer's or a related disorder, their concern about such matters is intensified. The older person cannot even communicate her wishes and needs, and staff is not as intimately familiar with his or her preferences. One daughter, for example, asked, "Will they know to give her the apple she loves every day?" Moreover, the nature of the disease is such that the patient cannot report instances of neglect or maltreatment.

The daughters speak:

> When we visited her in the nursing home, we could tell she was angry with us. She was among strangers. It was our fault.

* * *

> When I come home after visiting, I often have to sleep to forget. In the two years I've been going, I see the different ages and stages of aging and what illness can do.

* * *

> I felt very guilty.

* * *

> It still upsets me. I can't handle it.

* * *

> I got a horrendous bill from the nursing home and looked for another place.

* * *

> It's a lot of money for someone to be unhappy.

* * *

We thought we were covered for expenses for Mom in the nursing home, but they said she was not covered. We didn't leave her there. The reason was financial.

* * *

So there she is, and we have to make the best of it. When we realized she would have to stay in, I felt horrible. I don't know if we made the right decisions. Sometimes I think we did, sometimes I don't.

Sometimes the placement works well:

She came around beautifully. It was better than the first place. They keep a good check on her and they do take care of her but not like I would. I don't know if they'll keep her. I don't know yet if she will have to leave. I think that as long as they know we are waiting for a bed for Mother at the same place where my aunt is they will let her stay [a facility that will accept Medicaid].

To summarize, research and clinical practice are consistent in confirming the continuity of family bonds after nursing home placement as well as before. Although such placement is often unavoidable, it is most often the last option explored and is regarded with dread. Placement often is "successful" and the well-being of the older person and family members is enhanced. In other instances, however, family members suffer negative emotional effects that are similar to those of families providing home care, in both cases deriving from the parents' symptoms of Alzheimer's disease, competing demands on their time and energy, lifestyle disruptions, family conflict, and the parents' complaints and declining capacities. New strains may emerge, however, that are specific to the placement—dissatisfaction with the quality of care, staff attitudes and behavior, the physical environment of the institution, role ambiguity, fear of exhausting the older person's assets, and economic strains when the family is contributing toward the cost of care. Guilt is a pervasive feature of the caregivers' subjective experience.

The daughters who predominate as the significant relatives of nursing home residents continue to feel that it's up to them to do whatever they can to see to it that good care is provided and to make the parent happy. More than prior to placement, however, matters are out of the daughters' control. Perhaps the gap between what they feel they should do and what they actually do is even wider now, and that discrepancy reinforces the guilt they feel at having surrendered care to others.

Though total alleviation of the suffering of these family members is an unrealistic goal, much can be done. The most doable actions relate to reimbursement of care coupled with strict regulations regarding quality considerations and oversight. Families should not have to feel that they have consigned their relative to a "warehouse" or to outright mistreatment. Unfortunately, during the years since the first edition of this book was published, grim scandals continued to erupt periodically about neglect, poor care, unsanitary conditions, and even outright abuse of nursing home patients. All kinds of information are being re-discovered, and all sorts of "remedies" are being re-invented. In 1998, *Newsweek* printed an article about the increasing number of lawsuits brought about by injuries to patients (Reibstein, 1998). An investigative report in *U.S. News and World Report* (Schmitt, September 30, 2002) contradicted the claim of the nursing home industry that they are not reimbursed enough to provide needed care and quoted government officials and records to refute the contentions of the industry's powerful lobbying organizations.

A General Accounting Office (GAO) study reported in the *New York Times* that "nursing home residents have suffered serious injuries or, in some cases, have died as a result of abuse," but that many cases are unreported and prosecution is rare (Pear, 2002). Yet some governmental proposals aim to reduce inspections and penalties. Again, in the *New York Times*, a report notes that under the guise of improving the quality of care, the government would rely in part on data reported by the industry, a process described by consumer groups as " . . . the nursing home industry's deregulation dream come true" (Pear, September 7, 2001). A more promising development is the action by the U.S. to issue consumer data on nursing homes (beginning with six states) including the proportion of residents who need help with daily activities, who have pain or bed sores, who are in restraints, and so on (Pear, 2002).

Still another variation on the problems that exist in nursing homes is reminiscent of the events that occurred in the 1960s when there were large scale discharges of the elderly from state mental hospitals. Now there are reports about patients released from New York State psychiatric hospitals into nursing homes. Apparently, they are "being locked away on isolated floors . . . where they are barred from going outside on their own, have almost no contact with others, and have little ability to contest their confinement. . . . " (Levy, October 6, 2002). Apparently, the creation of the special units for the mentally ill was approved by the State administration, but left unregulated, and the nursing homes have not sought licenses to operate locked floors. The units are in nursing homes that care mostly for the elderly. The effectiveness of media publicity and public pressure was demonstrated when two weeks after the publicity, the United States Justice Department opened a review to determine whether federal laws that protect the rights of people who are institutionalized or have disabilities were being violated. Officials at New York State psychiatric hospitals then ended the six-year old practice by ordering social workers to stop sending discharged patients to locked units in private nursing homes (Levy, October 19, 2002, p. 1).

But the scandals never seem to cease. Less than a month later, a news story broke to the effect that New York State had been "exporting" mentally ill patents to "problem plagued" nursing homes and adult homes in New Jersey, Boston, and elsewhere. New York officials were shifting the burden of overseeing the care of difficult patients to other states (Levy, November 17, 2002). It is shameful that the problems have reached such proportions that it was necessary to hold a conference called Forensic Investigation of Crimes in Skilled Nursing Facilities in San Diego, CA, on November 1, 2002. The conference was under the auspices of the San Diego County District Attorney's Office.

Many authorities have written extensively about personnel problems with those in direct contact with elderly residents being inadequate in number, lacking adequate training, being grossly underpaid, minority women who are poorly screened (e.g., see Stone, 2000; Stone with Wiener, 2001; Olson, 2000). Many of these overburdened nurse's aides are attempting to care for their own families as well as for their patients in nursing homes and lack health benefits (Olson, 2000). Indeed, many of them have parallel, less visible "careers" as unpaid caregivers to disabled older people in their own families (Brody, E. M., 1994).

Though in many instances, the anxiety of old people and families about nursing homes are based on reality, the sanctimonious viewpoint has again been reinvented that many more disabled people can live outside institutions and that it is less expensive (see Pear, February 13, 2000). This, despite study after study showing that for severely disabled people institutional care is *not* more costly. A recent report quotes a research study, for example, that even for a group more difficult to care for—that is, Alzheimer's patients—the total annual cost of care (both paid and unpaid) is $47,083 at home and $47,591 at a nursing home. But unpaid care accounts for 73% of the cost of home care, compared to 12% of the cost of nursing home care (*National Academy on an Aging Society*, No. 11, Sept. 2000).

Among the reasons older people and their children are so wary of nursing homes is because of their appearance and how they operate and provide care. Most nursing homes look like institutions. They resemble hospitals with long double-loaded corridors, shared rooms, and a look of sterility. Care is often scheduled rigidly to be efficient rather than to meet the needs of the older people. Nursing and medical care is the paramount focus, with minimal attention to the residents' psychosocial requirements and need for enjoyable activities. Overall, there is lack of flexibility to meet the diverse human needs of the diverse nursing home population.

Despite the continuing problems, there also have been some positive developments in relation to nursing home care. Such efforts may be spurred by competition with other kinds of facilities such as the rapidly increasing number of Assisted Living facilities and services such as day care and home care. (See chapter 17 for discussion of Assisted Living facilities).

Among positive developments has been the emergence of Special Care Units for residents with Alzheimer's Disease (VanHaitsma & Rusckdeschel, 2001). Although there is no consensus about the definition of an Alzheimer's Unit, the criteria generally are: homogeneous groups of residents with dementing illness who are segregated from those who are intact cognitively; special training for staff; therapeutic environmental modifications; and an increased number and variety of activities programs. Such units hold potential for positive outcomes for the residents. Research found, for example, that in such units, short term reduction in residents' anxiety occur (VanHaitsma, Lawton, & Kleban, 2002). That benefit, as well as other positive resident behaviors associated with Special Care Units, can substantially diminish a family's distress about placement during the older person's stay at a nursing home.

By 1996, almost one-fifth of all nursing facilities had at least one special care unit containing 6.8% of all beds. There certainly are far more now. While the most common type of such units was for people with Alzheimer's Disease or a related disorder, others were for rehabilitation, subacute care, hospice, HIV/AIDS, and brain injury (Williams & Haines, 2000).

There also have been other efforts to effect favorable changes in nursing homes. Some are striving to make their physical environments more home-like by designing smaller units and using home-like decor and furniture—for example, replacing dayrooms with rooms that look like dining rooms, living rooms, and dens. The aim is to replace medical model of nursing homes with social models. Some facilities are experimenting with different ways of serving meals, including the use of smaller environments, family style service, and even allowing residents to choose when and what they prefer to eat. Many words and phrases are emerging to describe such changes such as client-centered care, cultural change, and empowerment of nursing assistants. Some states have been responsive by changing regulations and providing funds to support these changes. For example, New York State funds nursing homes to do what are called Cultural Change Projects.

There is consensus among researchers that positive organizational changes and improved environments pay dividends for residents and increase satisfaction for resident, staff, and families (Brawley, 1997; Calkins & Marsden, 2000; Cohen & Weisman, 1991; Diaz-Moore, 1999; Lawton, Weisman, Sloane, & Calkins, 1997). Diaz-Moore (2002) reports on his work in the Environmental Design Lexicon for Dementia Care Project's family groups that caregivers express greater satisfaction when their older family members are in nursing homes in which the environment and care reflect a home-like social model. Such environments appear to mitigate the family caregivers' dismay, anxiety, and guilt. Role ambiguity of staff and family requires attention in order to clarify for the different actors on the scene what each expects of the others and the problems each group experiences. Attention to the physical, socioemotional, and mental health problems of elderly residents is important in its own right, of course. It is underlined here that nursing homes are not "bad" places per se. Nursing homes are a necessary part of the continuum of care, and many are good places. It is up to all of us—including government—to eliminate abuses and poor care and to make all such facilities decent places to live.

Finally, different categories of relatives may experience different sources and amounts of strain, and all are deserving of attention. In the context of this book, however, it is reiterated that most family caregivers of nursing home residents are adult children, and three-fourths of those adult children are daughters—the women in the middle who continue to be in the middle.

Chapter 17

Some Developments in Community Services and Residential Facilities

*Avalie R. Saperstein**

This chapter does not undertake to identify, enumerate, or describe all the community services and facilities for the elderly that exist. There are many books that treat those subjects comprehensively. Nor are caregivers offered instructions or suggestions about how to provide care for disabled older people. Among many books on that subject is a comprehensive resource on how to take care of the various ailments and disabilities the elderly experience (Mezey, 2000). Rather, since the focus in this book is on women in the middle and their experiences, there will be a brief overview of some of the major services and kinds of living facilities that have developed, increased, or both during the past few decades and that are helpful not only to the elderly themselves, but to their caregivers. It is accepted as a given after decades of research that services for older people ease the strains of family caregivers—women in the middle—and are essential to improving their well-being. Similarly, as the pre-eminent environmental psychologist, M. Powell Lawton, emphasized repeatedly over several decades, the physical and social environments in which the elderly live enhance the well-being of the caring family members as well as that of the older people themselves (see Lawton, 1983; Lawton, Swisman, Sloane, & Calkins, 1997).

Many familiar services and living settings for older people that developed earlier will not be part of this chapter. Examples are single room occupancy (SROs), board and care facilities, foster homes, hotels, shared housing, and

---

*Ms. Saperstein's professional activities are detailed on p. 274.

so on. An excellent monograph by Stone (2000) synthesizes information on services, housing options, and policy in the overall context of long term care for the elderly with disabilities.

SERVICES

During the past two decades, there has been significant growth in the development of services for impaired older people living in the community. In addition to services offered through voluntary family and sectarian agencies, in some states (such as New York), government services funded through the Administration on Aging (AOA) and Medicaid began to focus on the elderly population. Often, they did so, not by the expenditure of new governmental monies, but by reallocating funds from the Older American Act and Social Service block grants, Medicaid waivers, and in some instances use of funds from State budgets that supported nursing home care. Subsequently, those early efforts spread into other areas of the country. Many were fairly sophisticated and multi-component programs for community-dwelling elderly to assist them to remain in their own homes. The services most frequently offered are home delivered meals, homemaker service, chore service, transportation, case management, counseling, nurse consultations, home modifications and friendly visitors. The provision of Medicare Home Health was also greatly expanded, but its services were limited to those who needed acute care.

In the main, informal caregivers were not and are not the explicit focus of these services. In fact, some Area Agencies on Aging exclude older people who have family caregivers. They develop policies based on the assumption that such older people are less needy, and target those who live alone. In other areas, however, the services are used to complement services being provided by informal caregivers. Thus, though the services were not designed to help caregivers and the picture is uneven, they and other family members often benefit from the provision of certain services that offer some relief so that their efforts can be redirected to other needs.

While service provision nationally was concentrating on developing services for the impaired elderly population itself, there was increasing concern from many quarters about the importance of family caregivers. Groups such as the Alzheimer's Association were gaining strength, providing and strongly advocating for services for caregivers. Efforts to develop adult daycare were also emerging with a similar dual focus.

Concurrently, there was continuing interest by researchers about family caregiving, and studies on the subject proliferated. Much of that research concerned the effects of caregiving to Alzheimer's patients. A recent thorough review of dementia caregiver intervention research concluded that the interventions have "shown promise of affecting important public health outcomes in areas such as service utilization, including delayed institutionalization; psychiatric symptomology including the successful treatment of major and minor depression; and providing services that are highly valued by caregivers" (Schultz et al., 2002). Research studies such as the Family Respite Care Service Program (Lawton, Brody, E. M., & Saperstein, 1991), apart from alleviating caregivers' strains, are important from a political standpoint. Like others before it, the study indicated that formal services to caregivers and their care recipients did not replace family care. This provides an additional policy rationale for helping informal providers without encouraging them to withdraw their own help.

It was the combination of these various activities, complemented by the experiences of professionals and the personal experiences of the public and of politicians with aging relatives, that began to turn attention toward family caregivers. The Family and Medical Leave Act, signed into law in 1993, was one result. Although the Act has limitations (for example, it excludes care for friends and non-nuclear family members, as well as any financial compensation), it is a beginning in the direction of addressing the needs of caregivers in the workforce (Older Women's League [OWL], 2001).

Despite such activities, the Federal government did not move to develop an agenda for services for caregivers. Some of the states did so, however, using their Medicaid dollars, general revenues, proceeds of lotteries, and Social Services Block Grants. Some health and social service agencies also moved in that direction. These programs often resulted from research-demonstration projects.

Two 1999 surveys by the California Family Caregiver Alliance and the National Association of State Units on Aging (Coleman, 2000) found that a wide range of programs for caregivers had been developed and were operational in many states. The programs ranged from being minimal to those comprehensive enough to include several components such as information and referral, family consultation or care planning, support groups, care management, and education and training. California and Pennsylvania are among those offering the more comprehensive statewide caregiver support programs (Pandya & Coleman, 2000). In addition, 35 of the 50 states have programs that provide some cash assistance to caregivers (Stone, 2000). Again, these programs vary widely, ranging from some cash reimbursement to caregivers for caring for the older person to reimbursement for out-of-pocket expenses.

Although many of these projects were not evaluated by research, anecdotal evidence indicates that caregivers felt helped by the services. In addition, some caregiver intervention studies such as those by Bass, Noelker, and Rechlin (1996) and Toseland, Rossiter, and Labrecque (1989) indicated that certain interventions led to positive outcomes for caregivers and that service use mitigated some of the negative consequences of caregiving. Toseland's use of caregiver groups led to improvements in psychological functioning, increases in informal support networks, and positive personal changes in coping with the challenges of caregiving.

An example of a successful program for caregivers is the Counseling for Caregivers Program in Philadelphia, PA. Beginning in 1985, it resulted from a research/demonstration project (Lawton, Brody, E. M., & Saperstein, 1991). This comprehensive program still exists under the sponsorship of the Madlyn and Leonard Abramson Center for Jewish Life (formerly the Philadelphia Geriatric Center), as well as with substantial funding from an array of foundations, such as The Pew Charitable Trusts, and fee for service. Its director reports that it provides approximately 500 caregivers annually in the greater Philadelphia area with information and referral, case management, education, counseling, and respite (Berdugo, Peninah), personal communication, 2002). Program evaluation data consistently indicate that as a result caregivers are linked to needed resources, experience significant improvements in solving caregiving problems, increase their competence in managing the caregiving situations, and enhance their knowledge and sensitivity to their elderly relatives' limitations.

It was not until 2001, that the Federal government began to make a modest investment in services designed specifically for caregivers (apart from Medicaid). In October 2000, Congress reauthorized the Older Americans Act amending it to include funding for a National Family Support Program under Title III. This program awarded funding to state departments on aging for the purpose of distributing funds to Area Agencies on Aging to develop and support respite care to families caring for their elderly relatives at home. Grants were made to an array of organizations to develop innovative strategies to provide services to caregivers. Funding was authorized at a very modest $125 million for 2001 and reauthorized at a slightly increased amount for 2002 (Pandya & Coleman, 2000).

In addition to the federal, state and social service agency programs listed above, adult daycare has experienced substantial growth, offering a range of services to both care recipients (medical, recreational, therapeutic, and socialization) and to their caregivers (respite, education, support groups). In eight years, the number of daycare centers doubled nationally, growing from 2,100 centers in 1989 to 4,000 centers in 1997. Daycare centers are extremely diverse in sponsorship (proprietary and voluntary), in their services (both medical and social models), in sources of revenues (subsidies from Medicaid, Older American Act monies, fee for service), and in target populations (dementia and physically impaired). Daycare serves mainly those with moderate cognitive and/or physical impairments, although there are a disproportionate number of persons with cognitive problems (Stone, 2000).

Caregivers who struggle to maintain their elderly relatives at home benefit from daycare which offers them respite, education, and relief from sharing the care with daycare staff. Starting attendance at daycare can be traumatic for older people and for their caregivers as well. Sending vulnerable relatives to new situations is difficult emotionally, and preparing the disabled to board a van or to be driven by the caregiver at a scheduled time to the site of daycare may be an arduous task. For those who persevere, studies such as the one by Zarit, Stephens, Townsend, and Greene (1998) have shown that caregivers who utilize adult daycare programs benefit in terms of reduced levels of stress and improved psychological well being.

There is a wide variety of services for caregivers under diverse kinds of sponsorship. The main resources for obtaining referrals to needed services are the local Area Agencies on Aging and family service agencies. Private geriatric care managers provide fee for service assistance to families in order to help them to understand what their older relatives need and want and to connect them with the appropriate services. Some large business corporations provide their employees with eldercare services including information/referral, education, and support groups. Caregivers can call some hospitals and social service agencies to obtain information and referrals. And of course, there are many fee-for-service homemaker agencies.

In sum, some progress in service development has been made. But there is also a great deal that remains to be done. At present, services are diverse and uneven regionally. Although some communities are resource rich in such services, most have few and many have none. On balance, there simply are not enough publicly financed services so that caregivers with low incomes can benefit. Government and foundation supported services are extremely significant because of their financial accessibility. Another limitation is that some caregivers, especially those with diverse ethnic and racial backgrounds simply lack knowledge that the service exists (see chapter 15).

Both increased amounts of existing kinds of services and an increased range of services and benefits are needed. The list is long and includes such benefits as dependant care accounts and tax credits for care of elderly family members and friends, financial benefits linked to The Family Medical Leave Act, as well as more flexible eligibility criteria for care recipients. (Dependent care accounts allow employees to set aside a certain amount of their paychecks prior to tax to spend on dependents.)

RESIDENTIAL FACILITIES

Chapter 16 reviewed the ample evidence to the effect that older people and their families dread nursing home placement, that they experience stress when the disabled elderly share adult children's homes, and that older people ardently wish to have their own living spaces. It follows, then, that a range of other kinds of residential facilities should exist and more should be invented. Some progress has been made in this direction.

Continued living in one's own home is not always an option. The older person may need more than the periodic scheduled help that a caregiver who lives separately can provide, even when complemented by help from community services. The elderly individual may require unscheduled intermittent help that is almost impossible to provide without some form of 24-hour supervision. Or, even if her needs can be met in a scheduled manner, she may be alone most of the day, becoming more and more isolated. Some of the newer forms of living arrangements that have been developed more closely approximate one's own home than does a nursing home. It is self-evident, however, that the environment and services of any facility must match the resident's capacities.

Congregate Housing with Supportive Services

Congregate Housing is residential housing, usually apartment buildings specifically designed for well older people, which include certain services such as meals and housekeeping. The very first such building opened at the Philadelphia Geriatric Center in 1960 and was replicated widely during the next several decades. Many of the earlier buildings had a minimal number of supportive services, and later added them or contracted with community services to do so as their residents aged in place. People continue to be attracted to this type of housing because it resembles "normal" housing and because it provides opportunities for socialization. In the main, people move to congregate housing when they have decided that they no longer want or can manage all the responsibilities of maintaining their own homes. The kinds and amounts of available services and resources vary significantly among different facilities. Generally, the family's role is the same as when the older people live in their own homes. Some of these congregate settings are supported through the Department of Housing and Urban Development (HUD).

Assisted Living (ALs)

Assisted living (AL) is the most rapidly growing kind of senior housing in the United States with an estimated 15–20% annual growth. Recently, it was estimated that approximately 600,000 residents were living in 25,000 to 30,000 such facilities (Citro & Hermanson, 1999). ALs are designed for older adults who require some help in their activities of daily living, but who do not require the medical management and oversight of nursing homes. While some voluntary nursing homes have been developing ALs as part of their overall operation, Stone (2000) points out that the industry includes more real estate developers and hotel managers than care providers.

There is no universally accepted definition of assisted living, but it is generally agreed that, ideally, it is characterized by a philosophy of resident autonomy, dignity, privacy, and independence, and is a social model of care as contrasted with the highly structured and medical environment of nursing homes. About two-thirds of ALs have between 11 and 50 beds. They have been defined as group settings that provide a range of services such as meals and personal care services (for example, bathing, medication administration, some health monitoring, and 24-hours-a-day supervision so that intermittent care can be provided as needed) (Hawes, Rose, & Phillips, 1999). These facilities are generally homelike environments with private rooms or apartments and private bathrooms. Some ALs are entirely for residents with a dementing illness; others provide special units for persons with such diagnoses.

Assisted living is not federally licensed and regulated, but is a state responsibility. There is significant diversity among the states in licensing and regulation and in definitions of AL. Most states have licensure regulations, and most are minimal, which has both positive and negative aspects. Ideally, minimal regulations allow facilities to adopt innovative ways of serving the particular needs of each resident. At the same time, using the rationale of providing a homelike and social environment, ALs may not provide the appropriate health and safety standards required by impaired residents. Competition among ALs in a given community often appears to be the quality regulator.

Some serious problems exist when facilities do not provide what is promised or add on fees to attend to the individual resident's needs. Although the "aging in place" concept is a major selling point for ALs, fewer than half (45%) retain residents with moderate or severe cognitive impairments or physical limitations (such as need for help in transferring), and only 28% would retain residents with behavioral symptoms such as wandering (Hawes et al., 1999). The Hawes survey found that 65% of the facilities they studied provided "low service"—that is, they did not have an RN on staff or did not provide nursing care, and another 5% did not provide personal care assistance.

The average cost per day of ALs in 2000 was $78 (ALFA, 2001), an amount beyond the resources of middle and moderate-income older persons and their families. Fewer than one-fifth of people over age 75 can afford this without spending down (Williams & Hawes, 2000). Although some states provide public support and subsidies, third party reimbursement is not widespread. Some states, however, have tried to use residential care as a less costly substitute for institutions (Stone, 2000). But such reimbursement is only for those residents who are nursing home and Medicaid eligible, excluding many who would choose the option but whose financial resources are too high to qualify for Medicaid but too low to pay privately, as well as those who don't quite meet nursing home eligibility standards.

There is an incentive for states and the federal government to become involved in the financing and maintenance of older people in ALs because they are less costly than nursing homes. Based on families' experiences with ALs, family availability and support may be a key factor in allowing some nursing home residents to choose that form of living in lieu of nursing homes. Another pressure for federal and state involvement is that families and older people prefer and are advocating for that option. Professional organizations (AAHSA, AARP, the Alzheimer's Association, the American Health Care Association's National Center for Assisted Living, the American Seniors Housing Association, and the Assisted Living Federation of America) are pressing for the development of low cost, quality facilities (AAHSA, 2002).

Some states are working with organizations to develop low cost assisted living facilities. Combining innovative financing approaches that may include housing financing agencies, Low Income Housing Tax Credits, and community development assistance, the number of assisted living facilities for low-income residents is beginning to grow (Citro & Hermanson, 1999). Moreover, the federal government (states often are already involved) is beginning to participate in promoting such affordable facilities. Appropriations in 2000 and 2001 for HUD included $50 million for converting elderly HUD projects to assisted living facilities. The FY 2001 bill also included an additional $50 million allocated to the Section 202 program to develop such new facilities (Wilden & Redfoot, 2002).

Although these are modest steps, they are promising beginnings toward enabling impaired elders and their caregivers to benefit from this housing option. At the same time, caution must be exercised in monitoring ALs to ensure that they deliver the services they promise.

No matter the living arrangement chosen, the family plays a major role in most situations, being instrumental in assisting the older person to choose the facility and to move there. Recognizing that there is enormous diversity in facilities, families need to be wise consumers. What families perceive as the best facilities may not in fact be "best." Some of the more costly ALs recognize that adult children have a strong need to place parents in the best possible environment, yet they do not educate those families about the fact that their notions of their elderly family member's needs may not reflect what is really best or even appropriate.

Further, though they need not do the daily hands-on care, families continue to provide service monitoring and advocacy on behalf of their elderly relatives; major assistance with medical appointments and medical care decision-making; and, of course, emotional support. Thus, the amount of supervision and service families must provide continues. And, of course, the families also must respond to their elderly relatives' changing capacities and may face the upsetting prospect of moving them elsewhere.

Continuing Care Retirement Communities (CCRCs)

To live in a CCRC is a lifestyle option available only to those with ample financial resources. CCRCs (also called Life Care Communities) are communities that provide housing, health care and residential services for the elderly for the lifetimes of the residents in what has been called a continuum of care. Depending on their changing needs, the older people generally enter the CCRC, first living in independent apartments, then moving to assisted living, and then to the nursing home. All of these elements are combined in one enriched community. The independence and well being of the residents are emphasized, as well as the opportunity for them to participate in community activities.

This form of living has grown rapidly. In 1981, there were about 300 of them in the nation (Winklevoss & Powell, 1982). Powell and MacMurtrie (1986) pointed out that over 40% of the communities in their 1981 survey opened during the 1970s. Sponsored by a variety of auspices, CCRCs have been proliferating during the past few decades and were reported in 1997 to number about 1,200 communities serving about 350,000 residents (Sanders, 1997). The average age at admission is almost 79 years, and the average age of all residents is slightly over 81 (Sanders, 1997). They are an attractive and stable retirement option for long-term care.

Most CCRSs are luxurious, with correspondingly luxurious prices, though there is a wide diversity in services, price and contract types. Usually there is a substantial entrance fee for purchase of the apartment that may or may not be partially or totally refundable when the resident dies or leaves. There also is a monthly charge, plus the cost of additional meals and medical supplies if needed. The contracts must be read carefully to fully understand entitlements and extra charges. For example, while nursing home care may be included, there may be a significant extra charge for a private room.

Basically CCRCs offer four types of contracts. *Life care contracts* provide independent living and health related services. No additional fees are generally required if a resident moves from one level of care to another. *Modified contracts* provide independent living and a specified number and amount of health related services such as nursing home care. *Fee for service contracts* provide independent living and guaranteed access to health related services which are provided at the full per diem rate. *Equity contracts* involve an actual real estate purchase with a transfer of ownership of the unit allowable almost invariably at a discounted price.

CCRCs are considered an insurance product and are regulated by state departments of insurance. They also are regulated by state agencies in accordance with the types of care they include, such as assisted living facilities and nursing homes. The Continuing Care Accreditation Commission of the American Association of Homes and Services for the Aging also licenses them.

There are certain advantages for older people and their caregivers when this option is chosen. In many ways, when people elect to enter a CCRC, they are simultaneously deciding what their future care, if needed, may be. When more care is required, the care is at hand, thus avoiding the emotional strain of choosing and moving to a different facility. In addition, since the older people enter this environment while they are well, they and their family members have opportunities to learn about the community and to develop relationships with staff and peers. Transitions, although always difficult, are accomplished in a known setting, among staff and friends who are familiar and nearby. At the same time, family caregivers remain active in their relatives' care.

As with all housing options, the consumer must be educated and knowledgeable. In the past, CCRCs have invested most heavily in the independent part of the living facilities in order to attract new residents to enter. This has sometimes led to less than adequate number of facilities and services in the assisted living and nursing home units. Change is occurring, however. With older residents aging in place and more sophisticated managers, some CCRCs are investing their talents and money to develop the more intensive levels of care.

Naturally Occurring Retirement Communities (NORCs)

A new name has emerged to define communities and/or buildings where large numbers of older people have aged in place. This newest form of living, which has attracted much attention is called "Natural Occurring Retirement Communities" (NORCs). According to a 1992 survey, 27% of older people live in a building or neighborhood where more than 50% of the residents are over the age of 60 (Lanspery, 1998).

NORCS develop in multiple ways. In some instances, as older people move into an area or building, the younger people move out. The area or building may be a condominium complex, a rental apartment building, a cooperative, a mobile home park, or a neighborhood of one- or two-family homes. It is self-evident that a NORC can only develop where there is a concentration of older people. Although they exist primarily in urban areas, there are some NORCs in rural and suburban areas as well.

Perhaps the best known and largest NORC is Co-op City in the Bronx, New York. It is under the direction of New York City's United Hospital Fund's Aging In Place Initiative. Of its 50,000 residents, 8,000 are 65 or older. Many moved in when the buildings opened in 1968 and have never moved out. The *New York Times* called it the "largest de facto retirement home in the nation" (Feuer, August 15, 2002, p. 1). It abounds with opportunities for a wide variety of activities and services including seminars, classes, trips, Meal on Wheels, mental health clinics, a daycare area, and many, many others.

NORCs have been receiving increasing interest in the last decade or so. Their residents have varied needs, and it is in the best interest of all concerned to meet those needs. From the service providers' perspectives, it is cost effective to serve people in high-density locations. From the building owners' perspectives, attending to the well being of the residents maintains a positive ambience and encourages good upkeep of apartments. Some NORCs have been targeted for special services by Area Agencies on Aging and family service agencies. Others have identified their own needs and invested in special contracts to provide services that are paid for by a blend of private pay, building owner contributions, foundations, and subsidies. Some NORCs have extremely sophisticated service systems including special activities and socialization, case management, health care services, and help with activities of daily living.

In 2002, the federal government awarded grants totaling $3.7 million to support community services to NORCs in five cities for the purpose of enhancing the residents' ability to remain in the community in a quality environment (U.S. Administration on Aging, 2002). Although a modest sum, it is a beginning. Because of the increasing amount of publicity about NORCs, they have captured the interest of both the housing and aging networks.

NORCs are advantageous for families as well as for their residents. An important advantage is that the services enable the older people to remain in their own homes and age in place surrounded by friends and neighbors. The family role remains basically the same as when older people live in their own homes, but finding and using resources and services is easier, since the NORC has identified reliable service providers and facilitates connections. The NORC may even have a monitoring system to be sure the in home services provide help as scheduled, thus alleviating some family concerns. The older person is not as isolated, as she may be living in the larger community with emergency help and assistance close by. Family members remain involved in decision making, medical issues, and advocacy, and are, of course, still emotionally connected. If the resident deteriorates beyond the point of continued NORC living, the family participates as always in the decision-making process and placement.

An additional advantage is that NORCs may enable people with cognitive and physical impairments to remain at home longer than if they living were in a separate home in the community. Anecdotal reports indicate that while other residents may complain about the deterioration of their friends and neighbors, they are generally helpful and resist moving them to more intensive levels of care unless their behavior is disturbing.

In conclusion, it is reiterated that no matter how much responsibility some facilities assume for the resident, ultimately the family assists in making the difficult decisions, provides the emotional support the older person most values, implements the move when one is indicated, and experiences the impact that may occur. The older person relies on the family regardless of the services available or housing arrangements.

New services and forms of housing should be evaluated, ways should be found to make those with favorable outcomes available, and invention as well as replication should occur.

Part V

Unfinished Business on the Parent-Care Agenda

Chapter 18

Unfinished Business on the Parent Care Agenda

The plight of women in the middle requires attention and action not only in their own interests, but in the interests of the elderly and their entire families. Unless solutions are sought, found, and implemented, reverberations will be felt down through the generations. While some progress has been made since the first edition of this book was written, there remains unfinished business that was noted at the time but that has not been addressed appropriately. In addition, new items have appeared on the agenda. It is to be hoped that knowledge will be developed about new trends and situations that have occurred and that actions based on such knowledge will be taken.

It cannot be assumed, however, that a neat list of unfinished agenda items can be drawn up and checked off in turn as each is accomplished. There will always be unfinished business because change is a constant in addressing issues concerning parent care. The number and proportion of older people in the population has changed and inevitably continues to change. Their characteristics and needs have changed and will continue to change in unpredictable ways as each new cohort enters the aging phase of life and as new scientific and social developments occur. The health status, values, lifestyles, preferences, and personal resources (including family resources) of the elderly change. Changes also occur in the environment in which caregiving takes place—in the social and economic climate, and in social policies that create, eliminate, or reduce services, entitlements, and facilities. Nor are values immutable, though they change slowly and unevenly.

This book has emphasized the interlocking of the well-being of the elderly and their family members. It follows that positive changes in the lives of caregivers are linked to positive changes in the lives of the older people and affirms that things can be done to effect such changes. The title of this chapter, "Unfinished Business," takes as its premise the proposition that the "business" of improving the plight of older people and their caregivers—the women in the middle—*can* take place.

Since the first edition of this book, some things have changed, some things have remained the same, and diversity has increased. Some developments have been beneficial to women in the middle, their elderly parents, and their families. But in some areas, the *lack* of developments has been disappointing. These will be noted in this chapter, as will some directions that can be taken.

PERSPECTIVE

It is important to recall that the continuing increase in the elderly population is a most positive development. Each new cohort of older people in past decades has been progressively healthier, better educated, and has enjoyed higher incomes and more leisure. Most of the aged are not sick and dependent and are able to enjoy the gift of longer life. People who have worked for many years can look forward to a retirement in which to rest from their labors or become involved in new activities, and enjoy their children, grandchildren, and great-grandchildren. At any given time, most do not need any more help than the normal, garden-variety of reciprocal services that family members of all ages exchange on a day-to-day basis and at times of emergency or temporary need. As we are all aware, however, some of the benefits achieved are threatened from time to time and vigilance is required to ensure that the gains that were made are not eroded.

The younger generations, too, benefit from the demographic developments and scientific advances that have resulted in a large aging population. Many more babies and children nowadays can expect to have both of their parents survive while they are growing up. Many more young parents can raise their children without fearing that epidemic diseases will carry those children off. Today's young children are fortunate in that they can learn to know many more grandparents and great-grandparents than earlier cohorts of children. Older people are often a resource to the younger generations in the family, giving them emotional support and financial aid, caring for young grandchildren, and providing other services. In fact, the proportions of old people who *give* help to their children exceed the proportions who *receive* help from their children. There are few people who would wish those opportunities away in order to return to the "good old days" of family life that weren't as good in those ways as nowadays.

It is undeniable, however, that one result of the vast increase in the number of very old and disabled people in the population is that parent care is now a normative experience. Although the burden falls differently on different population groups, most people need to help an elderly family member at some time during their lives. Adult children nowadays provide much more care and more arduous care to more older people for longer periods of time than ever before in history. Their capacity to supply all the help needed is often exceeded. The women who provide most of the needed help, therefore, often experience the severe strains documented in this book.

What the elderly want most from their children is affection, continuing warm relationships and contacts, and to be cared about. Above all, they do not want to be dependent on anyone. In one research study after another, older people consistently express their fear of dependency and emphasize their wish not to be "a burden." The last thing they want is to become a source of worry and strain to their children. They do expect, however, that if they become disabled and need help, their children will see to it that they are cared for. But most do not want their children's love to be demonstrated by cleaning, cooking, personal care, or financial help when these can be obtained from nonfamily sources.

For their part, adult children who are privileged to have surviving parents want them to live on and to do so in a state of well-being. They want to provide care when it is needed. These attitudes reflect strong family values and bonds of affection forged over many decades. Their commitment is a potent and constructive force, and they feel rewarded when they honor that commitment. Such loyalty has been shown to transcend ethnic and racial differences.

Against that background, women's profound and compelling conviction that care of the elderly is *their* responsibility has not changed. Women still feel and behave as though it's up to them to provide all the help older people need and to make their parents and parents-in-law happy as well. Indeed, they still try to do it all and to make everyone in their families happy.

Women set high standards for themselves in enacting all of the roles they play and in meeting what they perceive as their responsibilities to their parents, to other members of their families, and to their jobs or volunteer work. They put themselves at the bottom of their priority lists, giving up their own free time and chances to socialize and take vacations when need be. Many women are deprived of opportunities to meet their own needs. They even forego opportunities for their own development in the form of employment and education when they cannot manage to juggle all of the things they are called upon to do. Yet they often feel that somehow they are not doing enough. As the national surveys and research studies cited earlier in this book have shown, there is no evidence at all that women's commitment to caregiving to their old has diminished. That has continued despite the increased demands on their time and energy that have occurred.

Some of the values held by women have remained constant, and some have changed. Despite the pressures exerted by the demographic changes, the women's "old" values about family care of the elderly and about their responsibility to be the caregivers have not changed. Changes in other of their values have, however, been expressed by their continuing, large-scale participation in the labor force. When the new and old values compete and the women's actual behavior in caring for parents is scrutinized, in the main it is the old values that are controlling. It is thus clear that the new values have not driven out the deeply rooted old values.

Unquestionably, daughters and daughters-in-law remain in an uncomfortable middle position in many ways. In the middle generationally, in their middle years, in the middle of competing responsibilities to various people in their families and to their jobs, and in the middle between values that compete, they often ignore their responsibilities to themselves.

As the data and the women's narratives showed, parent-caring women are at various stages of life. It is not unusual for them to have caregiving careers that overlay several life stages as they take care of several older people simultaneously or sequentially. As a result, many of them experience negative effects on their emotional, physical, and economic well-being and on their own and their families' lifestyles. If things do not go well, many think that somehow they have failed. That has not changed either.

Among the reasons some adult daughters push themselves so hard is the feeling that they must return in kind the total care they were given by the parent in childhood—a goal that is unachievable. They confuse providing care with caring—as though they must give all the care the older person needs themselves, and if they do not, they don't care enough. They are subject to pressures to continue, not only from their own subjective processes, but also from societal values that stimulate and intensify such feelings. Whatever the reasons (and there are many), some women refuse even those services that are available and that could give them some relief during their parent-care years.

All indications are that the problem will increase. If help is to be offered to women in the middle and their families, several paths must be taken in the search for solutions. The various tasks to be accomplished require different approaches—separate, but interrelated and interdependent activities that have implications for each other. Since knowledge is incomplete and existing broad trends continue while new ones emerge, it is urgent that the problems be explored further and that the trends be monitored by research. Social policy must see to it that community services that can help are in place, that long-term care facilities are available when placement of the older people is necessary, and that those nursing homes are regulated so that scandals and abuses do not continue to erupt about the treatment received by the older people who live in such places. Service organizations and agencies and their workers must see to it that those in need know of the existence of services and can gain access to them. Women who do not use available services, even when their need is great, require help to do so. And the agenda for all of us is to see to it that we move in a positive direction toward those goals.

RESEARCH AGENDA

Social and economic trends are susceptible to change and are not always predictable. Moreover, new trends constantly emerge. Continuing and newly emerging tends require constant and systematic tracking and study to determine their effects on patterns of parent care and on the recipients and providers of care. Some of the trends described in this book are continuing. For example, there is no sign that the increase in women's labor force participation will change direction. Another trend is the demographic changes that are further reducing the supply of filial caregivers and increasing the pressures on women to care for several older people. The section of this book on Baby Boomers spells out their double jeopardy in growing old as part of a huge number of disabled very old people who have fewer children to provide them with care.

Multiple caring responsibilities may also increase because older people who have no children on whom to depend will be more numerous. Some older people will lack family caregivers either because they have always been childless or because being in advanced old age increases the possibility of outliving one or more of their children. Though other family members rise to the occasion to help the childless, they do not do as much as older people's own children. Caring for the childless elderly presents a special challenge to society and professionals.

Extremely important are the effects on parent care of certain changing patterns of family formation. How will those various patterns be enacted when the elderly members of the family need care? Examples are the increases in gay couples, inter-racial marriages, and single parent families. Because of high rates of divorce and lower marriage rates, more people will not have spouses to help them in old age. How will elderly people alone and without children be cared for? For that matter, who cares for such people now? At the same time, more remarriages mean more parents/step-parents and also more step-siblings in those "blended families." How will filial loyalties play out in caring for more elderly parents, step-parents, and in the ways in which caregiving may be shared with assorted step-siblings?

A surprising gap in data about family care of the elderly concerns older people with functional mental problems or with severely disturbed and disturbing behavior. As noted in chapter 2, there is no survey similar to the NLTCS for that population. Yet, what information is available tells us that such mental disabilities are severely stressful for family caregivers—even more than care of the physically disabled (see chapter 3).

In a related vein, other changing patterns cry out for attention. Developmentally disabled people are living longer, so that more caregivers will experience "double dependency" as they care for their elderly parents and disabled children at the same time (often well into the latter's adulthood). As Lebowitz has emphasized, surveys similar to the NLTC surveys have not been done for the under-65 chronically disabled with life-long mental illness (e.g., schizophrenia), physical impairment, or developmental disability for whom family caregiving remains the primary source of assistance (particularly for mothers, whose own aging in turn compromises their continuing ability to provide care) (Lebowitz, May 2001). Who will care for such "children"?

Another increasing form of double dependency derives from the later ages at which some women are electing to have their first child. More of them, therefore, will be in the parent-care years while they still have young children at home. The nests of some middle generation people are not only remaining filled with their offspring for longer periods of time, but are being refilled to a greater extent with young adults who return home, sometimes with their own young children. The nests of more families, then, are filled with young adult children as well as with disabled elderly parent(s).

Though adult daughters and daughters-in-law predominate as filial caregivers for elderly people, there are other patterns of care of the old by the younger generations that have barely been addressed. The differences between care of mothers and care of fathers and of in-laws of both genders have not been fully studied, for example. Some adult children help elderly parents who are caring for spouses, and some care for both parents at the same time. And some grandchildren become primary caregivers when deaths in the middle generation leave a caregiving gap. Indeed, some grandchildren find themselves responsible for two generations of older people—their parent(s) and grandparent(s). Even when not in primary caregiving roles, those grandchildren as well as other members of the caregivers' nuclear and extended families constitute an invisible backup system, making important appearances at times of emergency or special need. Study of the operation of that system—its composition, how it is mobilized, and how it functions is a fascinating and potentially fertile area for investigation.

And there are still other matters to monitor with respect to grandchildren. In 1997, well over a million children under the age of 18 lived in households of grandparents without a parent being present. Many times that number lived in three-generation family households. The increase in the number of grandparents who are rearing their grandchildren makes one wonder about grandparent care when generation two has been missing. Will those grandchildren substitute for adult children in helping disabled grandparents? And how old will those children be when such a contingency arises? How will their lives be affected? (See Fuller-Thomson and Minkler, 2001, for discussion of research needs about this subject.) Will children born of not-married couples behave in a fashion similar to those who are children of married couples? The number of unmarried couples in the U.S. nearly doubled in the 1990s. The number of families headed by women who have children grew almost 5 times faster in the 1990s than the number of married couples with children, reported the *New York Times* based on Census Bureau data (Schmitt, 2001).

There is a particular need for longitudinal studies to supplement cross-sectional surveys. People's situations change over time, and it is the trajectory of change that informs us of their needs. Moreover, parent care is not an event that is isolated from the continuum of life experience; the patterns have their roots in early childhood. We know little of the meaning of the parent-care years as they shape the contours of people's entire lives. What changes occur in the wake of the parent-care years? What are the sequelae even long after the parents' deaths? And how does the parent-care experience influence the lives of all concerned when the caregivers themselves grow old?

The focus of this book on caregiving women is not meant to ignore or exclude the disabled elderly themselves. The inner experiences of the older people themselves require exploration. How do they feel, and what are their reactions and their perspectives when they are dependent on adult children? They are the ones who fear becoming "a burden" on their children. What effects do they experience when their fears become reality?

There are many other research needs. The need for more knowledge about ethnic/racial differences in parent care is self-evident in view of the significant increases in various minority groups in the U.S. Still another trend is the increase in geographic mobility, which (combined with fewer children) creates special problems when distance separates parents and children. The new forms of housing options that provide supportive environments and services surely require monitoring. New "inventions" deserve evaluation.

PUBLIC POLICY AGENDA

It is not within the purpose of this book to set a comprehensive policy agenda; policy options have been explored in detail elsewhere (e.g., Brody, S. J., 1987; Binstock, 1999; Binstock & Day, 1996; Stone, 2000; AARP, 2001, OWL, 2001). Nevertheless, a word must be said, because public policy concerning the elderly has direct relevance for their family members as well. Maddox (1987) offered compelling evidence of the firm linkage between older people's socio-economic status and their functional capacities. In the major research he reported, improvements in socio-economic status were associated "dramatically and significantly with reduced levels of functional impairments" (p. 560). It follows that better functioning capacity translates into less help needed from caregiving family members—from our women in the middle. Ergo, an essential step toward alleviating the burdens of those caregivers is to improve the social and economic circumstances of the old people for whom they provide care.

Delineating what has been done and what remains to be done with the broadest of brush strokes, it is apparent that policy had moved forward primarily in the areas of income maintenance and acute medical services for the elderly. In the current political climate, however, even those gains are being threatened. Modest progress had been made in the direction to which the trends described have pointed—that is, the area of supportive health/social services. Most of the recently invented kinds of living facilities show promise, but are, unfortunately, beyond the economic capacities of most of the elderly. There is an urgent need to create the services and facilities dictated by acute, transitory, and long-term care needs dictated by chronicity. These are now incomplete and uneven regionally.

Income maintenance and payment of acute medical costs for older people have been of direct benefit to their families as well as to older people themselves. As was indicated, prior to Social Security (1935), SSI (1972), and Medicare (1965), to be old virtually meant to be poor. Although there are still some poor older people (and that should not be), poverty no longer characterizes most of the elderly. Only a very small proportion are now totally dependent on their children for day-to-day living expenses, in contrast to the more than half who were dependent before Social Security took hold. Similarly, because of Medicare, the elderly and their children do not have to worry about being wiped out financially because of acute catastrophic illnesses of the old (Brody, S. J., 1987). It is important to be vigilant, however, lest any Social Security or Medicare benefits be eroded. The well-documented care needs of mentally ill old people (and therefore the needs of their families) have been grossly neglected. Reimbursement for care under Medicare is much more limited than for physical ailments, for example.

A significant area of unfinished business on the social policy agenda is long term care insurance. It is *the major requirement* of the elderly population and their family caregivers. The attempt to develop a long-term care policy that was introduced in Congress during the late 1990s was defeated. It appears highly unlikely that new legislation will be introduced in the foreseeable future. Moreover, the pharmaceutical subsidy programs for older adults, promised in the 2000 presidential election, have not materialized. The proposals being put forward will do little to alleviate the problem. Our failure to enact a program of long-term care insurance and to incorporate pharmaceuticals as part of Medicare are major disappointments.

Until the political climate permits major advances, we could proceed incrementally to develop the essential components of a long-term care system. For example, more supportive community services can be developed, but require federal funding. Development of housing options with services should go forward. Funding through Medicaid and HUD could help provide some options.

Nursing homes continue to provide care for our most impaired elderly, but should move toward social models of care rather than routines and environments that resemble hospitals. In addition to adequate reimbursement, strict oversight and monitoring of facilities is needed if we are to avoid the scandals about outright abuses that occur. Neglect and abuses have persisted for many, many decades and erupt and are rediscovered periodically (see Chapter 13). Surely it is time for mistreatment of our old, disabled, helpless people to be ended by strict governmental surveillance and enforcement of standards. After so very many years of a variety of unacceptable conditions, when will that happen?

The lack of a national policy focusing directly on caregivers has resulted in the unofficial policy of simply cheering the family on to do more. However tentative steps are being taken toward recognizing the problems that confront women in the middle. In 2001 and 2002, the federal government allocated some monies for demonstration projects focusing on services for caregivers. While we have had a plethora of demonstration projects, that program is a beginning. State, local, and privately financed research/demonstration projects have consistently documented the advantages for caregivers when they utilize information and referral, respite care, counseling, case management, support groups, and education. But, again, the federal government is needed to support states' efforts and to expand programs nationally. Designating services as entitlements would encourage caregivers to utilize formal services to complement their caregiving efforts and would send a strong message to the effect that eldercare cannot be the sole responsibility of women in the middle.

A major problem is the crisis we are facing in the workforce because of a shortage of workers who provide 90% of the direct formal care to older people in their own homes and in facilities such as nursing homes. Based on the anticipated growth in the aging population and the rising levels of education of immigrant groups who will be less willing to work in such low-wage jobs, the crisis will grow to unprecedented levels. (See Stone, 2000, for an excellent discussion of this issue.)

At the root of this personnel crisis is the low value that we as a society place on such workers. Nursing assistants in residential facilities and home care workers in the community are predominantly women of color or recent immigrants (Olson, 2000). Their jobs in the community and nursing homes place them at the bottom of the staff hierarchies, subject to rigid rules and regulations, with minimal or no autonomy. They care for the most impaired elderly residents who are often of different racial/ethnic groups, work at times with insufficient staffing and resources, have difficult hours, engage in labor that is physically demanding, are paid minimum or slightly above minimum wage, and some do not have benefits. In addition, most deal with stressful situations at home resulting from living in poor neighborhoods, economic difficulties and responsibilities for their children and other family members (Foner, 1994; Tellis-Nayek & Tellis-Nayek, 1998). Indeed, many such workers have parallel, less visible, unpaid careers as caregivers to older people in their own families (Brody, E. M., 1994). Scarcity of such workers in the future is not simply a matter of demographics, but of role and wages as well. The net result is a situation in which frail older people are being taken care of by unpaid and stressed informal caregivers and underpaid, poor (often minority) women.

The policy trend for many years has been to embrace community care as an "alternative" to nursing home care and to create barriers to institutional placement. The "either/or" approach that places nursing homes in competition with community care has been proven to be inappropriate. Community care is not cheaper for the severely disabled. Yet at the very same time that the so-called alternative of community care is sanctimoniously encouraged, health and social services have been systematically reduced and housing subsidies have been virtually eliminated, increasing the burden on caregiving families by closing avenues that might relieve them.

The financing of long-term care, in the community and in nursing homes, must come from the federal government. As S. J. Brody has emphasized, the cost of public insurance would not be "a bottomless pit," but its development depends on the value judgment made by society: the issue is not our *ability* to take this step, but our *willingness* to do so (Brody, S. J., 1987). A quarter of a century ago, in a major report, The Brookings Institution strongly endorsed public long-term care insurance. It stated that private insurance should be encouraged but could not be afforded by most people (Rivlin & Wiener, 1988). Experts agree that the informal support system itself is in need of support and that provision of services would help the family continue to do what it has always done and is committed to doing.

Part of the problem is the confusion about the meaning of words such as "dependency" and family "reliability" and "responsibility." As this book has shown, there are different kinds of dependency—financial, physical, and emotional—that have quite different meanings to those involved. The elderly wish to depend on different people for different needs and services. Thus, their expectations for filial support vary when anchored to specific tasks. No one pretends that bureaucratic organizations can substitute for the emotional support (expressed by concern, continuing contacts, and help in emergencies) that families provide to older people. But family reliability does not necessarily mean giving ongoing personal and nursing care or performing household tasks. As many gerontologists have pointed out, some functions are appropriate for families and others for the "formal" support system. Unless such blurred distinctions are clarified, inappropriate value judgments will continue to hamper the development of social policy.

Money would also help. Some suggestions are to expand the Family and Medical Leave Act and the Dependant Care Tax Credit to include care for elder relatives (OWL, 2001). In September 2002, California took the lead by enacting an important expansion of the Act which allows employees to collect as much as 55% of their usual salaries for up to 5 weeks a year for that purpose. Twenty-seven other states are now considering similar legislation. Among other economic considerations are the opportunity costs incurred by caregivers (and their families) when parent care interferes with their vocational lives. We know little about the costs of health care (mental and physical) for those caregivers who are negatively affected by the help they provide to the old.

There is a long way to go in inventing flexible ways to buttress and complement family efforts. But enough information is at hand to enable policy-makers to mount a vigorous attack on the problems. Scapegoating the elderly by encouraging intergenerational competition in the allocation of resources belies understandings about the linkages in the well-being of the generations. "Filial responsibility" is seen in all-or-nothing terms as involving *total*, round-the-clock responsibility. The question is, *when does the public's expectation of filial responsibility mean abdication of social responsibility?*

PRACTICE AGENDA

The emotional strains of parent care would not be eliminated even in the best of all possible worlds in which all needed services existed and were available, accessible, and affordable. Though understanding of the psychological processes at work is by no means complete, the information already at hand has not been fully integrated into the curricula of professional schools or applied in practice. There is growing awareness among professionals of the needs (medical, psychological, and social) of older people themselves, but that interest has not been matched by interest in the intra- and interpersonal problems of family caregivers. There should be a shift from tunnel vision focus on the individual to a wide-angle lens view that includes other members of the family in the interest both of the caregivers and the of the elderly recipients of care.

There are subtle issues that impede service utilization and speak to the need for counseling. As the case studies in this book showed, there are psychological barriers that inhibit some women's use of needed services. In addition, the acceptability of services differs among older people with different socioeconomic, racial, and ethnic backgrounds and among individuals and families with diverse personalities and expectations. Therefore, whatever the label given to the process now most commonly referred to as "case management," it must include the enabling process called counseling.

Attitudinal barriers are not limited to the recipients of care. As the case studies showed, professionals and religious leaders often exhibit negative and judgemental attitudes, exhorting exhausted caregivers to exert further efforts. An example is Doty's description of a case in which a daughter did not want to take her disturbed father into her home because he had already set a boarding house on fire (Doty, 1995). The solution advocated by the hospital planner was for "the hospital staff to work on family members until by cajoling, browbeating, shaming, and bribing them with services to the extent possible, they could be convinced to do their duty" (p. 99).

Because of the complex nature of the problems with which case managers deal, effective case management is a highly skilled, knowledge- and values-based activity. It is not solely a mechanical manipulation or arrangement of tangible services, but should include the offering of sensitive help with psychosocial issues. The blending of these activities cannot be carried out by untrained people, no matter how well-meaning they may be.

The nonuse and underuse of services by some of the neediest caregivers is a constant frustration to service workers. Reports about subsidized respite services, for example, including those for caregivers of Alzheimer's patients, consistently report that they are grossly underutilized by caregivers and when used, are used very modestly. This, despite concerted efforts to educate and counsel them. Surely, the therapeutic professions must turn their attention to the subjective problems some caregivers experience that prevent them from using help to ease their distressing, even health-threatening, situations.

AN AGENDA FOR ALL OF US

In recent years, there has been a flow of books of advice on parent care. Women are being instructed in techniques of nursing care for older people and what symptoms to look for, the importance of assessment and treatment of the elderly, and so on. They are being told about methods of reducing the stress they experience from parent care (relaxation techniques, for example). They are being advised how to manage older people who have personality or behavior problems. Women are being told not to feel guilt or other of the symptoms they experience. Support groups have proliferated, and some women do indeed feel supported, though others need more or different forms of help than support groups can offer. All of those things are important and undoubtedly help some women in some ways.

But one of the most disturbing aspects of the caregiving drama is the resignation of some daughters and daughters-in-law—their acceptance that this is the way it has to be. That acceptance is given such sanction in our society—even powerful, crushing reinforcement—that few women can resist as individuals.

Women in the middle are victimized by the intense pressure to which they are subjected in being told to embrace caregiving exclusively as their lot no matter the effects on their lives. As a result, some not only have low expectations of help from others, but tend to belittle the value of such help. The expectations of others reinforce the women's expectations of themselves and loom large in producing the strains and symptoms to which daughters and daughters-in-law are so vulnerable. It may be that the underlying anger and feelings of helplessness these women experience (whether or not they are aware of those feelings) are components of the depression, anxiety, and other mental health symptoms so often reported as consequences of parent care.

That is not to say, of course, that women should not help elderly family members. No one would disagree with the value we all hold that older people should receive care. No one would disagree with the proposition that it is the responsibility of the family and society to see that the care is provided. In helping their elderly, however, some women go beyond what appear to be the limits of endurance and do so at the cost of severe deprivation and suffering to their own families and their own mental and physical health. Not all women do so, of course. In some instances, care is not unduly stressful. In some instances, help from other family members and nonfamily sources is obtained and utilized. But there are some women who do not seek or accept even the help that is available to them. Although there are those who have special, individual problems, they share with all of their counterparts the pressures of societal value about women's roles in parent care.

A major imponderable in the unfinished business of parent care is how the tension between changing and constant values will be resolved. Values determine not only what is done by society and professionals, but interact with socioeconomic conditions and people's subjective processes to determine behavior on the level of the individual and family.

When the Women's Movement began, some people assumed that the goal of women was to gain equality by broadening the scope of their activities in the world of men. But, as psychologist Corinne Weithorn was prescient in pointing out, that notion yielded to the realization that change must occur not only in women's roles but in men's roles as well. Realignment of male/female relationships in the division of labor, she argued, should use the concept of *equitable* rather than *equal*—that is, not equal sharing of identical tasks, but a fair sharing of the total load. Looking at women's roles in historical and cross-cultural perspective, Weithorn (1975) wrote, "Now that strength is no longer a requisite for survival, pregnancy no longer a consequence of sexual activity, and the infant no longer dependent on the mother's breast, women are demanding a revised contract, one more adaptive to survival in contemporary society" (p. 292).

A revised contract between men and women has by no means been drawn up and ratified. The new values about gender roles have taken hold unevenly. Many men have supported the Women's Movement, many accept women's working as a desirable lifestyle change or as an economic necessity, and some have made genuine efforts at a radical change in their own lifestyles. But all available evidence indicates that true equity has not been achieved.

The Women's Movement has not offered strong advocacy to middle generation women. It has emphasized the interests of young women and has also paid some attention to elderly women. But somehow the problems of women between the young and old have received only token attention. Today's young women should remember that they are destined to be the women in the middle of the future.

On balance, the socialization of women to the role as caregiver is powerful, and the behavior of today's adult children tells us that most women and men continue to accept the proposition that it is women's role to provide the day-to-day care of the old. An important (and not fully realized) fact is that, no matter the degree to which men share responsibilities, parent care and women's employment add to the total package of family responsibilities to be shared. Equity between men and women, then, is not a total solution. Additional help must come from other sources such as the "formal" system and from the business community as well. Such help serves men as well as women in the middle and the elderly.

There is a growing awareness among bewildered and beleaguered women in the middle that they are not alone in their predicament and that help in various forms can be obtained. It remains to be seen whether that awareness can be channeled into a force for effecting change. It is too much of a demand on individual women to deal with the pressures exerted by societal values and expectations. Perhaps attention to the problem requires a massive sea change of the magnitude of the women's movement itself. Women need the collaboration of all of society—professionals, researchers, policy-makers, and men.

Women will continue to pursue diverse lifestyles, and they should have the freedom to do so. Undoubtedly, in the future some women will prefer to work at full-time occupations, and some will adhere to "traditional" roles as wives, mothers, and homemakers. Others will move in and out of the work force as the needs of their families dictate. Each woman has to decide for herself what she wants the shape of her life to be.

It is now axiomatic, however, that women's changing roles inevitably affect men as well. Though most men undoubtedly feel the repercussions of parent care as husbands, brothers, and sons of women in the middle, some may be finding themselves "men in the middle" when they must become the principal "responsible" family member in helping the old. The demographic trends indicate that more of them will be in that position in the future.

An unanswered question is why women do not organize to lobby for change. The elderly and particularly the very old and disabled are predominantly women. Those who provide care are predominantly women, both in the informal and formal systems of care in nursing homes and in the community. Women and men have not joined with each other to press social policy-makers for the needed services, to demand flexibility and benefits from employers, and to urge the women's movement to make the cause of women in the middle its own.

We cannot do it all, of course. There is no simple or single solution. Women will continue to care for and about the elderly people in their families, to be concerned and sad at the declines of those old people, to provide affection and support, to do what they are able, and to arrange for the needed services that they cannot supply. (Perhaps those are the only appropriate "norms" for filial behavior.) The strains so many parent-caring women experience are not completely preventable or remediable. But those women deserve and should expect to receive the help they need to keep them from exceeding the limits of endurance, a point that so many reach now. True, we do not know all we need to know to accomplish that goal. But surely we know enough to move in the right direction.

References

Agency for Healthcare Research and Quality (AHRQ). (2000, February). Nursing home quality of care improved during the early 1990s. *AHRQ, 234,* 13–14.

Allen, I. (with collaboration from Levin, E., Sidell, M., & Vetter, N.). (1983). The elderly and their informal carers. In Department of Health and Social Security, *Research Contributions to the Development of Policy and Practice* (pp. 29–92). London: HMSO.

American Association of Homes and Services for the Aged (AAHSA). (2002). *Assisted living: Choice, flexibility, and affordability issue brief,* pp. 1, 2. Washington, DC: AAHSA.

American Association of Retired Persons (AARP). (1987, February).Caregivers in the workplace. Survey results. Overall summary. Washington, DC: AARP.

American Association of Retired Persons (AARP). (2001). *Executive summary of in the middle, a report on multicultural boomers coping with family and aging issues.* Washington, DC: AARP.

American Association for World Health. (1999). *Healthy aging, healthy living—start now,* Resource Booklet, 7.

Archbold, P. G. (1978). Impact of caring for an ill elderly parent of the middle-aged or elderly offspring caregiver. Paper presented at the 31st Annual Meeting of the Gerontological Society, Dallas, TX.

Archbold, P. G. (1983). The impact of parent caring on women. *Family Relations, 32,* 39–45.

Assisted Living Federation of America (ALFA). (2001). *ALFA's Overview: 2001 of the assisted living industry, supplemental report,* 1–10. Fairfax, VA: Assisted Living Federation.

Bass, D. M., Noelker, L. S., & Rechlin, L. R. (1996). The moderating influence of service use on negative caregiving consequences. *Journals of Gerontology Series B: Psychological Sciences and Social Sciences, 51*(3), 121–131.

Bengtson, V. L. (1975). Generation and family effects in value socialization. *American Sociological Review, 40,* 358–371. New York: Springer Publishing Company.

Bengtson, V. L., & Silverstein, M. (1993). Families, aging, and social change: Seven agendas for 21st century researchers. *Annual Review of Gerontology and Geriatrics, 13,* 15–38.

Bengtson, V. L., & Treas, J. (1980). The changing context of mental health and aging. In J. E. Birren & R. B. Sloane (Eds.), *Handbook of mental health and aging* (pp. 400–428). Englewood Cliffs, NJ: Prentice-Hall, Inc.

Binstock, R. H. (1999). Challenges to United States policies on aging in the new millennium. *Hallym International Journal of Aging, 1*(1), 3–13.

Binstock, R. H., & Day, C. L. (1966). Aging and politics. In R. H. Binstock & L. K. George (Eds.), *Handbook of aging and the social sciences* (4th ed.) (pp. 362–387). San Diego, CA: Academic Press.

Blenkner, M. (1965). Social work and family relationships in later life with some thoughts on filial maturity. In E. Shanas & G. Streib (Eds.), *Social structure and the family: Generational relations* (pp. 46–59). Englewood Cliffs, NJ: Prentice-Hall.

Boaz, R. F. (1996). Full-time employment and informal caregiving in the 1980s. *Medical Care, 34*(6), 524–536.

Boaz, R. F., Hu, J., & Ye, Y. (1999). The transfer of resources from middle-aged children to functionally limited elderly parents: Providing time, giving money, sharing space. *The Gerontologist, 39*(6), 648–657.

Boaz, R. F., & Muller, C. F. (1991). Why do some caregivers of disabled and frail elderly quit? *Health Care Financing Review, Winter, 13*(2), 41–47.

Bombeck, E., quoted by J. Skow. (July 1984). Erma in Bomburgia. *Time,* 56.

Brawley, E. (1997). *Designing for Alzheimer's disease*. New York: John Wiley & Sons.

Broder, J. M. (2002, September 24). Family leave in California now includes pay benefit. *The New York Times,* p. A20.

Brody, E. M. (1966a). The impaired aged: A follow-up study of applicants rejected by a voluntary home. *Journal of American Geriatrics Society, 14,* 414–120.

Brody, E. M. (1966b). The aging family. *The Gerontologist, 6,* 201–206.

Brody, E. M. (1969). Follow-up study of applicants and non-applicants to a voluntary home. *The Gerontologist, 9,* 187–196.

Brody, E. M. (1970). The etiquette of filial behavior. *Aging and Human Development, I,* 87–94.

Brody, E. M. (1974). Aging and family personality: A developmental view. *Family Process, 13,* 23–37.

Brody, E. M. (1977). *Long-term care of older people: a practical guide.* New York: Human Sciences Press.

Brody, E. M. (1978). The aging of the family. *Annals of the American Academy of Political and Social Science, 438,* 13–27.

Brody, E. M. (1979). Aging parents and aging children. In P. K. Ragen (Ed.), *Aging parents* (pp. 267–287). Los Angeles: University of Southern California Press.

Brody, E. M. (1981). Women in the middle and family help to older people. *The Gerontologist, 21,* 471–480.

Brody, E. M. (1985a). The role of the family in nursing homes: implications for research and public policy. In M. S. Harper & B. Lebowitz (Eds.), *Mental illness in nursing homes: agenda for research,* 234–264 (NIHM). Washington, DC: U.S. Government Printing Office.

Brody, E. M. (1985b). Parent care as a normative family stress. The Donald P. Kent Memorial Lecture. *The Gerontologist, 25,* 19–29.

Brody, E. M. (1986). Informal support systems in the rehabilitation of the handicapped elderly. In S. J. Brody & G. E. Ruff (Eds.), *Aging and rehabilitation* (pp. 87–108). New York: Springer Publishing Company.

Brody, E. M. (1988). *Marital status, parent care, and mental health.* (Project 1 of Caregiving and Mental Health: A Multifaceted Approach, NIMH grant number MH43371).

Brody, E. M. (1990a). *Women in the Middle: Their Parent-Care Years.* New York: Springer Publishing Company.

Brody, E. M. (1990b). Role reversal: an inaccurate and destructive concept. *Journal of Gerontological Social Work, 15*(1–2), 15–22.

Brody, E. M. (1992). Problems of carers: The United States' view. In J. B. Evans & T. F. Williams (Eds.), *Oxford Textbook of Geriatric Medicine.* Oxford: University Press.

Brody, E. M. (1994). Women as unpaid caregivers: The price they pay. In E. Friedman (Ed.), *An Unfinished Revolution: Women & Health Care in America* (pp. 67–86). United Hospital Fund of New York.

Brody, E. M. (1995). Prospects for family caregiving; response to change, continuity, and diversity. In R. A. Kane & J. D. Penrod (Eds.), *Family Caregiving in an Aging Society* (pp. 15–28). Thousand Oaks, CA: Sage Publications, Inc.

Brody, E. M. (2001). The Philadelphia Geriatric Center: How did it happen? *Contemporary Gerontology, 8*(1), 14–20.

Brody, E. M. & Contributors. (1974). *A social work guide for long-term care facilities.* Washington, DC: U.S. Government Printing Office.

Brody, E. M., Dempsey, N. P., & Pruchno, R. A. (1990). Mental health of sons and daughters of the institutionalized aged. *The Gerontologist, 30*(2), 212–219.

Brody, E. M., & Gummer, B. (1967). Aged applicants and non-applicants to a voluntary home: An exploratory comparison. *The Gerontologist, 7,* 234–243.

Brody, E. M., Hoffman, C., Kleban, M. H., & Schoonover, C. B. (1989). Caregiving daughters and their local siblings: Perceptions, strains, and interactions. *The Gerontologist, 29*(4).

Brody, E. M., Hoffman, C., & Winter, R. (1987). *Family relationships of depressed, dysphoric, and non-depressed residents of nursing homes and senior housing.* Presented at 40th Annual Meeting of The Gerontological Society of America, Washington, DC.

Brody, E. M., Johnsen, P. T., & Fulcomer, M. C. (1984). What should adult children do for elderly parents? Opinions and preferences of three generations of women. *Journal of Gerontology, 39,* 736–746.

Brody, E. M., Johnsen, P. T., Fulcomer, M. C., & Lang, A. M. (1982). *The dependent elderly and women's changing roles.* Final report on AoA grant number 90–A 1277).

Brody, E. M., Johnsen, P. T., Fulcomer, M. C., & Lang, A. M. (1983). Women's changing roles and help to the elderly: Attitudes of three generations of women. *Journal of Gerontology, 38,* 597–607.

Brody, E. M., Kleban, M. H., Hoffman, C., & Schoonover, C. B. (1988). Adult daughters and parent care: A comparison of one-, two-, and three-generation households. *Home Health Care Services Quarterly, 9,* 19–45.

Brody, E. M., Kleban, M. H., Johnsen, P. T., Hoffman, C., & Schoonover, C. B. (1987a). Work status and parent care: a comparison of four groups of women. *The Gerontologist, 27,* 301–208.

Brody, E. M., Litvin, S. J., Albert, S. J., & Hoffman, C. (1994). Marital status of daughters and patterns of parent care. *Journal of Gerontology, 49*(2), S95–S103.

Brody, E. M., Litvin, S. J., Hoffman, C., & Kleban, M. H. (1992). Differential effects of daughters' marital status on their parent care experiences. *The Gerontologist, 32*(1), 58–67.

Brody, E. M., Litvin, S. J., Hoffman, C., & Kleban, M. H. (1995a). Marital status of caregiving daughters and co-residence with dependent parents. *The Gerontologist, 35*(1), 75–85.

Brody, E. M., Litvin, S. J., Hoffman, C., & Kleban, M. H. (1995b). On having a "significant other" during the parent care years. *Journal of Applied Gerontology, 14*(2), 131–149.

Brody, E. M., & Schoonover, C. B. (1986). Patterns of parent care when adult daughters work and when they do not. *The Gerontologist, 26,* 372–381.

Brody, E. M., & Spark, G. (1966). Institutionalization of the aged: A family crisis. *Family Process, 5,* 76–90.

Brody, S. J. (1985). The future of nursing homes. *Rehabilitation Psychology, 30,* 109–120.

Brody, S. J. (1987). Strategic planning: The catastrophic approach. The Donald P. Kent Memorial Lecture. *The Gerontologist, 27,* 131–138.

Brody, S. J. (1990). Geriatrics and rehabilitation: Common ground and conflicts. In S. J. Brody & L. G. Pawlson (Eds.), *Aging and Rehabilitation II* (pp. 9–29). New York: Springer Publishing Company.

Brody, S. J., Poulshock, S. W., & Masciocchi, C. F. (1978). The family caring unit: A major consideration in the long-term support system. *The Gerontologist, 18,* 556–561.

Butler, R. N., & Lewis, M. (1973). *Aging and mental health: Positive psychosocial approaches.* St. Louis, MO: C. V. Mosby Company.

Calkins, M. P., & Marsden, J. P. (2000). Home is where the heart is: Designing to recreate Home. *Alzheimer's Care Quarterly, 1*(1), 8–16.

Campbell, R., & Brody, E. M. (1985). Women's changing roles and help to the elderly: Attitudes of women in the United States and Japan. *The Gerontologist, 25*(6), 584–592.

Cantor, M. H. (1983). Strain among caregivers: A study of experience in the United States. *The Gerontologist, 23,* 597–604.

Center on an Aging Society (1999). Analysis of data from the 1999 NLTCS-Beta Release Version 3.0, Washington, DC: Center on an Aging Society.

Chatters, L. M., Taylor, R. J., & Jackson, J. S. (1985). Size and composition of the informal helper networks of elderly blacks. *Journal of Gerontology, 40,* 605–614.

Cherlin, A., & Furstenberg, F. F. (1985). Styles and strategies of grandparenting. In V. L. Bengston & J. F. Robertson (Eds.), *Grandparenthood* (pp. 92–116). Beverly Hills, CA: Sage Publications.

Cicirelli, V. G. (1980). Relationships of family background variables to locus of control in the elderly. *Journal of Gerontology, 35,* 108–114.

Cicirelli, V. G. (1981). *Helping elderly parents: The role of adult children.* Boston, MA: Auburn Housing Publishing Company.

Cicirelli, V. G. (1982). Sibling influence throughout the lifespan. In M. E. Lamb & B. Sutton-Smith (Eds.), *Sibling relationships: Their nature and significance across the lifespan* (pp. 267–284). Hillsdale, NJ: Lawrence Erlbaum Associates

Citro, J., & Hermanson, S. (1999). Assisted living in the United States. Washington, D.C. *AARP Public Policy Institute* (pp. 1–11). American Association of Retired Persons.

Cohen, U., & Weisman, G. D. (1991). *Holding onto home: Designing environments for people with dementia.* Baltimore: John Hopkins Press.

Cohler, B. J. (1983). Autonomy and interdependence in the family of adulthood: A psychological perspective. *The Gerontologist, 23,* 33–39.

Cohler, B. J., & Grunebaum, H. U. (1981). *Mothers, grandmothers, and daughters: Personality and childcare in three-generation families.* New York: John Wiley and Sons, Inc.

Coleman, B. (2000). Helping the helpers: state-sponsored services for family caregivers. Executive Summary, *AARP Public Policy Institute, 2007-7,* (1–4). Washington, DC. American Association of Retired Persons.

Community Relations Letter (1987, February). The Center for Corporate Community Relations, Vol. 1, No. 7.

The Conference Board. (1997, Winter). *Work-family roundtable—juggling the demands of dependent care, 7*(4). New York: The Conference Board.

The Conference Board. (1999). *Work-life initiatives in a global context.* New York: The Conference Board.

Corson, W., Grannemann, T., Holden, N., & Thornton, C. (1986). Channeling effects on formal community-based services and housing. *Technical Report 86B-10.* Princeton, NJ: Mathematica Policy Research.

Crummins, E. M., Saito, Y., & Reynolds, S. L. (1997). Further evidence on recent trends in the prevalence and incidence of disability among older Americans from two sources: The LSOA and the NHIS. *Journal of Gerontology B Psychological Science and Social Science, 52,* 559–571.

Crystal, S. (1982). *America's old age crisis: Public policy and the two worlds of aging.* New York: Basic Books.

Daniels, N. (1988). *Am I my parents' keeper?* New York: Oxford University Press, Inc.

Deimling, G. T., & Bass, D. M. (1986). Symptoms of mental impairment among elderly adults and their effects on family caregivers. *Journal of Gerontology, 41,* 778–784.

Diaz-Moore, K. (1999). Dissonance in the dining room: A study of social interaction in a special care unit. *Qualitative Health Research,* 9(1), 133–155.

Diaz-Moore, K. (2002). [Personal communication.]

Dilworth-Anderson, P., Williams, I. C., & Gibson, B. E. (2002, April). Issues of race, ethnicity, and culture in caregiving research: A 20-year review (1980–2000). *The Gerontologist,* 42(2), 237–272.

Doty, P. (1986). Family care of the elderly: The role of public policy. *The Milbank Quarterly,* 64(1).

Doty, P. (1995). Family caregiving and access to publicly funded home care: Implicit and explicit influences on decision making. In R. A. Kane & J. D. Penrod (Eds.), *Family Caregiving in an Aging Society.* Thousand Oaks, CA: Sage Publications.

Doty, P., Jackson, M. E., & Crown, W. (1998). The impact of female caregivers' employment status on patterns of formal and informal eldercare. *The Gerontologist, 38*(3), 331–341.

Doty, P., Liu, K., & Wiener, J. (1985). An overview of long-term care. *Health Care Financing Review, 6,* 69–78.

English, O. S., & Pearson, G. H. J. (1937). *Common neuroses of children and adults.* New York: W. W. Norton and Company.

Enright, R. B., & Friss, L. (1987). *Employed caregivers of brain-impaired adults.* San Francisco, CA: Family Survival Project.

Erikson, E. (1950). *Childhood and society.* New York: W. W. Norton and Company.

Feuer, A. (2002, August 15). High-rise colony of workers evolves for their retirement. *The New York Times,* pp. A-1, A-15.

Foner, N. (1994). *The caregiving dilemma.* Berkeley, CA: University of California Press.

Frankfather, D., Smith, M. J., & Caro, F. G. (1981). *Family care of the elderly: Public initiatives and private obligations.* Lexington, MA: Lexington Books.

Freedman, V. A., Martin, L. G., & Schoeni, R. F. (2002). Recent trends in disability and functioning among older adults in the United States: A systematic review. *JAMA (Journal of the American Medical Association), 288, No. 24,* 3137–3146.

Friedan, B. (1963). *The feminine mystique.* New York: W. W. Norton and Company, Inc.

Friedman, D. E. (1986). Elder care: The employee benefit of the 1960s? In *Across the Board,* June, 46–511. New York: The Conference Board.

Fries, J. F. (1984). The compression of morbidity: Miscellaneous comments about a theme. *The Gerontologist, 24,* 354–359.

Fuller-Thomson, E., & Minkler, M. (2001). American grandparents providing extensive child care to their grandchildren: Prevalence and profile. *The Gerontologist, 41*(2), 201–209.

George, L. K. (1980). *Role transitions in late life.* Monterey, CA: Brooks/Cole Publishing Company.

George, L. K. (1984). The burden of caregiving: How much? What kinds? For Whom? In *Advances in Research,* 8(2). Durham, NC: Duke University, Center for the Study of Aging and Human Development.

George, L. K. (1984a). *The dynamics of caregiver burden.* Final report submitted to the AARP Andrus Foundation, December.

George, L. K. (1986). Caregiving burden: Conflict between norms of reciprocity and solidarity. In K. Pillemer & R. Wolf (Eds.), *Elder abuse: Conflict in the family* (pp. 67–92). Boston: Auburn House.

Gilligan, C. (1982). *In a different voice.* Cambridge, MA: Harvard University Press.

Gold, D. T. (1987). Siblings in old age: Something special. *Canadian Journal on Aging, 6,* 199–215.

Goldfarb, A. I. (1965). Psychodynamics and the three-generation family. In E. Shanas & G. F. Streib (Eds.), *Social structure and the family: Generational relations* (pp. 10–45). Englewood Cliffs, NJ: Prentice-Hall.

Grad, J., & Sainsbury, P. (1966). Evaluating the community psychiatric service in Chichester: Results. *Milbank Memorial Fund Quarterly, 44,* 246–278.

Greenberg, B. (1984). The sources speak. In *The Jewish women in the middle,* 16–22. Hadassah Study Series. The Women's Zionist Organization of America.

Gruenberg, E. M. (1977). The failures of success. *Milbank Memorial Fund Quarterly, Health and Society* [Winter], 3–24.

Gurland, B. (1990). Symposium on role reversal: A discussant responds. *Journal of Gerontological Social Work, 15*(1&2), 35–38.

Gurland, B., Dean, L., Gurland, R., & Cook, D. (1978). Personal time dependency in the elderly of New York City: Findings from the U.S.-U.K. cross-national geriatric community study. In *Dependency in the Elderly of New York City* (pp. 9–45). New York: Community Council of Greater New York.

Gwyther, L., & Blazer, D. (1984, May). Family therapy and the dementia patient. *American Family Physician,* 149–156.

Haley, W. E., Levine, E. G., Brown, L., Derry, J. W., & Hughes, G. H. (1987). Psychological, social, and health consequences of caring for a relative with senile dementia. *Journal of the American Geriatrics Society, 35,* 405–411.

Harel, Z., & Noelker, L. (1978). *The impact of social integration on the well-being and survival of institutionalized aged.* Presented at the Annual Meeting of the Gerontological Society, Dallas, TX.

Harris, P. B. (1998). Listening to caregiving sons: Misunderstood realities. *The Gerontologist, 38*(3), 342–352.

Hawes, C., Rose, M., & Phillips, C. D. (1999). A national study of assisted living for the frail elderly. *Myers Research Institute, Menorah Park Center for Senior Living,* Beachwood, Ohio.

Heuser, R. L. (1976). Fertility tables for birth cohorts by color: United States, 1917-73, Table 7A. Rockville, MD: U.S. DHEW, PHS, Pub. No. (HRA)76-1152, NCHS.

Hobbs, F. B. (1996). 65+ in the United States. *Current Population Reports, Special Studies, 2–13,* 23–190. U.S. Department of Commerce.

Hoenig, J., & Hamilton, M. (1966). Elderly patients and the burden on the household. *Psychiata et Neurologia, 152,* 281–293.

Hollender, M. H. (1988). House calls on housebound patients. In J. A. Talbott & A. Z. A. Manevitz (Eds.), *Psychiatric house calls* (pp. 105–106). Washington, DC: American Psychiatric Press, Inc.

Horowitz, A. (1982). *Predictors of caregiving involvement among adult children of the frail elderly*. Paper presented at Annual Meeting of the Gerontological Society of America, Boston, MA.

Horowitz A. (1985a). Family caregiving to the frail elderly. In C. Eisdorfer, M. P. Lawton, & G. L. Maddox (Eds.), *Annual review of gerontology and geriatrics, 5* (pp. 194–246). New York: Springer Publishing Company.

Horowitz, A. (1985b). Sons and daughters as caregivers to older parents: Differences in role performance and consequences. *The Gerontologist, 25,* 612–617.

Horowitz, A., & Dobrof, R. (1982, May). *The role of families in providing long-term care to the frail and chronically ill elderly living in the community*. Final report submitted to the Health Care Financing Administration, DHHS.

Horowitz, A., Sherman, R. H., & Durmaskin, S. C. (1983). *Employment and daughter caregivers: A working partnership for older people?* Paper presented at 36th Annual Meeting of the Gerontological Society of America, San Francisco, CA.

Horowitz, A., & Shindelman, L. W. (1981). *Reciprocity and affection: Past influences on current caregiving*. Paper presented at 34th Annual Meeting of The Gerontological Society of America, Toronto, Canada.

Hunt, A. (1978). *The elderly at home*. London: Office of Population Censuses and Surveys, Her Majesty's Stationer Office.

Ikels, C. (1983). The process of caretaker selection. *Research on Aging, 5,* 491–509.

Isaacs, B. (1971). Geriatric patients: Do their families care? *British Medical Journal, 4,* 282–286.

Jarvik, L. F. (1990). Role reversal: Implications for therapeutic intervention. *Journal of Gerontological Social Work, 15*(1&2), 23–34.

Johnson, C. L. (1983). Dyadic family relations and social support. *The Gerontologist, 23,* 377–383.

Kane, R. A., & Penrod, J. D. (1995). Toward a caregiving policy for the aging family. In R. A. Kane & J. D. Penrod (Eds.), *Family caregiving in an aging society*. Beverly Hills, CA: Sage Publications.

Kaplan, C. (1999, February 1). There's no gentle way to uproot someone you love [Op. Ed.]. *The New York Times.*

Katz, S., Ford, A. B., Moskowitz, R. W., Jackson, B. A., & Jaffee, M. W. (1963). Studies of illness in the aged: The index of ADL, a standardized measure of biological and psychological function. *JAMA (Journal of the American Medical Association), 185,* 914–919.

Katzman, R. (1995). Alzheimer's disease. *New England Journal of Medicine, 314,* 964–973.

Katzman, R., & Bick, K. (2000). *Alzheimer's disease, the changing view.* San Diego, CA: Academic Press.

Kemper and Associates. (1986). *The evaluation of the National Long-Term Care Demonstration: Final report.* Princeton, NJ: Mathematica Policy Research.

Kent, D. P. (1965). Aging—fact or fancy. *The Gerontologist, 5,* 51–56.

Kiecolt-Glaser, J. K., Glaser, R., Dyer, C., Shuttleworth, E. C., Ogrocki, P., & Speicher, C. E. (1987), Chronic stress and immune function in family caregivers of Alzheimer's disease victims. *Psychosomatic Medicine, 49,* 523–535.

Kingson, E. R., Hirshorn, B. A., & Cornman, J. M. (Eds.). (1986). *Ties that bind: The interdependence of generations.* Washington, DC: Seven Locks Press.

Kinnear, D., & Graycar, A. (1982). *Family care of elderly people: Australian perspectives.* Social Welfare Research Centre, Univesity of New South Wales, SWRC Reports and Proceedings, No. 23.

Kinnear, D., & Graycar, A. (1984). Aging and family dependency. *Australian Journal of Social Issues, 19,* 13–25.

Kleban, M. H., Brody, E. M., & Lawton, M. P. (1971). Personality traits in the mentally impaired aged and their relationship to improvements in current functioning. *The Gerontologist, 11,* 134–140.

Kleban, M. H., Brody, E. M., Schoonover, C. B., & Hoffman, C. (1989, May). Family help to the elderly: Perceptions of sons-in-law regarding parent care. *Journal of Marriage and the Family, 51.*

Lamb, M. E., & Sutton-Smith, B. (1982). *Sibling relationships: Their nature and significance across the lifespan.* Hillsdale, NJ: Lawrence Erlbaum Associates.

Land, H. (1978). Who cares for the family? *Journal of Social Policy, 7,* 257–284.

Lang, A., & Brody, E. M. (1983). Characteristics of middle-aged daughters and help to their elderly mothers. *Journal of Marriage and the Family, 45,* 193–202.

Lanspery, S. (1995). AAAs and naturally occurring retirement communities (NORCs). *The Supportive Housing Connection,* 1–4. Washington, DC: National Resource and Policy Center on Housing and Long Term Care.

Laslett, P. (1976). Societal development and aging. In R. H. Binstock & E. Shanas (Eds.), *Handbook on aging and the social sciences* (pp. 87–116). New York: Van Nostrand Reinhold.

Laurie, W. F. (1978). Employing the Duke OARS methodology in cost comparisons: Home services and institutionalization. In *Advances in Research, Vol.* 2, No. 2. Durham, NC: Duke University, Center for the Study of Aging and Human Development.

Lawton, M. P. (1971). The functional assessment of elderly people. *Journal of the American Geriatrics Society, 19,* 465–481.

Lawton, M. P. (1978). Institutions and alternatives for older people. *Health and Social Work, 3,* 109–134.

Lawton, M. P. (1980). *Environment and aging.* Monterey, CA: Brooks/Cole Publishing Co.

Lawton, M. P. (1983). Environment and other determinants of well-being in older people. The Robert W. Kleemeier Memorial Lecture. *The Gerontologist, 23,* 349–357.

Lawton, M. P., & Brody, E. M. (1969). Assessment of older people: Self-maintaining and instrumental activities of daily living. *The Geronologist, 9,* 179–186.

Lawton, M. P., Brody, E. M., & Saperstein, A. R. (1989). A controlled study of respite services for caregivers of Alzheimer's patients. *The Gerontologist, 29,* 8–16.

Lawton, M. P., Brody, E. M., & Saperstein, A. R. (1990). Social, behavioral, and environmental issues. In S. J. Brody & L. G. Pawlson (Eds.), *Aging and rehabilitation: II.* New York: Springer Publishing Company.

Lawton, M. P., Brody, E. M., & Saperstein, A. R. (1991). *Respite for caregivers of Alzheimer patients: Research and practice.* New York: Springer Publishing Company.

Lawton, M. P., Rajagopol, D., Brody, E. M., & Kleban, M. H. (1992). The dynamics of caregiving for a demented elder among black and white families. *Journal of Gerontology: Social Sciences, 47,* S156–S164.

Lawton, M. P., Weisman, G. D., Sloane, P., & Calkins, M. (1997). Assessing environments for older people with chronic illness. In J. Teresi, M. P. Lawton, D. Holmes & M. Ory (Eds.), *Measurement in Elderly Care Populations.* New York: Springer Publishing Company.

Lebowitz, B. D. (1978). Old age and family functioning. *Journal of Gerontological Social Work, 1,* 111–118.

Lebowitz, B. D. (1985). Family caregiving in old age. *Hospital and Community Psychiatry, 36,* 457–458.

Lebowitz, B. D. (1988). Mental health services. In G. L. Maddox (Ed.), *Encyclopedia of Aging.* New York: Springer Publishing Company.

Lebowitz, B. D. (1990). Rehabilitation and geriatric education: Mental health perspectives. In S. J. Brody & G. Pawlson (Eds.), *Rehabilitation and the Elderly II* (pp. 290–298). New York: Springer Publishing Company, Inc.

Lebowitz, B. D. (2001, May, personal communication).

Lebowitz, B. D., & Light, E. (1993). Caregiver stress. Chapter 6 in T. Y. Yoshikaiwa, E. L. Cobbs, & K. Brummel-Smith (Eds.), *Ambulatory Geriatric Care.* St. Louis, Mosby Year Book.

Lebowitz, B. D., & Light, E. (1996). The aging caregivers of psychiatric patients: health care perspectives. *Psychiatric Annals, 26,* 785–791.

Levkoff, S. E., Levy, B. R., & Weitzman, P. F. (1999). The role of religion and ethnicity in the help seeking family caregivers of elders with Alzheimer's disease and related disorders. *Journal of Cross-Cultural Gerontology, 14,* 335–356.

Levy, C. J. (2002, October 6). Mentally ill and locked up in New York nursing homes. *The New York Times,* pp. 1, 29.

Levy, C. J. (2002, November 17). New York restricts confinements of mentally ill. *The New York Times,* p. 1.

Levy, C. J. (2002, November 17). New York exports mentally ill, shifting burden to other states. *The New York Times,* pp. 1, 32.

Lewin, T. (2000, October 24). Now a majority: Families with two parents who work. *New York Times,* p. A14.

Lewis, K. (1980). Services for families of the institutionalized aged. *Aging* [Fall], 15–19.

Liebowitz, B., Lawton, M. P., & Waldman, A. (1979). Designing for confused elderly people: Lessons from the Weiss Institute. *American Institute of Architects Journal, 68,* 59–61.

Lingg, B. A. (1975). Women Social Security beneficiaries aged 62 and older, 1960–1974. *Research and Statistics Notes,* No. 13, 9/29.

Litvin, S. J., Albert, S. M., Brody, E. M., & Hoffman, C. (1995, December). Marital status, competing demands, and role priorities of parent caring daughters. *Journal of Applied Gerontology, 14*(4), 372–390.

Liu, K., Manton, K. G., & Liu, B. M. (1985). Home care expenses for the disabled elderly. *Health Care Financing Review, 7,* 51–58.

Liu, K., & Palesch, Y. (1981). The nursing home population: Different perspectives and implications for policy. *Health Care Financing Review, 3,* 15–23.

Locker, R. (1976, 1981). Elderly couples and the institution. *Social Work, 21,* 149–150.

Lopata, H. Z. (1973). *Widowhood in an American city.* Cambridge, MA: Schenkman Publishing Company.

Lopata, H. Z., & Norr, K. F. (1980). Changing commitments of American women to work and family roles. *Social Security Bulletin, 43,* 3–14.

Lowenthal, M. F. (1964). *Lives in Distress.* New York: Basic Books.

Lowenthal, M. F., & Haven, C. (1968). Interaction and adaption: Intimacy as a critical variable. *American Sociological Review, 33,* 20–30.

Maddox, G. L. (1987). Aging differently. *The Gerontologist, 27*(5), 557–564.

Manney, J. D. (1975). *Aging in American Society.* Ann Arbor, MI: Institute of Gerontology.

Manton, K. G. (1988). Planning long-term care for heterogeneous older populations. In G. L. Maddox & M. P. Lawton (Eds.), *Varieties of aging. Annual review of gerontology and geriatrics, 8.* New York: Springer Publishing Company.

Manton, K. G., Corder, L., & Stallard, E. (1997). Chronic disability trends in elderly United States populations, 1982–1994. *Proceedings of the National Academy of Science, 94,* 2593–2598.

Manton, K. G., & Gu, X. (2001). Changes in the prevalence of chronic disability in the United States' black and non-black population above age 65 from 1982 to 1999. *Proceedings of the National Academy of Science, USA, 98,* 6354–6359.

Marshall, V. W., & Rosenthal, C. J. (1985). *The relevance of geographical proximity in intergenerational relations.* Presented at 38th Annual Meeting of the Geronological Society of America, New Orleans, LA.

Matthews, S. H. (1987). Provision of care to old parents: Division of responsibility among adult children. *Research on Aging, 9,* 45–60.

Mercier, J. M., Paulson, L., & Morris, E. W. (1987). *The effect of proximity on the aging parent/child relationship.* Presented at 40th Annual Meeting of The Gerontological Society of America, Washington, DC.

Metropolitan Life Insurance Company (1997, June). *Metlife study of employer cost of working caregivers.* Westport, CT: Metlife Mature Market Group.

Metropolitan Life Insurance Company (1999). *Metlife juggling act study.* Westport, CT: Metlife Mature Market Institute.

Mezey, M. D. *Encyclopedia of elder care.* New York: Springer Publishing Co.

Montgomery, R. J. V., & Kosloski, K. D. (2001). *Change, continuity, and diversity.* U.S. Administration on Aging.

Moore, M. J., Zahn, C. W., & Clipp, E. C. (2001). Informal costs of dementia care: Estimates from the National Longitudinal Caregiver Study. *Journal of Gerontology, 56B*(No. 4), S219–S228.

Moss, M., & Kurland, P. (1979). Family visiting with institutionalized mentally impaired aged. *Journal of Gerontological Social Work, 1,* 271–278.

Murray, J. (1973). Family structure in the preretirement years. *Social Security Bulletin, 36,* 25–45.

National Academy on Aging. (1997). *Facts on long-term care.* Washington, DC: National Academy on Aging.

National Academy on an Aging Society. (2000). *Caregiving: Helping the elderly with activity limitations,* No. 7. Washington, DC.

National Academy on an Aging Society. (2000, September). *2000 Progress Report on Alzheimer's Disease* [No. 11]. National Institute on Aging.

National Alliance for Caregiving, & American Association for Retired Persons. (1997). *Family Caregiving in the U.S.: Findings From a National Survey. Final report.* Bethesda, MD: National Alliance for Caregiving.

National Alliance for Caregiving and the American Association of Retired Persons (AARP). (1997). *Family Caregiving in the U.S.: Findings from a National Survey, 33.* Bethesda, MD.

National Center for Infectious Diseases. (2001, October 13). Trends in deaths caused by infectious diseases in the United States, 1900–1994. *Centers for Disease Control and Prevention.* Atlanta, GA: Box 1.

National Council on Aging (NCOA). (1999). Centers offering adult day services have nearly doubled since 1989 as demand mushrooms. *News Archives NCOA.* Washington, DC: NCOA, Inc.

Neugarten, B. L. (1968). *Middle age and aging.* Chicago, IL: University of Chicago Press.

Neugarten, B. L. (1968a). Adult personality: Toward a psychology of life cycle. In B. L. Neugarten (Ed.), *Middle age and aging,* 137–147. Chicago, IL: University of Chicago, Press.

Neugarten, B. L. (1973) Personality changes in later life: A developmental perspective. In C. Eisdorfer & M. P. Lawton (Eds.), *Psychological processes in aging,* 311–335. Washington, DC: American Psychological Association.

Neugarten, B. L., & Hagestad, G. O. (1976). Age and the life course. In R. H. Binstock & E. Shanas (Eds.), *Handbook of aging and the social sciences,* 35–57. New York: Van Nostrand Reinhold Co.

Noelker, L. S., & Poulshock, S. W. (1982). *The effects on families of caring for impaired elderly in residence.* Final report of AOA grant number 90-AR-2112. Cleveland, OH: Benjamin Rose Institute.

Older Women's League (OWL). (2001). 2001 Mothers Day Report. Family caregiving and the Older American Act: Caring for the caregiver. Special Committee on Aging. United States Senate. Washington, DC. Serial No. 107-5, 46–75.

Olson, L. K. (2000). The public and private worlds of women and elder care in the U.S. *Hallym International Journal of Aging, 2*(1), 11–25.

Ory, M. G., Hoffman, R. R., Yee, J. L., Tennstedt, S., & Schultz, R. (1999). Prevalence and impact of caregiving: A detailed comparison between dementia and nondementia caregivers. *The Gerontologist, 39*(2), 177–185.

Pandya, S. M., & Coleman, B. (2000, December). In American Association of Retired Persons (AARP) publication FS82, 1–5. Washington, DC: Public Policy Institute, AARP.

Parmelee, P. A., Katz, I. R., & Lawton, M. P. (1989). Depression among institionalized aged: Assessment and prevalence estimation. *Journal of Gerontology, 44*(1), 22–29.

Parsons, T., & Bales, R. (1955). *Family, socialization, and interaction process.* Glencoe, IL: Free Press.

Patterson, T. L., Semple, S. J., Shaw, W. S., Yu, E., He, Y., Zhang, M. Y., Wu, W., & Grant, I. (1998). The cultural context of caregiving: A comparison of Alzheimer's caregivers in Shanghai, China and San Diego, California. *Psychological Medicine, 28,* 1071–1084.

Pear, R. (2001, September 7). U.S. may ease rein on nursing homes. *The New York Times,* pp. A1, A16.

Pear, R. (2002, February 13). U.S. seeks more care for disabled outside institutions. *New York Times National.*

Pear, R. (2002, April 9). Many on Medicaid lack drugs, study says. *The New York Times,* p. A22.

Pear, R. (2002, April 25). U.S. begins issuing consumer data on nursing homes. *New York Times National,* p A27.

Pearlin, L. J. Pioli, M. F., & McLaughlin, A. E. (2001). Caregiving by adult children, involvement, role disruption, and health. *Handbook of aging and the social sciences, Fifth Edition.* Academic Press.

Peck, R. C. (1968). Psychological developments in the second half of life. In B. L. Neugarten (Ed.), *Middle age and aging: A reader in social psychology,* 88–92. Chicago, IL: University of Chicago Press.

Penning, M. J. (2002). Hydra revisited: Substituting formal for self- and informal in-home care among older adults with disabilities. *The Gerontologist, 42*(1), 4–16.

Peters-Davis, N. D., Moss, S., & Pruchno, R. A. (1999). Children-in-law in caregiving families. *The Gerontologist, 39*(1), 66–75.

Phillipson, C., Bernard, M., Phillips, J., & Ogg, J. (2001). *The family and community life of older people.* New York: Routledge.

Port, C. L., Gruber-Baldini, A. L., Burton, L., Baumgarten, M., Hebel, J. R., Zimmerman, S. I., & Magaziner, J. (2001). Resident contact with family and friends following nursing home admission. *The Gerontologist, 41*(5), 589–596.

Posner, W. (1961). Basic issues in casework with older people. *Social Casework, 42,* 234–240.

Powell, A. V., & MacMurtrie, A. (1986). Continuing care retirement communities: An approach to privately financed housing and long-term care for the elderly. In R. J. Newcomer, M. P. Lawton, & T. B. Byerts (Eds.), *Housing in an aging society* (pp. 234–253). New York: Van Nostrand Reinhold.

Prince, M. (1996, July 29). Elder care benefits valued. *Business Insurance,* 3, 21.

Punch [cartoon]. (1988, October 21).

Reece, D., Walz, T., & Hageboech, H. (1983). Intergenerational care providers of non-institutionalized frail elderly: Characteristics and consequences. *Journal of Gerontological Social Work, 5,* 21–34.

Reibstein, L. (1998, July 27). Nursing home verdicts: There's guilt all round. *Newsweek,* 34.

Reid, O. M. (1966). Aging Americans. A review of cooperative research projects. *Welfare in Review, 4.* U.S. DHEW, 1–2.

Rice, D., Fox, P., Max, W., Webber, P., Hauck, D., & Segura, E. (1993). The economic burden of Alzheimer's disease care. *Health Affairs, 12*(2), 164–176.

Rivlin, A. M., & Wiener, J. M. (1988). *Caring for the disabled elderly: Who will pay?* Washington, DC: Brookings Institution.

Robinson, B., & Thurnher, M. (1979). Taking care of aged parents: A family cycle transition. *The Gerontologist, 19,* 586–593.

Rosenheim, M. K. (1965). Social welfare and its implications for family planning. In E. Shanas & G. F. Streib (Eds.), *Social structure and the family: Generational relations,* 206–240. Englewood Cliffs, NJ: Prentice-Hall, Inc.

Rosenmayhr, L., & Kockeis, E. (1963). Propositions for a sociological theory of aging and the family. *International Social Science Journal, 15,* 410–426.

Rosow, I. (1965). Intergenerational relationships: Problems and proposals. In E. Shanas & G. F. Streib (Eds.), *Social structure and the family: Generational relations,* 341–378. Englewood Cliffs, NJ: Prentice-Hall, Inc.

Ross, H. G., & Milgram, J. J. (1982). Important variables in adult sibling relationships: A qualitative study. In M. E. Lamb & B. Sutton-Smith (Eds.) *Sibling relationships: Their nature and significance across the lifespan,* 225–250. Hillsdale, NJ: Lawrence Erlbaum Associates.

Rossiter, C., & Wicks, M. (1982. *Crisis or challenge? Family care, elderly people, and social policy.* Occasional Paper No. 8. London: Study Commission on the Family.

Sainsbury, P., & Grad de Alercon, J. (1970). The effects of community care in the family of the geriatric patient. *Journal of Geriatric Psychiatry, 4,* 23–41.

Sainsbury, P., & Grad, J. (1966). Evaluating the community psychiatric services in Chichester: Aims and methods of research. *Milbank Memorial Fund Quarterly, XLIV,* 231–242.

Sanders, J. (1997). Continuing care retirement communities: a background and summary of current issues, *U.S. Department of Health and Human Services,* Washington, DC, 1–28.

Sanford, J. R. A. (1975). Tolerance of debility in elderly dependents by supporters at home: Its significance for hospital practice. *British Medical Journal, 3,* 471–473.

Scanlon, W., & Layton, B. D. (1997). Report to congressional requesters: How continuous care retirement communities manage services for the elderly. Washington, DC: U.S. General Accounting Office.

Schmitt, E. (2001). For the first time, nuclear families drop below 25% of households. *The New York Times,* p. A-1.

Schmitt, C. H. (2002, September). The new math of old age. *U.S. News and World Report,* 67–74.

Schneider, E. L., & Brody, J. A. (1983). Aging, natural death, and the compression of morbidity: Another view. *The New England Journal of Medicine, 309,* 854–856.

Schoen, R. (1985). Marriage and divorce in twentieth century American cohorts. *Demography, 22,* 101–114.

Schoeni, R., Freedman, V. A., & Wallace, R. (2001). Persistent, consistent, widespread, and robust? Another look at recent trends in old-age disability. *Journal of Gerontology B Psychological Science and Social Sciences, 51,* S-206–S218.

Schoonover, C. B., Brody, E. M., Hoffman, C., & Kleban, M. H. (1988). Parent care and geographically distant children. *Research on Aging, 10,* 472–492.

Schorr, A. L. (1960, June). *Filial responsibility in the modern American family.* Washington, DC: U.S. Department of Health, Education and Welfare, Social Security Administration, Government Printing Office.

Schultz, R., O'Brien, A., Czaja, S., Ory, M., Norris, M. A., Martire, L. M., Belle, S. H., Burgio, L., Gittin, L., Coon, D., Burns, R., Gallagher-Thompson, D., & Stevens, A. (2002). Dementia caregiver intervention research: In search of clinical significance. *The Gerontologist, 42*(5), 589–602.

Schulz, R., & Beach, S. R. (1999). Caregiving as a risk factor for mortality. *Journal of the American Medical Association, 282*(25), 2215–2219.

Schulz, R., Visintainer, P., & Williamson, G. M. (1990). Psychiatric and physical morbidity effects of caregiving. *Journal of Gerontology, Psychological Sciences, 45*(5), 181–191.

Schwartz, A. N. (1979). Psychological dependency: An emphasis on the later years. In P. K. Ragan (Ed.), *Aging parents* (pp. 116–125). Los Angeles: Ethel Andrus Gerontology Center, University of Southern California Press.

Seelbach, W. C. (1977). Gender differences in expectations for filial responsibility. *The Gerontologist, 17,* 421–425.

Seltzer, M. M. (1990). Role reversal: You don't go home again. *Journal of Gerontological: Social Work, 15*(1/2), 5–14.

Seltzer, M. M., & Li, L. W. (2000). The dynamics of caregiving: Transitions during a three-year prospective study. *The Gerontologist, 40*(2), 165–178.

Shanas, E. (1960). Family responsibility and the health of older people. *Journal of Gerontology, 15,* 408–411.

Shanas, E. (1961). *Family relationships of older people.* Health Information Foundation, Research Series 20. Chicago, IL: University of Chicago.

Shanas, E. (1979a). Social myth as hypothesis: The case of the family relations of old people. *The Gerontologist, 19,* 3–9.

Shanas, E. (1979b). The family as a social support system in old age. *The Gerontologist, 19,* 169–174.

Shanas, E., & Streib, G. F. (Eds.) (1965). *Social structure and the family: Generational relations.* Englewood Cliffs, NJ: Prentice-Hall.

Shanas, E., Townsend, P., Wedderburn, D., Friis, H., Milhog, P., & Stehouwer, J. (1968). *Old people in three industrial societies.* New York: Atherton Press.

Simos, B. G. (1973). Adult children and their aging parents. *Social Work, 18,* 78–84.

Smith, K. F., & Bengtson, V. L. (1979). Positive consequences of institutionalization: Solidarity between elderly parents and their middle-aged children. *The Gerontologist, 19,* 438–447.

Soldo, B. J. (1982b). *Effects of number and sex of adult children on LTC service use patterns.* Presented at 1982 Annual Meeting of Social Security Administration, Boston, MA.

Soldo, B. J. (1996). Cross pressures on middle-aged adults: A broader view. *Journal of Gerontology: Social Sciences, 51*(B), S271–S273.

Soldo, B. J., & Hill, M. S. (1993). Intergenerational transfers: Economic, demographic, and social perspectives. In G. L. Maddox & M. P. Lawton (Eds.), *Annual review of gerontology and geriatrics, 13,* 187–216. New York: Springer Publisher Company.

Soldo, B. J., & Myllyluoma, J. (1983). Caregivers who live with dependent elderly. *The Gerontologist, 23,* 605–611.

Spark, G., & Brody, E. M. (1970). The aged are family members. *Family Process, 9,* 195–210.

Spillman, B. C., & Pezzin, L. E. (2000). Potential and active family caregivers: Changing networks and the "sandwich generation." *The Milbank Quarterly, 78*(3).

Stephens, M. A., & Townsend, A. L. (1988). *Daily stressors for family caregivers to institutionalized AD patients.* Presented at 41st Annual Meeting of The Gerontological Society of America, San Francisco, CA.

Stephens, M. A., Townsend, A. L., Martire, L. M., & Druley, A. L. (2001). Balancing parent care with other roles: Interrole conflict of adult daughter caregivers. *Journal of Gerontology, 56B*(1), 24–34.

Stoller, E. P. (1983). Parental caregiving by adult children. *Journal of Marriage and the Family, 45,* 851–858.

Stoller, E. P., & Cutter, S. J. (1993). Predictors of use of paid help among older people living in the community. *The Gerontologist, 33*(1), 31–40.

Stone, R. J. (2000). *Long-term care for the elderly with disabilities: Current policy, emerging trends, and implications for the twenty-first century.* New York: Milbank Memorial Fund.

Stone, R. J. (2001). Alzheimer's disease and related dementias: Important policy issues. *Aging and Mental Health, 5*[Supplement 1], S146–S148.

Stone, R. J., Cafferata, G. L., & Sangl, J. (1987). Caregivers of the frail elderly: A national profile. *The Gerontologist, 27,* 616–626.

Stone, R. I., & Kemper, P. (1989). Spouses and children of disabled elders: How large a constituency for long-term care reform? *Milbank Quarterly, 67, (Nos. 3–4).*

Stone, R. I., & Short, P. F. (1990, June). The competing demands of employment and informal caregiving of disabled elders. *Medical Care, 28*(6), 513–526.

Stone, R. I. (with Wiener, J. M.). (2001). Who will care for us? *The Urban Institute* and the *American Association of Homes and Services for the Aging.*

Streib, G. F. (1958). Family patterns in retirement. *Journal of Social Issues, 14*(2).

Streib, G. F., & Shanas, E. (1965). [An introduction.] In E. Shanas & G. F. Streib (Eds.), *Social structure and the family: Generational relations,* 2–8. Englewood Cliffs, NJ: Prentice-Hall, Inc.

Strom, S. (2001, April 22). The rise in Japan: Assertive daughters-in-law. *The New York Times International,* p. 3.

Sussman, M. (1965). Relationships of adult children with their parents in the United States. In E. Shanas & G. F. Shanas (Eds.), *Social structure and the family: Generational relations,* 62–92. Englewood Cliffs, NJ: Prentice-Hall, Inc.

Taeuber, C. M. (1983). *America in transition: An aging society.* U.S. Bureau of the Census, Current Population Reports, Special Studies Series P-23, No. 128. Washington, DC: Government Printing Office.

Tellis-Nayak, V., & Tellis-Nayak, M. (1989). Quality of care and the burden of two cultures: When the world of the nurse's aide enters the world of nursing homes. *The Gerontologist, 29*(3), 307–313.

Tennstedt, S. (1999). Family caregiving in an Aging Society. Presented at the U.S. Administration on Aging Symposium; Longevity in the New American Century, Baltimore, MD, 24.

Tennstedt, S., & Chang, B. (1998). The relative contribution of ethnicity vs. socioeconomic status in explaining difference in disability and receipt of national care. *Journal of Gerontology: Social Sciences, 53B*(2), 816–870.

Tobin, S. S., & Lieberman, M. A. (1976). *Last home for the aged: Critical implications of institutionalization.* San Francisco, CA: Jossey-Bass.

Tornatore, J. B., & Grant, L. A. (2002). Burden among family caregivers of persons with Alzheimer's disease in nursing homes. *The Gerontologist, 42*(4), 497–506.

Toseland, R. W., Rossiter, C. M., & Labrecque, M. S. (1989). The effectiveness of peer-led and professionally led groups to support family caregivers. *The Gerontologist, 29*(4), 465–471.

Townsend, A., Deimling, G., & Noelker, L. (1988). *Transition to nursing home care: Sources of stress and family members mental health.* Presented at 41st Annual Meeting of The Gerontological Society of America, San Francisco, CA.

Townsend, P. (1965). The effects of family structure on the likelihood of admission to an institution in old age: The application of a general theory. In E. Shanas & G. F. Streib (Eds.), *Social structure and the family: Generational relations,* 163–187. Englewood Cliffs, NJ: Prentice-Hall, Inc.

Townsend, P. (1968). The household and family relations of old people. In E. Shanas, P. Townsend, D. Wedderburn, D. Friis, P. Milhoj, & J. Stebouwer (Eds.), *Old people in three industrial societies,* 178. New York: Atherton Press.

The Travelers Companies, & American Association of Retired Persons. (1985, June). *The Travelers Employee Caregiver Survey.* Hartford, CT: The Travelers Companies.

Troll, L. E., & Bengston, V. L. (1979). Generations in the family. In W. Burr, R. Hill, F. I. Nye, & I. Reiss (Eds.), *Contemporary theories about the family: Research-based theories, I,* 127–161. New York: Free Press.

Troll, L. E., & Stapley, J. (1985). Elders and extended family system: Health, family salience, and affect. In J. M. A. Munnich (Ed.), *Life span and change in a gerontological perspective,* 211. New York: Academic Press.

Trupin, L., & Rice, D. (1995, June). Health status, medical care use, and number of disabling conditions in the United States. *Disability statistics abstract number 9.* Washington, DC: National Institute on Disability and Rehabilitation Research.

Turnbull, A. P., Summers, J. A., & Brotherson, M. J. (1984). *Manual 5, working with families with disabled members: A family systems approach.* Salinas, KS: University of Kansas.

Uchitelle, L. (2001, June 26). Lacking pensions, older divorced women remain at work. *The New York Times,* p. 1.

Uhlenberg, P. (1974). Cohort variations in family life cycle experiences of U.S. females. *Journal of Marriage and the Family, 36,* 284–292.

U.S. Administration on Aging. (1998). *A profile of older Americans: 1998.* Washington, DC.

U.S. Administration on Aging. (2000, Fall). *America's families care.* Washington, DC: U.S. Department of Health and Human Services.

U.S. Administration on Aging. (2000, Fall). *Implementing the National Family Caregiver Support Program, America's families care: A report on the needs of america's family caregivers*. Washington, DC.

U.S. Administration on Aging (AOA). (2002). Health and Human Services awards $3.7 million to support community services for seniors in naturally occurring retirement communities in five cities. *AOA News*. Washington, DC.

U.S. Bureau of the Census. (1984). *Projections of the population of the United States, by age, sex, and race: 1983–2080*. Publication P-25, No. 952. Washington, DC: Government Printing Office.

U.S. Bureau of the Census. (1986, December). *Statistical brief: Age structure of the U.S. population in the 21st century*. SB-1–86. Washington, DC: Government Printing Office.

U.S. Bureau of the Census. (2001, June). *America's Families and Living Arrangements: Population Characteristics: Current Population Reports*. Washington, DC: Government Printing Office.

U.S. Bureau of the Census, Department of Commerce. (1995, May). *Statistical Brief: Sixty-Five Plus in the United States*, SB 95–8. Washington, DC: Government Printing Office.

U.S. Bureau of the Census, Vital Statistics. (2001). *Statistical abstract of the United States, 2001*. Washington, DC: Government Printing Office.

U.S. Census Bureau. (2001).Table 68, Vital Statistical Abstract of the U.S.

U.S. Department of Commerce, Bureau of the Census. (1982a, October). Decennial census of population, 1900-1980 and projections of the population of the United States; 1982-2050 (Advance Report). *Current Population Reports*. Series P-25, No. 922.

U.S. Department of Commerce, Bureau of Census. (1982b, March). Fertility of American Women: June 1981 [Advance Report]. *Current Population Reports*, Series P-20, No. 369.

U.S. Department of Health and Human Services, Administration on Aging [Fall]. (2000). p.1

U.S. Department of Health and Human Services, *The National Nursing Home Survey: 1997–2000*, p. 2.

U.S. Department of Health and Human Services (DHHS), Public Health Services [PHS]. (1985). *Women's health: Report of the Public Health Service Task Force on Women's Health, Vol. II*.

U.S. Department of Health and Human Services, National Center for Health Statistics. (1997). Data from the 1997 National Nursing Home Survey, Table 3. Washington, DC.

U.S. Department of Health and Human Services, National Center for Health Statistics. (1999). Unpublished data from the 1999 National Nursing Home Survey, Table 3. Washington, DC.

U.S. Department of Health and Human Services, National Center for Health Statistics. (2000, July). *National Nursing Home Survey*. Washington, DC.

U.S. Department of Health and Human Services, National Center for Health Statistics. (1998, July). *Monthly Vital Statistics Report, 46*(12). Washington, DC.

U.S. Department of Health, Education and Welfare (DHEW), Public Health Services (PHS). (1972, July). *Home care for persons aged 55 and over in the U.S.: July 1966–June 1968*. Vital and Health Statistics, Series 10, No. 73.

U.S. Department of Health, Education and Welfare (DHEW), Public Health Services (PHS). (1985). *Women's health: Report of the Public Health Service Task Force on Women's Health, Vol. II*.

U.S. Department of Labor, Bureau of Labor Statistics. (1999, Winter). Working in the 21st Century. *Occupational Outlook Quarterly*. Washington, DC.

U.S. Department of Labor, Bureau of Labor Statistics. (2000, February 16). Changes in women's labor force participation in the 20th century. *Monthly Labor Review: The Editor's Desk*. Washington, DC.

U.S. Department of Labor, Women's Bureau. (1986, October). *Facts on U.S. working women*. Caring for Elderly Family Members, Fact Sheet No. 86-4. Washington, DC.

U.S. General Accounting Office, Comptroller General of the United States. (1977, April 19). *The Well-Being of Older People in Cleveland, Ohio*. Number RD-77–70. Washington, DC.

U.S. House of Representatives Select Committee on Aging. (1979). *Mid-life women: Policy proposals on their problems*. Washington, DC: Government Printing Office.

U.S. National Center for Health Statistics (NCHS). (1973). National Health Survey. *Characteristics of residents in nursing home and personal care homes. U.S. June–August 1969*. Series 121, No. 19, HSMHA.

U.S. National Center for Health Statistics (NCHS). (1978, September 6). *Advance data. An overview of nursing home characteristics: Provisional data from the 1977 National Nursing Home Survey*. U.S. DHEW, No. 35.

U.S. National Center for Health Statistics (NCHS). (1985, December). DHHS publications number PHS 86-1232, Table 10, p. 38.

U.S. National Center for Health Statistics (NCHS). (1985). *Preliminary data from the 1985 National Nursing Home Survey*. Division of Health Care Statistics.

U.S. National Center for Health Statistics (NCHS). (1986, May 2). *Advance Report of Final Marriage Statistics, 1983, Vol. 35,* No. 1, Supplement, PHS.

U.S. National Center for Health Statistics (NCHS). (1998, July). *Monthly Vital Statistics Report, Vol. 46,* No. 12.

U.S. National Committee on Vital and Health Statistics. (1978, September 8). *Long-term health care: Minimum data set*. Preliminary Report of the Technical Consultant panel on the Long-Term Health Care Data Set, PHS, NCHS.

U.S. News and World Report (Schmitt, September 30, 2002).

Upp, M. (1982). A look at the economic status of the aged then and now. *Social Security Bulletin, 45,* No. 3, 16–22.

VanHaitsma, K., Lawton, M. P., & Kleban, M. (2000). Does segregation help or hinder? Examining the role of homogeneity in behavioral and emotional aspects of quality of life for persons with cognitive impairment. *Research and Practice in Alzheimer's Disease: Special Edition—Alzheimer's Disease Special Care Units,* 4, 163–178.

VanHaitsma, K., & Rusckdeschel, K. (2001). Special care for dementia in nursing homes; overview of innovations in programs and activities. *Alzheimer's Care Quarterly,* 2(3), 49–56.

Wagner, D. (1997). Comparative analysis of caregiver data for caregivers to the elderly, 1987 and 1997. *National Alliance for Caregiving*. Bethesda, MD.

Wagner, D. L. (2000). Dimensions of family caregiving: A look into the future, the development of future of workplace eldercare. Westport, CT: Metlife Mature Market Institute.

Walsh, F. (1980). The family in later life. In E. Carter & M. C. McGoldrick (Eds.), *The family life cycle: A framework for family therapy,* 198–220. New York: Gardner Press, Inc.

Wardman, T. A., & Liu, K. (2000). Disability trends among elderly persons and implications for the future. *Journal of Gerontology, 55B*(5), S298–S307.

Weed, J. A. (1981). *National estimates of marital dissolution and survivorship, vital and health statistics: Series III, analytic studies.* No. 19. DHHS publication number (PHS) 81–1403.

Weinberg, J. (1976). On adding insight to injury. *The Gerontologist, 16,* 4–10.

Weithorn, C. J. (1975). Women's role in cross-cultural perspective. In R. K. Unger & F. L. Denmark (Eds.), *Woman: Dependent or independent variable?,* 276–292. New York: Psychological Dimensions, Inc.

Wenger, G. C., Brody, E. M., & Jingming, L. (2000). Family support in Beijing (China) and Liverpool (UK): Differences and similarities. *Hallym International Journal of Aging, 2*(1), 85–91.

Winklevoss, H. E., & Powell, A. V. (1982). *1982 Reference Directory of Continuing Care Communities.* Philadelphia, PA: Human Services Research.

Whitlatch, C. J., Schur, D., Noelker, L. S., Ejaz, F. K., & Looman, W. J. (2001). The stress process of family caregiving in institutional settings. *The Gerontologist, 41*(No. 4), 462–473.

Wilden, R., & Redfoot, D. L. (2002). Adding assisted living services to subsidized housing: Serving frail older persons with low income, American Association of Retired Persons (AARP) Public Policy Institute, Washington, DC, 1–85.

Williams, C. G., & Hawes, C. (2000). Expanding long-term care choices for the elderly: Identifying users. Workshop held in San Diego, CA (2000, September 11–13). Washington, DC: Agency for Health Care Research Quality [AHACPR; formerly AHCP& R: Agency for Health Care Policy & Research].

Wisensale, S. (2001). *Family leave policy: The political economy of work and family in America.* Armonk, NY: M. E. Sharpe.

Wolf, D. A., & Soldo, B. J. (1986). *The households of older unmarried: Micro-decision model of shared living arrangements.* Presented at Annual Meeting of the Population Association of America, San Francisco, CA.

Wood, V., & Robertson, J. F. (1978, May). Friendship and kinship interaction: Differential effect on the morale of the elderly. *Journal of Marriage and the Family,* 367–375.

Yee, J. L., & Schultz, R. (2002). Gender differences in psychiatric morbidity among family caregivers: A review and analysis. *The Gerontologist, 40*(2), 147–164.

York, J. L., & Caslyn, R. J. (1977). Family involvement in nursing homes. *The Gerontologist, 17,* 500–505.

Zarit, S. H., Reever, K. E., & Bach-Peterson, J. (1980). Relatives of the impaired aged: Correlates of feelings of burden. *The Gerontologist, 20,* 649–655.

Zarit, S. H., Stephens, M. A., Townsend, A., & Greene, R. (1998). Stress reduction for family caregivers: Effects of adult day care use. *Journal of Gerontology Series B: Psychological Sciences and Social Sciences, 53,* S267–S277.

Index